# STUDIES ON THE
# INTERIOR OF
# RUSSIA

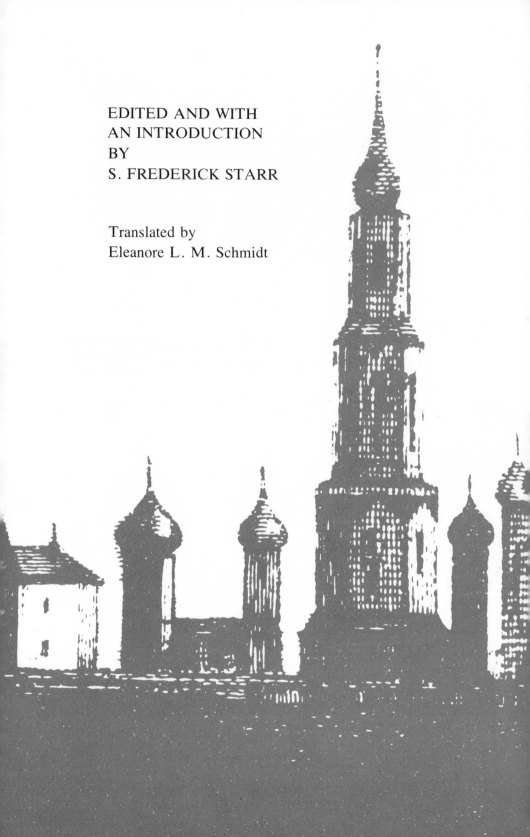

EDITED AND WITH
AN INTRODUCTION
BY
S. FREDERICK STARR

Translated by
Eleanore L. M. Schmidt

# STUDIES ON THE
# INTERIOR OF
# RUSSIA

*August von Haxthausen*

**THE UNIVERSITY OF CHICAGO PRESS**
Chicago & London

The University of Chicago Press, Chicago 60637
The University of Chicago Press, Ltd., London

International Standard Book Number: 0-226-32022-7
Library of Congress Catalog Card Number: 71-190692

2-26-79

# Contents

# Introduction

Considering his preeminence among western European experts on Russia, Baron August von Haxthausen was a strangely obscure figure.[1] Numerous Russians acknowledged that he told them more about their society than had any foreign writer before. Yet few of those thinkers who so fervently debated his ideas knew much about the half-century of his life that passed before his 1843 tour to the east. Even those who met and talked with him in Moscow salons seem to have been little conscious of his personal motives in studying Russian life. Nor were his German compatriots generally better acquainted with the deeper concerns of this landholding scholar. Beyond the circle of a few close friends he seemed only an austere and bookish aristocrat with a consuming interest in the politics of his class. Even his family found him a forbidding bachelor and his endless travels an eccentric indulgence. No *bon mot* of his ever attracted a great memoirist to treat him. And when he died his obituaries were brief and quite insubstantial.

The century intervening since his death renders it all but impossible to recapture the personality which eluded contemporaries. At the same time the longer perspective enables us today to perceive relationships between Haxthausen's life and times that might not have been evident in his own day. It is clear now that Haxthausen, like many people of our own century, became interested in Russia as a result of his preoccupation with the broader problem of revolutionary

1. Sections of this essay are reprinted from S. Frederick Starr, ''August von Haxthausen and Russia,'' *Slavonic and East European Review* 44 (July 1968): 462–78.

change. In the early nineteenth century, though, it was not Russia but western Europe that seemed to lie in the grip of social and political turmoil. All his life Haxthausen labored to come to grips with the titanic forces unleashed by the great French Revolution of 1789. Of all of his attempts to do so, his writings on Russia were the most significant.

August Franz Ludwig Maria Baron von Haxthausen-Abbenburg was born on the eve of the revolutionary Terror, in 1792, but a world away from Paris at his family's estate at Abbenburg in Westphalia.[2] Though French books and "manners" had long since invaded the German lands, the deeper cultural horizons of Abbenburg scarcely extended beyond the nearby bishopric of Paderborn until the Napoleonic occupation in 1806. Haxthausen's father traced his lineage at least to the fifteenth century and boasted the title of Chamberlain and High Bailiff of the Magistracy of Lichtenau, and Lord of Thienhausen, Bökendorf, Abbenburg, and Hellersen. Notwithstanding this ringing appellation, he appears to have been a typical prosperous backwater planter, content to manage local affairs from the disheveled office in his *Fachwerk* manor house and occasionally to visit his relatives at the nearby estates of Bökendorf and Thienhausen. August's mother was entirely of the same mold. When the brothers Grimm first made her acquaintance she was milking the cows, and though she herself was well educated, she never yearned for the salon life that lured so many German aristocrats in the late eighteenth century.

The Haxthausens produced a family of nine daughters and eight sons, of whom August was the youngest. Out of practical necessity August was sent off to the Warburg estate of an uncle, the Baron Kalenberg, to be reared. There he received the same upbringing his father had known, Catholic to the core and centered on the agrarian life of the Weser valley. His early schooling was completed under the tutelage of the priest at Bökendorf and then at the Mining School at Clausthal, near Göttingen. The register of that institution indicates that Haxthausen studied there until 1812 but gives no indication that he in any way distinguished himself.[3]

2. For information on Haxthausen's youth see Karl Schulte-Kemmingshausen, "August von Haxthausen," in *Westfälische Lebensbilder*, ed. Alois Bömer and Otto Leunenschloss (Münster, 1930) 1:87–92; and Anon. (Ludwig von der Osten), *Franz Ludwig August Maria Freiherr von Haxthausen: Ein photographische Versuch von Freundeshand* (Hanover, 1868), pp. 1–12.
3. *Die preussische Bergakademie zu Claustal, 1775–1925* (Leipzig, 1925), p. 462.

## Introduction

The decisive series of events in Haxthausen's life was set off by the French occupation and the establishment of the Kingdom of Westphalia under Jerome Bonaparte in 1806. At once the new ruler set about imposing the full range of reforms and regulations associated with his brother's two-year-old empire. Among these, he bid for the favor of the peasantry by nullifying the remaining feudal duties owed to the landowners. At the same time, however, the revolutionary regime imposed severe new taxes and required local lords to join in the task of collecting them. By 1809 the mounting popular opposition exploded in widespread tax withholdings, desertion from the Bonapartist army, and local violence directed both against Bonapartist rule and against the German lords who acquiesced in it.

This insurgence reached the Haxthausen estates on 4 March 1812, when the peasants of the village of Altenhagen refused to pay taxes and resisted by force the gendarme detachment called to quell the rising. Altogether ten peasants were arrested. According to the district police files, those who were apprehended refused to give their names to the officials, stating instead, "We all go by one name: 'Members of the Commune.'"[4] The proud tone of this sally anticipates the sense of dignity that Haxthausen was later to find in the Russian peasantry.

Tax withholdings by Westphalian peasants were in some measure a rebuke to the dominant landed class. But the Haxthausens chose to interpret it instead as an act of defiance by true Germans against conditions created by the foreign domination. Such a view is not so naïvely conservative as it may at first appear. A recent scholar who has explored the collection of feudal dues in the Paderborn area confirms that in the years immediately prior to the occupation such families as the Haxthausens were sufficiently well off to be able to postpone payment in cases of acute need.[5] Under the Bonapartes such *noblesse oblige* became impossible. To be sure, the peasantry had received new civil rights, but, as August von Haxthausen later so frequently pointed out, they were at the same time torn from the web of mutual relationships that the hierarchical rural society of the *ancien régime* in Westphalia had afforded.

If this interpretation of the peasant movement exonerated German lords from one form of guilt, it plunged them deep into another.

4. Heinz Heitzer, *Insurrectionen zwischen Weser und Elbe. Volksbewegungen gegen die französische Fremdherrschaft in Königreich Westfalen 1806–1813* (Berlin, 1959), p. 208.

5. Ibid., p. 209.

For had not the peasantry shown itself more irreconcilably opposed to foreign domination than the nobility? Answering in the affirmative, numerous Westphalian noblemen banded together in 1812 and 1813 to take command of the movement for national liberation that had long germinated in the lower classes. Several members of the Haxthausen family were deeply involved in this movement and August's older brother Werner figured so prominently in the leadership of the insurrection and the secret Tugendbund that he was later invited to attend the Congress of Vienna as a representative of Westphalia.[6] August himself volunteered for service with the Hanoverian forces and saw action in the fighting against the debris of the Grand Army in Holstein and in the region of the Elbe. It was at this time that he penned verses with such inflammatory titles as "Der Sachsen Heerfahrt" (The Journey of the Saxon Army) and "Kriegslied" (War Song).[7] His closest friends of this period, the eminent folklorists Jakob and Wilhelm Grimm, left further evidence of Haxthausen's military activities during the northern campaign. With admiration the brothers related in letters how even as his squadron was under siege the young August took time to listen to and note down the popular legends and fairy tales told by his fellow soldiers.[8] Several of his brothers and sisters shared this interest. During the war of liberation August and his sister worked closely with the Grimms on their great collection of fairy tales and recorded the songs and lore of their native district with the intent of publishing an extensive collection of Westphalian folk lyrics.[9] This passion for the local peasant culture, like the aristocratic bid for leadership of the insurrection, reveals the sense of guilt which the landed class experienced

6. Arthur Kleinschmidt, *Geschichte des Königreichs Westfalen* (Gotha, n.d.), pp. 184, 564, 565; Werner Engel, *Politische Geschichte Westfalen* (Cologne and Berlin, 1968), p. 235.

7. Universitätsbibliothek Münster (UBM), Haxthausen archive, correspondence, 1812–14.

8. *Briefwechsel zwischen Jakob und Wilhelm Grimm aus der Jugendzeit*, ed. Hermann Grimm and Gustav Hinrichs (Weimar, 1881), pp. 223, 422.

9. Selections of this collection were published posthumously as *Westfälische Volkslieder in Wort und Weise mit Klavierbegleitung und liedervergleichenden Anim*, ed. A. Reisserchein (Heilbronn, 1879). See also J. Grauheer, *August von Haxthausen und seine Beziehungen zu Annette von Droste-Hülshoff* (Altena, 1933), esp. pp. 37 ff.; and Karl Schulte-Kemmingshausen, "Eine neue aufgefundene Volksliedersammlung aus der Zeit der Romantik," *Zeitschrift für rheinisch.-westfäl. Volkskunde*, 1933, Heft 1-4; and "Freundesbriefe der Familie v. Haxthausen an die Brüder Grimm," ed. Wilhelm Schoof, *Westfälische Zeitschrift*, vol. 94.

upon seeing the anti-French initiative of the peasantry. With the military effort, it strove to re-create, or perhaps to create, the hierarchically based social cohesion that class antagonisms under the Bonaparte regime had torn asunder. Moreover, it assuaged the guilt that the aristocratic proclivity for "enlightened" learning had left.

During his student years at the University of Göttingen (1814–18) Haxthausen pursued this romantic interest in the literary and musical culture of traditional Germany. Along with the poet Clemens Brentano, Ernst Moritz Arndt, the brothers Grimm, and several other friends and teachers, most of them noblemen,[10] he participated in a literary journal, *Die Wünschelruthe* (The Magic Wand) in which he and other subsequently distinguished writers presented essays, stories, and adaptations of folk poetry. Haxthausen served as editor and contributed two groups of folk songs, a rather preposterously complex adventure novel, *Die Geschichte eines Algierer Sklaven* (The History of an Algerian Slave), and a long study of medieval German folk epics entitled "Über die altdeutschen Volks- und Meisterlieder."[11] During the year of its existence (1818) this weekly review was the center of Göttingen literary life and attracted the notice of several German luminaries of the day, among them the journalist Josef Görres.[12]

The sponsoring body for *Die Wünschelruthe* was a society called the Poetic Cobbler's Guild (*Die poetische Schustergild*), one of the many fraternal circles that flourished in the years before the German student movement was suppressed.[13] The bylaws, of which Haxthausen was the author, reveal that the society was strongly Masonic in form, with weekly secret meetings, handshakes, etc., but that its purpose was to promote the cause of German culture.[14] For the time being at least, Haxthausen was still an ardent German

10. *Achim von Arnim und Clemens Brentano*, ed. Reinhold Steig, 3 vols. (Stuttgart, 1894), 1:396.

11. *Die Wünschelruthe*, 1818, no. 9, contains the folk song collection; nos. 11, 13, 14, 15 contain *Die Geschichte eines Algierer Sklaven*, and nos. 42–45 contain Haxthausen's essay on folk epics. The few papers relating to the life of this little-known journal are preserved in Schloss Thienhausen (ST) unnumbered vol. 1, and in the UBM collection.

12. Görres to Haxthausen, 1818 undated, UBM.

13. The main figures in this group besides Haxthausen were J. P. Hornthal and August von Arnswaldt, the latter the son of the curator of Göttingen University. See Wolfgang Bobke, "August von Haxthausen: eine Studie zur Ideengeschichte der politischen Romantik," Ph.D. diss., Munich, 1954, pp. 20 ff.

14. UBM, and ST, unnumbered vol. 1.

nationalist, "Tannhauser," as he was known to his fellow initiates in the lodge.

Members of the Poetic Cobbler's Guild hoped to defend German culture from alien influences by uniting the divided Christian churches in Germany under the banner of the mystical faith preached by the seventeenth-century Görlitz cobbler Jakob Böhme. Though Haxthausen never wavered in his Catholicism, throughout his life he was drawn toward the zealous religiosity of the antirationalist sectarians. Their unvarnished piety he saw as a shield against the revolutionary ideas of the French Enlightenment and as a rebuke to the Catholic nobility for its rationalism. This attitude, first elaborated in an essay of 1826,[15] was reflected again two decades later in his study of Russia. Its implication that religion serves chiefly as a unifying force among classes corresponds closely to the socially conscious form of Catholicism preached in the 1820s by Haxthausen's friends Josef Görres and Franz von Baader. Haxthausen criticized the Catholic nobility for abandoning its traditional faith and thereby divorcing itself from the peasantry whose care had been entrusted to it. There could be no question that the nobility was better fitted to exercise civil authority than any generalized and impersonal state administration. But until aristocrats regenerated themselves through contact with the wellsprings of the indigenous culture, their authority could be neither legitimate nor real.

Haxthausen's formal studies at Göttingen served to reinforce his antirationalism and traditionalism. Through the philologist Georg Friedrich von Benecke he discovered the old German poetry of which the folk tales were a living echo. And through the anthropologist and natural historian Johann Friedrich von Blumenbach he was introduced to the notion of studying man in his total physical environment (*Totalhabitus*), instead of merely his political or intellectual activities. Most important were his studies in the faculty of law. In the years after the national awakening, German jurists saw their primary task to be to purge German law of the baneful influence of poorly assimilated Roman and French legal notions and to erect a new law based upon historial experience rather than "mere reason." To this end, Jakob Grimm, now a professor, expounded the teachings of Edmund Burke and Friedrich Savigny to eager Göttingen disciples.

The historical jurisprudence which Haxthausen absorbed was ultimately mystical in character, for it held that social processes

<hr>

15. August von Haxthausen, "Die Kirche und ihre Institutionen im Verhältnis zu den Tendenzen der Zeit," *Der Katholik* (Mainz), 21 (1826):74.

might be described but not explained. Paradoxically, though, it was at the same time far closer to life than the view which it superseded, for it required the student to seek the fundamental principles of a society in its historical and everyday existence. Under the influence of this school, legal scholars abandoned *a priori* speculations for fieldwork. This vital interest in all the apparent confusion of actuality reverberated through the German academic world. By the early nineteenth century the detailed study of economic and social institutions, or the field of *Statistik* as it was termed, had taken its place as an important adjunct to the syllabus of jurisprudence. Each student of *Statistik* was expected to select a nation or region whose social customs, economy, and laws he would examine through searching historical and statistical studies. Such training developed Haxthausen from an amateur folklorist into a serious-minded social scientist.

His studies completed, Haxthausen returned in 1819 to inherit one of his family's estates at Bökendorf, close by Abbenburg in Westphalia. There he continued his avocation of folklore collecting. Together with a local friend, Paul Wigand, he founded a "Westphalian Society for Historic and Antiquarian Studies" and enlisted his university friends, including Wilhelm Grimm, to aid in the work of recording oral traditions and folk poetry.[16] At the same time he continued the project of publishing folk songs, making contact with musical amateurs who could assist him in writing instrumental accompaniments. None of these activities did he pursue with any real dedication, however, and as they one by one came to naught, his attention turned to the legal studies of his student days. At length, in 1829 he published a slim volume on the laws of land tenure in his immediate neighborhood. The full title of this work reflects its polemic character: *On Agrarian Relations in the Princedoms of Paderborn and Corvey and Their Conflicts in the Present Time, Including Proposals for Releasing the Ground and Soil from Encumbering Laws and Liabilities.*[17] His goal was to prevent the land from becoming a mere commodity like other forms of capital; the means he proposed for achieving this were simply to repeal most of the Bonapartist legislation passed since 1806.

Such an extreme conclusion was entirely compatible with Haxt-

16. *Unbekannte Briefe der Brüder Grimm*, ed. Wilhelm Schoof (Bonn, 1960), pp. 119–20.
17. August Freiherr von Haxthausen, *Über die Agrarverfassung in den Fürstenthümern Paderborn und Corvey, und deren Conflikte in der gegenwärtigen Zeit nebst Vorschlägen, die den Grund und Boden belastenden Rechte und Verbindlichkeiten dasselbst aufzulösen* (Berlin, 1829).

hausen's personal experience in managing his family's holdings. The Napoleonic legislation had had a peculiarly strong impact on the economy of the large estates that dominated the rural economy of eastern Westphalia. For the first time major lords were required to employ hired labor to work their lands. Not only did this place an unprecedented financial burden on them but it also forced them to enter into scores of individual contracts and to become embroiled in endless lawsuits, the records of which swell the estate archives of the region to this day. Nor did the peasant fare much better. The abolition of communal institutions proved a boon to the more enterprising peasants who rapidly became farmers with their own farmhands and hired labor. But many more failed under the new conditions and sold their property back to the lords for the price of a ticket to America.[18] Hence, in the locality which Haxthausen knew best, the short-term impact of the reform seemed to justify his gloomy verdict.

The antirevolutionary tone of the study on Paderborn and Corvey was blatant but sophisticated. This, combined with the author's obvious command of the methods of *Statistik*, attracted the attention of the heir to the Prussian throne, the future Friedrich Wilhelm IV. Honoring Haxthausen with the title *Geheimer Regierungsrat*, the crown prince invited him to Berlin and there offered him an attractive stipend to conduct the same analysis for all the provinces of Prussia. Haxthausen accepted the assignment and spent a full decade on the research, traveling each summer throughout Prussia to gather legislation pertaining to land tenure. In that the compilation was intended to serve as the basis for future "organic" legislation, the project bears comparison to Count Mikhail Speranskii's attempt to assemble all the laws and acts of the Russian government during the same years; like Speranskii, Haxthausen was never to complete the task upon which he had embarked.

His whole background and training had sensitized Haxthausen to detecting the living survivals of the golden age that he never doubted lay in the past. In surveying the entire northern empire, though, he quickly perceived that in most places the indigenous systems of land tenure and peasant organization had been all but obliterated by the effects of legislation passed during the last century. Haxthausen was forced to acknowledge how unusual had been the corporative spirit of the peasants in his own native region, and how exceptional

18. ST, vol. 17, includes documents on this process at Thienhausen as well as some of the accounts of Bökendorf.

had been the relatively harmonious relations among classes that prevailed there before the French occupation. At the same time, his curiosity was aroused by what appeared to be survivals of another ancient but non-Germanic tradition of communal peasant organization in those eastern regions once occupied by Slavic peoples. In his report of 1838 and again in a supplement published in 1842 he brought together the results of his research on this subject.[19]

Primitive Slavic farming communes, or *Gemeinden*, were still partially preserved as the basis of Pomeranian peasant organization even after the dislocation caused by the freeing of the serfs during the revolutionary years. In praising these institutions, Haxthausen argued that such corporate bodies could mediate between the individual and society and between classes within the society, thus protecting each from the other.[20] Here at last was evidence of an ideal yet real social system in which individuals were integrated into their society without revolution, an achievement made possible, Haxthausen believed, by custom alone and not through the legal machinations of meddling bureaucrats and revolutionaries.

This discovery prompted Haxthausen to propose a series of legislative measures designed to untrammel peasant institutions from excessive legal and administrative impediments. In numerous memorandums he urged the Prussian government to pursue his own brand of conservatism by reducing the role of the state bureaucracy and allowing loyal and free local forces — the aristocracy and peasantry together — to play a greater role in rural affairs. But opposition to his ideas had been growing in administrative, Lutheran, nationalist, and liberal quarters since the mid-1830s.[21] Professional civil servants resented the fact that Haxthausen had received a titled appointment directly from the royal family on the strength of one essay and some folksongs, without passing any examination. Lutherans were angered by his outspoken participation from 1831 to 1841 in the Catholic and Evangelical organ *Das Berliner politische Wochenblatt*. And Prussian nationalists took umbrage at his evident hostility toward their schemes for German unity. His experience with the bureau-

19. August Freiherr von Haxthausen, *Die ländliche Verfassung in den einzelnen Provinzen der preussischen Monarchie* (Königsberg, 1839), and *Über den Ursprung und die Grundlagen der Verfassung in ehemals slavischen Ländern Deutschlands im Allgemeinen und dem Herzogthum Pommern im Besondern* (Berlin, 1842).
20. *Über den Ursprung*, p. 24.
21. For Haxthausen's political conflicts see Bobke, "August von Haxthausen," pp. 59–66.

tions to acquire Thienhausen.[24] His work as a landed proprietor had given him the security which the Prussian state had denied him.

Disillusioned with the Prussians, no longer able to gain a hearing at home for his views, and having brought his private affairs to a successful conclusion, Haxthausen had reached a point in his career at which new directions were both necessary and possible. In the late summer of 1842 he turned to his old friend Count Peter von Meyendorff, Russian ambassador at Berlin. Several years earlier Meyendorff had proposed that Haxthausen continue his research on land and communal institutions in the Slavic lands of the Russian Empire. With Meyendorff's encouragement Haxthausen in 1837 had already journeyed as far east as Dorpat in Russian-ruled Estonia to discuss peasant institutions with the Russian and German professors at the university there.[25] Now, in 1842, Meyendorff's proposal for more extensive study suddenly appeared most attractive. Like many western Europeans before and since, Haxthausen was eager to find in Russia a nation fated to achieve the social and religious ideals that his own fellow countrymen had spurned.

The incident that opened the way for Haxthausen to pursue research in the east was the publication by the tsarist government of an important *ukaz* on "obligated" (*obiazannye*) peasants.[26] This law, issued a month before Haxthausen's petition to the throne was rejected, permitted Russian lords to put land at the disposal of peasants through voluntary agreements between the parties. To assure that the power of the lords would not be impaired, the state left them title to the land; but it was hoped that with more land for themselves and their obligations precisely specified, peasants would find their lot improved. Haxthausen strongly praised this legislation in an essay which he published under the initials "A.H." in the *Preussische Staatsanzeiger*; this was promptly reprinted in the *Allgemeine Zeitung*, the *Journal des Débats* and the Times.[27] A copy reached Nicholas I in Petersburg, presumably through Meyendorff. The tsar

24. ST, vol. 17, pt. 7, August von Haxthausen to Guido von Haxthausen, 1838–42, vol. 18, *Actum*, 31 January 1840, setting forth the order of inheritance among the surviving brothers.

25. Haxthausen's travel diaries from this expedition are preserved in UBM, as is his correspondence with the Dorpat scholar Evers.

26. For details on this law see N. M. Druzhinin, *Gosudarstvennye krestiane i reformy P. D. Kiseleva*, 2 vols. (Moscow, 1946–58), 2:7–80.

27. *Preussische Staatsanzeiger*, 7 May 1842; Schulte-Kemmingshausen, "August von Haxthausen," p. 97.

immediately wrote a note of congratulations and an invitation to visit Russia, which he mistakenly sent to Alexander von Humboldt, who had also shown a keen interest in Russia over the years. Fortunately, Humboldt passed the letter on to Haxthausen, who received it with enthusiasm. Early the next spring the former *Geheimer Regierungsrat* was on his way by sleigh to Russia, where he was to spend a year investigating agrarian conditions and the state of the nation.

Baron Haxthausen's research on Russia was initiated and supported by the Russian crown. Royal backing brought significant benefits to the Westphalian guest, not the least of which were the services of an interpreter, letters of introduction, a court coachman, and a supply wagon. At the same time, it brought inconveniences that were to become irksome before the report on the research was finally in print. Haxthausen's chief official contact, Count Meyendorff, was himself seriously interested in law and ethnography and had actually led an expedition to study the Russian interior. In addition to sending letters of introduction to friends throughout Russia, he considered it essential to provide the distinguished German with cadastral surveys and other such data.[28] This prospect alarmed the Russian chief of the gendarmes, Count Benckendorff, who, unimpressed by Haxthausen's recent clash with Prussian liberals, circulated a series of secret memorandums on the researcher's supposedly dangerous political affiliations. These unnerved the timid Meyendorff to such a degree that he became reluctant to bear the responsibility for his friend's project. Count P. D. Kiselev, the Russian minister of state domains, did not view a clash with Benckendorff with any greater enthusiasm, though privately he considered Haxthausen to be an ally in reform. Finally, the security problem was resolved and the archives opened to Haxthausen by means of a compromise. To please his friends and patrons, the guest was overwhelmed with more than four hundred pounds of statistical surveys and memorandums on agrarian law and administration. But, as a concession to Benckendorff, his activities were monitored at every turn. No further data was forwarded to Haxthausen after he left Russia and the secretary whom Kiselev had graciously made available to him reported

28. The best secondary accounts of Haxthausen's Russian expedition are to be found in P. O. Morozov, "Baron Gakstgauzen i ego sochinenie o Rossii," *Istoricheskie materialy iz arkhivov ministerstva gosudarstvennykh imushchestv* (St. Petersburg, 1891), pp. 189–207; and V. I. Semevskii, *Krestianskii vopros v XVII i pervoi polovine XIX-ogo veka*, 2 vols. (St. Petersburg, 1888), 2:428–43.

secretly to Petersburg on his later activities in Berlin. Fifteen years after his Russian trip Haxthausen was still being warned by his former hosts that he should break off his correspondence with Alexander Herzen.

Benckendorff's caution was not entirely unwarranted, considering the importance of Haxthausen's mission to the Russians. As Meyendorff conceived the project, Haxthausen was to interpret the Russian experience to western Europeans. Petersburg officials were still enraged over the phenomenal popularity abroad of the Marquis de Custine's witty and vicious *La Russie en 1839*, published only shortly before in Paris. Though he knew no Russian and spoke French poorly, Haxthausen's assertion that Russia's internal life was unique and "could not be judged by analogy with that of any other people"[29] seemed to dovetail nicely with the official doctrine of Russian uniqueness. It was in this spirit of public relations that the tsar agreed to back the research and to bear the cost of publishing the results in Germany. To the same end, a French edition was to appear simultaneously with the German.[30] Though there is no evidence of official interference in the actual process of research and writing, there can be no question that support would have been withheld had Haxthausen reached conclusions incompatible with the Russian ideology of "official nationality." It was Haxthausen's good fortune, however, to have received an ample pension from his former patron, Friedrich Wilhelm IV. This fund, evidently created by the Prussian ruler in embarrassment over his own failure to stand up to his friend's liberal critics, assured Haxthausen a greater independence in his dealings with the Russians than might otherwise have been the case. Indeed, he was able to refuse the tsar's offer of direct financial assistance.

Soon after the spring thaw in 1843, Haxthausen and his entourage left Moscow for six months in the field. With him was Dr. Heinrich Kosegarten, an assistant who was to write several sections of the *Studies*, and the young Russian aide and interpreter provided by the tsar. The route took him via Novgorod to Moscow, then north to the Vladimir-Iaroslavl area and from there through the Volga region to Nizhnii Novgorod and Kazan and eventually across the steppe to the Caucasus and the Crimea. Late in the summer he turned northward once more, traversing the southern Ukraine to

29. Morozov, "Baron Gakstgauzen," pp. 191–93.

30. For complete bibliographic information on the German, French, and English editions of the *Studies*, see "A Note on the Translation," below p. xliii.

Kiev and thence to Moscow with a brief visit en route to Tula. Along the way he interviewed peasants, priests, landlords, and officials and during brief stops drew the pen sketches that were later to adorn his volumes.

By the time he reached Moscow late in the autumn, Haxthausen was probably among the most widely traveled men in Russia. This alone should have opened the salons of Moscow to him at once. In fact, though, he had at first to overcome hostilities that he had unwittingly caused while in Petersburg at the beginning of his tour. Among the officials and court figures who met him, Haxthausen had encountered a twenty-nine-year-old German historian, Ernst-Eduard Kunik, who had left Berlin to seek his academic fortunes to the east. Opposed to the new visitor's politics and probably seeing in him a potential rival, Kunik wrote to the Moscow historian Mikhail Pogodin expressing his hope that the intellectual leaders of that city would sharply protest Haxthausen's views.[31] This, added to the fact that just at this point the travel memoirs by the Marquis de Custine were outraging many Russians who had cordially received that Frenchman in 1839, at first created a difficult situation for Haxthausen in Moscow.

His keen enthusiasm for all things Russian finally set to rest the fears that these circumstances had aroused. The historian Pogodin, who had at first suspected him of being a spy,[32] eventually gave a dinner in his honor, as did innumerable other figures prominent in the social and intellectual *haut monde* of Moscow. It was at these soirees that Haxthausen met and conversed with members of the gifted Aksakov family, particularly the twenty-five-year-old Konstantin.[33] He in turn introduced the Westphalian aristocrat to all his fellow Slavophiles. Alexander Herzen also met him on several occasions, and the aging curmudgeon Peter Chaadaev seems to have made a particularly strong impression on the guest. The discussions of this busy winter enabled Haxthausen later to write more knowledgeably of contemporary Russian thought than practically anyone

31. N. P. Barsukov, *Zhizn i trudy M. P. Pogodina*, 22 vols. (Moscow, 1883–1906), 7:281.

32. Ibid., 7:282.

33. Aksakov had earlier shown his zeal for enlightening foreign tourists when in 1840 he prepared a long memorandum on Russia for Pierre Manguin, of the French Chamber of Deputies. Manguin had theretofore believed Russia to be a Moslem nation. Another person to host Haxthausen frequently in Moscow was the poetess Karolina Pavlova, the German wife of the mediocre writer Nikolai Pavlov. See *Russkii arkhiv*, 1890, no. 2.

else in the West. At length, armed with his field notes and a wagon load of local records and official documents, Baron Haxthausen returned to his native Germany in the spring of 1844 to set down his impressions.

Four years were to elapse before the first volumes of the *Studies* were set in print. This delay, which exasperated Petersburg officialdom, was not occasioned by conflicting responsibilities, for although Haxthausen did make a brief trip to Vienna and Rome in 1844, his busy two-year service in the upper house of the United Prussian *Landtag* did not begin until 1847. Rather, it seems to have been due chiefly to the "want of diligence and orderly work habits" that the poet Achim von Arnim had observed in him thirty years before.[34] At the same time, Haxthausen compounded his difficulties by choosing for the publication a narrative style in which he had never before worked. His earlier studies on Prussian land law, like most German works on *Statistik*, had been presented in a turgid, thematic form. Though he was at best a mediocre stylist, Baron Haxthausen rejected this model in favor of the lighter, less academic format of the travel account; only in the last volume of the *Studies* did he attempt to pull the many threads together into analytic essays on defined topics. The choice of this mode of expression was probably made under the influence of Custine's work and the discursive but popular *Travels in European Russia* published by the Brunswick professor Blasius in 1844.[35] By following these successful examples, Haxthausen hoped to assure for his work a broad readership, a prospect which could only have pleased his publicity-conscious backers.

This was a wise choice in every respect. Never was travel writing more popular than in the 1830s and 1840s. During these last decades before steamboats and railroads made travel swift and inexpensive, the most modest trip might still appear an adventure. The literary genre of the travel record was ideally suited to register this excitement. Under the pen of an adept writer, the subtlest moods of local color could be blended with anecdotes, learned observations, and

34. *Achim von Arnim und Clemens Brentano*, 3:424.

35. J. G. Blasius, *Reise im europäischen Russland in den Jahren 1840 und 1841*, 2 vols. (Brunswick, 1844). Blasius was also supported by Count Meyendorff. Blasius's general itinerary, the length of his stay, the format of his work, and even the pen-and-ink sketches all anticipate Haxthausen's work. Haxthausen knew Blasius personally and had a well-thumbed copy of his *Reise* in his library, now in UBM.

philosophical digressions to produce a diverting yet edifying whole.[36] Of course, the more exotic the surroundings, the broader was the range of possibilities opened to the writer. Russia under Nicholas I was a favorite for western European travel writers precisely because of its colorful "differentness." Over thirty writers had successfully exploited this element in the twenty years before Haxthausen's volumes appeared.[37] By mid-century, the specifically Russian genre had taken on a defined character, with the form itself determining the points at which the reader was prompted to register awe, admiration, or horror.

In all the voluminous travel literature produced by wandering Europeans in these years the true focus of interest is never far beneath the surface — western Europe itself. Just as writers of the Enlightenment had brought their fictional Persians to Paris and sent fictional Parisians to China as a means of providing Frenchmen with insights on their own civilization, so now this less playful age utilized realistic descriptions of different cultures to achieve the same end. Travel accounts, for all their apparent superficiality, performed the very serious function of orienting Europeans in space and in time at a moment in their history when domestic changes threatened to disorient them at every turn. As Alexis de Tocqueville frankly announces in the introduction to his remarkable *Democracy in America*, "It

36. For the origins of this genre see H. Roddier, "De quelques voyageurs observateurs des moeurs. Naissance d'une forme et d'une mores littéraire," *Connaissance de l'étranger: Mélanges offerts à la mémoire de Jean-Marie Carrét* (Paris, 1964), pp. 440–61.
37. Among the more widely read accounts were: James Stanislas Bell, *Journal d'une résidence en Circasie*, 2 vols. (London, 1839); Robert Bremner, *Excursions in the Interior of Russia*, 2 vols. (London, 1839); John D. Cochrane, *Narrative of a Pedestrian Journey through Russia and Siberian Tartery*, 2 vols. (London, 1825); M. Demidoff, *Travels in South Russia and the Crimea*, 2 vols. (London, 1855); Capt. C. Colville Frankland, *Narrative of a Visit to the Courts of Russia and Sweden in the Years 1830 and 1831*, 2 vols. (London, 1832); A. B. Granville, *St. Petersburg*, 2 vols. (London, 1829); Charles F. Hennigson, *Revelations of Russia in 1836 by an English Resident*, 2 vols. (London, 1846); J. G. Kohl, *Reisen im Innern von Russland und Polen* (Dresden and Leipzig, 1841); L. Leouzon le Duc, *La Russie contemporaine*, 2d ed. (Paris, 1854); E. Dupré de Saint Maur, *L'Hermite en Russie*, 3 vols. (Paris, 1829); Henri Merimée, *Une année en Russie: Lettres à M. Saint-Marc Girardin* (Paris, 1847); Laurence Oliphant, *The Russian Shores of the Black Sea* (New York, 1854); Leitch Ritchie, *A Journey to St. Petersburg and Moscow* (London, 1836); A.M.X.-B. Saintines, *Six mois en Russie* (Paris, 1827); Xavier Hommaire de Hell, *Les steppes de la mer Caspienne, le Caucase, la Crimée et la Russie méridionale*, 3 vols. (Paris 1843–45).

is not merely to satisfy a legitimate curiosity that I have examined America; my wish has been to find there instruction by which we may ourselves profit."[38] Though his subject matter and form of presentation differed sharply from those of Tocqueville, Haxthausen resembled him in endeavoring to identify the forces that were changing European society, to examine the problems to which they gave rise, and to estimate what role, if any, traditional habits and institutions might play in the modern world thus created.

Haxthausen was stimulated to write his *Studies* because of his belief that there were perpetuated in Russia features of the traditional society that had been obliterated in western Europe. This interest determined his itinerary, the topics of his conversations with Russians, the subjects of his pen sketches, and the underlying theme of the final publication. In contrast to Custine and other travelers, he hurried from the Italianate capital of Saint Petersburg as soon as he had outfitted himself for the road. Though he was received by the tsar, he did not bother to mention the fact — the functions of the westernized court held no attraction for him whatsoever. A true Romantic, he was bent instead upon seeking out the authentic customs of the land, the simple yet noble modes of life to whose existence the cataclysmic events of his youth in Westphalia had first awakened him. Haxthausen's romanticism led him not to verse but to a cool consideration of the total society, an analysis that is surprisingly devoid of exoticism or overindulgence in local flavor. Even in sections on the colorful Black Sea region not translated here, the tone remains scholarly, more comparable to works by modern social historians, ethnographers, or anthropologists than to a tourist brochure. Yet thanks to the aesthetic cast of his thought, Haxthausen was more sensitive than his predecessors to the characteristic act, the typical habit, and the representative artifact — anything, in fact, that served to elucidate the continuing presence of traditional life in Russia.

From the outset, this Westphalian scholar assumes that the roots of Slavic Russian society will differ from those of Germanic and Romance peoples of western Europe. Such a belief underlies the constant juxtaposition of Russia and Germany throughout the *Studies*. Each people possesses its own unique cultural heritage which influences and, in part, determines the manner in which the people will face modernity. Haxthausen did not intend this emphasis to be an invitation to nationalist self-praise. On the contrary, he was

38. Modern Library (New York, 1956), p. 36.

critical of what he considered the narrow nationalism of the Moscow Slavophiles and took particular pains in the *Studies* to dissociate himself from this aspect of their movement.[39]

What characterized the traditional Russian society which Haxthausen so admired? Because of the long-winded and often disjointed style of his *Studies*, Haxthausen's answer to this question must be pieced together from numerous comments scattered throughout the work. Recognizing the problems inherent in imposing generalizations on what were intended as distinct observations, it might be said that two themes sound throughout the *Studies*: that Russian society still maintained in its peasant communes and other institutions the basis for a unity and cohesion within and among classes that was lacking in western Europe, and that this social cohesion was founded on hierarchical and patriarchal lines that embraced every individual in Russia from tsar to peasant.

Conservative Catholic thinkers had long maintained that the individual did not constitute a foundation upon which social unity could be built.[40] Long accustomed to detecting evidence on this issue, Haxthausen was quick to observe that in Russia the building blocks of national unity were not individuals but family groups. At home the Russian family, in contrast to its French or German counterpart, might still occupy all rooms of the house in common. Though tightly knit within, the Russian family easily integrated itself into larger units, specifically the communes (*obshchina*), which were "the family enlarged."[41]

Haxthausen's name is inseparably linked with the primitive communism of the Russian countryside, which he is credited with having "discovered." Actually, Haxthausen was not the first to extol the peasant commune; nor were Alexander Herzen, Alexander Khomiakov, the Polish historian Joachim Lelewel, or Haxthausen's brother Werner, all of whom have been mentioned in this connection.[42] Haxthausen had been anticipated by the Russian scholar Ivan Boltin as early as the eighteenth century.[43] But Haxthausen's role

39. *Studien*, 1:31.

40. See C. Haller, *Die Restauration der Staatswissenschaft* (Winterthur, 1816).

41. *Studien*, 2:85; 1:xvi.

42. Werner Freiherr von Haxthausen, *Uber die Grundlagen unserer Urfassung* (n.p., 1833), p. 80. See Eduard Arens, *Werner von Haxthausen und sein Verwandtenkreis als Romantiker* (Aichach, 1927). On Lelewel see Boris Nikolaevskii, "Za vashu i nashu volnost," *Novyi zhurnal* 7 (1944): 261–69.

43. Ivan Nikitich Boltin, *Primechaniia na istoriiu drevnei i nyneshei Rossii g. Leklerka*, 2 vols. (St. Petersburg, 1788), 2:340 ff.

was more than that of a mere publicist. Having been preoccupied with the vision of peasant communitarianism since his youth, he could approach the Russian village commune with far greater breadth of understanding than anyone else of his era. The remarkably full account of the institutions of rural Russia contained in the *Studies* was undeniably the first attempt to bring the Russian commune into the sphere of European social thought.

Haxthausen pictured Russia as covered with small communal organizations, each integrated internally by ties of blood and by common ownership of land and each sharing these properties with every other communal group. Because of the identity of communal institutions everywhere, families and individuals could move from one region to another and be "adopted" into a new commune, thus preserving the overall social unity and preventing rootlessness. This practice, coupled with the widespread seasonal migration of labor, tended to encourage the spirit of national cohesion at the expense of localism. Throughout his journey, this German traveler from Westphalia was astonished by the Russian's consciousness of his own nationhood, and he enthusiastically predicted that future colonization would only further the cause of national integration.

Haxthausen also observed that Russia's unity existed vertically through society, from class to class. This he attributed to the existence of a national Russian church and a single, centralized national government. As in the earlier essays on Germany, he continued to view the church principally as the bearer of a public ideology, and, as such, a societal institution no less important than the government itself. The spectacle of the tsar kissing a peasant after Easter mass symbolized for him the social unity fostered by both church and state. The Russian nobility, too, though corrupted by its inveterate Francophilia, was no less a part of this overall oneness.

The second general characteristic of traditional Russia was the pervasiveness of the hierarchical principle in all social organizations. Like the tendency toward unity, the hierarchical structuring of all group relationships was rooted in the Russian family itself. The sanctity of paternal authority was so thoroughly inculcated in the home that the family could serve as the model for all other relationships up to and including that of man to God. Thus far Haxthausen did not expand beyond the Catholic image of society, but in commending the communes and artels he emphasized an aspect of hierarchical authority often muted in the West. These unifying institutions, he argued, were not based on democratic equality among the members but on absolute authority, the "despotic power" *(despotische Macht)* of the communal elders and, through them, of the group over its individual components. Habituated to living under such hierarchical relationships, Russians established them whenever they came together in groups; at village meetings, monasteries, prisons, or *Singfeste* an elder was immediately selected and patriarchal authority renewed.

It is in this context that the Westphalian baron argued the need for the perpetuation of the Russian gentry or, as he called it, the nobility, not as a reward to that class for its past services or present worth, but as a necessity in terms of the organization of society as a whole. The paternal relationship between nobleman and peasant was a necessary link in the hierarchical chain that eventually united tsar and people. In agreement with the historian Pogodin and other exponents of the doctrine of "official nationality," Haxthausen insisted that Russia was an autocracy. Since this autocracy was founded on the unity of the Russian people — a tenet which Haxthausen shared with the official ideologists and the Slavophiles alike — its authority was *ipso facto* legitimate.

Haxthausen believed that unity and hierarchy were the fundamental principles underlying Russian society and to these he traced all the welfare of the Russian nation. His praise for the resulting system was lavish and at times one-sided. Divisive factions and competing interest groups scarcely enter his analysis and, to the extent that they do, they lead to no consideration of institutional means for resolving conflicts. Politics did not exist in Haxthausen's Russia either, and the influence of the administration was felt only as a necessary inconvenience and bothersome foreign transplant. The resulting picture could scarcely be made more attractive for Europeans of the mid-nineteenth century. Observing the unity and hierarchy imparted to Russian society by the family, the state, and especially the communes, Haxthausen concluded that Russia had already achieved the utopia of which Saint-Simonians dreamed, yet without the atheism which alone vitiated the French socialists' system.[44]

Haxthausen was convinced that Russia's traditional institutions would shield her from the revolutionary upheavals which had so shaken western Europe and that, accordingly, Russia was destined to follow an unprecedented course of national development. On the eve of the Crimean War he represented Russia as the modern successor to the Roman Empire and in a long appendix not included among these selections, portrayed her armies as being invincible. At the same time, doubts gnawed at the German traveler and found

44. *Studien*, 1:141–54.

expression in a strong pessimism running throughout *Studies*. This countercurrent flowed from his recognition of the extent to which Russia had already entered an age of transition by 1843. Haxthausen was no materialist; he held that modernization of institutions resulted from prior intellectual changes rather than from developments in the economy. On his expedition he discerned that modern rationalism had already made inroads in Russia. The nobility had long since been exposed to the secular culture of France, and such diverse phenomena as the system of education and the chant of the Orthodox Church already bore the stamp of this modernizing influence.

Haxthausen adduced further evidence on the rapid pace of change in Russian society from the economic realm. Industrialization was already advancing rapidly, especially in Moscow. He was among the first scholars to devote serious attention to industrial Moscow and the first western observer to characterize Moscow as an industrial city. Change was less marked in agriculture but was already observable in the beet sugar factories of the south and in the work of a few progressive landlords. With great candor he predicted flatly that economic growth might be impeded by the rural communes. "It must be confessed," he wrote, "that the fundamental principle of the communal system — equal division of land — is not conducive to agricultural progress; at the very least, it will render progress more difficult." Indeed, it was not unlikely that "agriculture and all branches of farming would remain at a low level on account of [the communes]."[45] But the primitive communism of the peasantry would likely not remain static. The day when modern notions of society and economics would infect the peasant commune already loomed in 1843. "How long will this institution remain," Haxthausen asked, "if intellectual culture, which signifies progress, makes headway among the people on the Russian land?"[46]

Having acknowledged the extent to which the tsarist empire was in a state of flux, Haxthausen then drew the reader's attention to the reaction that these changes evoked from traditional Russia. Opposition to the imported ideology of secular individualism gave rise to the Old Believer schism in Russian Orthodoxy and to the smaller pietistic sects. Haxthausen was among the first scholars to analyze the Russian schismatic and sectarian movements in detail and actually devoted a long and now lost manuscript to this subject.[47]

45. Ibid., 1:129–30.
46. Ibid.
47. An earlier study on these movements is Le P. Thiener, *L'Eglise schismatique Russe* (Paris, 1846). Haxthausen's manuscript may be in Leningrad,

He concluded that these groups, seeking the simplicity and purity of the primitive church, were a living rebuke to Orthodoxy for having lost touch with traditional Russia. Though their Gnostic beliefs were objectionable to Haxthausen, their morality, sobriety, and piety were not. Even in industrial Moscow, the Old Believer retained these qualities. Their efforts to better the spiritual and physical welfare of their coreligionists impressed Haxthausen deeply and convinced him that the Orthodox Church should be doing precisely the same things. The alternative appeared clear to Haxthausen: the large-scale desertion of the populace from the church, and social revolution.

No innovation was received passively by traditional Russia; each force set up its own counter-force. Urbanization was retarded by colonization, efforts to develop commercial agriculture were countered by the recalcitrance of the peasantry, and bureaucraticization was opposed by rural noblemen. Yet Haxthausen's fastidious cataloging of the interaction of the old with the new does not signify that he rigidly opposed all modification of the old order. Whatever his instinctual reaction may have been, his historical sense was too keen not to accept change as inevitable. This qualified acceptance of "progress" was the easier for Haxthausen because he acknowledged the presence of many discordant elements in the otherwise idyllic Russian past. A case in point is the enserfment of the peasantry, which Haxthausen traced to fundamental movements in Russian history and not to chance or to alien forces acting on Russia from without. Similarly, he realized that Peter I had greatly sharpened class conflict in Russia, but professed a lively respect for his achievement nonetheless. In sharp contrast to the romantic Slavophiles, Haxthausen depicted the destruction of Muscovite Russia as a heroic feat integral to the process by which Russia's historical identity unfolded.

However all-embracing his view of the past, Baron Haxthausen remained, in his own words, "not one to sing the praises of modern culture."[48] This culture was sweeping into Russia, and not even the traditions of unity and hierarchy could avail to stop it. At bottom a pessimist, Haxthausen nonetheless did not yield completely to gloom. The example of the communal manufacturing artel, fostering simple industry yet thwarting the formation in Russia of a rootless proletariat, seemed to justify at least some hope. If traditional Russia

---

since the accession list for 1929 of the Manuscript Division of the Leningrad Public Library lists a work by Haxthausen on the sectarians, but the present archivists are unable to locate it.

48. *Studien*, 1:147.

could not stop the incursion of the international culture of modernity, it could at least reshape it somewhat and adapt it to Russian circumstances.

To bring about this eventuality, Haxthausen sprinkled his *Studies* with advice for the Russian government and public. No area was too trivial for his attention, and his policy suggestions range from forestry and matters of dress to communications, colonization, and local government. Such proposals, like those he had advanced in Prussia earlier, had one objective: to free Russia's indigenous institutions from legal fetters and thereby to forestall the advance of secularism, the formation of a rootless proletariat, and the onslaught of revolutionary anarchy. His application of these principles in the two northern empires imparts unity to Haxthausen's career and serves to link his analysis of Russia with conservative social thought in Europe as a whole.

The principal interest of the Russian government in supporting Haxthausen's research was to improve Russia's image in western Europe. For generations this image had oscillated between extremes. Catherine's support of Voltaire, Diderot, and other Encyclopedists encouraged the view that Russia was ruled by doctrinaire reformers; this caricature was reinforced by the liberal and constitutional interests of Catherine's grandson, Alexander I. Under Nicholas I, the pendulum swung hard to the right. The *Quarterly Review*'s blunt assertion that Russia "had not contributed one single iota to the advancement of human knowledge"[49] and the *Times*'s allusion to "the headstrong and fanatical character of Nicholas, confident to excess in his resources, and elated by the consciousness of brute force"[50] revealed attitudes calculated to give pause to the most self-possessed Russian. The tsar's diplomats turned to public relations none too soon!

Did their campaign succeed? There can be no question that Haxthausen's *Studies* was widely read across the continent. His chief sponsor, Count Meyendorff, avidly collected the reviews and reported with pride to the Russian empress that his protégé had become a literary celebrity.[51] The *Spectator*'s general assessment of the *Studies* as being "occupied with deeper and more important subjects than almost any other work on modern Russia"[52] seems

49. *Quarterly Review* 94 (1854): 434.
50. *Times* (London), 18 May, 1842.
51. Peter von Meyendorff, *Ein russischer Diplomat an den Höfen von Berlin und Wien*, ed. Otto Hoetzsch, 3 vols. (Berlin and Leipzig, 1923), 3:317.
52. *Spectator*, 14 June 1856, p. 643.

to have been shared by most western readers. Given such reviews, Meyendorff was quite justified in concluding that "the existence of this man is an advantage for us."[53]

The specific message that readers gained from the *Studies* was highly colored by their personal political convictions. For continental radicals the appearance of the *Studies* could not have been more timely. Many who read these volumes while reeling from the defeat of the revolutions of 1848 found significance in the notion of a "Russian socialism" vaunted by Haxthausen. To them he seemed to be announcing that the communitarian ideal which had just been discredited on the streets of Paris, Berlin, and Vienna was alive and well on the eastern border of Europe. This was the essence of the praise lavished on Haxthausen by the French radical historian Jules Michelet in his polemical *Légendes démocratiques du Nord*. Until 1847, he claimed, Russia had been "scarcely better known than America before Columbus."[54] Haxthausen was Russia's discoverer, and the welcome news that he brought Europe was that Russia's indigenous institutions were communistic. Other enthusiasts of the left closed their eyes to the broader message of the *Studies* and eagerly expounded this same view. One to do so was the émigré Russian anarchist, Mikhail Bakunin, who promoted Russia's homegrown socialism in one of his last works before his forced return to Russia in 1849.[55] This boldly populist interpretation of Russian society was to endure for some years. So widespread was it in radical circles that Marx and Engels both felt obliged to denounce it in the succeeding decades.[56]

Conservatives in western Europe were scarcely less delighted with the *Studies*, though for reasons different from those of the Forty-eighters. They relished Haxthausen's belief in the possibility of achieving social harmony within the framework of traditional society and applauded as he argued that the institutional heritage of the past should be buttressed rather than ripped away. The baron's fear of despotism and anarchy and his underlying cultural pessimism also struck sympathetic chords among a diverse readership in France

53. Meyendorff, *Ein russischer Diplomat*, 3:397.
54. Jules Michelet, *Légendes démocratiques du Nord* (Paris, 1854), p. 25.
55. Michael Bakunin, *Die russische Zustände: Ein Bild aus der Jetztzeit* (Leipzig, 1849); see Franco Venturi, *Roots of Revolution* (New York, 1960), p. 60.
56. Karl Marx and Friedrich Engels, *Marx und Engels Werke*, 39 vols. (Berlin, 1962), 18:562.

and Germany. Finally, the implication in the third volume of the *Studies* that the simple Christian piety of the Russians might be instilled into western Catholicism through a union of the churches was singled out for commendation. Haxthausen had long supported every effort to reunite Orthodoxy and the Holy See, and in 1844 had even journeyed to Rome at the behest of Nicholas I to make preliminary arrangements for the papal-Russian concordat of 1847. Subsequently he traveled to England and France to meet with church leaders there,[57] and he carried on a lively correspondence on the issue of Christian unity with such diverse figures as the poet Alexander Khomiakov, Andrei Muraviev, Metropolitan Philaret of Moscow and the French philosopher Baron Montalambert.[58] Subsequently he brought together at Thienhausen a large assembly of German bishops, the Russian Catholic Prince Gagarin, and others to establish the society "Petruswerk" as a means of promoting church unity and social regeneration.[59] This program, already spelled out in the *Studies*, helped endear Haxthausen to those readers who drew back in horror from the radicalism of the day.

The only quarter in which the *Studies* appears not to have been well received was liberal, industrial England, where it was met with skepticism, criticism, and outright derision. One reviewer found the work "incoherent . . . , perplexing and often insipid."[60] Unlike continental conservatives, English readers took note of the discussions of the Russian village commune but denied the validity of Haxthausen's conclusions. As a critic put it, "The general description of the rural institutions . . . we believe to be theory; indeed, with serfdom, they seem scarcely compatible with practice."[61] Reviewers confounded Haxthausen's effusive commendations of Russia as a society untainted by proletarian influence by citing pas-

57. August von Haxthausen, "Fünf Briefe über die Stellung der Katholizismus in Frankreich und England," *Westfäl. Merkur,* 1850, nos. 244, 246, 249, 250, 252.

58. This valuable correspondence is preserved in the Archivstelle beim Erzbischöflichen Generalvikariat, Paderborn (AEGP). See also "Une correspondance entre le Baron de Haxthausen et André Mouravieff," ed. P. Haring, *Istina* (Paris, 1969), and *Chteniia v obshchestve liubitelei dukhovnogo prosveshcheniia,* 1887, bk. 9, pp. 149–99.

59. Eduard Winter, *Russland und das Papsttum,* 2 vols. (Berlin, 1960–61), 2:297–98, 301–4; also Haxthausen's introduction to I. Gagarin's *La Russie sera-t-elle catholique?* (Paris, 1856); German ed., *Wird Russlands Kirche das Papsttum anerkennen?* (Münster, 1857).

60. *Westminster Review* 66 (1856): 223.

61. *Spectator,* 14 June 1856, p. 642; cf. *Quarterly Review* 93 (1853): 25–46; 94 (1854): 423–60.

sages from the *Studies* describing the droves of paupers in public places. These particular criticisms were but the prelude to a more fundamental attack on Haxthausen's impartiality as an observer. The *Westminster Review* correctly discerned that Haxthausen, "who wrote the latter part of his work after the revolution of 1848, evidently writes throughout at the German democrats; and he praises everything Russian almost avowedly, because he thinks that Russian stability will counteract the liberal movement in Germany. We therefore distrust his fairness, and think he is biased in his conclusions by a wish to serve what is called the party of order."[62]

Haxthausen's *Studies* inculcated no single image of Russia among western European readers. But it did more than merely enable representatives of each political faction to discover in Russia tendencies analogous to those they favored or opposed at home. On the one hand, the work deepened the general interest in Russia and helped broaden that interest to include the social institutions of the Russian interior as well as the urban-centered life of the state. On the other hand, it served to integrate the terms used to describe Russia's social and political life with the framework within which western Europeans perceived their own changing institutions — all this at the moment when western armies were departing to engage tsarist troops in the Crimea.

Haxthausen surprised western Europeans with his challenging account of Russia, but the most decisive impact of his writings was in Russia itself. The empress assured Haxthausen that the *Studies* was the greatest work ever written on Russia and the distinguished Imperial Geographical Society immediately offered him full membership.[63] The Slavophile Alexander Koshelëv remarked, "A German visiting our country pointed the way for our so-called learned men to study earnestly matters which they had not taken seriously before,"[64] to which Alexander Herzen retorted, "Isn't that a disgrace!"[65] The considerable discussion of the *Studies* within Russia took place despite the stringent conditions prevailing under the "censorship terror" of 1848–55. Nicholas himself read and approved a draft of the *Studies* and sent a large diamond to Haxthausen in gratitude, but then, as if doubting his own judgment, forbade a

62. *Westminster Review* 66 (1856): 224.

63. Von der Osten, *Haxthausen*, p. 33; Eugène Lamansky to Haxthausen, 17 November 1855, AEGP.

64. *Russkaia Beseda* 8 (1858): 108.

65. A. I. Herzen, foreword to Russian edition of *From the Other Shore, Sobranie sochinenii*, 30 vols., ed. V. P. Volgin et al. (Moscow, 1954–66), 6:18.

full translation to appear in Russia during his lifetime. Yet the wide-spread memory of Haxthausen's winter in Moscow and the enthusiastic notices on the work appearing in western journals aroused a curiosity that defied censorship. No sooner did the *Studies* appear than members of the reformist Petrashevskii circle in Petersburg discussed its revelation at their gatherings, and the leader, Mikhail Petrashevskii, began translating the chapters devoted to the sectarians.[66] Thanks to such informal channels of communication, many educated Russians were introduced to the essentials of Haxthausen's argument long before the *Studies* could be discussed legally in 1856.

The Russian intelligentsia found the most intriguing aspect of the *Studies* to be its panegyric of a unique "Russian socialism." Alexander Herzen was the first to be converted to this populist perspective in 1848–49, but others quickly followed.[67] In a series of forthright essays written for western European and Russian readers, Herzen declared his new faith in peasant communism and in so doing took a long step toward the position of his old antagonists, the Slavophiles. "Haxthausen is completely right," he wrote. "The social structure of the rural commune in Russia embodies a great truth. The commune is the proprietor and the object of taxation; it renders a rural proletariat in Russia impossible."[68]

Nikolai Chernyshevskii, editor of the influential *Contemporary (Sovremennik)*, echoed Herzen's judgment. In 1848 Chernyshevskii had watched in helpless frustration as the revolutionary cause went down to defeat, and now he vented his pent-up hatred for the forces of order by pointing out the conservatism in Haxthausen's work. He would very likely have turned against Haxthausen completely had the liberal economist Ivan Vernadskii and the statist historian Boris Chicherin not launched their own frontal attack on the *Studies*. Both scholars garnered voluminous data to support the point that rural communes lacked the historical and economic significance ascribed to them by Haxthausen.[69] They held that the communes,

66. *Delo Petrashevtsev*, ed. V. Desnitskii (Moscow, 1936) 3:225, 513 514; *Biografiia pisma i zametki iz zapisnoi knizhki F. M. Dostoevskogo: Materialy dlya zhizneopisaniia F. M. D. -ogo*, ed. O. Miller (Leningrad, 1933), 1:92.
67. See N. M. Druzhinin, "A. Gakstgauzen i russkie revoliutsionnye-demokraty," *Istoriia SSSR*, 1967, no. 3, pp. 73–75.
68. Herzen, *Sobranie sochinenii*, 6:199–201.
69. I. V. Vernadskii (1821–84), professor, civil servant, and editor, carried his attacks on Haxthausen in his *Ekonomicheskii ukazatel*, vol. 1 (St. Petersburg, 1857); B. N. Chicherin (1828–1904) devoted his important *Oblastnye uchrezhdeniia Rossii v XVII v.* (Moscow, 1857), to a consideration of the state's role in communal institutions.

far from being evidence of the creative force of the simple peasantry before they were ensnared by serfdom and the state, were actually themselves created by the state. The implication was clearly that the Russian state would today be acting entirely within its powers if it chose to modify or abolish peasant institutions to suit its changing needs. This unexpected attack from such an odious quarter prompted Chernyshevskii to drop his own critique and sally forth in Haxthausen's defense.

The widely read polemics on history and economics established no conclusions. But they did succeed in airing many issues crucial to the serf problem in Russia at a time when emancipation could not be openly debated in the press. Attacked or defended, the *Studies* did much to establish the framework in which aspects of this important issue were to be considered over the next years.

Haxthausen's involvement with the emancipation of the Russian serfs was not limited to the role his *Studies* played in the unofficial debates of 1855–56. As early as 1842 he had forwarded his general views on this vital issue to the minister of state domains, Count Kiselev, who disseminated them in the ruling circles of Petersburg. Count Meyendorff acknowledged at the time that "many people who know Haxthausen seem to think that his trip would be of great use to our government in explaining the measures through which a permanent emancipation of the serfs could be achieved."[70] Fulfilling Meyendorff's hopes, Haxthausen had met in Petersburg with representatives of the German nobility from Russia's Baltic provinces who had gathered at the tsar's request to consider means of improving the condition of Latvian and Estonian peasants in their charge. The Westphalian baron offended them by declaring bluntly that their peasants could be saved from poverty only if they were provided with land.[71] He offered the same advice to the Russian minister of justice, Panin, in 1848.[72]

In 1856, with Alexander II now on the throne, Haxthausen intensified his abolitionist campaign. First, he drafted two articles on the process of emancipation in the Prussian and Austrian monarchies.[73] These received the censors' imprimatur only because they did not deal directly with Russian affairs. Even the censors,

70. Morozov, "Baron Gakstgauzen," pp. 194–95.
71. Barsukov, *Zhizn . . . Pogodina*, 7:281.
72. Haxthausen to Panin, 4 August 1848, UBM.
73. August von Haxthausen, "Ob otmenenii i vykupe pomeshchichikh gospodskikh prav v Prussii," and "Ob otmenenii i vykupe pomeshchichikh gospodskikh prav v Avstrii," *Russkii Vestnik* 12 (1857): 426–42, 571–82.

though, must have realized that they were loaded with thinly veiled advice for the government, the first such advice to appear in print. In these articles he argued the case for the Prussian as opposed to the Austrian pattern for liberating the peasantry. Specifically, he praised the legislation of Friedrich Wilhelm I and Friedrich II for guaranteeing the peasant's right to his own land, and the later legislation of 1806–15 for assuring both that the gentry would be repaid in full for land turned over to the peasantry and that the interests of the peasantry would be defended by official commissions constituted at the provincial level. Of course, these measures had the obvious benefit of shoring up the large estates. At the same time, Haxthausen insisted that the peasantry be made truly independent by being granted acreage adequate for its needs, which had not been done in Prussia. Whatever its cost, the peasants themselves should prefer such a settlement to the Austrian method, which he claimed had crippled agricultural productivity and reduced the rural populace to a state of profound misery. To guide future Russian legislators in their work, Haxthausen appended to his essays a Russian translation of the principal legislative acts covering the Prussian emancipation.

Even while these articles were in preparation, the author of the *Studies* was resorting to more direct means of influencing Russian policy. Since the 1840s a particularly enthusiastic supporter of Haxthausen's work on both church and secular problems had been the Russian grand duchess Elena Pavlovna. Haxthausen had visited her in Petersburg and she had met him frequently at the spas of her native Germany. In 1856 she had petitioned the young tsar for permission to carry out a test emancipation at her estates at Karlovka in Poltava province.[74] Alexander had refused on the grounds that the gentry rather than the state should lead the process. Temporarily thwarted, the grand duchess resolved to continue her campaign by gaining the backing of the leading experts on the serf question. To this end, she convened a gathering of distinguished experts at Wildbad in the Schwarzwald during the summer of 1857. Among those present were Kiselev, now ambassador in Paris, the jurist Konstantin Kavelin, two Poltava lords, A. A. Abaza and V. V. Tarnovskii, and Haxthausen. Most of the participants came in the expectation of working out further details of the Karlovka project, which they in fact did. But the assembly had another far more impor-

74. On this project see W. Bruce Lincoln, "The Karlovka Reform," *Slavic Review* 28 (September 1969): 463–70.

tant purpose, which became evident at the first session. A Russian nobleman vacationing in Germany recorded that the group was engaged in "a detailed study of the peasant question in general and of the communes in Russia and other Slavic lands in particular."[75] This study was by no means merely academic. Though largely unknown to contemporaries, the Wildbad group was delving deeper into the emancipation issue than had any governmental or gentry body in Russia before, and was setting down proposals that anticipated many of the provisions of the actual emancipation statutes of 1861.

The complete working papers of the sessions preserved in Haxthausen's archive indicate that he dominated the meetings and was principally responsible for drafting the documents produced by the self-appointed commission. To guide the members in their work he had prepared ahead a paper entitled "Observations on the Broader Development and Extension of the Present Provincial Order in Russia, Especially in Relation to the Imminent Abolition of Serfdom."[76] Here once more he stressed the need for the gentry to be directly involved in the emancipation process, both because the administrative hierarchy lacked the physical capability and moral authority to accomplish the task alone and because the nobility desperately needed the practical involvement in local affairs that such work would entail. But it was the responsibility of the government to monitor and guide the work by placing the provincial marshals of the nobility in charge of elected twelve-man juries or commissions which would make local arrangements for the emancipation and adjudicate disputes over its implementation. These groups, similar to the provincial committees and arbiters of the peace that were actually instituted, would work closely with the *ispravniki* representing the executive police and, of course, with the central agencies of government. Finally, he emphasized the importance of expanding state-sponsored mortgage credit to lords to such a degree that the abolition of serfdom would be as nearly voluntary as possible from the lords' side. Haxthausen's lack of attention to the peasants themselves at this stage indicates that he considered the problem of the future political and social position of the nobility to be the most critical aspect of the issue.

75. D. A. Obolenskii, "Moi vospominaniia o velikoi kniagine Elene Pavlovne," *Russkaia Starina* 137 (1909):42.

76. "Bemerkungen. Die weitere Entwickelung und den Ausbau der jetzigen Gouvernements Verfassung in Russland betreffend, besonders in Beziehung auf die bevorstehende Auflösung der Leibeigenschaft," AEGP.

The vitriolic confrontations in Petersburg in 1859–60 were to prove him right on this.

The organization of peasant life and the role of the state were the subjects of two further *Promemoriae* addressed to the grand duchess.[77] The first of these reviewed the history of communal institutions in general terms, making reference to west European and other Slavic nations as well as Russia. The second, thirty-four pages long, detailed the need for an unprecedented Russian form of emancipation that would utilize the best of all previous methods. Such a program would have to enable peasants to remain in their villages rather than be set adrift toward the cities or isolated on individual farmsteads. By citing his earlier research on Estonia he was able to argue convincingly that this goal could be achieved only if the peasants received an adequate amount of land and if this land were granted in communal rather than individual tenure. If this were to be done, he claimed, future industrial development would occur not in the cities but in the countryside, where its most dangerous effects would be meliorated by rural institutions. Haxthausen, it need hardly be said, agreed heartily with Count Bismarck, who had declared only two years before that big cities should disappear from the face of the earth. A further result of maintaining communal tenure would be that taxes on new industries would be credited to the rural areas and would help repay the lord for the land he turned over to the communes, hence reducing the burden on the peasantry of redemption payments in the form of labor or gold. In this document Haxthausen stressed once more the critical role of government-sponsored credit in the emancipation process. Here, though, he added that the treasury should guarantee that any peasant commune unable to meet its obligations must be able to borrow from the treasury at a reasonable rate of interest. Analogous arrangements were proposed for state-owned peasants as well. All these procedures were to be worked out by the government for the entire country but were to be adjusted to local conditions by the provincial commissions of noblemen.

This memorandum stands unique among all the many manuscript proposals of the era in that (1) it argues the need for organized groups of gentry to be involved locally but stresses that the general

77. Both AEGP, both unnumbered pages. The longer one has the fuller title "Promemoria zu den anliegen Vorschlagen zu Gesetzgebungsaktion über die aufzuhebende Leibeigenschaft und die Dotirung des Bauernstandes in Russland." This MS is incorrectly dated 4 September 1857 in a pencil note not in Haxthausen's hand or that of his secretary.

terms of the emancipation must be worked out by the government itself, and (2) it underscores the importance of state credit as a tool for avoiding undue hardship to either lords or peasants. It is further noteworthy for viewing the long-term implications of continued communal tenure in economic as well as political terms.

Whether it would have any practical effect depended upon the response to it of Alexander II, who was scheduled to arrive in Bad Kissingen late in June 1857. As the imperial train steamed up to the station at the renowned spa, the grand duchess, Kiselev, and Haxthausen were on the platform waiting. The strategy of the self-designated lobbyists called for the enlistment of a fourth accomplice, the foreign minister S. M. Gorchakov. To bring this tottering champion of European stability to their side, Haxthausen had penned yet another memorandum, this one stressing the inevitability of emancipation.[78] He pointed out that serfdom in its present form was less than two centuries old and that for a half-century the Russian state had been seeking means of eliminating it. The attempt to contractualize the relation of lord and peasant in 1842 was only the most important of a series of measures that were bearing fruit today. Haxthausen then reviewed the benefits to be derived from the abolition of serfdom by each segment of society — lords, peasants, urban craftsmen, merchants, and the state. The conclusion reiterated the points that he had earlier made to the grand duchess regarding credit. As an afterthought, Haxthausen inserted in the foreign minister's copy a paragraph, not in his original draft, in which he played heavily on the danger of revolution:

> The question of the emancipation of the serfs, while a problem special to Russia, is at the same time a political problem and hence most important not only for Russia but for the rest of Europe as well. I become more convinced of this daily, especially after learning on good authority that the radical party of Mazzini and his brothers in England now puts great hope in a social revolution taking place in Russia. Experience itself shows us that the leaders of that party are not empty dreamers, but truly calculating and perceptive men.[79]

This awesome picture apparently convinced the minister of the neces-

78. "Promemoria den Fürsten Gortschakoff nach Kissingen gesandt," AEGP.

79. Gorchakov's copy was passed on to Alexander II and is preserved in the Central State Historical Archive of the USSR (TsGIA-SSSR), f. 1160. 81, pp. 383–84. Partially quoted by P. A. Zaionchkovskii, *Otmena krepostnogo prava v Rossii*, 2d ed. (Moscow, 1960) pp. 78–81.

sity of bringing the views of the abolitionists to the tsar's attention. Gorchakov delivered to Alexander II Haxthausen's memorandum, as well as a further disquisition on the necessity of emancipating the serfs. This was also the work of Haxthausen.

Alexander had earlier declared himself in favor of abolishing serfdom, warned the nobility of his intentions, and appointed a secret committee to investigate the issue. As yet, though, he remained opposed to the notion of a single, nationwide emancipation worked out by the government rather than by local lords alone, and he was uncommitted on the question of using state credit organs to aid in the process. On the same day that he was given Haxthausen's memorandum (21 June) he received from Petersburg a dispatch that made it clear that the secret committee had interpreted its charge in an exceedingly cautious manner. Eager to recess for the summer, its members had confined themselves to considering the problem of law and order after emancipation without establishing any general principles of emancipation itself or a timetable. Given this situation, the presence in Kissingen of three distinguished abolitionists and especially the memorandums from a respected German scholar who had been strongly supported by Alexander's father, Nicholas I, became factors of paramount importance in forming the young tsar's views and firming his resolve to act. He read with the keenest interest the lines in the memorandum to Gorchakov declaring that the sole effective bulwark against revolution lay in creating a contented peasantry:

> We live in an epoch when thoughts and ideas do not wait years and centuries to be fully developed and disseminated. Spread by the press, steam, and electricity, they sweep Europe like lightning from one end to the other; there is no nation and no country which can preserve itself from their influence. I say this so as to remind you that in Russia one cannot stop half way. It is impossible to leave the most important questions of national existence to their own development. The state is obliged to act first by taking a considered and active part in their solution, so that events, having outstripped it, do not lay hold of the government and lead to its downfall.[80]

Haxthausen clearly had struck a note to which the reticent tsar could respond from deepest instinct and conviction. Alarmed at the prospect of violent upheaval, Alexander penciled in the margin, "Completely true; herin lies my chief concern."

80. Ibid., pp. 385 ff.

Within days, the imperial suite embarked posthaste for Petersburg. Couriers sped ahead to inform the reformist Grand Duke Konstantin that he should reconvene the secret committee forthwith and take over its direction. Henceforth it was clear that whatever role the gentry would play, the Russian government would participate actively in the process of emancipation. And in Russia, reforming statesmen and abolitionist noblemen mobilized for the work that lay ahead. Meanwhile, the Kissingen group continued to exert pressure, this time by publishing the full text of the final confidential memorandum that had so sparked Alexander's anxiety.

Haxthausen was by no means the first foreigner to decry the plight of the Russian peasantry.[81] But his many proposals for dealing with the issue were among the most concrete available to the imperial government. In an early letter to Kiselev, he warned that "to give the peasant personal freedom without first binding him by his own interests to agrarian pursuits would be not only a mistaken measure but a dangerous one."[82] This led the otherwise sympathetic Herzen to denounce Haxthausen's "passionate love of slavery."[83] After 1856, this issue crystallized in the debate over whether communes should be maintained as the basis of rural organization. Over the years and especially in his most recent memorandums Haxthausen presented one of the strongest defenses of communal ownership of land to reach the tsar and his advisers. General Yakov Rostovtsev, who as head of the editing commission that drafted the reform was the target for much of this barrage, finally announced the decision of the government. "In our literature," he concluded, "one can find many discussions and debates on how the commune was formed; but communes do exist in Russia, are still needed, and consequently should be preserved."[84]

The wisdom of this decision has long been questioned by economists, who argue convincingly that it perpetuated conditions of labor inimical to the development of a modern western European type of industrial order in Russia. The decision to require the peasants rather than the state to repay the nobility for their freedom has been criticized no less sharply for binding the peasantry to further decades of rural servitude and thereby hampering the formation of a free labor force

81. See, for example, M. P. D. de Passenans, *La Russie et l'esclavage dans leurs rapports avec la civilisation* (Paris, 1822).

82. Morozov, "Baron Gakstgauzen," p. 194.

83. Herzen, *Sobranie sochinenii*, 12:114.

84. P. P. Semenev-Tian-Shanskii, *Epokha osvobozhdeniia krestian v Rossii, (1857–1861 gg.) v vospominaniiakh P. P. Semeneva-Tian-Shanskogo*, 4 vols. (St. Petersburg, 1911–16), 3:232.

in the cities. That Haxthausen would have welcomed both of these consequences cannot be doubted, given his lingering hope that Russia might be saved from the intellectual, social, and economic upheavals that were fast obliterating the rural society which he had known and loved in Westphalia. Yet it must be acknowledged that if Russia's village communes had not originally been created by the state, it was state action which preserved them in 1861 and which consigned them to further decades of interference and control by both landlords and bureaucrats. Ironically the proposal that Haxthausen endorsed for freeing the indigenous social forces of rural Russia ended by subjecting those forces to the very sort of meddling that he most despised.

August von Haxthausen's interest in Russian affairs did not cease with the abolition of serfdom. In the years before his death in 1866 he maintained an active correspondence with numerous Russian leaders and kept open house at Schloss Thienhausen for all of his many Russian friends who came to Germany to take the waters. In 1865 he succeeded in publishing a study of the means by which a constitutional form of government could be introduced without destroying the sovereignty of the tsar, and in the year of his death he completed a lengthy analysis of the statutes of emancipation.[85]

The constitutional proposal, clearly at odds with Haxthausen's earlier doctrine of Russian uniqueness, indicates the extent to which he was prepared to make strategic concessions to ward off the threat of revolution. In his first correspondence with officials of the Russian government in 1842 he had spoken candidly of his youth in Westphalia and the roots of his fear: "I was witness then to the disorders wreaked on all classes and estates by the revolutionary regime in France; I saw how freedom vanished before the ideas of equality and liberty, and how all privelege of birth and even the patriarchal power of the seigneurs vanished, along with the respect often earned over centuries of good works."[86] This fear, which first drove Haxthausen

---

85. August von Haxthausen, *Das constitutionelle Princep* (Leipzig, 1864); French translation, *Considérations sur la Nature, les conditions et les effets du princip constitutionnel* (Leipzig, 1865); Russian translation, *Konstitutionnoe upravlenie* (St. Petersburg, 1866). *Die ländliche Verfassung Russlands. Ihre Entwickelungen und ihre Feststellung in der Gesetzgebung von 1861* (Leipzig, 1866). In the years after 1861 Haxthausen also assisted in editing A. Skrebitskii's monumental collection of documents on the emancipation.

86. Haxthausen to Kiselev, 17 January 1843, in Semevskii, *Krestianskii vopros* 2:421.

into public life in Prussia, carried him eventually to Russia, which he described in the *Studies* as the one nation in Europe immune to revolutionary change.

The *Studies* is a monument to this personal history of Baron Haxthausen, but it is more. First, it stands as an event in Russian intellectual history, for it reinforced and popularized what hitherto had been an exotic infatuation of a handful of scholars with the peasant institutions of Russia. Second, it is an event in the history of Russian state policy, for it bears witness both to Nicholas I's preoccupation with his reputation in Europe, and to his government's willingness at least to consider basic reforms. Third, it is an event in European thought, for it encouraged readers across the continent to include Russia in their consideration of the changes taking place in Germany, France, and England. Finally, it remains among the best travel accounts of its era and, as such, marks an important stage in the continuing process by which men become conscious of the implications of modernization for the societies in which they live.

S. FREDERICK STARR

# A Note on the Translation

Haxthausen's *Studien über die innern Zustände, das Volksleben, und insbesondere die ländlichen Einrichtungen Russlands* first appeared in 1847–52 (vols. 1 and 2, Hanover, 1847; and vol. 3, Berlin, 1852). The authorized French translation was issued a year later, as *Etudes sur la situation intérieure, la vie nationale et les institutions rurales de la Russie* (vols. 1 and 2, Hanover, 1848; vol. 3, Berlin, 1853). This edition, though encompassing the entire three volumes of the original, was rendered with more spirit than accuracy. Sentences and whole paragraphs were deleted without note, comments by the translator were freely interpolated into the narrative, and both Russian and German technical terms were misleadingly rendered in French. Shortly afterward a drastically shortened English version was prepared. This truncated edition, issued as *The Russian Empire, Its People, Institutions and Resources* (R. Farie, translator; 2 vols., London, 1856), was abridged so as to accord with the interests of the British reading public at the time of the Crimean War. Accordingly, sections describing south Russia and the Crimea were translated *in toto*, as was the long appendix on the military potential of Russia, whereas analytical chapters and passages devoted to agrarian issues were shortened or simply deleted. The English version, while not as free a rendering as the French, is nonetheless marred by frequent mistranslations and by excessive Germanisms in syntax. An authoritative Russian language version of the *Studies* appeared only in 1870 as *Issledovaniia vnutrennykh otnoshenii, narodnoi zhizni, i v osobennosti selskikh uchrezhdenii Rossii barona Gakstgauzena* (L. I. Ragozin, translator; Moscow, 1870).

xliii

## A Note on the Translation

The present edition is translated from the German original. Wherever possible, the style of the German is preserved, though Haxthausen's more clumsy Victorianisms must occasionally be recast to render them intelligible. The frequent repetitions that encumber the German original have been deleted. These and all other abridgments are registered in the text by ellipsis dots. Footnotes indicated by symbols are Haxthausen's; the numbered notes are the editor's. The small illustrations that appear at the end of several chapters are from woodcuts of Haxthausen's original drawings.

The principle of selection applied throughout has been to translate those sections most closely connected with Haxthausen's own deepest concerns and with those of contemporary social thought in western Europe and Russia. Accordingly, the descriptions of village life in central Russia and especially the extensive accounts of Iaroslavl and Nizhnii Novgorod provinces are translated almost in full from volume 1. Also included from volume 1 is the excellent discussion of the sectarian communities, a theme followed up later in the chapter on the Mennonites from volume 2. Haxthausen's thoughtful analysis of colonization and national integration from volume 2 is translated and abridged. Finally, the lengthy essays from volume 3 on Moscow, the nobility, the religiosity of Russians, and the peasant commune are included. These passages, along with the analysis of colonization, present a convenient summary of Haxthausen's investigations and form the basis for the author's concluding prognostications in "The Mission of Russia."

For those interested in reading at greater length in the original text, the following listing of chapters not translated here may prove useful. From volume 1, a chapter on Petersburg (1) was excluded, as were those on the Saint Petersburg Forestry Institute (2), the trip from Moscow to the Trinity–Saint Sergius Monastery (5), parts of the chapters on Vologda (8–9) and on Kostroma (11), as well as the concluding chapters on the Kazan area (15–16). The chapters deleted from volume 2 provide an interesting travelogue on the southern part of the empire and are particularly valuable for the archaeological and ethnographical data they contain. These chapters cover the trip from Kazan to Samara (17), Penza (18), and Voronezh (19), and include discussions of the prehistory of the steppe country (22), of the Nogai Tartars (23) and of the entire Crimean peninsula (24–25). From the third volume we have excluded the long section on the military (6), since it was less the result of original research than the other parts and since it is already available in a nineteenth-century

English translation, and also the chapter on the crown lands (7), which largely repeats arguments presented earlier.

It is our hope that the selections we have chosen will represent the *Studien* faithfully and in a sufficiently comprehensive fashion for the modern reader to form his own impression of August von Haxthausen's thought.

For the use of the archival materials cited in the Introduction and notes we are grateful to Dr. Alfred Cohausz of the Archivstelle beim Erzbischöflichen Generalvikariat, Paderborn; to Dr. Ruth Steffen of the Universitätsbibliothek, Münster; and particularly to Guido Freiherr von Haxthausen, Schloss Thienhausen, Westphalia. Our thanks also to Mr. Arthur Bunce for his editorial assistance.

S.F.S.
E.M.S.

# STUDIES ON THE
# INTERIOR OF
# RUSSIA

August von Haxthausen, 1843. Unpublished lithograph. Schloss
Thienhausen archive. Courtesy of Guido Freiherr von Haxthausen.

# *Preface*

For long years the author of this book has dedicated himself to the detailed study of rural institutions. In particular, he has studied the nature of the peasant commune and the peasant's relationships to it, as well as his relationship to agriculture, to his family, his landlord (in those cases where he is still in a condition of dependence), and to the state. The author has endeavored to observe and to study directly the life of the so-called lower classes. He later found the time, opportunity, and support for his scholarly pursuits when the Prussian government commissioned him to investigate thoroughly the institutions of the peasant class in all the royal provinces and to substantiate his results through detailed descriptions and the historical development of these institutions. The materials he collected were to provide the necessary foundations for future legislation. For this purpose he traveled from 1830 to 1838 through the Prussian Empire and through a large part of the neighboring countries.

In reviewing the historical development of certain rural institutions in all of western Germany, the author discovered conditions which could not be explained from the known development of Germanic society. He attributed the origin of these anomalous institutions to the Slavic peoples who inhabited these originally Germanic lands from the sixth to the twelfth century. These Slavic tribes were either Germanized or gradually disappeared.

He found it essential for his historical studies to submit the national life and institutions of the Slavic peoples to a somewhat more comprehensive study. Never able to gain an understanding of the institutions of peoples simply from historical documents and literature, he always considered direct observation imperative. Subsequent study of the literature of a people helped him to understand its national life, but it was not the primary source of his insight. For this reason he urgently desired to visit the original Slavic countries, which have always been inhabited by Slavs and whose national institutions developed independently.

In those parts of the Prussian Empire still populated by Slavic peoples such as the Cassubians, the Masurians, Upper Silesians, and even the Poles, the original Slavic structure of rural institutions has not remained pure, nor did it develop along purely indigenous lines. The infiltration of so many Germanic elements often makes it impossible to distinguish the Germanic from the Slavic. The author therefore desired to visit and study carefully those countries in which the genuinely Slavic elements of the rural institutions had been able to develop free from external influences. For this reason he could consider only the southern parts of the Austrian Empire, Serbia, Bulgaria, and above all Russia.

But such an investigation involved great difficulties. It could, of course, be undertaken only with the special protection and support of the governments in question. He found the greatest willingness on the part of the Russian government to support his scholarly research. The emperor ordered not only that the author be provided with the protection of all the administrative authorities but also that the requisite reports and notes from the archives and registries be made accessible to him.

After having procured everything needed for such an important trip in Petersburg, he began his journey from Moscow in the spring of 1843. First he traveled to the north, traversed a part of the vast woodlands, and returned to the Volga. He journeyed eastward to Kazan and as far south as Saratov and then proceeded to the rich grain areas of Penza, Tambov, Voronezh, and Kharkov. After crossing the steppes from Ekaterinoslav to Kerch in the Crimea, he made a special short excursion into the southern Caucasian districts and then traveled along the Crimean coast to Odessa. He reached Kiev after journeying through Podolia and Volhynia and returned to Moscow in November via Chernigov, Orel, and Tula.

This book contains a part of the personal experiences, observations, and materials which he gathered in Russia.

In dealing with these investigations, one must keep in mind as a basic principle that for each people rural institutions, both material and legal, have a distinctively national quality. Only when one has fully recognized this, will he be able to interpret and represent those institutions accurately. Although every people, indeed every group, exhibits in this respect particular characteristics, we encounter them to a greater degree in the two large families of nations, the Germanic and the Romanic. Nevertheless, these two peoples have very much in common. The leveling and amalgamation of rural institutions was brought about over the past thousand years through a manifold interpenetration of customs, languages, interests, and all aspects of popular life, through the common church and the diffusion of Roman law.

This amalgamation is also revealed in the Germanic and Romance languages. All of these languages have created words and concepts with precisely the same meaning. In each of these languages one can describe the rural institutions of one's own people as well as those of a foreign people. Indeed, they can be represented with such accuracy that, not only will the foreign scholar acknowledge this, but, should he translate the book into his own tongue, the public would find it generally intelligible and correct. If, for example, one analyzes the concepts *Gemeinde, commune* or *Pächter, farmer, fermier,* one finds that they signify in each of the three languages essentially the same social and legal institutions. And one can describe them in each of these languages and be correctly understood even by a foreign people. . . .

German customs, practices, and concepts have influenced the Poles and Bohemians for centuries. They have adopted German and Roman legal concepts and institutions; for centuries their legislation has exhibited the same character as that of the Germanic and Romanic peoples. The indigenous Slavic institutions have thus been significantly modified here, and the entire constitutional and legal structure of these peoples resembles that of the Germanic and Romanic peoples so closely that in general the above statements apply to them as well. . . .

This cannot be said, however, of those Slavic peoples who either have not drawn near to the intellectual and cultural milieu of the other European peoples or have not adopted European ideas into their national life, such as the Serbians, Bosnians, and Bulgarians, or where this has been the case only in recent times . . . as with the Russians.

The social and legal institutions of those Slavic peoples untouched by modern European civilization differ so completely in principle (as well as in the development of this principle) from those of the other nations that our languages often lack the precise words to

5

designate them correctly. To find the correct formulation, we have to describe and circumscribe them. The linguistic and legal concept of the word *Gemeinde, commune*, for example, is so uniform and well defined in all the European languages that one can use it in any one of these languages without the fear of being misunderstood. How extraordinarily different on the other hand is the concept of an old Slavic and Russian *commune*! In Europe it is an aggregation, a division made from above, a group of people who dwell together by chance and whose relations are ordered by custom, habit, and law. In the Slavic countries, the commune is a family organism. Originally an expanded patriarchal family, it is still today at least a fictive family based on collective property and headed by an elder.

Among those Slavic peoples who remained completely untouched by civilization, such as the Serbians, Bulgarians, etc., this fact is so obvious that scholars could not but discover it long ago. Consequently they avoided the mistake of interpreting these institutions with an outsider's eye. The works of Ranke on the Serbians and of Cyprien Robert on the Slavs in general give honorable testimony to this, which is the more surprising because Ranke, as far as we know, was never in Serbia and never observed Serbian national life directly.[1]

Descriptions of Russian conditions are different. Russia already constituted a political entity quite early. At a very early date she acquired political institutions from Constantinople and very likely through Germanic (Varangian) influences. Ever since Russia cast off the Mongol yoke in the sixteenth century, she has drawn decidedly nearer to western Europe. For one hundred and forty years she has energetically sought to adopt modern civilization. The upper classes have been raised and educated entirely in a European manner, and all her political institutions have been copied from those of western Europe. Russian legislation has assumed not only the character but even the forms of European legislation. The results, however, are visible in general only among the upper classes. Foreign culture has not affected the customs and habits, the family and communal institutions, the farming methods and rural institutions in general of the lower classes. The populace has hardly been touched by

1. Leopold von Ranke (1795–1886) was professor of history at Berlin and founder of the research seminar as a form of instruction. His *Fürsten und Völker von Südeuropa im 16. und 17. Jahrhundert* (Berlin, 1827) was based on Italian documents discovered in Berlin. Cyprien Robert (1807–58) professor of Slavic languages and literature at the Collège de France, also wrote his *Les Slaves de Turquie* (Paris, 1844) without resort to field research.

foreign culture through legislation and only slightly through the administration.

However, because of the schism between the culture of the upper and lower classes, the upper classes' understanding of indigenous rural institutions has suffered infinitely. Because the upper classes were accustomed to foreign tongues and customs, and because their education was based only on a knowledge of foreign jurisprudence and foreign institutions, they also viewed their own native institutions with a somewhat alienated eye. They sought to explain them on the basis of superficially similar foreign institutions or, in those cases where they could influence legislation, to reshape them according to the foreign model. Only most recently, with the rise of a more national spirit in Russia as in all the nations of Europe, and with the manifestation of a vigorous effort in the Russian world of scholarship dedicated to research on the sources and true nature of popular institutions,* have changes come about in this respect. However, even today the foreign culture introduced in times past and the cultivated language of the upper classes, which at one time

---

*One must say in praise of German scholars in particular that they provided the initial impetus for this trend. Men like Schlözer, Müller, Evers, Georgi, Storch, and others, and, above all, more recently Reutz, were the teachers of the younger Russian scholars and played the major role in arousing their love for national institutions and their enthusiasm to research them.[2]

2. August Ludwig von Schlözer (1735–1809) was a Göttingen scholar and publicist who lived in Petersburg between 1760 and 1764 and thereafter encouraged Russian studies from Germany. Renowned for his pioneering research into Russian chronicles, especially his *Nestor*, 5 pts. (Göttingen, 1803–9). Gerhard Friedrich Müller 1705–83) was editor of *Sammlung russischer Geschichte,* 9 vols. (St. Petersburg, 1732–65), which considerably advanced western knowledge of Russian history. Müller edited the first scientific and literary periodical in the Russian language, the *Ezhemesiachnye sochineniia k polze i uveseleniiu sluzhashchikh*, but was widely criticized by colleagues at the Academy of Sciences in Petersburg for advancing the so-called Norman theory of the origin of the Russian state. Johann Philipp Gerhard Ewers (1781–1830) was rector of Dorpat University from 1818 and author of *Das älteste Recht der Russen in seiner geschichtlichen Entwickelung dargestellt* (Dorpat, 1826). Johann Gottlieb Georgi (1762–1802), was a German traveler, ethnographer, and author of *Geographisch-physikalische und naturhistorische Beschreibung des russischen Reiches*, 9 vols. (Königsberg, 1797–1802). Heinrich Storch (1766–1835), a Baltic German economist, was tutor to the Russian royal family and explicator of the theories of Smith, Bentham, Sismondi, and Say in Russia. Alexander Magnus Reutz (1799–1862) was a Baltic German professor of Russian law at Dorpat University and author of *Versuch der Ausbildung der russischen Staats- und Rechtsverfassung* (Mitau, 1829).

7

stamped a foreign concept on Russian words designating national institutions, continue to act as obstacles.

Even learned native Russians no longer have or have not yet reacquired an understanding of genuinely Russian conditions and institutions; * they still have not been able to impart to their language the spirit to describe them clearly to us and to themselves. Only now, with the founding of a literary school in the tradition of Walter Scott and Irving, are their poets beginning to discover and to depict national and family life, its customs and characteristics. If I must maintain the above to be true of native Russians, then, of course, it must be said to an even greater degree of foreigners who have written about Russia. Whoever wants to travel to Russia to investigate thoroughly conditions there and to view national life with an unprejudiced eye must first of all forget everything he has read about it.

The author of this book was in Russia for slightly more than one year. For this reason he can in no way boast that he has plumbed the depths of Russian national life. His conscience dictated that he set about making his observations with an open mind. In Russia, as everywhere on his trips, he observed with love, for he has always stood in awe of all genuine, vigorous, and untainted popular institutions! More than twenty years of studies and travels have sharpened his eye for precisely this kind of observation. With this book he hopes he has contributed not only new and useful information but also food for thought and research.

To a certain extent the author believes he has indicated a new method for observing Russian institutions. However, he specifically does not mean to imply that he intended or was in a position to present a complete, universally valid, and irrefutable work. The book contains studies; it is not a critical work. The author does not want to be held responsible for single errors. He does believe, however, that he has included those points on which every work must be based that attempts to represent current social conditions

---

* A noteworthy example of this was the now deceased Alexander Turgenev.[3] Provided with a completely European cosmopolitan education, imbued with the most profound and fervid love for his native country and very knowledgeable in its history, he nonetheless nearly lost his understanding of genuine Russian national life.

3. Alexander Ivanovich Turgenev (1784–1846), educated at Moscow University and Göttingen, was a noted scholar, publicist, and editor of a collection of western documents on early Russian history, *Historica Russiae monumenta ex antiquis exterarum gentium archivis et bibliotecis deprompta ab A. I. Turgenevio*, 2 vols. (Moscow, 1841–42).

in Russia in accordance with their national principle. Likewise, anyone who is qualified and in the proper position to develop these institutions in harmony with their national character and not merely to correct and promote them on paper must consider these points. May enlightened and well-intentioned men observe his method and examine his results. (He hopes this will be the case with the Russian government in particular!) Whether they agree with him or correct him, he only hopes that the book may provide the occasion for improvements and a stimulus to progress.

In order to substantiate to a certain extent what has already been stated, I want at this time to mention briefly some of the results of my observations and researches.

While the other European nations in their origin and development can be designated as feudal states, one must call Russia a patriarchal state. This simple sentence contains vast implications and explains in essence almost the entire political and social structure of Russia.

The Russian family is the microcosm of the Russian nation. In the Russian family there prevails a perfect equality of rights. However, as long as the family remains together as one, the father is its head or, after his death, the eldest son. He alone is entitled to the absolute disposition of all property and allots to every family member within the community what he considers to be essential. The expanded family is the Russian commune. The land belongs to the family or the commune with the individual enjoying only the right to use it. Because everyone in the community has exactly the same rights, the land is equally divided among all the living for temporary use. Consequently, the right of the children to inherit their father's allotment cannot exist. Rather, the sons claim their share (which is equal to all others) of the communal property on the basis of their own right, as members of the commune. The commune, too, has its fictive father, the elder, the *starosta*, who is obeyed unconditionally.

According to traditional popular belief Russia belongs to the Russian people, who, although divided into communal groups, constitute a single family under the authority of its head, its father, the tsar. Thus the tsar alone is authorized to manage all affairs and is obeyed without question. A restriction of his power would be totally unthinkable to the Russian people. "How can a father's authority be limited in any other way than by divine law?" The true core of the people would ask this question today, as it did 230 years ago at the elevation of the Romanovs. All attempts to limit the absolute power of the tsar made then or subsequently failed quite simply and without leaving a trace owing to that profound traditional conviction of the people, their political faith! The constitutional position of the Russian tsar in relation to the Russian populace is thus completely different from that of any other monarch. Only as the emperor of the Russian monarchy, does his position correspond to that of other monarchs.

Since every Russian belongs to a commune and is entitled as a member thereof to an equal share of land, there are no born proletarians in Russia. In all the other European countries the harbingers of social revolution agitate against wealth and property. The abolition of the rights of inheritance, the equal division of the land is their shibboleth! In Russia such a revolution is impossible because the utopia of the European revolutionaries already exists there, well rooted in Russian national life!

European liberalism seeks to eradicate every organic distinction between city and countryside, to destroy everywhere medieval institutions such as the guilds, and in general to spread freedom in the trades. These social conditions have existed in Russia from time immemorial, but they have impeded all domestic progress. In its attempt to overcome these obstacles by means of legislation, the government founded and extended privileges to the cities, established merchant and craft guilds, and sought to create a true middle class, an effort which up to this point has been rather unsuccessful.[4]

The aristocracy, an element which originally may have been missing in the Slavic race, was relatively small in number before Peter I. In every age the nobility has owed its influence and importance more to the confidence of the princes than to its status among the people. Peter I created an aristocracy based on merit, which almost completely forced the hereditary nobility into the background.* The career of an aristocrat is open to everyone; through distinguished service, anyone from the populace can under certain conditions acquire personal and then hereditary nobility. In reality, however,

---

*In all other countries, even in the constitutional nations, nobility is acquired by the favor of the princes and according to their whim. In autocratic Russia, not the emperor, but merit and the law bestow nobility! Nevertheless, there exists in general no worse aristocracy than this aristocracy based on merit (the system of state service).

4. Though Catherine II's patronage of city building encouraged the development of a middle class, the efforts to which Haxthausen refers took place under the leadership of Ct. E. P. Kankrin, chiefly in his guild law of 1824. See Walter McKenzie Pintner, *Russian Economic Policy under Nicholas I* (Ithaca, 1967), pp. 55–67, "The Dream of a Middle Class."

this system has in no way proved to be an outstanding one, and the need for a competent rural gentry in Russia is unmistakable.

In recent times Russia has taken enormous strides forward in modern manufacturing. A large percentage of the aristocracy have become entrepreneurs. Moscow has been transformed from a city of the aristocracy to an industrial city, the center of manufacturing. It is very doubtful whether the consequences of this are universally commendable. In part as a result of the rise of industry, the daily wage in Russia has gone up enormously. If all circumstances are taken into account, the daily wage is relatively higher in Russia than in any other country.[5]

Removed from the European markets and lacking the necessary means of transportation, agricultural products command a very low price in the Russian interior. Since the daily wage is so high and since all labor is extremely expensive, agriculture is clearly the least remunerative industry. If hired hands must be used, the revenues from the land are totally unrealistic. The result is that farming in all its branches is pursued without energy or diligence, thus contributing to its lack of progress. It would decline even more if serfdom with its various unpaid services did not sustain it in many regions. [Because the lucrative wages offered by industry would entice many peasants away from the land,] manufacturing is one of the most powerful obstacles to the abolition of serfdom, which, moreover, is gradually becoming inevitable even in Russia.

Since time immemorial there has existed in many parts of Russia an industry based on the structure of the Russian commune which is a kind of national association-factory system. Indeed, these factories represent what Saint-Simon theorized to be necessary for the social reform of Europe and held up as a model. Out of preference for the modern factory system, the government has hitherto not paid nearly enough attention to these national association-factories.

Regarding her internal development, Russia is approaching a promising future. Her political unity is a physical necessity; nature

5. Comparative estimates of Russian wages at this time are rendered difficult by the fact that a substantial part of the industrial labor force worked on a seasonal basis and that Russian industries generally paid maintenance costs which could exceed actual wages by as much as 200 percent. Haxthausen's figure appears exaggerated nonetheless, especially considering that, adding wages and maintenance, workers in the Russian metallurgical industries still received less than half the wages of their counterparts in France and Germany. See M. L. de Tengoborski, *Commentaries on the Productive Forces of Russia*, 2 vols. (London, 1855), 1: 449; 2: 127–28.

divided the country into four colossal parts which, individually, even if they are some day adequately populated, do not have the prerequisites for true independence. Only united do they constitute a powerful and autonomous state. In the north there are only woodlands, including an unbroken forest larger than the kingdom of Spain! Then there is a slightly to moderately fertile tract of land stretching from the Ural to Smolensk, comprising eighteen thousand square miles with more than sixteen million inhabitants and filled with the most varied industry. . . . To the south of this area lies the so-called Black Earth region, which in productivity and expanse has hardly an equal on earth. It is twice as large as all of France! For one hundred consecutive years wheat has been growing on the same unfertilized field. Almost nowhere does the soil need to be fertilized for sowing; in many places it does not have to be plowed at all but merely raked gently! Straw and dung serve as fuel, since there are no forests.

To the south and southeast begin the vast steppes, which nomads have traversed with their herds for thousands of years. The steppes, which are for the most part fertile, are now gradually being cultivated by colonists from the interior, living in oasis-like settlements. Should the efforts to afforest and populate adequately the areas bordering the Black Sea ever be successful, that region would be counted among the most flourishing in Europe. This huge region situated between four seas and not inferior in size to the rest of Europe is inhabited by a robust and totally homogeneous people.

The Russians are divided into two groups, the Great Russians and the Little Russians, whose linguistic differences, however, are not so great as those of the Low Germans and the Upper Germans. The thirty-four million Great Russians comprise the most numerous and homogeneous national group in Europe. In their character there is not a trace of petty jealousy or separatism, but rather a general feeling of national and religious unity as found among no other people. Only the Little Russians, a more contemplative and intellectually gifted people, represent a slight shade of contrast to the Great Russians. But they, too, cling tenaciously to Russian unity.[6]

For one century the Russian upper classes have received a European rather than a national education issuing from the development

6. An important exception to this view were the federalist schemes of the Ukrainian ''Brotherhood of Saints Cyril and Methodius,'' founded in Kiev in 1846 by N. I. Kostomarov and P. Kulish and closed by the government the following year. See P. A. Zaionchkovskii, *Kirillo-Mefodievskoe obshchestvo, 1846–1847* (Moscow, 1959).

of their own people. In regard to education, one thus finds in Russia two peoples standing side by side. Fostered by a vastly expanding industry, a strong desire for intellectual improvement is presently stirring in the lower classes. One of the greatest tasks of the government will be to provide the proper direction for this desire and great need for education. The national church alone can assume leadership in this field, but first the clergy itself requires a more practical education to qualify it for this task. Only recently have efforts in this direction been made, owing to the encouragement of the government.

If I must maintain the political unity and indivisibility of Russia to be a physical necessity, then I must also assert that Russia cannot become a power bent on conquest. In order to secure internal unity and independence as well as a strong external position, Russia had to pursue an expansionist policy. Without the Baltic and Black Sea coasts she simply could never have become a compact, self-sufficient, and outwardly powerful state.

But each subsequent annexation has already become more of a liability than an advantage or accretion of power. If it were compatible with the dignity of the state, then it would be advisable for Russia to surrender all her burdensome conquests. Every village which she might presently subjugate would represent an incalculable increase in the burden and a weakening of domestic power. Russia will have to spend more than a century subduing her interior! Of what use to Russia could a million unreliable subjects be in a defeated country that must be watched over by a large army, when she can acquire ten million trustworthy and homogeneous subjects in a few years by conquering her own interior?

# 1
# *Moscow*

It has often been observed that one cannot gain an accurate impression of Russia from a sojourn in Petersburg. Petersburg has been called an attractive window which Peter I opened in order to look out upon Europe and to let in western European air. Petersburg is a European city throughout with less national character than, for instance, London and Paris. It has somewhat more Russian churches than those of other denominations and is inhabited by Russian soldiers, civil servants, some Russian burghers and quite a few Russian peasants, as well as by Germans, Finns, French, and English, etc. Petersburg is not even located on national Russian territory but on Finnish soil. The Russians are merely colonists, who have been living there for scarcely 140 years. . . .

Moscow has a meaning for the Russian people unlike that of any city for any people. It is the focal point of all the national and religious sentiments of the Russians. There is not a Great Russian in the vast empire, in Archangel or in Odessa, in Tobolsk or in Novgorod, who would not speak of Moscow, "the Holy Mother," with deep respect and enthusiastic love. After having journeyed hundreds of miles, every Russian peasant at the first sight of Moscow's towers will reverently remove his cap and bless himself. In Moscow I have often seen an *izvozchik* (*drozhkii*-driver) turn into a street in the early morning, take off his cap and make the sign of the cross upon catching a glimpse of the Kremlin towers for the first time that day. This profound attachment, however, is innate not only in the common uncultured Russian; I have seen it in every social class, the upper and lower classes, the educated and the uneducated. Several blasé inhabitants of Petersburg may be the sole exception to this rule.

Napoleon did not know or anticipate this; otherwise he would have abandoned his expedition to Moscow. Had he led his army to Petersburg or southern Russia instead, he would not have stirred the Russian national consciousness to such a degree, and the outcome might have been different. With the occupation of Moscow it became a war to the death, rendering any peace impossible as long as there was a Frenchman in Russia!

After the fire of 1812 most of the dwellings in Moscow were rebuilt in the modern western European taste and style. This must necessarily affect the customs and way of life of their residents in many respects. Approximately eight to ten thousand Germans, French, etc., live there.[1] In addition there may be about fifteen to eighteen thousand residents who have received a more or less European education and upbringing: government officials, officers, aristocrats, merchants of the first and second guild, etc. All the others, perhaps three hundred thousand persons, are still true Russians in their thinking, their education, customs, and way of life and are untouched by the ostentation of modern civilization.

The preponderance of genuine Russian customs in Moscow was, of course, far greater in the sixteenth and seventeenth centuries. However, for a long time the rulers of Russia felt that the Russians were culturally far behind the other European peoples, even though they were equal to them in origin, in intelligence, physical abilities, religion, and political status. They believed that it was necessary to bring Russia into closer contact with western Europe and to introduce its advanced culture. They thought this could be accomplished most easily by drawing as many foreigners as possible to the empire, by entrusting foreign teachers with the education of Russians wherever practical, by introducing western European political institutions, or by modeling Russian institutions after them.

Ivan Vasilevich had already summoned many foreigners, especially Germans, and sought to organize his army on a European footing. The regents of the house of Romanov enthusiastically pursued this course.[2]

1. In 1858 the number of foreign subjects living in Moscow was 37,900; for details on Moscow's population in this period see A. G. Rashin, *Naselenie Rossii za 100 let* (Moscow, 1956), pp. 120, 124.

2. For evidence on Russian contacts with western Europe under Ivan IV see M. Gukovskii, "Soobshchenie o Rossii moskovskogo posla v Milane, 1486 g.," *Voprosy istoriografii i istochnikovedeniia istorii SSSR*, ed. S. Valk (Moscow-Leningrad, 1963), pp. 648 ff.

No one, however, recognized more clearly the need to put Russia on the cultural level of western Europe and took more drastic and energetic steps in this direction than Peter I. It was not in Peter's lively and intense nature to sow seeds without wanting to reap the harvest and enjoy the fruits. In carrying out his designs he encountered difficulties everywhere. The natural dislike of the people for innovations and things foreign acted everywhere as obstacles in his path. But he was not the man to be deterred or to take half-measures. He felt that every thoroughgoing change, every vigorous and rapid innovation, would be impossible as long as he continued to reside in Moscow, the center of ancient, genuine Russian tradition. Like Archimedes he looked for a firm point (beyond the earth) with which to move it. He found this point in the construction of Petersburg. Through a successful war he had acquired for Russia the Baltic seacoasts, which made possible stronger and closer ties to western Europe. His sharp eye recognized the incalculable advantages that the location of Petersburg offered for Russia's entire trade with western Europe. With his plans for the construction of canals leading to the Russian interior, he believed that this city would become one of the most important trade centers in the world. Trade, of course, is the most natural means of communication among nations and is the most convenient bridge for cultural exchange. He therefore decided to make Petersburg his residence and from this point to reform Russia with all his energy. Who can deny that he succeeded?

The direction which he gave to Russia still remains; the impulse which he instilled in the country lives on in all of Russia's political and social institutions. It is a *fait accompli* whose effects cannot be destroyed by any human power. Every investigation as to whether this course has been beneficial and necessary for Russia must therefore be rejected as useless. Who can deny that Peter I took far too little consideration of many genuinely national institutions? Who can deny that he wanted to transplant many mediocre and even bad foreign elements prematurely, without investigating whether they could take root and whether they were compatible with existing patterns and the national character? Today, however, the question is: Should Russia continue even more intensely and comprehensively in this direction? Or, should she be content with the results gained from this course and, using the acquired western European culture, pursue a more national policy by cultivating and preserving the good aspects of her own traditions? I shall return later to this most important problem of Russia's domestic policy.

The sight of Moscow as one approaches the city is extraordinary, and I know of no European city with which to compare it. The most splendid view is from the so-called Sparrow Hills. From here one sees innumerable golden and green cupolas and spires in a sea of red-roofed houses. Every church has at least three cupolas; most, however, have five and even thirteen, and there are about four hundred churches! On a hill in the center, hovering above the city like a crown, is the Kremlin with its thirty-two churches and 170 spires and cupolas clustered closely together. Surrounded by his guard, Napoleon once stopped here on horseback, expecting that the boyars and municipal authorities of the imperial city would appear and humbly present him with the keys of the city. No one came; the inhabitants had deserted the "holy" city, and during the night Moscow went up in flames. Napoleon had reached his zenith and from that time on his star began to wane.

As one enters the gates of Moscow, the magnificent impression one had from outside vanishes. The city is then like any other. Indeed it has less of a historical appearance than Nuremberg, Lübeck, or Danzig for instance, where churches and dwellings from the tenth century on stand snuggly next to one another. Cities which have a history and whose buildings from various centuries silently tell this history, cities where in every house many generations have borne joy and sorrow and then died, leaving the house to the children and grandchildren so that they could start a new life — these cities captivate me. I prefer them and even find them to be more beautiful than such modern cities as Petersburg or most of Berlin, which look as if they shot up out of the earth overnight at the order of some potentate. I do not like, much less admire, their long straight streets, monotonous houses resembling barracks, all with one and the same pretentious taste, houses which in truth do not even meet the demands of real taste and art. . . . I expect a house to appear original, characteristic, picturesque, or to be an architectural masterpiece.

After 1812 Moscow was rebuilt completely in the usual modern style, although, in keeping with a national Russian fancy, an excessive number of columns and balconies has been added. One finds almost no old, interesting, and quaint private homes. Only in the suburbs and in the side streets are the houses truly Russian dwellings constructed of horizontal beams with the gables facing the street. Next to the homes there is a courtyard with a wooden fence and an entrance gate. As one can see, there was originally in Russia absolutely no difference between urban and rural architecture.

The churches, of course, break up the monotony of this modern architecture. When one turns a corner or is in the back of the court, these churches appear everywhere before one's eyes. They look unique enough, almost like exotic plants among common indigenous shrubs. Like everything related to the Eastern Catholic cult, the architecture of the Russian churches is restricted to established styles from which there has been almost no deviation. Consequently the older churches in Russia are very much alike and have a certain monotony, although the style is actually simple and noble. Many of our so-called Byzantine churches in western Europe are built in this style, and even the modern Italian style, as perfected in Saint Peter's in Rome, is actually based on the same architectural principles. The nave of the church is nearly square; in the center is a high vault supported by columns. In the oldest churches, such as the cathedral in Novgorod and the Hagia Sophia in Kiev, which was probably modeled after the Hagia Sophia in Constantinople, the inner part of the vault contains a fresco of Christ blessing the world. The interior is divided into two main parts by the iconostasis, a thin partition with three doors, which is decorated from top to bottom with icons. The front part is for the congregation, and the sanctuary, which is divided into three sections, is meant only for the priests; the center section contains the detached altar. On either side of the main vault there are at least two smaller vaults, although as a rule there is also one small vault in each of the four corners. There are even churches with thirteen vaults. The number is not arbitrary but has a symbolical meaning. The three vaults symbolize the Trinity, five vaults Christ and the four Evangelists, and thirteen Christ with the twelve apostles. The bells generally hang in a separate tower adjacent to the church. In those churches without a tower the bells are suspended from the side vaults, which usually have a tower-like extension. Of course, the bells never hang from the main vault, since this is part of the soul of the church. The old churches actually have no windows in the nave. Only now and again does one find a single window or several very narrow ones behind the altar. Light enters only through the vault. As a result there is a magical semidarkness in all Russian churches. The daylight is weak; the churches are illuminated more by the candles on the altar and on the iconostasis.

The exterior of the modern Russian church is generally in the style of Saint Peter's in Rome, as for example the cathedrals of Saint Isaac and Kazan in Petersburg. The huge, as yet uncompleted cathedral of the Redeemer in Moscow is being built in Byzantine style by the architect Thon[3] and approaches the Old Russian style. From the time of Catherine II, one also finds churches built entirely in the modern Italian style, the so-called (corrupted) Jesuit style, for example, Saint Andrei's in Kiev.[4]

Although most of the streets and private buildings in Moscow appear thoroughly modern, this is not true of one relatively small part of the huge city. We are speaking of the Kremlin, situated on a rather high hill and surrounded by a high wall, as well as a part of the adjoining Kitaigorod.

The distinctive features of this part of the city and of Moscow in general have been described in adequate detail in other works. I therefore omit a description and add only a few basic remarks.

The Kremlin occupies the area of a moderately small city. It takes approximately thirty minutes to walk around it and well over an hour if one includes the Kitaigorod. Except for the churches most of the buildings in the Kremlin are modern, having been built after the beginning of the eighteenth century. Only the remains of the old Palace of the Tsars, the small Granavitaia Palace, and the high circular wall with its towers and three gates are older, although they do not go beyond the sixteenth century. Several of the churches, however, are older. *Spas na Goru*, the Church of the Redeemer on the Hill, which is located in the middle of the courtyard of the new palace, dates back to the twelfth century.[5] This church existed before Moscow was a city. Russia has only a few ruins from prehistoric times, since it was not customary to construct buildings of stone. From the pre-Christian era there are no buildings or ruins. After the eleventh century only a few churches in famous cities were built of stone. Even the city walls were formerly constructed of wooden beams placed one on top of the other. The dwellings were always made of wood. According to Olearius (1633) even

3. Konstantin Andreevich Thon (1794–1881); this church was intended by its sponsor, Nicholas I, to mark the revival of true Russian architecture. The Moscow swimming pool now occupies the site.

4. Saint Andrei's was designed by the Italian B. Rastrelli and built in 1747–58; see S. V. Bezsonov, *Arkhitektura Andreevskoi tserkvi v Kieve* (Moscow, 1851).

5. The original church on this site was built of wood in the thirteenth century and was replaced by the present structure in the fourteenth century; it was restored under Nicholas I. See A. Martynov, *Moskva, Podrobnoe istoricheskoe i arkheologicheskoe opisanie goroda*, 2 vols. (Moscow, 1873), 2: 28–40.

the tsar continued to live in a wooden palace in the Kremlin although a stone palace had been completed, since wooden buildings were formerly thought to be much healthier in Russia. . . .[6]

One of the most unusual and magnificent buildings is the cathedral of Saint Basil, located on the square which separates the Kremlin from the Kitaigorod. It reflects all the colors of the rainbow, and from a certain distance or in foggy weather one might think it was a huge dragon ready to pounce on its prey. Ivan Vasilevich had an Italian build the church in 1554 to commemorate the conquest of Kazan.[7] After the church had been completed, Ivan is said to have asked the architect if he thought he could draw up a plan for an even more extraordinary building. When the conceited man said he could, Ivan had him blinded. A master with rather strange and unpleasant moods! But curiously enough, in the memory and opinion of the Russian people and in extant popular legends he was a pious and good-natured man who could easily be duped and who was occasionally inclined to play practical jokes. The Attila of the German version of the Nibelung legend is also a pious and good soul, as is Charlemagne among his peers. Legend always tells a different version than history and is nevertheless just as true. What we call history presents the truth from one point of view only.

A large, modern imperial palace is now being built in the Kremlin. When viewed from the river Moskva, where it can be seen in its entire breadth, the palace towers high above all the buildings. Among all the graceful and beautiful spires and cupolas its rectangular shape produces an extremely unromantic effect and ruins the entire view of the Kremlin.

The most splendid view of the Kremlin is from the bridge over the Moskva. One beautiful evening in May as I drove across the bridge at midnight in a *drozhkii* with deep silence everywhere and only the soft murmuring of the Moskva below me, the Kremlin appeared before my eyes in the magic of the moonlight: I thought I was beholding a fairy-tale from the Arabian Nights carved in stone.

The Kitaigorod begins on the other side of the large square located in front of the two large gates leading to the Kremlin. The first building of the Kitaigorod is the huge emporium or bazaar which

6. In fact, Olearius stresses throughout the opulence of royal life. Adam Olearius (1600–1671), *The Travels of Olearius in Seventeenth-Century Russia*, ed. Samuel H. Baron (Stanford, Calif., 1967).

7. It is now generally accepted that the architects were the Russians Barma and Postnik.

is also called the *gorod*. I believe, one could walk for an hour before having explored the innumerable passages with their rows of shops on either side. (It is a fair which lasts year in and year out!) Whoever does not know his way around, however, has a rather difficult time finding what he is looking for, since there is a special row of shops for each type of article. The leather goods are in one place, the calicoes somewhere else, and the linens in still another place, etc. The uninitiated owes it to pure luck if his wanderings soon lead him in the right direction. These bazaars can be found in every Russian city. They are obviously of Oriental origin, although perfectly suited to the gregarious spirit of the Russians. Of course, the Gostinyi Dvor in Moscow surpasses all the others. In the entire world there is probably no store under one roof which offers a better quality or a greater variety of articles than the Moscow bazaar. One can have everything his heart desires, but to be sure for a dear price. The temptation, however, is great. In most of the shops there are boys aged twelve to fifteen dressed in long cloth caftans, which are generally blue. Like the very best retrievers they are trained to fetch every foreign passerby. As soon as we come within range of the shop, the well-trained lad surrounds us and tries with the most ingratiating gestures and words to maneuver us into the shop. He blocks our path by standing directly in front of us, yielding only step by step as we push our way forward. At the border of his territory he makes a last desperate attempt; he grabs us, clinging obstinately to our coat or arm and tries to drag us into the shop by force. If we continue to resist, he suddenly releases us and goes away quietly in order to chase the next passerby in the same way. We escape him only to fall into the territory of the next, equally persistent retriever. One has only to cope with one youth at a time, if one does not happen to be standing in between two shops; in such a case one is of course attacked from two sides, since each of them strictly defends his border and his territorial rights.

In a Russian store one never sees female sales personnel. Even in the modern millinery and fashion shops one sees French and German women as managers and sales clerks, but no Russians. . . .

Saint-Simon's followers journeyed to Egypt looking for the emancipated woman. Had they gone to Russia they might have returned more satisfied. In a constitutional monarchy the king is supposed to reign but not rule. In a well-ordered family it is the man who reigns, but the woman who rules. In Russia, at least in Moscow, it is just the opposite: the woman reigns and her husband rules. In Russia the female sex occupies a different position from its counterpart in the rest of Europe. This position, however, varies depending upon social class. Among the *muzhik*s, or peasants, who in Moscow number more than one hundred thousand, the women work far less than the men and German women. As a rule the man even does the household chores; he fetches the water and wood and makes the fire.* His wife watches, shuffles about, holds the children, etc.

Among the burghers the wives, especially of the merchants and artisans, do nothing all day; they are not the least bit interested in the household. They have absolutely no idea of what a German housewife is or what she does. Their husbands do everything and even keep house.

Among the wealthy the girls are brought up for the most part in various boarding schools, where they acquire a refinement and an education far superior to that of the men. But these institutes turn out fashionable ladies but no housewives. In the upper classes this is especially the case.

Today, of course, even the households of Moscow are beginning more and more to Europeanize. In a genuine Russian household it is still common for men to perform every type of chore. There are no cuisinières, but only chefs, no scullery maids, no housemaids, no female housekeepers, etc. All their duties are performed by male

---

*There is a good Russian joke which expresses beautifully in the form of a conversation the patience and meekness of the peasant and the dogmatic rule of his wife.

*Peasant:* Dear wife, let us sow this barley.
*Wife:* Mate, it isn't barley, it's buckwheat.
*Peasant:* Have it your way. I don't want to argue.

*Peasant:* Look at how beautifully our barley is sprouting.
*Wife:* It isn't barley, it's buckwheat.
*Peasant:* Fine, it's buckwheat. I don't want to quarrel.

*Peasant:* The barley is ripe; let us harvest it.
*Wife:* It isn't barley, it's buckwheat.
*Peasant:* Fine, it's buckwheat. I don't want to argue.

*Peasant:* The barley has now been threshed. How fine it is.
*Wife:* It isn't barley, it's buckwheat.
*Peasant:* All right, it's buckwheat. I don't want to quarrel.

*Peasant:* What fine barley malt. Let us brew our beer from it.
*Wife:* It isn't barley malt, it's buckwheat malt.
*Peasant:* Fine. it's buckwheat malt. I don't want to argue.

*Peasant:* What good beer we brewed from our barley malt.
*Wife:* It wasn't barley malt, but buckwheat malt.
*Peasant:* All right, I don't want to argue, but I have never heard of buckwheat malt or of brewing beer from it.

servants. This accounts for the extraordinary disproportion of males in Moscow, who nearly double the female population. The statistics for 1834 list 214,778 men but only 133,784 women.[8]

A large part of the real estate is also in the hands of women. In front of every house in Moscow and Petersburg is a sign with the name of the owner. In walking along the streets, one can be certain to find the name of a woman before every third house. This is also the case with real estate in the rural areas; perhaps one-fifth to one-quarter of this property is in the hands of the female sex.

It is easy to understand what a great influence women enjoy in society as a result. The entire development of social life has been leading up to this. Nowhere does property change hands as frequently as in Russia. In public service, in commerce, in manufacturing, and in the trades large fortunes are quickly amassed but are lost just as quickly. Cases of embezzlement in public service are discovered, and the property of the guilty party is confiscated. Poor business ventures (and at bottom the Russian is a gambler) destroy the merchant and the manufacturer. In such cases the families are completely ruined. This occurs all too frequently, and from the outset the husband has to prepare for such probabilities by providing the family with a financial reserve. He puts a part of the property, specifically the house and the land, in his wife's name; at the beginning it is more *pro forma*, but after a time it becomes a legally binding arrangement. In this way the movable property has come to belong to the husband whereas the wife holds the real property. The latter remains even after her husband's property has been scattered to the four winds. Russian legislation is more partial to women concerning the administration and the disposition of their property than that of any other nation.[9]

Just as Moscow assumed an entirely different outward appearance after the great fire of 1812, so too did it undergo a profound change with respect to its population. Today the elements of the population are completely different from those of former times. Moscow was once the city of the Russian aristocracy; today it is a modern industrial city.

Fifty years ago it was estimated that of the 8,360 private homes

8. Haxthausen's figure indicates that for every thousand males in Moscow there were only 623 females; this grew to only 700 by 1871 and 803 by 1907. For peasants and house servants the figure was even lower; in 1830 for every thousand gentry-owned male house servants there were only 153 females; Rashin, *Naseleine,* p. 274.

9. These laws were enacted under Paul I, 1796–1801.

cratized regime in Berlin had convinced Haxthausen that the nationalism he had earlier preached would lead only to the further Prussianization of German life and that the only hope lay in the creation of a broad and tolerant greater Germany that would embrace Catholic Austria as well as Lutheran Prussia.[22]

These points of tension were by no means negligible, but it was the opposition of the Prussian liberals that was Haxthausen's undoing. This exploded in a series of bitter denunciations of his proposed inheritance law, which would have reduced (but not eliminated) state interference in the transfer of landed property. Haxthausen reciprocated by lashing out at his arch-foes, the liberal constitutionalists. Even his old friends the Grimms were critical of the "audacious statements" he made in self-defense.[23] Officials in the Rhenish provinces supported his opponents in Berlin and closed important cadastral surveys to his research. By 1842 he had few supporters left in Berlin. In that year the Diet cut off all support for his investigations and, defeated, he returned to Westphalia. From Bökendorf Haxthausen gloomily petitioned his royal patron, Friedrich Wilhelm IV, who lamely turned the case over to the Ministry of State. Finally, on 11 May 1842, the ministry bluntly rejected Haxthausen's petition for support to be renewed. With his work far from complete, Baron Haxthausen was released from the state service.

During 1841–42 Haxthausen's domestic circumstances changed no less dramatically, though fortunately for the better. For years he had worked to consolidate his holdings at Bökendorf, buying back tracts of land that had been lost with the emancipation of the peasantry. Under the capable hand of his manager he succeeded in turning his expanded domain into one of the most lucrative in the region. Nearby lay the sizable estate of Thienhausen, the debt-ridden property of the Danish branch of the Haxthausen family since 1688. This holding was to revert to August's branch should the Danish line die out, and from the late 1830s that prospect was imminent as the last heir in Copenhagen lay mortally ill. In order to obtain the land and moated castle at Thienhausen, however, all outstanding debts and mortgages had to be paid, and August was the only one of the surviving brothers able to do this. Just as he lost his position in Berlin, Haxthausen was completing the negotia-

22. See August von Haxthausen, "Die deutsche Einheit," *Kölnische Zeitung*, no. 156, 5 June 1842.

23. Jakob Grimm to Ernst Johann Friedrich Dronke, 12 April 1839, *Unbekannte Briefe*, pp. 266–67.

approximately 6,400 still belonged to the aristocracy. At that time the majority of the Russian aristocracy resided in Moscow, at least during the winter. This aristocracy was too proud to tolerate tenants in their homes; furthermore, the entire arrangement of these dwellings was such that stores could not be conveniently housed in them (on the first floor for example), nor could trades and manufacturing be carried on in them. The homes were located either in the back of a courtyard or on the street, in which case there was a courtyard with an entrance gate next to the residence. Some were large palaces with two and even three stories; others, one-story Russian-style homes constructed of horizontally arranged beams and elegantly ornamented. Streets with houses directly next to each other with two, three, four, and more stories, the first of which is used for stores, etc., as in our western European cities, were unknown in Moscow.

The aristocracy lived in those homes with their families and domestic serfs in a combination of Oriental and European luxury. The peasant worked and paid his master; as a rule, the lord, his family, and his servants spent everything in Moscow. The greatest luxury consisted in the number of horses and domestics. With respect to the luxury of horses the government found it necessary several times to issue regulations for equipages. It was determined who could drive with six, four, and two horses, etc. In western Europe one simply cannot imagine such a wealth of domestic servants. It is said that more than a thousand domestics lived in the larger palaces. Even unimportant and impecunious aristocrats had at least twenty to thirty servants, and one could find no lazier, more idle, and more disorderly crew than these. Of course, it was impossible to provide this horde with an adequate amount of work. I was told that the manner in which the chores were divided among them often bordered on the ridiculous. For his whole life one man had nothing more to do than sweep a single flight of stairs; another did nothing but bring the drinking water to his master and mistress for the midday meal, and a third fetched the water for supper, etc. However, it was not very expensive to keep them. Like the Russian peasant they lived on bread, porridge, *shchi* (cabbage soup) and *kvas* (a kind of sour beer). They dressed like peasants and dwelled in *izbas* (small outbuildings) located in the yard. . . . The aristocracy and its servants constituted at that time the majority of Moscow's population, perhaps 250,000 persons.[10] In the summer, half of them, or

10. In 1788–94, 4.9 percent (8,600) of the Moscow population were gentry and 35 percent were house serfs. An additional 30.7 percent of

maybe two-thirds, moved to the country, and Moscow was then deserted until winter.

Since 1812 a complete change has gradually come about. All the homes of the aristocrats were burned down; the aristocratic families withdrew to the interior of the country. They suffered tremendous losses and therefore lacked the means to restore their courts and to begin anew their former life of indolence and luxury. The aristocracy remained in the provinces and began to winter in the provincial capitals, which have thrived since then. About this time the government began to encourage manufacturing, and Moscow soon became the center and headquarters of all industrial activity. If one now asks, "To whom does that palace belong?" he gets as reply, "the manufacturer N, or the merchant O, etc., but formerly Prince A. or G."

With the burgeoning of manufacturing the makeup of Moscow's population has changed completely. In the better sections of the city one house adjoins the next. Today one rarely finds large courtyards with their entrance gates, which still predominate only in secluded parts of the city. The houses usually have two or three stories, but seldom more, and on the ground floor there is store after store. Certain streets, Kuznetskii Most, for example, can compare in this respect with the most elegant streets in the leading European cities.

The aristocracy with its huge staff of indolent servants has now been replaced by the manufacturers with their equally large number of workers. A large number of noblemen have become entrepreneurs, and their former domestics now work in factories for a wage.

But even that part of the aristocracy which has not entered manufacturing and is serving in the government or living off its wealth in Moscow leads an entirely different life than formerly. The luxury of horses has decreased considerably; one restricts oneself to one's needs. The way of life with respect to domestics has changed completely, and people do not have more than are required. One may still keep more servants than in Berlin, for example; a family which gets along with two or three servants in Berlin has at least four to six in Moscow. Nevertheless, that horde of unoccupied domestics has completely vanished. It is now a rare exception to have twenty or thirty persons working in the household. Only now and again does one hear some important Russian mention the unusual case of an aged boyar who in the old manner still has several hundred

the populace were peasants; *Statisticheskoe opisanie Moskvy* (Moscow, 1841), pt. 1, pp. 262–64.

servants gathered about him. Among others a certain Prince Sergei Golitsyn was mentioned to me in this connection.[11] In general the aristocracy now finds it most compatible with its present way of living as well as in its interest to allow those formerly indolent servants to work for a wage in one of the numerous factories in return for a fee to be paid their master. In this way the serfs can earn their own bread and often acquire some property. Indeed, at the present time that part of the aristocracy which has adopted European customs generally does not even keep its own serfs as servants, but hires domestics instead. While his servants may be working for board and wages in the homes of other aristocrats in Moscow, he has hired the serfs of another nobleman. Thus in the past thirty years Moscow's face and character have changed so completely that someone who investigated social conditions there fifty years ago would not recognize them today. He might think he was in an altogether different Russian city.

Hitherto the political influence that Moscow, as the center of industry, exercises on the policy and the decisions of the government has been neither examined nor commented on. Even though the government might like to strike out in other directions for reasons of foreign policy, several factors compel it to take very close notice of Moscow's opinion, particularly regarding the system of protective duties: first, the love and respect which all Russians have for the "Holy Mother Moscow"; second, Moscow's inestimable importance as the center of manufacturing and hence as the representative of the empire's industrial region; third, the size of this region, which has the area of a large empire and sixteen million inhabitants. Some time ago when the issue of the complete incorporation of Poland was being discussed, a deputation from Moscow pointed out the great losses that domestic and above all Moscow's industry would suffer as a result, and the matter was dropped for the time being.

I have already indicated that I consider the absence of a genuine middle class to be one of the most serious shortcomings of the Russian social order. Through its education and social position the middle class of the West cultivated that municipal and corporate spirit, that honorable self-reliance and pride which contributed so much to the cultural development of the Germanic and Romanic nations from the Middle Ages on.

11. Prince Sergei Mikhailovich Golitsyn ("senior") (1774–1859) was director of the Moscow School District from 1830 to 1835 and in 1834 president of the second investigating commission of Herzen and Ogarev. See A. I. Herzen, *Byloe i Dumy*, 8 pts., 3 vols. (Moscow, 1967), 1:187 ff.

It seems as if there are mysterious forces in the character and the history of the Slavic peoples unfavorable to the development of a bourgeoisie. Not only among the Russians but also among the other Slavic peoples there is no dynamic unfolding of a middle class. Neither the Poles nor the southern Slavs have created a bourgeoisie, and among the Bohemians it is an institution introduced by the Germans. Indeed, to this very day the Bohemian cities are inhabited for the most part by Germans.

For more than half a century the government has been trying to organize a middle class in Russia. Catherine II provided a municipal structure in the German spirit and several other municipal statutes based on the German model. One must admit that this legislation was a failure and that it did not have the anticipated results. The German corporate spirit on which the legislation is based is entirely alien to the Russian national character with its strong associative spirit. The corporate spirit contradicts the national customs, the social habits and views of the Russian people, and I really do not believe that it will ever take firm root.

This is not the case with manufacturing, which has been growing vigorously for the past twenty-five years. Considering its vast expansion, industrialization will indubitably have a marked and as yet incalculable influence on the rise of a middle class. The form which this class will assume is still completely hidden in the future.

The Russian has a talent for everything. Of all peoples he may have the most practical sense for acquiring a suitable vocation. The attachment and love for his station, his trade and his work which is so characteristic of the German is wholly unknown to the Russian. The true German loves his station; he does not want to exchange it for any other. He remains steadfast to the craft or trade to which he first dedicated himself. He practices his trade with perseverance, love, and a certain pride, seeking honor and self-fulfillment in it. He derives pleasure from a piece of work which he has successfully produced with his hands. He believes that his station in life is a definite God-given calling, which he is duty bound to follow.

Not so the Russian. For the most part chance determines which of the youth's many talents should first be cultivated. Without much deliberation the master decides who among his serfs' sons is to become a shoemaker, a smith, a cook, a scribe, etc. In order to get better artisans, conscientious seigneurs apprentice the youths to master craftsmen on the basis of contracts extending from three to eight years. Without taking aptitude into consideration, the colonel of a regiment orders so and so many men to become saddlers, smiths, wheelwrights, musicians, and scribes in the chancery. And they do become skilled craftsmen and almost always with facility. From their ranks proceed as a rule the best artisans and workers, since an outside force compels them to stick to their trade. Among the crown peasants, however, the youth receives his first inducement from his parents or relatives, or he chooses an occupation on his own. If he takes up a trade, he does not receive the same training as a German craftsman. The German spends a certain number of years as an apprentice with regular masters and then advances from apprentice to journeyman. Finally, after submitting a sample of his work, he becomes a master recognized by the fellow members of his guild and entitled to the important rights of a master craftsman. The Russian learns by watching this man or that man, tries something on his own, invents something, and seeks to earn a living as best he can. One cannot speak of particular loyalty to his station or a love for his trade. The Russian does not have any scruples regarding the price of his labor but takes whatever he can get. He feels no sense of duty or honor to supply a good, solid piece of work. He works only for the money and only to sell his wares and is quite unconcerned about his reputation.

If he does not get anywhere in his trade, he immediately takes up another. How often does a man start out as a shoemaker or a tailor, give up his occupation, and become, let us say, a *kalachi* vendor, roaming the streets of Petersburg or Moscow all day selling various kinds of baked goods. After he has made some money and bought horses and a wagon, he becomes a driver, traveling far and wide in the empire. He also engages in small business ventures and soon begins a peddler's trade. Finally he settles somewhere and, if luck is with him, he may become a powerful merchant. The careers of most of the wealthy merchants and factory owners, if one were to check into them, resemble this pattern.

However, even after the Russian has become a wealthy merchant or factory owner, this does not at all mean that he loves his station and his occupation. He regards his trade only as a means to get rich. If he has children, he may train one child for his business, but only in order to have a reliable helper. He seeks to provide the others with an education that will qualify them for military or public service and in this way to give them the hope of acquiring nobility. Hunger for money and inordinate ambition are the rocks on which everyone's character is wrecked in Russia. The common man, the peasant, is kind and good-hearted, but as soon as he comes into money and becomes a speculator or a merchant, he is corrupted and becomes a wicked rogue. The government has recognized the injurious consequences of this tremendous fluctuation and has made various attempts to check it somewhat. The government wants to create a stable bourgeoisie, and the law instituting a class of honorary burghers is convincing evidence of this.[12]

The increase in industrial activity also contributes somewhat, of course, to the formation of a more stable middle class. The simple merchant, especially the Russian merchant, is more a huckster than a first-rate businessman. This explains why, in proportion to his great numbers, he is seldom involved in the empire's foreign trade and why he leaves international commerce mostly to the Germans and the English living in Petersburg. He can easily close his shop and give up his business if he so desires.

Not so the factory owner. A factory requires a certain stability and is almost like a demesne. There is a great amount of immovable capital in the buildings and machinery and an equally large investment in workers and minds. Hence it is much more difficult to dissolve the entire enterprise, and it always involves considerable loss. In addition, a manufacturer must be more versatile and must have a better-rounded education than the merchant. The perpetuation and the stability of the factory require the owner to train his children for the business. A good education is necessary, and once acquired it produces in every man a certain love for the business in which he will apply this knowledge. Hence Russia can cherish the hope that in the class of industrialists at least the promising beginnings of an upper middle class are gradually emerging.

But the true core, the lower middle class, will always be missing. In Russia the upper middle class will sooner or later merge with the aristocracy. For the present, there is absolutely no hope for the creation of an honorable and numerous petty bourgeoisie. The classes which represent the latter, the artisans, shopkeepers, and small businessmen, are generally thoroughly demoralized in Russia.

I do not think it is possible to free them from this demoralization by means of stringent guild regulations because, as I have said, the corporate spirit of the guild and the guild system are totally alien to the Russian national character. Example and competition

12. This special class of citizens was free from bodily punishment, could maintain carriages with two or four horses, build factories, etc., and was founded by Catherine II in 1785 and reestablished in 1832, at which time its members were divided into hereditary and nonhereditary honorary citizens. See A. Ianovskii, "Grazhdanstvo pochetnoe," in Brockhaus and Efron, *Entsiklopedicheskii slovar* 9:523–24.

have had the best influence on these classes. In almost all the larger cities there are German artisans, and when the Russian especially wants to praise and recommend an article he will say that it is German made. Hence competition and example now and again force the Russian artisan to produce a respectable piece of work and to charge honest prices. In recent times one has unfortunately had occasion to observe that the newly immigrated German artisans have not tried to uphold their old reputation for solid craftsmanship but have sometimes become boastful and unreliable.

The genuinely Russian system of producing handwork is a community of artisans organized like a factory. All the inhabitants of a village or an area work at the same trade. There are villages which make only boots, others which produce only tables and chairs, and others which manufacture only pottery, etc. One or several families work according to the factory system, dividing the work among themselves; they have their outlets in the large cities and at the fairs. This method of production is common throughout the empire and is the genuinely national system. The Russians are in general excellent factory workers but poor artisans; they like the trade associations but not the guild system.

There are no so-called little people in Moscow as in the German cities and especially Berlin, who live in attic and cellar apartments. I have not seen any cellar apartments in Moscow and if there are any rented apartments they are indeed unusual. Formerly there was also no proletariat at all in Moscow; today there are only the small beginnings of one. Heretofore there have existed only two lower classes in Russia; one was either a peasant and belonged to a commune and had the right to a plot of land like every other commune member or was a domestic and belonged to a master who was obligated to provide lodging, clothing, and food. No one was without a home, without property, or without a master who had to provide for him. In general no one was destitute.

One of the ways to attain freedom in Russia is to become a soldier. The serf who enters the military is freed from his master. When he is discharged he is a completely free man, but actually it is the freedom of a bird in the air. Formerly the soldier left all the bourgeois conventions of life behind forever. After a twenty-five-year tour of duty the number of soldiers who returned to civilian life was negligible. Very seldom did they establish a new family. Isolated and alone they wasted away in the vast empire. They could not be regarded as the seed and basis of a future proletariat. The present emperor has reduced the tour of duty and introduced a system of furloughs extending over a period of years.[13] This system permits the soldier to return to civilian life, but his former ties to his community, his family, and his master are not renewed. It is a dangerous experiment. For the first time we see in Russia the seed for the growth of a mob, a future proletariat.*

In all of the large cities one still sees unique figures and unusual costumes. In the German cities, too, people can still be found wearing their national dress, but they are already rare exceptions. Everywhere the townspeople have doffed their native costume. Only the peasants from neighboring villages and areas continue to dress in this fashion, as for example the Vierländer in Hamburg, the peasants from the Oder Moor in Berlin, and the Altenburger in Leipzig. But the native costume is beginning to be replaced everywhere by modern fashions. In Moscow, however, the entire population of the lower classes, perhaps nine-tenths of the total population, still wears national costumes. Among them one sees unusual and occasionally very characteristic figures. Of course, specific vocations have also created certain classes with their own customs and practices. Of these the *dvornik* should be mentioned as one of the most characteristic figures. His position is that of house attendant and doorkeeper. Summer and winter the *dvornik* lives in the courtyard, in the entrance hall under the gateway, or on the street. He has to keep the street respectably clean. If he fails to do so, he had better be careful, for his good master, the *budochnik*, is not to be trifled with. Morning and evening one sees him armed with his broom indefatigably cleaning the sidewalks or the inner courtyard, whose absolute master he is and from which he derives his name in fee (*dvor*, court). Charged by the owner with the supervision of the house and the premises, he serves as the intermediary between the owner and the tenants, whose factotum he is. Besides dealing with the tenants he is also in charge of all repairs, the inspection of chimneys, etc. If the tenants need a residence permit, a visa for their passport, or any kind of certificate from the police, they always look to the *dvornik* for help. He is everybody's man and is indispensable to the owner, the tenant, and

---

*A new regulation permits every discharged soldier to join any state commune. The commune is obligated to accept him and to allow him to participate in the division of the land. However, the soldiers do not take the intended advantage of this regulation. To be sure, they become members of the commune, but they never become farmers.

13. This law of 1834 did not apply to Jews, cantonists, and several other groups; although successful, it was criticized for creating a class of idlers; John Shelton Curtiss, *The Russian Army under Nicholas I, 1825–1855* (Durham, N.C., 1965), pp. 252–54.

the police. The police also turn to him in every matter concerning the tenants. They make him their right arm in each house. The position of *dvornik* is generally held by old soldiers, although any peasant gladly accepts the post.

The *dvornik*'s first cousin is the *budochnik*. Just as the *dvornik* tends the courtyard, the *budochnik* minds the streets. On the corner of every main street there is a wooden booth which serves as living quarters for the *budochnik*. As the lowest police official, he is directly in charge of the streets. He is supposed to see to it that there is no disorder and that the street is kept clean. His charge is to observe everything and to know who lives in every house. One should be able to get all kinds of information from him. As a rule, the *budochnik* stands majestically in front of his booth in perfect idleness. Leaning on his strong halberd, he lets the sun beat down on his sheepskin coat around his broad shoulders. If a stranger asks him, "Does so and so live on this street and in which house?" the first reply he gets is a laconic "nyet." If the stranger continues to pester him, he points to the *budochnik* in the next street. However, if the stranger reaches into his pocket or weighs a *grivennik* in his hand, the indolent figure becomes alive, and the stranger receives the best of service. But the *budochnik* also expects his legitimate hope to be fulfilled and meekly reminds the forgetful stranger of his debt with a "na vodki" (for some vodka). I cannot refrain from commenting on a national difference between the Petersburgers and the Muscovites who expect or request a tip. It is a well-known fact that everyone in Russia asks for and accepts a tip.* But the Petersburger, who has been touched by European culture, asks in an affected manner and in a hushed tone for a tip "na chai" (for tea); the Muscovite, however, is honest and says "na vodki."

A very characteristic figure in every Russian city, but particularly in Moscow, is the *izvozchik (drozhkii*-driver). The Great Russian is a born coachman. Riding is actually not his métier. With the exception of the Cossack tribes one seldom sees the ordinary man on horseback, but as far as driving talent is concerned he surpasses all the other peoples. The quintessence of the Russian coachman is the *izvozchik*. In God's whole wide world there is no kinder,

---

*After God had created the world He wanted to populate it. He created the various nations and provided them abundantly. The Russians also received much land and bountiful resources. Then He asked each nation individually if it were satisfied. All replied that they had plenty. But when God asked the Russian he took off his cap and grinned, "na vodki, Lord." (Russian popular joke.)

more courteous, craftier, and cleverer rogue. He receives his initial training as a postilion on the equipage of an aristocrat. One sees ten- to twelve-year-old boys sitting on one of the first horses all day and in the party season for most of the night. He eats, drinks, plays, and sleeps on the horse; in brief he actually becomes one with his horse. How often have I seen such youths sweetly sleeping on the horse at temperatures of $-50°F$. And can he drive! How sturdily he sits in the saddle, how cautiously and correctly he steers his two horses at every turn and at a fast trot at that.

At age seventeen or eighteen he becomes either a full-fledged driver on the coachbox or an *izvozchik* hired out to a wealthy man, until he has saved and gambled enough to buy his own horse and *drozhkii* as well as a sled for the winter. From now on he actually lives on the narrow front seat of the *drozhkii* or sled. He and his horse live most frugally on the hay, oats, and bread which he carries along in the *drozhkii*. In Moscow and Petersburg there are, in addition to the day *drozhkii*s, the night *drozhkii*s which drive about the streets from ten until five. Generally two *izvozchiki* form a partnership. They have three horses between them and use them in such a way that each horse always has a day of rest every third day. At five in the morning the night coachman drives to certain *kabaki* (inns). The day *izvozchiki*, who get up at this time, assemble at the inn and leisurely drink their tea together, their only warm food for the day. Consequently, one finds almost no *drozhkii*s on the streets from five to seven. The good behavior, patience, and courtesy of the *izvozchik* surpass the manners of every other class of the population. When a well-dressed man walks along the street and turns around just once, he can be sure to see half a dozen coachmen driving toward him who most courteously offer their services. There is a tremendous amount of competition among them, but they never curse at one another or at the man who gets the job. They never lay hands on one another, drive into each other, or ruin anything. In Petersburg and Moscow the transportation system is on the whole wonderfully well supervised by the police. The most stringent regulations are enforced. The coachman or *izvozchik* who runs over someone, killing or simply injuring him, or who damages another carriage is immediately arrested. In the first case he is sent into the army and in the other cases he is dealt corporal punishment. However, he always loses his horse, which is sent to the police and turned over to the fire department.

The *plotniki* (carpenters) are another very characteristic class of the population. Since the great majority of all the buildings in Russia

33

are constructed entirely of wood, the carpenters in Russia are more numerous and more important than in any other land. In the country every peasant is actually a carpenter as well. Every peasant knows how to build a house, to put up the roof, and to make the furnishings. The *plotniki* in the cities, and particularly in Moscow, are nothing more than the elite of those ordinary peasants and not at all like the artisans in Germany, especially those who have received their training in the guilds. And yet they are wonderfully skilled. They manifest the character and the talents of the Russian people, which have already assigned to Russia an important place in world history, a position which may be enhanced in the future: absolute obedience, a correct sense of proportion, the practical talent for suitable arrangements, and finally the talent of knowing how to produce an excellent piece of work with simple tools and a modest amount of material. The *plotniki* in Moscow constitute a well-organized community with divisions and subdivisions, with common households and elected leaders whom they obey unconditionally. The order and discipline are exemplary. This entire system was not instituted from above by means of regulations and laws but arose from below out of necessity, the people's natural inclinations, and their love of order.

The *plotniki*, or rather the entire Russian nation, are to be admired for their sense of proportion and their quick ability to see and use every advantage. The true Russian *plotnik* actually uses only an ax and a chisel. With an ax in his belt he traverses the empire from one end to the other, looking for and finding work. It is unbelievable what he can accomplish with the ax. All the various tools used by our trained artisans are completely unknown to him, and nevertheless his work is not of inferior quality. Indeed it often answers the purpose better than the work produced by our craftsmen despite their far more extensive training. Often one cannot imagine that it is possible to produce with a clumsy ax and a crude chisel the lovely ornamentation and carvings such as one finds on ships and Russian houses.

Lycurgus forbade the Spartans to use any implements other than the ax and the saw in order to guard against any kind of ornamentation, which he considered to be a sign of effeminacy. The Russian *plotniki* could have showed him that the natural desire for decoration and embellishment is not suffocated by depriving men of the means to create beauty. Man helps himself as best he can with inadequate resources and in the end reaches his goal nonetheless. The real *plotnik* in the interior even despises the use of the saw, which the Muscovite carpenter knows how to wield very well. In the north where wood is still plentiful, he fells an entire tree if he needs one board and chips away at both sides until only the desired board remains.

Given the common Russian's extraordinary passion for travel and the millions of Russian pilgrims, coachmen, peddlers, artisans, workers, etc., who annually journey from one part of the empire to another, and given the Russian's profound love and respect for Moscow and his desire to visit the holy city at least once in his lifetime — given these factors, it is in this city that one can best study and compare the physiognomies, the outward appearance, and the character of the various Russian tribes as well as of the inhabitants of the different provinces and regions.

# 2
## *Iaroslavl Province* I

The province of Iaroslavl is at the core of that part of the monarchy inhabited by the Great Russians. The soil is not very fertile, particularly in the northern and northwestern regions; the climate is raw but healthful. The Volga and the several other rivers which flow through the province render its location advantageous. The people are recognized as the most handsome and robust of the Great Russians.

For the method of researching Russian institutions which I have chosen, this region is one of the most interesting of the Russian empire. As we have said, one finds here a robust people of a distinctive nationality, struggling with the rigors of climate and poor soil. For this reason they have been dependent in great part on industrial trades since ancient times. Recently, however, they have also been sucked into the whirl of manufacturing which is stirring in Russia.

Among primitive peoples agriculture is the stage of development which marks the dawn of civilization. In the beginning, agriculture generally satisfies only the simple needs of peoples. However, with the growth of the population and a more sophisticated way of life, new and different needs arise, which vary according to locality, time, and the culture of a people.

It cannot be proved historically that there were peoples who bypassed agriculture and turned immediately to commerce and industry. Yet this seems to have been the case with the Phoenicians and their colonies as well as with some Greek cities. But who can say that they did not have an unknown period in their early history when they shifted from agriculture to commerce? Of the larger historical nations that inhabited a sizable landlocked area, there was none that did not first rest upon an agricultural foundation. However, we frequently find that peoples or tribes whom we originally knew only as agricultural transfer at a certain stage of their culture to industrial and commercial activities. Unproductive soil, a growing population, and the resultant scarcity of arable land often force this change.

This was the case with sections of Russia and especially with part of the present province of Iaroslavl. In the Middle Ages we already find there extensive industrial and commercial activity. Iaroslavl maintained contacts with the Hanseatic cities to the west through Novgorod and Pskov, and to the east it had commercial ties with Asia. Ever since the time that Peter I opened the Baltic Sea to direct Russian trade and since the vast new canal systems established splendid connections between the interior and Petersburg on the Baltic Sea, the province of Iaroslavl has become an industrial and commercial center. It is true that the poor soil and the scarcity of land contributed to this tendency, but the natural inclinations and talents of the Russian people have also played a part.

The soil in the province is not very fertile and you can count on an average yield only a third that of the productive zones. This natural unproductivity could be remedied considerably through increased fertilization and more intensive efforts at cultivation. However, next to nothing is being done to improve the land. Whatever several landowners such as Mr. Karnovich have done in this respect has hitherto been little imitated on the whole and has been virtually ignored by the peasants.[1] As we have said, the reason for this is obvious: commerce and industry yield adequate profits, but agriculture does not repay the additional effort required and the capital invested for improvements. Moreover, in judging local conditions one must not apply the criteria one is accustomed to use in countries farther to the south and west, such as France, England, and central Germany. Disregarding the quality of the soil, agriculture requires more effort on the part of man and beast in these northern regions than in the southern climes and thus yields less net profit. The work required in the most important branch of farming, namely, the planting and the harvesting of crops, is distributed over a much longer period in the southern regions and is proportionately much

1. A planter of Iaroslavl province. See chap. 3, n. 3. For governmental efforts to encourage modern agriculture see M. L. de Tengoborski, *Commentaries on the Productive Forces of Russia*, 2 vols. (London, 1855), 1:437 ff.

less expensive than in the north. Around Orléans and Mainz and in the lands along the Danube, for example, the farm work is spread out over seven months, whereas in Iaroslavl this same work has to be performed in four months because of the short summer. The work that I can accomplish there with four people and four horses here requires, on a field of equal size and quality, seven men and seven horses. To cultivate an estate of a thousand morgens of plow-lands and pastures near Mainz, I would need four teams of horses, eight male farmhands, six female workers, and perhaps an additional fifteen hundred working days furnished by independent hired laborers. The expenses for the work performed by men and animals would amount to about 3,500 thalers. After these expenses have been deducted from the gross profit of the estate, which is about 8,500 thalers, a net profit of 5,000 thalers remains. Let us assume that an estate of the same size and with the same quality of soil is located north of the Volga, and that the average price for produce and all other factors are equal. Simply owing to the climate one would need about seven teams of horses, fourteen male farmhands, ten female workers, and twenty-one hundred working days from independent day laborers to do the same cultivation. Instead of 5,000 thalers the net profit would amount to only 2,600 thalers. This dis-proportion could be offset if one could get rid of the animals and discharge the workers in the winter, when field work is at a standstill.*
The expenses are the same if I have to feed four teams of horses for seven months or seven teams for four months. If one could dispose of the teams and the workers for five months near Mainz and for eight months north of Iaroslavl both farms would have equal expenses. However, this arrangement is hardly possible even in a single case and is certainly out of the question for an entire province. Given this impossibility, circumstances turn out to be infinitely more favorable for the farm near Mainz than for the estate in the vicinity of Iaroslavl. In the winter the estate near Mainz has to feed only four-sevenths the number of horses and workers as the latter; the former has to provide for them for only five months, whereas the estate near Iaroslavl must sustain them for eight months. Disregarding this circumstance, the farm near Mainz can provide both men and animals with considerably more worthwhile and profitable jobs than the estate near Iaroslavl. The winter is neither as severe nor as

---

*Many peasants actually do get rid of their horses after the harvest and purchase others in the spring. Since the coachmen do most of their business in the winter, they buy the horses from the peasants in the fall.

long, and the earth is not covered with an impenetrable blanket of snow. One can use the costly human and animal labor for a variety of tasks; they can spread the fields with manure, earth, marl, and calcium; they can haul firewood and timber for the entire year, and they can drive produce to market. When the temperature is above freezing, they can dig ditches, construct so-called "fontanelles" [small wells] and irrigate the fields. In their free time the female workers can ret and spin flax, etc. In brief, one is able to employ men and animals on the farm itself for the entire five winter months. It is true that they cannot perform as much farm work as in the summer because of the short days. Yet at the most only about two horses and one farmhand would be superfluous and could be dispensed with for the five winter months. But even this is not necessary. In heavily populated industrial areas one can always find extra employment for idle teams and hands, for example, pulling or driving a hackney. Hence one can assume that on such a well-organized farm in Mainz there would be absolutely no manpower or pecuniary losses in winter.

None of these conditions applies to the estate north of Iaroslavl. There winter farm work consists only of hauling the necessary supply of wood and driving the produce to market, which barely occupies one team full time. The winter or at least the period of inactivity lasts eight months, and the working force of men and animals would be three-sevenths greater. If one also considers the relatively low prices for farm produce, the distance to the markets, the sparse population and thus the high wages, as well as the fact that the German and French farm horses pull much better and longer and also that the Russian workers cannot be compared with the Germans for perseverance — if one considers these factors, it is very clear that most of the net profit is absorbed. However, we also assumed that the farm near Iaroslavl possesses land as fertile as that on the plain near Mainz. But for every six or seven bushels' yield in Mainz one would in fact get scarcely three bushels on an equal area in Iaroslavl.

From this hypothetical arithmetic example, one can see clearly that if someone were given a tract of land near Iaroslavl on the condition that he set up and run a farm there and purchase the appropriate stock and equipment as is the custom in central Europe, he would have to express his polite thanks and decline. Not only would he make absolutely no profit, but he would even have to provide considerable subsidies each year. It is evident that agriculture by itself is not a remunerative enterprise on large estates in these regions. And yet one cannot abandon farming, for it provides absolute necessities.

Agriculture must be examined from two points of view. Since it is an office or a duty imposed on men by God ("In the sweat of thy brow shalt thou cultivate the fields"), one is not permitted to abandon agriculture. Even if one's labors are not remunerated in terms of money, one must till the soil, for on the whole, and particularly for a continental country, agriculture alone provides the means for nourishing man and beast. Second, we must consider agriculture as an industrial activity. This aspect emerges only gradually with the progress of civilization. In this respect agriculture is an object of calculation. One must ask to what extent farming should be carried on when there is a pecuniary loss.

In examining the present-day situation, I must express the opinion that in the northern regions of Russia only two forms of large farms can exist. First, estates which employ serf labor are possible. In this case the owner himself does not have to provide for the farmhands and the animals; in other words, he has no expenses. Second, there can exist farms which hire hands and draft animals and to which home industries are joined. On these farms the men and animals not needed for field work can be profitably used.

I consider it absolutely essential that there should be a certain, although not excessive, number of large farms in these areas. Without them agricultural progress, which is more necessary in Russia than anyone has hitherto realized, is unthinkable. But, for the development of a higher form of agriculture Russia needs an aristocracy residing in the country as well as a bourgeoisie in the cities. This will not come about, however, if the aristocracy does not have any estates and farms which make its residence in the countryside both pleasant and necessary. Until now most of the noblemen either have been in the government service or have lived in the cities. Like the Italian aristocracy, the Russian nobility resides in the cities and lives off the revenues from the land (*obrok*). Since such large farms are necessary for agricultural progress and consequently for the welfare of the nation, serfdom cannot be abolished now.* However, it can

*The abolition or alteration of serfdom in Russia should be treated in local terms and not as a general political issue. However, Russia lacks territories which have developed their own particular form of government such as Germany's small principalities, each of which has its own appropriate legal institutions. Because the borders of the old petty principalities in Russia are completely obliterated, legislation at the provincial level, which represents a real need with respect to rural institutions, is hardly thinkable. . . .

be transformed into an institution regulated by law with fixed exact-
ments and a check on personal authority as was intended in the
*ukaz* of 2 September, 1842.[2] The second kind of farm mentioned
above, large estates, economically run in a completely western European fashion and joined with home industries, would certainly be
a great blessing for the northern regions, although they can never
become a national institution. Excellent schooling, intelligence, untir-
ing effort, and ambition are required to establish, maintain, and
run such estates. Of course, one will find this combination only
as a rare exception. The government should try to preserve and
support these farms in every way possible, wherever they are located,
for they alone as model farms can disseminate improved methods
of agriculture. Everywhere experience teaches us that the innovators
of these farms usually become martyrs to a good cause and go
to ruin. Mr. Karnovich, a man of very modest needs, began most
cautiously and will not be ruined. Yet I do not believe that the
capital he invested in improvements has yielded a fantastic profit
up to now.

In Iaroslavl province the cultivation of land owned by the peasants
is confined to providing bare necessities. Here, too, the infertile
soil and inclement climate play a decisive role. The crop scarcely
remunerates the peasant for his labor; the produce has to be driven
long distances to market and commands a very low price. The farmers' draft animals are weak, and the Russian worker does not
like heavy, continuous work in the fields. Is it not natural for the
Russian peasant in such areas to engage in farming only in order
to obtain sustenance for himself and his cattle and not in order
to make a profit, a goal which is hardly attainable anyway? It is
not in his interest to employ the men and animals at his disposal,
but to spare them. He cultivates as large an area as possible in
the simplest manner and with the least amount of effort and then,
of course, reaps only a small quantity of grain. If he wanted to
improve a small field and cultivate it carefully, he would indubitably
harvest a better crop. But produce has a very low price. When
considering his work in terms of money, he would easily be able
to figure out, by adding the amount spent to improve the land,
that production was far too expensive to make any profit.

There are areas in Europe and certainly also in Russia where
the peasant cannot take into account the work he spends in cultivating
the land simply because he has no other means of converting his

2. See Introduction, n. 26. The text of the law is published in *PSZ*,
2d series, no. 15462, 16:261–62.

labor into money. In such a case he cannot speak of a loss, however much energy he expends in tilling the fields; the smallest profit is still a profit and is better than nothing. We then have a situation similar to that of the French peasant whom Arthur Young tells about![3] However, this does not apply to the Russian peasant in Iaroslavl province; there his labor has a high pecuniary value for which the industries that flourish in the province are responsible.

We have already mentioned that farm work in these regions is restricted to the four summer months. At this time all the forces available are engaged in cultivating the land. But in the remaining eight months, when all farm work is at a standstill, they are without work. What consequence has this had over the ages? The result has been a truly remarkable growth of industrial activity, as vigorous in rural areas as in the cities.

The location of the province has always been most favorable for industry. In the Middle Ages we already find industry and commerce flourishing here. But particularly since Petersburg began to prosper as the main commercial city of the empire, industry has grown immensely in Iaroslavl province. In accordance with Peter I's grandiose plan, the main harbor on the Baltic Sea, Petersburg, was connected with the most important river in the entire empire, the Volga, and consequently with all its tributaries by means of three remarkable canal systems. In the vicinity of Rybinsk the canals empty into the Volga. Because the cargo has to be transferred to other kinds of vessels here, this formerly unimportant town became the largest entrepôt in all of Russia. This was the starting point for the rise of industry in the province.

At first industry utilized the raw materials from the province itself. During the eight winter months, when the farm work allowed them sufficient free time, the inhabitants and producers manufactured articles and sent them to market. Their individual disposition and talents provided the inhabitants of this province with the impetus toward industrial activity. The local Russian is intelligent, lively, very inventive and imitative, greedy for gain, and has a leaning toward trade. The conditions of serfdom provided another powerful stimulus to industrial activity. For the most part the serfs were not underlings who tilled the lord's fields in return for the right to a plot of land but tenants who paid a tax in money (*obrok*). The masters' own

3. Arthur Young (1741–1820), author of *Travels during the Years 1787, 1788, 1790. . . ,*2 vols. (Bury St. Edmunds, 1792–94); German translation: *Reisen durch Frankreich und einen Theil von Italien, in den Jahren 1788 bis 1790*, 2 vols. (Berlin, 1793–94).

interest produced this arrangement centuries ago, for it was most convenient for the indolent aristocracy residing in the cities. This practice greatly encouraged the rise of industry.

Agriculture provided sustenance but no profit. However, money was required to pay the *obrok*. Raw materials sold cheaply but every manufactured article commanded a high price. (The above statement still holds today throughout Russia; although this point has already been mentioned several times, it cannot be repeated often enough.) As we have said, articles were first manufactured from the raw materials of the province: wheelwrights, cabinet makers, wooden-shoe and bast-shoe makers, bast weavers, pitchboilers, ship and bark builders supplied the market with a great variety of wood produce. Spinners, linen weavers, rope and sail makers, etc., provided articles manufactured from hemp and flax for the market; saddlers, harness makers, tanners, and shoemakers produced leather goods from animal hides, etc.

These industries were not organized into craft guilds in such a way that each village had all the necessary artisans, shoemakers, tailors, saddlers, etc., to satisfy the immediate needs of the surrounding area. Rather, as we have said, goods were mass produced and sent directly to the markets. This system gave birth to that remarkable national associative spirit which is based on the organization of the Russian commune.

In other countries an individual dedicates himself to the particular trade for which he has a bent and for which he feels he has a certain talent. In Russia it is assumed that everyone has a penchant, the skill, and the talent for every occupation. And there is a great deal of truth to this. The aptitude which every Russian, almost without exception, has for all kinds of technical skills is unbelievable. As a rule even a roving Russian works at every possible trade . . . until he abides by the one that seems to promise him the most gain.

For the most part the communities here specialize in one industry. For example, all the inhabitants in one village are shoemakers, in another smiths, in a third community tanners, and so forth. This arrangement has great advantages. Since the Russians are accustomed to remaining together in large families spanning the generations, a natural division of labor is introduced which is so essential for factory-like production. The members of the community continually help each other with capital and workers; the purchases, and as a rule the sales, too, are made in common. The artisan communities send their wares to the cities and markets and have their shops everywhere. Unlike the German craft corporations, these artisan communities do not form a closed guild; rather they are loose associations united only by communal bonds. Every member of the commune can freely take up the village trade or abandon it and start another. This seldom happens though, because there is little to be gained. If an individual wanted to practice another trade, he would move to a community where this particular trade predominates. There is not the least bit of coercion, corporative or otherwise. The factories are free associations, which recall Saint-Simon's theories to mind.

The trades practiced in this manner offer the artisan communities considerable advantages, and the province of Iaroslavl, which nature otherwise endowed so niggardly, enjoys great prosperity because of them. But does this system lay the foundation for agricultural progress in the province, and is there a visible improvement in the individual crafts and industries? The answers to these questions are negative, and one should not praise this arrangement too highly. The manufactured articles are largely shoddy and not reliable; as a rule they remain at a constant level of imperfection and show no improvement whatever. As profitable as this institution is for the people themselves, the consumers must be rather dissatisfied.

Nevertheless, from an economic point of view, the artisan communities are enormously advantageous. Workers not employed in agriculture are engaged in useful work without causing agriculture to suffer appreciably. It seems to us that the government should have made every effort to protect and support this popular institution and if possible to have perfected it. However, it let these industries go their own way. Instead of taking an interest in them, the government introduced the western European system and encouraged the inhabitants to found all kinds of factories.[4]

There are now many factories, silk and cotton mills, etc., some of which are flourishing. This is not the place for me to express my judgment of the entire system. The opinions which one hears on the subject in western Europe are on the whole seldom right. Russia is, after all, a country different from all others and cannot be judged from a foreign point of view. Are not the following well-known economic principles? Factories which utilize the raw materials of the country to produce goods to satisfy domestic needs are the most advantageous; the government should found, protect, and improve them in every way. Factories which use foreign raw materials

4. This development began well before the reign of Peter I. See P. I. Liashchenko, *Istoriia narodnogo khoziaistva SSSR*, 2 vols. 4th ed. (Moscow, 1956), 1:290.

to produce goods for domestic consumption should be tolerated and protected, but the government should do nothing to encourage their foundation. Lastly, factories which take foreign raw materials to manufacture articles for foreign markets are dangerous. They breed a menacing population which endangers the security of the state in time of internal unrest or foreign wars. In Russia, however, the cotton mills, which of course belong to the second and in part to the third category, have proved to be the most beneficial and advantageous; without a doubt they are the most important factories. Cotton clothing is worn throughout Russia and is becoming more and more common. Travelogues from the seventeenth century even mention this; cotton shirts are widely worn among the peasantry and are becoming more popular every day. Every country lad prides himself on acquiring a motley striped shirt as soon as possible. Such a shirt worn over the pants and belted at the waist is the genuinely national summer dress. The government is thus forced to act in contradiction to the above economic principles and to do everything in its power to further the manufacture of cotton goods, which satisfies a national need!

I do not want to express an opinion on the system employed in Russia to improve and encourage manufacturing; I simply want to discuss its form. Western European entrepreneurial factories were introduced in contradistinction to the national associative factories. Instead of urging and teaching the peasants to perfect and promulgate the system of the national associative factories, the state encouraged the aristocracy to become manufacturers and to establish factories based on the foreign model.

Why should it not have been possible, given the inborn obedience of all common Russians, to found a cotton mill in the state villages, for example? Instructors and managers from England and Germany were required as it was, for the factories established by the aristocracy hired these foreigners. Today they may still be in the majority of mills. Of course, the crown would have had to provide the buildings and the machinery; to cover the interest it could have fixed the price of the yarn. At the beginning the crown would have had to supply the looms and employ teachers to instruct the people in their jobs. Then it could have turned over the trade, etc., entirely to the old Russian communal factory association. It is obvious that at first a good deal of training, regimentation, and enforced obedience would have been necessary. However, considering the Russians' great flexibility and technical abilities everything would have run smoothly very soon, and these new factories would have quickly amalgamated with the existing old Russian ones. Just how talented and intelligent the people are in grasping technical things is clearly revealed by the great number of modern factories established and run by Russian peasants who can neither read nor write and who acquired their technical knowledge on their own. Some of the most respectable, most competent, and wealthiest fabricants in Russia, the calico manufacturer Guchkov in Moscow and the Petersburg tobacco producer Shchukov, belong to this category.[5]

One might reply that the system and form of western European factories are the result of long experience and experimentation, that they are the product of a more advanced culture than exists by and large in Russia. Why should we not secure this fruit of civilization? Why should we not borrow it from our neighbors, since this could be done without too much effort? The Russian people possess many abilities and above all the ability to acquire every kind of technical skill, which is most essential in manufacturing. Is it not a government's duty to adopt and imitate useful institutions, wherever one finds them? Does not every nation learn from the other?

In this reasoning there is one point which I must refute: a nation cannot take true culture as a mature fruit and transplant it at home. Culture is only the product of a long internal evolutionary process and is not the memorized knowledge of the moment. The nations of the Occident passed through this long school of evolution in the course of many centuries; they always had the culture of the ancient world before them. Taking this culture as a model, the Western nations gradually raised themselves to a higher level. By no means did they put ancient culture on, ready made. For many centuries we have possessed the works of classical antiquity, and every generation has served its apprenticeship in the school of ancients. But only now that we have grown to their level are we truly beginning to understand and to use their works. Admittedly Russia occupies a more favorable position than did the Occident and she will necessarily advance more rapidly. Unlike the Occident the Russian peoples have living masters, with whom they have had the most vigorous and direct contact for several centuries. One can learn much more quickly from example, lively communication, and the exchange of ideas than from dead masters from the dead past. But nevertheless, in order to partake of the true fruits of civilization, a nation must first serve the years of apprenticeship; it cannot skip over them,

5. For a competent study of the Guchkov family and the later growth of such dynasties see Louis Menashe, ''Alexander Guchkov and the Origins of the Octobrist Party,'' Ph.D. diss., New York University, 1966.

and as a nation it must have undergone an internal, evolutionary process.

Civilization is composed of two elements, one universal, the other national. The first element is the flower of a higher civilization such as Christianity brought forth in the nations of Europe by using and synthesizing the classical tradition; this culture has thus become the common patrimony of all the European peoples. The second element is the preparation for this flowering, or the growth and moral education of nations, which is necessarily different in the case of each people.

Today the first element is not lacking in Russia. Christianity, which is the foundation of modern civilization in its entirety, was also present in Russia, and for more than a century the upper strata of Russian society have been learning from other peoples. In this respect it seems to me that the development of this higher element of culture in Russia has been completed. The educated class of Russians has the same education, the same customs and philosophies of life as the cultured class of every other nation. But as a result they are as little Russian as highly cultured Englishmen are English and cultured Germans German. Culture at this level is cosmopolitan in nature.

Was this higher culture attained in one generation in Russia? Peter I transplanted European customs and knowledge to Russia, but did he actually succeed? He could force the Russians to shave their beards and dress in the fashion of the French court. But did they become cultured individuals as a result? Only now, after four generations, after they have had foreign teachers and governesses from childhood on, after they were permitted to live abroad for years, after mammoth schools were founded where every upper-class Russian can attain the traditional European education that is the prerequisite for higher culture, only after a Russian national literature was gradually created for the upper classes — only now after a hundred and thirty years can one recognize that these upper classes have become cultured.

However, up to now nothing has been done for the education of the common people. Peter I and his successors obviously believed that one must first educate the upper classes and train them to be the teachers of the common people. Until around twenty years ago, however, no important steps had been taken to secure a genuine basis for popular education.

In my opinion this was to Russia's good fortune. Had one been satisfied here simply with laying the groundwork for a worldly culture, with drilling in knowledge without religious and moral foundations, the government would have made a sturdy rod for its own back. Only through its national church and its clergy can the Russian people acquire a moral and national education. Only from the church can one expect progress. However, until recently the church was not called upon for this purpose and may even have been prevented from attending to the education of the people. Only now is the clergy being trained in the seminaries to assume this task.

The Russian populace is thus separated from the upper classes by a gulf which will not be bridged for many years. Meanwhile, what are the people to do with the fruits of western European civilization, including the entire system of manufacturing? What clear advantage does it offer the people? Should the people simply be trained for a variety of technical skills? Or does the government want to seduce them in to acquiring a taste and penchant for foreign luxury and fashions? Can anyone think that this might elevate the cultural level?

What purpose do the factories in Russia serve that produce fashions and luxury items? For whom do they work? For the upper classes, for those who are truly cultured, or only for those who have borrowed the external refinement of European culture? Certainly not! They do not use the articles produced by Russian factories. There is something mysterious about the luxury and fashions of recent times. What does the word "taste" mean with respect to luxury and fashion? Why is it that only Paris and London and to a lesser degree Vienna tyrannically dominate styles in Europe? Why is it that the most artistic people, the Italians, that Rome and Florence, that Berlin, the intellectual center, do not have the slightest influence on fashion? There is a certain mysterious atmosphere hovering over those centers of fashion, the only places where mode thrives. Only the factories which are in direct contact with these centers can create articles recognized by this capricious queen, fashion. This is not the case with the Russian factories, for they do not live in that atmosphere of style. For this reason they are not in a position to create high fashion but can only imitate. Since their products never meet with the satisfaction of the elegant cultured individuals in Russian high society, these people surround themselves only with luxuries and fashions from Paris and London.

If the Russian articles do not meet the demands of high society, are they then meant to give the retinue of "apers," the ostentatious middle class, the mere outward appearance of modern elegance? Is it necessary for the wives of Russian merchants, who are inwardly rude and ignorant, to look almost like elegant ladies? Would it not be better for them to have kept the national dress and with it the simplicity and poetry of national customs and fashion? Or is it necessary for the families of lower officials to parade in the attire of European elegance, to indulge in their passion for luxury and fashion and thereby to force the poorly paid official to practice extortion and fraud, which they are strongly inclined to do anyway?

In concluding this discussion I must therefore maintain that with certain exceptions it was not necessary for Russia to introduce an extensive factory system in its modern European form. Also I must add that it has an unfavorable influence on the morality of the middle and wealthy classes.

Instead they should have tried to further the already existing national associative factories and to improve them by introducing modern machines. It is true that the most important branches of manufacturing, the linen, woolen, cotton, and silk industries, would not have produced fashionable articles, whose elegant styles and designs can never be matched anyway. But they could have made clothing which is suitable, comfortable, and decent for the majority of the people, for the well-to-do core of the population.

I have already mentioned that this factory system has had a profound influence on the social conditions of the lower classes and particularly on the institution of serfdom. In another place I may discuss this again in greater detail.

The modern factory system is now a *fait accompli* in Russia and is deeply entrenched in the entire social order. As much as one would like to object to its having been introduced, one can only think now in terms of organizing these factories in a more national manner and perhaps of changing them in part into national associative factories.

The idea behind the factories established by Peter I is national and correct. . . . He wanted to base them on the conditions of serfdom. The manufacturer was supposed to be able to use the people assigned to the factory but at the same time to assume the obligation of providing for them in a very broad sense: he was to feed, clothe, and care for them. When they were no longer able to work, he was not allowed to turn them out but had to care for them until death. As long as serfdom continues to exist, this idea must be carried on.

The majority of the factories no longer employ their own serfs. Instead, workers voluntarily apply for a job and receive a fixed wage. In various ways one could prevent many evils that this entails and particularly the demoralization of the factory workers, at least in part. The factory owners could be forced to organize their workers into a kind of Russian commune, to assume the complete and strict duties of a seigneur, to establish a communal granary for them, to provide schools, maintain hospitals, etc. Also they should not be allowed to dismiss workers without definite reasons as set down by the law and particularly not because of infirmity and old age, etc. One can justifiably make these demands on the factory owners, since they have been given such enormous advantages through protective duties. The threat to drop the protective tariffs would readily persuade the existing factories to submit to these demands. One could impose this condition in advance on factories established in the future.

The fact that many factory owners have seized upon these ideas on their own is clear proof that such an arrangement is feasible. I shall later describe some factories in Moscow, namely, those owned by Prokhorov, where schools, hospitals, and so forth are already to be found.

Although the large factories would be able to bear the burden, it would be difficult or impossible for the small mills. It might even cause their gradual decline. However, the community would not suffer any injury as a result. Like the great estate owners in Russia, the large fabricants do not oppress their people as do the small manufacturers and seigneurs of small estates.

## The *Polovnik* System of Agriculture

To my great surprise I encountered in the far north of Russia a rural institution familiar to me from a part of southern Europe. I had hitherto believed that given the soil climate and transportation situation this institution could not possibly exist in the north. It is well known that in most of Italy and in southern France most of the plowlands and meadows belong to the townspeople. Specifically they own either all or a part of the village fields; the houses, however, are the peasants' private property. (This arrangement formerly existed along the Rhine up as far as Cologne, but has been replaced in recent times by ordinary leaseholds granted in return for a fixed sum of money.) At the same time, there are also cases where the townspeople own entire farms, the buildings and the land (*Métairiewirtschaft*, known as *Halfenwirtschaft* on the Rhine). The lands or farms are leased to peasants in return for half of the harvest. This institution admits of many local variations. In those areas where only the land is leased, the owner sometimes receives half the grain but not half of the fodder. Occasionally he gets only half of the winter grain and the tenant keeps the straw. On the smaller farms (*métairies*) the owner provides the farm buildings and dwellings; the tenant, however, is responsible for their maintenance. Sometimes the cattle and the equipment belong to the tenant; in other instances the lessor permits him to use the stock and implements. The lessor usually provides the seed and pays the taxes. The tenant always keeps all the straw. The lessor's share is determined by the financial burdens the tenant has assumed, whereby the fertility of the soil is also taken into account. He may receive half of the winter wheat, half of all the grain, or half of all the grain and the hay.

It is an economic view or principle that the leasing of farms for payment in a share of the harvest is suitable only in southern grain lands, where fertile soil, a temperate climate, light work, and quick transportation enable the tenant to pay as much as one-half of the gross harvest in rent. In the central regions, from the North Sea and the Baltic Sea in the north to the Danube in the south, it has always been the rule that the owner is entitled only to one-third of the gross harvest. The agricultural system which employs serf labor is based on the latter principle. The owner turned over two-thirds of the arable land to a number of peasants (a village) for their own use. In return they had to perform all the work on that third of the land which had been set aside as the lord's estate. The gross harvest of this third constituted the actual rent for all the land.

In central Europe the farms based on serf labor have disappeared for the most part. They were attacked from two sides. First of all they were dealt a blow by the more advanced knowledge in the field of economics. Practical economists claimed that progress on such estates was hardly possible in that so many workers were superfluous but were kept on anyway. Second, this system was assailed by modern ideas that criticize serfdom as inhuman. In those countries where the institution of serfdom was not destroyed by revolution as in France, it was gradually abolished by legislation. Nearly everywhere it was replaced by a system of leaseholding whereby the tenant paid the rent in cash. In the Russian Empire the institution of serfdom still exists. In Courland the agricultural system employed prior to the abolition of serfdom there is still the most common.[6] As a rule two-thirds of the land is leased to the

---

6. Peasants gained personal freedom but without land or other necessities in Estonia in 1811, Courland in 1817, and Livonia in 1819, thanks to Alexander I.

peasants. Instead of paying the rent in the form of money, they have to cultivate the other third at their own expense.

This same principle holds in Russia proper. However, in the north the inclement climate often makes it impossible for the peasants to work the third in payment for the two-thirds assigned to them. Frequently they have to be given three-fourths of the arable land. In this case only the gross harvest of the last quarter constitutes the rent. Of course, the rent increases toward the south. On the enormously fertile land of the so-called Black Earth region, it can be as high as the gross harvest of half the land under cultivation. In the end effect this corresponds to the *métairie* or *Halfenwirtschaften* in Italy.

I did not expect, however, to find this agricultural system fully developed in the far north between 59° and 64° latitude, and yet this is the case.

As is generally true in all of northern Russia, there is no indigenous resident aristocracy in these areas. Most of the aristocrats living here are government officials. They come and go and do not set up permanent residence here. Several aristocratic families have been living in the cities, for example, in Ustiug, since time immemorial, although they do not own any property with serfs. However, they and a number of townspeople do own large areas, plowlands, and meadows, and even entire villages but there are none of the usual Russian nobiliary privileges attached to this land, which is to say that they do not have the right to use serfs for cultivating their lands. However, they can lease the land on the basis of the *polovnik* law.* This means that they simply have the right to lease the land to Russian peasants in return for payment in kind, a portion or half the harvest. This corresponds to the practice followed in Italy and southern France.

Two systems of cultivating these lands are common. Either the lands are located near a state village and may even be incorporated in the latter's plowlands and meadows, . . . or the lands are together in one area and separate from those of the state village. In the first case the plowlands and meadows are turned over to the people in the neighboring state village in return for half of the grain harvest: the owner provides the seed and also lets the people keep all the straw. I do not know for certain whether the hay is divided. In several places, where there were few meadows, the hay was left

*The word *polovnik* is derived from *polovina* (half) and has the same meaning as the West German provincial expression *Halfe* or *Halbbauer* (a peasant who turns over half the harvest as rent).

to the people, and the owners did not receive a share. I was told, however, that in areas where there were many meadows leased on the basis of a *polovnik* contract the hay was divided or a special payment in cash or in kind was stipulated.[7]

In the second case the *métairie* system is fully developed. A village is built on the fields belonging to the community, and the fields are distributed equally among the inhabitants. If the *polovniki* have built the houses entirely at their own expense, they belong to them; in those cases where the landowner provided the timber, the houses are his property. The stock, the buildings, and the implements belong to the peasants. All the fields are divided into large lots in such a way that an equal amount of plowland is assigned to each, . . . about six desiatins. Depending upon its manpower and its stock, each family takes over a half to a whole lot and sometimes up to two. The master has to pay the grain tax for the peasants and also supplies the seed. In lean years he has to provide the peasants with some or all of their food. Instead of payment in cash, the owner receives half the harvest. (If the meadows are few and the plowlands poor, he is given only half of the grain.)

The contracts are signed for a six- to twenty-year period. With the expiration of the contract and with one year's notice, each of the parties is free to cancel the agreement. The form of the contract is extremely simple. The parties appear before the district court and register their names in the *polovnik* books. "Mr. W. has ceded to the peasants N. N. N. the village A. and its fields in accordance with *polovnik* law for six, ten, or twenty years." At his departure the peasant takes the farm stock and sells the house, or if the house belongs to him and if he has built it, he dismantles it. If the material was supplied by the master, the peasant is paid a fair price for the labor involved in constructing the house. If one individual withdraws from the *polovnik* agreement of a village and moves away, the remaining peasants of the village are obligated to transport his dismantled house and his personal belongings to his new place of residence.

According to the last census the true *polovnik* peasants (those who dwell together in their own villages) numbered 3,920 males in the three districts of Ustiug, Solvueshchegodsk, and Nikolsk. I found that the views on the expedience and advantages of this institution differed somewhat in the various districts. In Ustiug the

7. On the *polovnik* or sharecropper system in Russia see Jerome Blum, *Lord and Peasant in Russia from the Ninth to the Nineteenth Century* (Princeton, 1964), pp. 100, 101, 484–85.

opinion was most favorable. I was told that the arrangement is very profitable for both parties and consequently very lasting, which brings economic benefit to the peasants and owners as well as to the commonweal. The contract is a binding legal agreement, and it is the greatest social evil that such does not apply to the other peasant institutions of Russia. The landowner and the *polovnik* both know exactly what their obligations are, and the fulfillment of these duties is to the advantage of both parties. The master attends to the peasant's interests at all times and protects him from outside oppression. The master frees him of life's bothers, paying the taxes to the crown for him and supporting him in lean years. However, should the master and the peasants be dissatisfied with one another, the agreement can be dissolved. . . . But in reality this almost never happens; the agreement is hereditary. The peasant is reluctant to leave the place that has become home, and the master does not like to lose upright and diligent people; the arrangement is obviously enormously advantageous for the owner.

The rent to be paid in kind appears to be unreasonably high in regions so far to the north. At first glance one cannot understand how the peasant can exist. It is obvious that the half of the harvest which he keeps is hardly adequate to provide food for himself, his family, and his cattle. However, the nature of the climate, Russian agriculture, and the Russian national character adequately explain the appropriateness of the system. All the work in the fields is at a standstill for seven to eight months, and the Russians have the talent and skill for all trades. The *polovnik* regards his farm as a permanent home and a center from which he can carry on his activity safely and conveniently. The work on the farm occupies him for four months, and although farming does not bring him a real profit or surplus, it does provide his sustenance. He can thus spend the following eight months attending to his other domestic needs and above all earning money. During this time the *polovnik* works at various trades like all the other Russian peasants; he speculates, trades, hunts and deals in furs, engages in business ventures or drives a coach. The result is that these people are generally well-to-do and that a great many are rich. They are even wealthier than the state peasants[8] despite the fact that the *obrok* paid by the latter

8. Throughout this and subsequent chapters Haxthausen incorrectly refers to crown lands when he means "state lands," and "the Ministry of Crown Lands" (*Ministerstvo udelov*) when he means the newly founded (1837) Ministry of State Domains (*Ministerstvo gosudarstvennykh imushchestv*). The error has been corrected here and elsewhere.

represents far less than the value of half the harvest. Also, wealth and prosperity are more evident among the *polovniki* than among the state peasants. The former have less need to avoid showing their wealth than the state peasants, since through the display of wealth the latter were more liable to attempts at blackmail on the part of the officials — at least this was the case until a few years ago before the introduction of the most recent regulations pertaining to the state lands. The security of their position also gave the *polovniki* great moral ballast. They are more reliable and honest in all their dealings, upright, simple and decent. There is no example of conflicts having arisen among them and with their masters.

In the district of Nikolsk the opinions on the *polovnik* institution were less favorable. Many peasants there are afraid to enter into this relationship, not because it is disadvantageous (the advantages are recognized here as well), but because they sense dangers to their freedom. They believe that the usual obligations included in the contract could lead to a kind of temporary and even lifelong serfdom and then perhaps to hereditary bondage, such as they have actually seen happen in the southern part of the district. I was unable to determine whether the conduct of several masters was responsible for this opinion or prejudice. Clearly it is only a prejudice, since the institution is very well regulated by law.

The consequence of this prejudice, however, has been a considerable decrease in the number of *polovniki* in the district of Nikolsk. Formerly there may have been well over a thousand male *polovniki*; now they hardly number three hundred. The owners of *polovnik* land are thus forced to pay to have the land cultivated or to enter into an ordinary lease.

Since this prejudice has spread here in recent times and since the departing *polovniki* applied for admission to the state villages, the Ministry of State Domains found it had to facilitate their departure and their admission to the state villages. The state villages now are supposed to accept them. However, if they do not want to admit them, the *polovniki* are allowed to settle in the depths of the forests. The inhabitants of the state villages are obligated to help them by felling trees and building a path for them. However, since the matter involves considerable difficulties for both parties, the *polovniki* generally remain in the state villages and are satisfied with the small share of state land.

The history of the origin and the rise of this institution is still very obscure, and I have been unable to elucidate it sufficiently. I have collected some material on the subject but nothing adequate.

In Ustiug Mr. Rakov gave me a short historical treatise containing some good notes. In Petersburg I found a treatise on polovnik agriculture in the Ministry of State Domains. I was also given the French translation of a chapter from a Russian book by Uspenskii, *Ancient Russian Institutions*.[9] However, as I said, I have been unable to procure an exhaustive study on the history of the *polovniki*. Moreover, there is little hope of getting such a work, since the older documents and reports on the institution were destroyed in 1710 in the great fire of Ustiug. Some few documents were salvaged but not the oldest ones.

In the above-mentioned book Uspenskii alleges that reference is made to *polovnik* law as early as the beginning of the eleventh century. In the laws which Iaroslav Vladimirovich gave the inhabitants of Novgorod, two systems of land cultivation are mentioned. Wealthy individuals, who inherited land or took it as the first occupants or who received it as a gift from the princes, hired freemen to farm the land. In return they paid the owner with half the harvest. They were called *polovniki*. Other freemen did not wish to enter into such an agreement with the large landowners. Instead they moved into the forests, burned down parts of the woods, and sowed their crops there. They were called *ognichane*.* The latter method of cultivation was, of course, not very stable, since the scorched land yielded a harvest for only a couple of years. It was then necessary to burn down another grove.

We obviously have here the two systems of land cultivation which have always coexisted in northern Russia: the Russo-Slavic system and the old Finnish method. The *polovnik* arrangement is what remains of the oldest Russian agricultural system. The majority of landowners assigned land to free peasants in return for a share of the harvest as here in the north, or in return for working the master's part of the land as in the central and southern regions. Sometimes they leased the land for payment in grain or perhaps even for payment in cash (*obrok*). The abolition of the freedom of movement under Tsar Boris Godunov and the turning over of the peasants to the seigneurs in the revisions under Peter I effected an enormous change in the original institution and gave rise to the present system.

Legislators have always regarded the *polovnik* agreement as favor-

*Ognichane* is said to be derived from *ogon* (fire). Etymologists disagree as to whether the name refers to someone who burns the earth for the purpose of cultivating the land or someone who has his own hearth.

9. Gavrilo Petrovich Uspenskii, *Opyt povestvovaniia o drevnostiakh russkikh*, 2d ed. (Kharkov, 1818).

able for agriculture in these regions (perhaps when compared to burning down the forests). In granting lands the princes included the condition that the *polovnik* system be applied. The oldest document salvaged in the fire at Ustiug which was issued by Tsar Ivan Vasilevich in 1552 states this explicitly.

Another still extant privilege of 8 June, 1652 granted by Tsar Alexei Mikhailovich states that everyone in the district of Ustiug who had bought land or held it in pledge could do as he wanted with the plowlands and meadows and could also enter into agreements with the *chernoslobodniki*[10] in accordance with *polovnik* law.

A privilege from 31 March 1699 likewise states that individuals who could not farm the land themselves had the right to sign contracts with the *chernososhchnik* peasants for half the harvest.[11] Included in this category were merchants who traded in Archangel and Siberia, and persons employed by the customs, and those engaged in distilling liquor. On a trip through these regions in the year 1690 Peter I remarked that judging from their appearance the *polovnik* villages were tidier and more prosperous than the state villages. He created a commission under the chairmanship of General Letarev to investigate the matter and its causes.

The commission's report convinced Peter I of the expediency and the salutariness of the institution. At the personal request of the *posadskie*[12] from Ustiug he therefore extended the privilege of 1699 to them and to all the *posadskie* of the region and issued the order to proceed at all times according to the old law.

The emperor later rewarded many merchants and some nobles with land in these areas. For the most part the descendants of these aristocrats have now joined the merchant class, for example, the Tvesovs, Chelbyshevs, Plotnikovs, etc. All of them were also given the right to buy, sell, and exchange such property, albeit always

10. *Chernoslobodniki* in ancient Muscovy were inhabitants of a *sloboda*, or settlement, who were exempt from the duties of serfs or residents of a *posad* and were under the jurisdiction of the state rather than a lord or the church. See V. O. Kliuchevskii, "Terminologiia russkoi istorii," *Sochineniia,* 6 vols. (Moscow, 1959), vol. 6, and Sergei G. Pushkarev, *Dictionary of Russian Historical Terms from the Eleventh Century to 1917* (New Haven, 1970), pp. 127–28.

11. A *chernososhchnik* from the thirteenth to the seventeenth century was a peasant living on state lands and subject to the head tax but otherwise free. See Kliuchevskii, *Sochineniia,* 4:63.

12. An inhabitant of a *posad*; according to the charter of 1785, one of the six categories of townspeople. Pushkarev discusses the process by which their freedoms were reduced, *Russian Historical Terms*, pp. 55–56, 95.

with the stipulation that the lands be leased to peasants in accordance with *polovnik* law.

On the basis of those investigations the order was given in the *ukaz* of 25 October 1723 to work out detailed regulations concerning the conditions of the *polovnik* peasants. The chief reason was so that the payment of crown taxes would not fall behind, when these peasants moved from one place to another. While taking the census ordered at that time the assessors were called upon to make suggestions for regulations dealing with the above-mentioned situation. The examiners of the provinces of Archangel, Kazan, and Siberia actually did make suggestions to the senate.* The latter concluded on 11 January and 22 February 1725 that the peasants should be allowed to move about freely, since they were freemen and not serfs. However, when the peasants changed their place of residence the landowner whom they left as well as the landowner to whom they moved was required to notify the authorities, to agree to pay the taxes, etc. Under threat of severe punishment no one was allowed to accept those peasants who left secretly, etc.

All the rights were confirmed again in the *ukaz* of 8 March 1753. With the general survey of the entire empire ordered at that time, all the *polovnik* land was measured as private property and the taxes to which the crown was entitled imposed. The plans and the new registries and books were first certified by the senate and later by the imperial *ukaz* of 1789. Around 1788 Kanikin, the governor of Vologda, collected the various documents and sent them to the senate, which confirmed all the rights of 27 June 1800 and again in 1805. A senate decision of 31 March 1783 also gave permission to the crown peasants who did not own any land or who could not pay the *obrok* to enter into a *polovnik* agreement with landowners upon previous notice and request.

Finally the Minister of Internal Affairs issued a regulation on 1 December 1827, which stated: (1) the *polovnik* system is based on the principle that the *polovnik* must give half of all the produce to his master; the contract determines whether payment is to be made in kind or in cash. (2) The *polovniki* purchase the farm implements and cattle at their own expense. The property owner supplies the material for constructing and repairing the buildings, and the *polovnik* provides the labor. (3) As freemen the *polovniki* can leave after the contract has expired, although they must always give a

---

*It seems that at least at that time the institution was also common in other provinces. I cannot say whether this is still the case today. There were no reports and notes in the ministries in Petersburg.

year's notice. (4) However, if the *polovniki* move to state villages, they are considered to be state peasants. (5) When they leave, the houses for which the masters supplied the material are left to the latter. However, the houses built without the master's assistance belong to the *polovniki*; they can sell them or dismantle and move them. (6) The *polovnik* agreements can be made for a period of six to twenty years. Upon expiration of the contract, new agreements can be entered into. (7) If the landowner wants to use the land for a different purpose, he must give special notice a year before the contract expires. (8) When the peasant settles on the land, the master must provide him with the seed. (9) No services and work other than those directly connected with farming the land turned over to him can be required of the *polovnik*. (10) Upon the death of the *polovnik* the contract agreement is terminated; the widow and the minor children do not inherit it. However, if they insist, the owner must pay the taxes for them, although he does have the right to send them off with [internal] passports so that they can work for him and earn some money.

# 3
# Jaroslavl Province II

Now that we have settled down for the first time in a hostel in the Russian interior, I want to make some general remarks on the subject. The European inn was formerly unknown in Russia. Instead, Asian caravansaries were customary. These are large, empty, unfurnished buildings, where for a modest price the traveler can find shelter for himself and his animals but nothing more. There is no innkeeper in the real sense; beds are not to be had, and one has to provide one's own food. It is impossible to speak of a friendly reception by the innkeeper or of the service. There are still such caravansaries in the southern part of the Russian Empire, in Astrakhan and the Caucasian provinces. Throughout these areas there are inns without lodging, where one can get prepared meals and tea or, in the regions around the Black Sea, Turkish coffee. Formerly, when Russians traveled in the interior they had everything they needed with them — beds, provisions, etc. With the spread of European civilization in Russia, European-style inns are being introduced, but only very gradually. Even in Petersburg there is no hotel which one could compare in terms of comfort with an inn in a moderate-sized or even small German city on the Rhine. Hotel Demuth and Hotel Coulon in Petersburg can hardly be ranked with a third-class inn in Germany in respect to elegance and comfort, even though they look like huge palaces from the outside. The beds and furniture are poor, I would say almost shabby. Very seldom is there a table d'hôte. If one wants to eat something in the hotel, it has to be specially prepared. Occasionally the owner leases the restaurant rights. One can hardly speak of service. Moreover, it is scarcely worth the effort to furnish an inn elegantly, since it would be appreciated only by foreigners and consequently would not be very profitable. The modern hotels in Petersburg and Moscow are, moreover, run exclusively by Germans, French, and Englishmen. The Russian merchant still prefers the Russian inns resembling caravansaries; as in former times the Russian aristocrat continues to take along his beds, etc. The very wealthy aristocrat takes with him even his cook and everything he needs. He makes himself at home in the inn and has his servants buy all the provisions. . . .

In Iaroslavl we found a typical Russian inn and accommodated ourselves as best we could. While Mr. A. went out to pay introductory visits to the governor and the chairman of the local bureau of state lands, I took advantage of the fine weather and strolled about the city a bit. Iaroslavl is a very modern city, and if one did not see the characteristically Russian cupolas on the large squares, one would hardly think one was in Russia. The city is picturesquely situated on the high right bank of the Volga. Most of the large Russian rivers that flow south or southeast have a high right bank (the mountain side) and a flat, often marshy left bank (the meadow side); this represents the original geological formation of the vast country. From the left side of the river, Iaroslavl appears grandiose with its two hundred spires and cupolas and its palaces along the bank. One might take it for a city like Hamburg, though it has scarcely twenty-five thousand inhabitants. This is the picture of every Russian city: the outer limits are fixed, and the city is simply waiting to be filled in. At the present moment no country or people makes a greater impression of growing and advancing than Russia.

Gostinyi Dvor,[1] the bazaar in Iaroslavl, is a lively place; the hustle and bustle, the shouting and clamoring, are reminiscent of Moscow. In the milling crowd I noticed more dark-haired people than previously; also the hair is cropped short in the back. The people are husky and often well built; their faces are lively and attractive. The women of this province are considered to be the most beautiful in Russia. . . .

Late in the afternoon we visited the governor and the chairman of the Bureau of State Domains, a Mr. von Hahn, who owns estates in the province. We drove out of the city with them to an area with very pretty parks, called the Summer Garden, at the far end

---

1. Such institutions date from medieval Novgorod, where they were opened for foreign traders. In the eighteenth century Peter I and Catherine II constructed *gostinye dvora* in numerous provincial towns, as well as the capitals.

of which a mental institution was located. The next morning the governor, General Baratinskii, paid me a visit and extended an invitation for noonday dinner.[2] Together with him and his Armenian wife, Princess Abamelek (a genuine Oriental beauty), we drove about to the churches. Later we visited a wealthy Russian merchant who had requested the honor of showing us a special work of art. However, it turned out to be nothing more than a good Viennese music box, which played a large selection of overtures, marches, and symphonies, and which had cost the good man no less than 30,000 rubles banco or more than 9,000 thalers. Through the widespread popularity of the piano, people have come to know and love modern music. But since there are no wandering music companies or musicians' guilds in the cities, music boxes serve as substitutes. . . .

From Moscow I had obtained a letter of introduction addressed to a Russian aristocrat living several miles from Iaroslavl. I wrote him and received an invitation to visit him on his estate.

On the morning of the sixteenth we went first to the bank of the Volga to look at a huge sturgeon that had been caught eight days before. It had been put into a container constructed of posts and boards which stood on the bank of the river. Only a river like the Volga can harbor such a monster. It measured eight to ten feet in length and about the same in circumference. No one could remember ever having seen such a large fish.

I asked to see the chancery and the registry of the office of the Ministry of State Domains as well as the way things were run there and found that in general they were analogous to the German, and especially the Prussian institutions. However, the system of controls and charts is infinitely more complicated and extensive. Bureaucratic red tape has gotten more out of control in Russia than in Prussia. And with respect to the essentials, such as education, thoroughness, diligence, and honesty, the Russian officials are far inferior to the German bureaucrats.

Around six o'clock in the evening I drove with Mr. von Hahn to Goropiatnitskaia, the estate owned by the aforementioned country

2. Iraklii Abramovich Baratinskii (1802–59), like many civil administrators of the reign of Nicholas I, was a former military officer. Von Hahn was a German. Contrary to Haxthausen's view, foreign civil administrators were not a numerous group in the first half of the nineteenth century. See Walter M. Pintner, "The Social characteristics of the Early Nineteenth Century Russian Bureaucracy," *Slavic Review* 29, no. 3 (September 1970): 429–43.

squire, Mr. Karnovich.[3] The road led through a rather well-cultivated region, although we also passed large tracts of low brush and marsh land. Some of this land could not really be cultivated, and in other areas agriculture would not be sufficiently profitable. After covering half the distance, we stopped to change horses. All the inhabitants of this village, which had burned down just a year ago and was now very attractively rebuilt, assembled. Since some business had to be taken care of, Mr. von Hahn immediately held an impromptu communal meeting to show me how such meetings are conducted in Russia. All of the men formed a circle around us in the street; the *golova* (the head of the *volost* or several associated communities), the village *starosta*, and the "white heads" stepped up to us. A rather lively discussion began, of which I understood not a word, since it was carried on in Russian. However, I was told the topics, which involved some general community matters and some minor differences among individual members. After a brief consultation among the "white heads" the disputes were settled by the *golova* with the approval of the chairman of the local bureau of the Ministry of State Domains. Everything was carried on in a most orderly fashion. Only the *golova*, the *starosta*, and the "white heads" spoke; the younger men in the circle were perfectly quiet and attentive. The discussion was animate and appeared to be clear and coherent, at least no one seemed to be at a loss for words. No one shouted or blustered; no one interrupted, and everyone was most polite to his neighbors. Their behavior toward the chairman of the bureau spoke well for both parties; the people were confiding, friendly, respectful, and not at all servile or fawning. With tears and cries of woe a man asked Mr. von Hahn to exempt his son from military service. For legal reasons the chairman had to turn down his request, but he consoled the man in a tender and friendly manner.

Accompanied by the *golova*, the *starosta*, and the "white heads," we went to the community house. The communal scribe presented Mr. von Hahn with all kinds of documents which of course were completely incomprehensible to me. From these papers, however,

3. Efim Stepanovich Karnovich (1783–1855) was educated at home and at a Moscow pension and then at Moscow University. After work in the Ministry of Finances and the Iaroslavl Provincial Directorate, he settled on his estate and devoted himself to modern agriculture, the civic affairs of his fellow gentry, and the life of the Moscow and the Iaroslavl agricultural societies. *Russkii biograficheskii slovar* (St. Petersburg, 1908), 8:530.

one can see how the use of records is also becoming common in the most isolated areas of Russia.

At my request, I was given the following information on the village. It consisted of twenty-three farms with a population of eighty-two male souls. The village had formerly belonged to a Prince Kozlovskii. The peasants, however, had bought their freedom. For the land, the stock, and their freedom they paid 50,000 rubles banco (14,286 silver rubles); 30,000 rubles were paid outright and the remainder within the next seven years.* Consequently, at present they did not have to pay any taxes other than the head tax and communal duties. The land has heretofore been divided not according to the number of souls, as is the common procedure in Russia, but according to the amount that each one contributed to the purchase money. But this method of land apportionment is so alien and inconvenient that they have already decided to introduce the usual practice of land distribution with the next revision. They plan to divide the total amount of the purchase money and to consider it a purely personal debt.

The sun had already begun to sink as we drove off. A peasant had asked for permission to ride along on the *kalasha*. Soon he started an animated and coherent conversation with the chairman, which I did not understand. My traveling companion assured me, however, that his comments were remarkably logical. He continued by saying that the man had discussed the topic of land distribution so intelligently that one could have printed it. The upper and lower classes, the educated and the uneducated, speak the same language in Russia; because there is no patois, it would be unusually easy to disseminate learning of a certain kind and to a certain degree. The written language is completely intelligible to the common Russian.

Since we arrived at Mr. Karnovich's around midnight, we sought the rest we needed. A splendid morning roused us from our beds; together with our host we were soon very busily inspecting every branch of the farm. This estate is by no means based exclusively on old Russian practices, but at the same time it is not a western European farm founded on the principles of scientific agriculture.

*Russian serfdom is indeed a strange institution. Not only did the families and their fields belong to Prince Kozlovskii, but also all their possessions, including the 50,000 rubles that they paid for their freedom. Why did he not take the money and keep the people as serfs? No law would have prevented him from doing this. However, Russian custom forbids this, and it carries more force than laws.

Rather, in every branch it is a national Russian farm with the addition and application of those inventions and improvements that European science offers and which local experience has shown to be useful. Mr. Karnovich has a scientific education. When he visited Germany, France, and England, he obtained first-hand information everywhere on agriculture. Full of enthusiasm and patriotism, he returned home to apply and try out what he had learned and to become the teacher and model of his area. He is unmarried (a widower, I believe) and has no family. Together with an old unmarried aunt he lives in the countryside among his people. He has tried many things on his farm, some of which failed, and others of which were success- ful. He had to fight the obstinancy and ignorance of the people, their blind attachment to tradition, and their hatred of every innova- tion. But he surmounted these obstacles and brought his farm up to a level which, comparatively speaking, was higher than any I had seen in Russia and which is certainly not often surpassed there. Although the modern, scientific improvements which he had introduced on his farm were not new to me, it was interesting to discover them in Russia.

For this otherwise rather infertile province, the estate of Goropiat- nitskaia is situated in a relatively fertile and pleasant region, inter- sected by small chains of hills. It is at about the same latitude as Livonia. The soil is predominantly sandy and contains granite pebbles. Here there is a good mixture of humus. The region has a rich supply of water and adequate brooks, ponds, lakes, and marshes; there are forests of conifers, lindens, birches, etc.

The farmyard is situated on a hill at the head of a small village with a church. Before the house there is a rectangular shaped yard surrounded by farm buildings. The garden behind the residence is attractively laid out but somewhat neglected. In general the entire complex does not look any different from a Livonian or Prussian farmstead. Like all genuinely Russian houses the manor house is constructed of beams placed one on top of the other; but what is otherwise unusual, it has two stories, the upper one of which is occupied by the master.

After looking around the farm, we descended the hill, where the fields and also some of the sheds and sheepfolds were located. Our host took us there to convince us of the feasibility and usefulness of an experiment he had made for storing potatoes during the winter. In the fall, on a dry piece of earth out of doors, he had heaped the potatoes into piles twenty feet long, ten feet wide, and four feet high. He covered them with a six-inch layer of straw, which was in turn covered with an eighteen-inch layer of earth. They had survived the winter, and the layer of earth was removed in our presence. Although there were still (17/29 May) frozen clods in the soil, the potatoes were well preserved, as we were able to prove to ourselves at dinner. In a nearby barn which, along with the drying room, was constructed in the style of a Livonian barn with foundation and pillars of stone, we found a peculiar threshing machine of a sort used widely in the province of Simbirsk. Since there was nothing to be threshed, we are unable to give any first-hand information on its merit. The people were plowing the fields for the summer sowing under the supervision of an old man, who nimbly drove the first plow. He had an unusually handsome old face, with long white hair and a beard. Considering his vigor I guessed his age to be sixty some odd years. But he was eighty and had a little five- or six-year-old son.

From here we went to a small village nearby to inspect a peasant farmstead. . . . The gable side of the house faced the street, and next to it there was a long narrow yard with an entrance gate. The house which we examined rather closely, had its main entrance from the street, which is not very common. The main door was to the left, and to the right there was a second little door leading to the lower room of the house, where small animals are kept. To get to the actual living room one has to climb a short flight of stairs. The *izba* contained no furniture other than a bench which ran along the entire room. Standing in the corner opposite the door was the icon illuminated by a lamp. Some shelves had been built along the walls for keeping dishes and various utensils. Spinning wheels and a loom were evidence of the very widespread linen industry in this region. An enormous brick stove, which serves as a sleeping place in winter, occupied one-third of the room. Next to the stove a small staircase leads to the above-mentioned lower room of the house (*podpole*) which is used as a storage room and where small animals, chickens and pigs, spend the night. In winter the cows are also milked here. There were some small rooms with tiny windows on the other side of the staircase which likewise serve as storage space for all kinds of things. In these rooms there were also several chests, one for each member of the family for storing clothing. In the summer the family usually sleeps here. Since the stove in the living room is also used for cooking, the living room is heated all year. The barn is attached directly to the living quarters and can be entered from the house. The passageway was covered by two roofs in such a way that the house and the barn together have three [stepped] roofs, the second of which is somewhat lower than the first and the third a bit lower than the second. The horses and cows are kept in the barn, separated by posts rather than partitions; in winter it is very cold, but the animals are accustomed to it.

Standing behind the barn and in the same line with it was the *sarai*, a building used for keeping the carts and agricultural implements. Since the salt and flour provisions are also stored here, a strong padlock is on the door. Several steps away, but in the same line, was a cellar with a superstructure used for keeping cabbage, fruit, etc. Behind the cellar there was a small cabbage garden, at the end of which stood the drying barn, and in back of the garden an area where the farmer dries the hay and also piles up his grain, before it is taken to the drying room. The bathhouse is always last in this row of buildings. Every farmyard is therefore very long and narrow and not round or square as in Germany.

Considering that there are cattle below and next to the living quarters and that the ceiling is low and the room hot, one would think that the dwelling would be very dirty and the air foul-smelling. But this was not the case. The air was better than I had expected, as a result of the open windows and the fire which was always blazing. Moreover, at least in this house, the living room was kept so clean that it was a pleasure to see. Our host told us that the living quarters of the peasants here were cleaner and better than those of the city dwellers.

We found the people in this house busily working at the spinning wheel and loom. They were friendly and confiding toward us; they behaved naturally and were not at all timid. They willingly answered all my questions.

The composition of this family was very strange. The head of the family and the farm was an elderly man who had been a widower for more than twenty years and who had no children. At his side was an old woman who was a distant relative, a widow with an attractive fourteen-year-old daughter. The husband of another, deceased daughter had remarried, and together with his wife and five children he performed the main tasks on the farm. Mr. Karnovich assured us that they lived in perfect harmony and were very fond of one another, even though they were not joined by blood ties. This kind of relationship is not at all unusual. The Russian cannot live without secure family ties; if he has no family, he creates a substitute. If his father is deceased, he seeks and selects one; he respects and loves him like a real father. Similarly, if a man has no children, he adopts some. One might ask why the old man did not marry the elderly woman, so that at least an outer bond, that of stepfatherhood, could have been established. Custom in these regions does not tolerate this, however, and considers it improper for a widower or a widow beyond fifty to remarry. But since a man at this age requires female care more than ever, the above relationships are formed very naturally.

We were assured in Moscow that Mr. Karnovich was the first in Russia to try to transform the condition of the Russian peasant into a tenant relationship. About one verst from the village he built a farm, with a house and farm buildings, to which he assigned twelve and a half desiatins (50 morgens) of plowland along with adequate meadows and pastures. He settled a peasant family on this farm. The construction and arrangement of the house is completely different from the Russian-style houses; it is modeled more after the English farmhouses. The cultivation of the fields and the rotation of the crops were based exclusively on the principles of scientific farming and were appropriate to the climate, the soil, and the geography. The farm implements were above criticism. Before he put the family on its own as new tenants, he gave them a thorough and practical training on his own farm. He signed a lease with them, but since this kind of contract arrangement was not legally valid before the promulgation of the *ukaz* of 2 April 1842,[4] he actually issued a deed of concession in which all the conditions were set down as binding. The experiment can be interpreted as a complete success in that the farm has existed for a number of years and the harvests are improving from year to year.

I expressed my doubts about his radical departure from existing common Russian customs in regard to the setup of the house and farm, as well as the kinds of tools, the methods of cultivation, etc. It was my opinion that the people could never be expected to imitate this system. Like a single exotic plant the entire farm would someday disappear without leaving a trace. I would have thought it more natural and effective if he had based his plans directly on existing institutions, Russian customs, and the national way of life. Then they would have represented an attainable model for the surrounding area. After all, he had followed these principles on his own farm and had without a doubt achieved so much precisely for this reason.

Mr. Karnovich was not of this opinion. He said that his estate

4. See Introduction above, n. 10.

was an old one that had been established before he had taken it over. Consequently, he was only able to make gradual improvements there and blend the new with the old. He had to accustom people, who had had an entirely different training to various new practices which were alien to them and which they despised; hence [on his own estate] he was able to introduce improvements but was unable to effect a complete change. He denied that this was the case with the small farm, which was an entirely new creation. This meant that he could but in fact proceed according to scientific principles. The people to whom he had assigned the farm had been adequately trained for their task. But they were Russians nevertheless. Let us assume that they had been placed on a farm that retained the fundamental national characteristics except for the addition of improvements and changes. Lured by example, national sentiment, childhood memories, and attachment to native customs, they might soon have ignored the innovations and improvements and slipped back into the old methods prevalent in their milieu. Now, however, with these new conditions completely different from all those around them, they have been directed along a path they can never abandon. According to Mr. Karnovich the agricultural system would thus be secure; it was so unlike the national institutions, and the setup of the entire establishment, as imposed by the arrangement of the house, was so entirely different from the former that a transition to national practices and a gradual lapse into the old way of doing things was utterly impossible.

He added that it would of course be difficult to get the Russian peasants to accept these alien agricultural institutions. However, his own farm was a good training center, in that it represented a transition. The Russian is, moreover, by nature teachable and has the greatest ability to imitate. Lastly the Russian is unusually clever at doing everything that is in his own interest. As soon as he sees that this agricultural system and the setup of the farm offer a distinct advantage, he will not hesitate to take it as a model. Of course, the farm is not a hothouse plant and must therefore take root gradually. . . .

In the afternoon of 17 May we drove to Velikoe Selo[5] (literally,

5. Velikoe Selo or simply Velikoe, situated south of Iaroslavl and east of the Moscow highway, subsequently famous for stock breeding and a center of mechanized cottage manufacture of shoes and shingles as well as large-scale linen weaving. V. P. Semenev-Tian-Shanskii, *Rossiia*, 19 vols. (St. Petersburg, 1899–1913), 1:150, 286.

"great village"), a community of 1,500 souls* or 3,000 inhabitants, located about three to four versts from Mr. Karnovich's estate.† The land and the inhabitants were the property of seven sisters, two of whom were already deceased. Because they neither lived nor had a manor there, they had imposed *obrok* payments on the peasants. However, they did not tax the individual *tiaglo* (family) but rather the village as a whole in the form of a tribute, taking into consideration the number of souls, the extent and quality of the plowlands, meadows, and forests and the industry in the village. (A large linen mill was located here.) In calculating and fixing the amount of tribute, three factors were taken into account: first, the sum for which the land might be leased; second, the number of persons to whom the land was assigned; third, the particular implements which the inhabitants possessed as well as the skill with which they carried on certain industries.

With the infiltration of western European civilization and industry Russian serfdom has undergone a complete change in many regions of the empire. Originally, only the very numerous domestic and farm servants (prisoners of war and their descendants) were serfs or rather slaves. The peasants were free tenants who could cancel their lease every Iuriev's Day (Saint George's Day) and leave. However, since no petty prince of Russia allowed his subjects to leave his territory, the area within which they could move about was limited.

When the petty principalities ceased to exist and Russia became a unified state, these restrictions were, of course, dropped, and the peasants enjoyed an unlimited freedom of movement. The Russian has always been unsettled and fond of roving; he has a strong allegiance to his country but little attachment to his place of birth. Unlike the German he engages in farming only out of necessity

*It is curious that in all matters involving the state and the individual in Russia one counts *souls*. In the rest of Europe one counts *heads*, men and women. In brief, the physical element is dominant. But in Russia, where the mechanical state flourishes and serfdom prevails, the spiritual aspect is emphasized in that souls are counted. In fine Mohammedan fashion, however, not the women, but only the men have souls and are souls! In this way an aristocratic lady, who herself is not a soul, can nevertheless possess many souls![6]

†According to a note in the *Zhurnal ministerstvo vnutrennykh del* of 1839, no. 6, p. 739, the village has around 2,700 souls or 5,400 inhabitants and only 700 desiatins of land.

6. This footnote has been moved from volume II, p. 280, of the German text, which is not translated here.

and not out of love for his work; he avoids heavy and especially continuous labor. Great inconveniences and confusion resulted from this unrestricted freedom of movement. Regions in which farming was difficult or not very profitable were completely depopulated and nearly became wasteland. However, in other areas, along the rivers and in the cities where lighter work could be found and earning more easily acquired, the population grew enormously. This led Tsar Boris Godunov to issue a *ukaz* 21 November 1601 abolishing the freedom of movement and binding all the peasants to the land on which they had been living the previous Iuriev's Day. From that time on, the peasant fell under the jurisdiction of the landowners, although he was not yet a serf; only after the reign of Peter I did he gradually become a serf.[7] One can claim that this happened almost by accident and not by law, as we shall demonstrate in greater detail elsewhere.

As long as Russia remained a purely agricultural state, serfdom was not very oppressive for the true peasants. This was especially so in Great Russia, where there were formerly few seignorial estates and where the peasant did not have to till the lord's land. Instead, for a certain amount of rent, the master turned over all his land without conditions to a community of his peasants. This practice is still common and is followed on all the state domains. (To my knowledge, the crown does not have a single estate in all of Great Russia where the serfs are required to perform special services for the seigneur.) In these cases the amount of rent was self-regulating and the master had to be content with the modest net proceeds. If he demanded more, the peasants were reduced to poverty; their livestock and equipment deteriorated or completely disappeared. Agriculture declined, and it became impossible to pay the taxes. However, the state was strict in its demand that the master himself should pay the taxes which the peasant owed to the state and at the same time compelled him to feed his peasants if they themselves had nothing. Hence pure self-interest forced the master to be gentle, considerate, and helpful to his peasants. He even had to try to keep the quality of their farm stock at a certain level; otherwise he could not expect to receive the full payment of the rent. But he did not live among them in their village. Because there were no manorial lands he resided in the city. Consequently, he could not possibly

7. Here Haxthausen minimizes the extent to which serfdom had been extended and codified in the seventeenth century, particularly in the ulozhenie (code) of 1649. See Blum, *Lord and Peasant*, chaps. 14, 21; and R. E. F. Smith, *The Enserfment of the Peasantry in Russia* (London, 1968).

look into the abilities and the financial situation of the individual peasants. Since he could not peek into the pot, as the saying goes, he had to be satisfied with imposing a collective tax on the entire community based on the number of inhabitants. This arrangement strengthened the already powerful Russian communal institution in its relationship to the lord. A Russian commune such as this one had, as it were, become an unusually well-organized free republic, dependent only in the sense that it paid a fixed amount of tribute to its seigneur.

The situation has now changed and is threatening to change in greater degree through the infiltration of western European civilization, industry, and luxury. Peter I and his immediate successors introduced factories artificially: they summoned foreign manufacturers, provided capital or loans, and turned over land to them for their establishments. At the same time they assigned a number of persons to them as factory workers, usually an entire village. The relationship of the workers to the factory owner was the same as that of the serfs to their master. They worked for the factory, and the owners were in turn responsible for providing their food, clothing, and lodging.* These factories actually gave rise to the notion in Russia that all the work performed by the serf belongs to his master and that the latter could use the serfs for any kind of work that would bring him a profit. Formerly the master knew of only two ways to employ his serfs as tillers of the soil or as personal domestics. With governmental support, industry continued to grow in Russia and the government itself summoned the aristocracy to build factories everywhere. In the past twenty-five years too many were established. The result was that the masters employed the serfs as workers in their factories as had been done earlier in the so-called crown factories. At first the masters used their unemployed domestics. Since they were poor workers at least in the beginnning, the seigneurs soon turned to their superfluous peasants. Because farming yielded less profit in the poor and moderately fertile regions than the factory, agriculture was frequently neglected and abandoned. Soon someone discovered the secret that every Russian was a poor factory worker as long as he toiled only for his master but that he could become an excellent laborer if he worked for his own benefit. The seigneur therefore gave his serf permission to look for work wherever he

*Factories of this type still exist in Russia, and I shall describe one that I visited in Iaroslavl. However, they are gradually declining compared to the new factories founded on modern principles.

could and wherever he wanted on condition that he pay a certain tax.*

Today this is the most common arrangement. It developed very naturally and consistently, and one cannot say that the peasants or the ordinary Russians on the whole complain about it. On the contrary, this practice is perfectly suited to the national temperament. As we have said, farming is not their favorite occupation. Now they can give up farming or leave it to the women, children, and the elderly. They can travel about, as they have always preferred to do, as hucksters and merchants, as artisans, factory workers, and coachmen. (The number of people engaged in the latter occupation has, of course, increased tremendously as a result of the enormous growth of industry.) They speculate, work for their own gain, and pay their master only a fixed tax, the amount of which is almost always arrived at by haggling. For the masters or the Russian aristocracy, this arrangement is likewise most convenient and agreeable.

Since 1812 the less well-to-do Russian aristocracy has come to know the rest of Europe, its luxuries and its comforts. (This was always true of the very wealthy or court nobility.) They grew dissatisfied with life at home, came to despise the national customs, and endeavored to transplant European life to their country. This became tremendously expensive! Russian aristocrats always had a weakness for luxury, with the result that they accumulated enormous debts. Their estates were put up for sale and came into the hands of parvenus who had amassed fortunes by the most reprehensible means, through speculation or in government service. The old bonds of reciprocal affection and loyalty that had been passed on from generation to generation and that alone could make the institution of serfdom humane or, at least tolerable, were torn asunder. The new masters regarded serfs purely as a means, as machines for earning them money.

Through government service more and more parvenus acquired nobility. A certain superficial modern culture spread in ever larger circles throughout Russia. It was a veneer too pitiable to be considered

---

*I have long believed that the government committed an error by encouraging industrialization in Russia to such an extent twenty-five years ago, before having legally normalized the relationship of the serfs to their master. This is indeed possible and in Germany was actually done. Furthermore, the government neglected to examine and determine the future relationship of the serfs to the factories. This is becoming more necessary with each passing day. It is much more difficult today than it would have been then, and is becoming increasingly difficult.

cultural betterment, but adequate to destroy every noble and national sentiment in the heart of man and to engender hatred and disgust for national customs. Everyone who had acquired this veneer entered government service and in this way attained the rank of nobility, if he did not already have an aristocratic title. Prestige and all real power was concentrated in this dangerous hierarchy of officials. Since honor, authority, and prestige could not be acquired without an official rank and since one could not serve his country and emperor outside the circle of officialdom, everyone, including the members of the old aristocratic families, entered the ranks of the civil servants. Everyone was more or less contaminated by the spirit of depravity which prevailed there. The result is that the aristocracy in Russia has swollen to a people of masters, as opposed to the old Russian populace of servants. Separated by a foreign culture, by foreign philosophies of life, customs, and mode of dress, the nobility has only its religion and its language in common with the peasantry.

Formerly, serfdom was not an unnatural, pernicious, and unsuitable institution, and it may even have been necessary for Russia's political development. I am speaking of the time when the aristocracy was not as numerous, when the nobility's customs, culture, and views of life differed little from those of the masses. At this time the aristocracy together with the serfs constituted *one* people. Serfdom then applied only to agriculture. The old village communes, embodying a powerful principle of true and disciplined freedom, had not yet been ruptured by destructive partitions. Today serfdom has become an unnatural relationship, and it is becoming more and more evident that in time it will be impossible to maintain this institution in its present form. No informed person in Russia hides this fact from himself. But how can serfdom be abolished and restructured without bringing about a great social revolution? This is the important question of the day.

Today serfdom in Russia is Saint-Simonism in reverse. As we know, this doctrine requires that men should be evaluated on the basis of their needs and abilities and that they should be paid accordingly. Their remuneration is, so to speak, the interest on the capital represented by their personal value. This also applies to the Russian serf. His value is formally assessed by his master. The latter says to him: "You are so many years old; your physical condition and health are such and such; you have so much physical strength, such and such a capacity for work and endurance; your intelligence, training, talents, and skills are such and such. Hence you represent so much capital." But instead of continuing like Saint-Simon: "Because you have a certain value, you are entitled to so many fruits of the earth,'' the Russian seigneur says to his serf, ''Since you have this value, you must earn so and so much. You bring in this amount as the interest on the capital which you represent but which belongs to me, and thus you pay me.''

After this brief digression let us return to conditions in Velikoe Selo. The village resembles a small city, with its bazaar and some good modern houses that testify to the prosperity of their residents. There is a rather large linen industry here. The inhabitants do not spin the yarn but purchase it instead. For every *arshin* of linen cloth the weaver gets 65 kopeks banco. Even a woman, if she is a skilled weaver, can easily earn a daily wage of 1 to 1½ rubles banco (9–14 silver *groschen*). This is a high wage when compared to the price of farm produce. In good years the price of a *chetvert* (four Berlin bushels) of rye generally sinks to 5 rubles banco (1 thaler, 17 silver *groschen*)! How can agriculture flourish, how can one demand that people diligently apply themselves to farming if it yields such a small profit and if they can earn more money in every other trade? Here a woman can earn enough by weaving to buy almost one bushel of grain for a single day's wage. In Bielefeld in Westphalia she can earn at the most 5 silver *groschen*, with which she can hardly buy one-tenth of a bushel of grain. . . .[8]

We learned the following about the commune and the system of land apportionment. Some of the inhabitants have amassed a considerable fortune through linen weaving and have acquired a large market. Others are engaged in farming, and a few in the crafts. The seigneurs took these commercial and manufacturing activities into account and imposed a higher *obrok* than could have been borne by agriculture alone. Had the owners demanded an equal tax from every male, as is customary, they would have squeezed the poorer people, while the rich would have paid a disproportionately small sum. The owners' absence made it too difficult for them to tax everyone according to his means. Since the entire village and all the inhabitants belonged to them anyway, the masters preferred to impose a collective tax and to leave it up to the community to apportion the tax burden among the individual members.

In view of these circumstances the commune employs a unique

8. It is exceedingly difficult to evaluate this statement, for it takes into account only money wages and not cost of living or real wages. For comparative data on the Rhineland, see Wolfgang Köllmann, *Sozialgeschichte der Stadt Barmen im 19. Jahrhundert* (Tübingen, 1960), chap. 4 (Barmen was the birthplace of Engels).

procedure to determine the individual tax. It divides the entire sum according to the amount of land held. But instead of apportioning the land equally among its members, the community has forced the rich to take more land than they can use and more than they would have been entitled to had the land been divided equally. As a result the wealthy have to pay higher taxes than can possibly be realized by farming. Of course, those who do not engage in agriculture cannot use the land. They either lease it to the true farmers for an amount so small as to be wholly insufficient to cover the tax on the land, or they let the land lie fallow. The power of the Russian commune and the obedience it exacts from its members are evident everywhere, and we shall have further opportunity to study its uniqueness. . . .

Upon returning [to Mr. Karnovich's estate], we took another walk through the gardens and fields; on this occasion our host gave us some interesting information, particularly on the relationship between masters and serfs, the nobility and peasants. The ordinary Russian is in general extremely genial. And if the master is good, just, and truly well meaning, a genuinely close, benevolent relationship usually develops. Mr. Karnovich told us of an old local bachelor who had died several years ago. This Mr. Archakov was cherished not only by his own peasants but through the entire region, which is unusual. He dwelt in a small Russian house among his peasants, toward whom he was in every sense benefactor and father. He was not rich and he shared everything with his people. Yet at his death he possessed three times the number of peasants he had had at the beginning. Whenever a village in the area was to be sold, as a rule the peasants of the community came to him and asked him to buy them. He would reply that they knew, of course, that he had no money, to which they would answer, "But *batushka* (dear father) if you don't have any, we do; we want to bring it to you so that you can buy us." Everyone brought his money to him for safekeeping. He was the peacemaker for the entire region.

Wherever we went, we saw and were told that our host enjoyed the same love and respect, although his modesty did not permit him to boast of this. Who could look into his gentle, friendly eyes and not be convinced that his heart was imbued only with the purest love for humanity! Because of his keen gift of observation and his long association with the lower classes of the population, each of his remarks was accurate and valuable. Unfortunately I neglected to write down each evening what I had heard and consequently some things have been erased from memory. I also heard many remarks elsewhere, repeated by others, and then forgot that I had also heard them here. At this point I want therefore to include some of these individual observations even though they have no real connection with each other.

Among other things, he made the following comment on the character of the Russian peasants. "The man in charge of giving orders, the peasant's master or superior, must avoid being vague in his actions as well as speech. The Russian always wants to have a definite decision, especially regarding quarrels among peers. Whether it be favorable or unfavorable, just or unjust, wise or foolish, he always accepts the decision. If an order is imprecise, he immediately becomes fractious and hard to handle. For him a resolute 'it is ordered' is a magical word, which he never defies.

"As welcome as such strict obedience must be to every authority, one must always relate it to the patriarchal idea. In every order the people must see only the father's command. If the order issues from a sense of paternal care and the obedience from childlike love, then no harm is done if now and again an order appears to be inexpedient, absurd, or even unfair. Respect forbids one to place a father's orders on a scale. The *chinovniki* (officials) are corrupting the people; they are suffocating every sense of justice in them; their orders appear everywhere to represent the caprice of petty despots. Their orders manifest base avarice or arrogance and never paternal concern or even a father's uncompromising and absolute will. For this reason the official engenders only servile but not childlike obedience. The Minister of State Domains, Count Kiselev, had an excellent idea for reawakening and strengthening a sense of justice in the people. He found that the Russian commune was the bastion of self-reliance and disciplined freedom. He wanted to elevate the Russian commune, to invest it with the power of self-government and to free it from the despotism and selfishness of officials, the *ispravnik* and so forth.[9] The peasants were to acquire the feeling that they must unconditionally obey their elected leaders, the *golova*, the *starosta*, and the 'white heads.' Moreover, they must feel that their leaders do not merely offer them protection but are themselves protected by all the authorities including the minister and even the emperor. The peasants complained at first because their direct taxes had been raised somewhat to achieve this, although the amount for the individual was insignificant. But, when they realized that

9. The *ispravnik* was the district (*uezd*) chief of police, an office established in 1775 by Catherine II. The *ispravnik* was elected by local gentry until 1862.

the oppressive demands of the *ispravniki*, which exceeded by far the direct taxes, ceased or were at least greatly reduced, they were satisfied. The growing awareness among the peasants that one can seek protection and redress for injustice is by far the most important result. Complaints, which are often delivered personally, are frequently passed on to the minister himself; a speedy and thorough investigation always follows and often very severe punishment.''

Mr. Karnovich was of the opinion that great inconveniences were caused by the insufficient number of small courts and a legal procedure too cumbersome for the simple conditions of the countryside. If a man has to travel forty to fifty versts over poor roads in order to present a minor complaint in person before the judicial authorities (there are no lawyers in Russia), he would rather give up his rights or try to take the law into his own hands. There is no institution like that of the *juge de paix* [peacemaker] in France. According to Mr. Karnovich it should not be difficult to find suitable candidates for such an office everywhere. However, they must not become a link in the long chain of officials, and the post can only be an honorary one. The late Mr. Archakov demonstrated this need and the possibility of satisfying it. Another local resident, Mr. Polovtsov, enjoys almost the same confidence among the people as the late Mr. Archakov and has also been asked to settle many quarrels. According to Mr. Karnovich there are several good men like these.

Mr. Karnovich also acknowledged that the greatest evil in this part of Russia is that agriculture yields too little profit. No one invests capital to improve his stock or farm in general, since it does not yield any interest. Whoever has capital or ready cash buys up more land, but it does not occur to anyone to carry out intensive improvements on the land he already owns. Sales show that the price of property is constantly going up, not because the land has been improved but because the demand is great. The revenues from the land are increasing somewhat, but only because the growth of industry has made it possible to utilize many things that formerly had no value.*

In a farmer's house we met a tailor working on a caftan and were told that there are villages in the province where all the inhabitants are tailors. They travel about looking for work at certain times of the year, usually in winter. Upon arriving in a village, they

---

*The best examples of the rising cost of property are said to be found along the southern coast of the Crimea. Whoever bought land there sixty years ago can now sell it for fifty times the original price. But the southern Crimea has been converted from a wasteland into a flourishing garden.

go from house to house, working everywhere until the entire village has been outfitted in new clothes; then they move on to another village. They receive food and drink and are paid a certain amount for each article rather than a daily wage. For a gray jacket they receive 50–70 kopeks banco and 2–4 rubles banco for a blue caftan. . . .

We were given the following notes on the apportionment of the land in Russian village communes. The distribution of land is based on the principle that the entire population of a village community represents a collective, to which all the fields, meadows, pastures, forests, streams, and lakes belong. Every living male has the right to use an equal share of the land. In accordance with this principle the allotment always varies, since every male born to a family of commune members is entitled to his share. Similarly, the portion of each deceased member reverts to the commune. The forests and pasture lands, hunting and fishing grounds, are not divided, and everyone shares equally in their use. The plowlands and meadows, however, are apportioned equally according to the value among all the males. It is, of course, very difficult to distribute these lands evenly. The village plowlands contain good, mediocre, and poor lots; they may be far away or nearby, convenient or inconvenient for the individual. How can these differences be compensated for? Although the problem is difficult, the Russians have surmounted it with facility. In each community there are experienced surveyors with traditional training who perform their work intelligently and to everyone's satisfaction. First of all, the fields are divided into square plots in such a way that all parts are roughly equal in respect to their distance from the village and the quality of soil. Each of these plots is then divided into as many long strips as there are shareholders in the community and distributed by drawing lots.* This is the common procedure, although local usages, deviations, and special systems have been established in every region and often in individual communities. It would be very interesting to collect them.† In the province of Iaroslavl, for example, many communities

---

*As a rule the entire community with women and children gathers for the distribution of the land and the drawing of the lots, but everyone is perfectly orderly and quiet. Quarrels never arise, because the system is very just and fair. If one thinks that his allotment is inferior to the others, he is given an additional piece of land from the reserve.

†Minister Kiselev had scientifically educated experts survey and classify the land in several villages in the province of Voronezh. A comparison showed that the results arrived at by the communal surveyors agreed within 3 to 4 percent with those based on scientific principles. And who knows who was right in the end!

have measuring rods, which are regarded almost as sacred objects. The length of the rods is in inverse proportion to the quality of the soil. The rod used for measuring the best land, for instance, is the shortest, the rod for the somewhat less fertile land is a bit longer. The longest rod is used for the worst land. Although the lots differ greatly in size, they are absolutely equal in value.

We have described here the free Russian commune, which owns the village fields. There are actually a large number of these free communes in Russia. All the Cossack communes, for example, belong to this category. In principle, however, it makes absolutely no difference whether the communes own the fields outright, whether they have limited possession of the land as in the case of the state communes, or whether they are tenants, as are the communes of serfs.

The principle of equal division is an indigenous Slavic legal concept. This principle, which is based on the indivisibility of all family property and the periodical division of the fruits, may have existed at one time among all the Slavic peoples and is perhaps still prevalent in some areas of Serbia, Croatic, Slovenia, and elsewhere. The cultivation of the land is a communal enterprise supervised by the elders. According to this principle the land is not divided annually but rather the harvest is distributed equally among the commune members.

The same principle holds in Russia, even among *obrok*-paying serfs. (While it was formerly common for only Great Russian serfs to pay *obrok* [pecuniary tax], today this applies to the majority of all Russian serfs.) The principle has been modified, however, among those serfs who have to render services to their master. The oldest form of this system consists of setting aside a part of the arable land, usually one-fourth to one-third, for the exclusive use of the seigneur.* The peasants keep the remaining three-fourths or two-thirds for their own use. In return they have to cultivate the lord's land without pay. They must fertilize, plow and harrow the land, sow and harvest the crop (the lord provides the seed), and drive the produce to market all at their own expense. In this primitive system the lord of the manor has no farm stock, no employees, and not even a steward; the village *starosta* usually fills this role. He does not have a residence and may have only a barn and drying room. The peasants do not pay any taxes but

---

*In Great Russia, when the peasants can no longer pay the *obrok*, the master is forced to establish a manor based on this system.

instead perform services for their master, which are determined by the work necessary to farm his third or fourth of the land. To prevent abuses, the government once and for all established that the work performed on the lord's demesne may under no circumstances exceed three days of the week.

The agricultural system based on services also has a decisive effect on the apportionment of the land in the community. With the *obrok* system every male receives an equal share of the land and must also assume an equal share of the taxes (*obrok*). In the system based on services, however, those unable to work, i.e., the young boys and the elderly, cannot claim a share of the land, since it is turned over to the people in return for their labor. Hence a different principle of land division must be employed, and the land is distributed on the basis of *tiagla*.

The word *tiaglo* has a very general meaning and cannot be translated. It does not mean simply a married couple or a family, but something in between. Let us take as an example a peasant who has a father unable to work, a grown son and several children who are underage. All of these persons together constitute only one *tiaglo*; they have to perform a single amount of work and receive only one portion of the land. Let us now assume that the son marries but stays on his father's farm. The family which now constitutes two *tiagla* is obligated to assume double the amount of work on the demesne and receives two shares of the land. Because marriage is a prerequisite for the formation of a *tiaglo*, the three parties concerned [the seigneur, the commune, and the head of the family] encourage marriage, albeit for different reasons. As a rule the seigneur is primarily interested in having as many *tiagla* as possible. However, if his estate is small, an overcrowded commune could become a burden for him, in that he would have more laborers than he can use. If the shares of land are so small that the peasants cannot earn a living, the master would either have to purchase additional land or provide the surplus population with another livelihood. This problem is not likely to occur at the present time. In view of the ubiquitous expansion of industry, he would turn over his surplus people to a manufacturer as factory workers. Another possibility would be to put them on *obrok* and give them passports so that they can leave the commune and seek employment as workers, artisans, hucksters, coachmen, or the like.

The commune, too, can be interested in the formation of a *tiaglo*. If it has more land than the members can profitably cultivate on their own, every increase in the number of workers or *tiagla* represents a real advantage for the others. The amount of work that any individual performs on the master's land is thereby decreased.

Lastly, the heads of the family themselves are usually most interested in having their sons marry and create new *tiagla*. It is a custom in Russia that a married son does not set up a separate household as long as his father is alive.* Every marriage thus brings the greatest gain to the head of the family in that he acquires another portion of land. And although he has to assume an extra share of the work on the master's land, this is completely compensated for by the fact that he obtains an additional worker in the person of his daugher-in-law. Even if she is poor and has nothing to offer but her healthy arms, the arrival of a daughter-in-law is always a welcome blessing for the family. (This is additional proof of the aforementioned favorable position of the female sex, even in the lowest classes of Russian society!)

Since these converging interests greatly encourage marriage, single status is almost unheard of among the common Russians. Up to very recent times the pressure to marry early gave rise to strange abuses. Lads were married off at such a tender age that Wichelhaus in his description of Moscow tells of having frequently seen robust women of twenty-four carrying their six-year-old husbands around in their arms. I was told that recently the government has strictly forbidden men to marry before their eighteenth birthday. Today this abuse seems to have disappeared.

The conditions which I have sketched here constitute the foundation of the Russian commune, which is certainly one of the most remarkable and interesting political institutions. It cannot be denied that the commune offers immense advantages for the inner social conditions of the country. The Russian communes present an organic unity and a compact social order not to be found anywhere else. Owing to the communes, there is no proletariat in Russia today. As long as the institution of the commune exists, a proletariat cannot

*Nowhere is a large family a greater blessing than among the Russian peasants. Sons always mean additional shares of land for the head of the family. Daughters are in such great demand that one hardly asks for a dowry and may even pay for a bride. In western Europe a large family is an immense burden and nuisance for the lower classes; in Russia a large family represents the peasant's greatest wealth. This explains the great increase in the population in Russia. The population would be far larger if the children were not sacrificed to the grave at a tender age owing to the parents' neglect in feeding and caring for them. Russian marriages are enormously fecund; ten to twelve children are common, although hardly one-third reaches adulthood.

emerge. A man can become poor and squander everything, but his children do not suffer as a result; they always retain or receive their share of the communal property, since they do not derive their right from him. Rather, by virtue of birth they are entitled as members of the commune to a portion. Hence they do not inherit their father's poverty.

On the other hand, one must also admit that the basic principle of the commune, namely, the equal division of the land, is not conducive to agricultural progress. At any rate it renders progress very difficult. As a result of this system every branch of farming will undoubtedly remain at a primitive level for many years to come. But will this institution remain intact if civilization makes significant inroads among the rural population in Russia? Who can say? Intelligent agronomists such as Mr. Karnovich are opposed to the practice and are of the opinion that agriculture cannot advance if the principle of equal apportionment is strictly applied. But this is the important point: the principle has not been rigorously upheld for years, although it has by no means been abandoned anywhere. It is subject to natural, convenient, and advantageous modification. As a whole the Russian peasants are far too practical-minded to shut their eyes to their real interests. This may be more true of the Russian than of other peoples. Long ago they recognized the disadvantages and inconveniences that result from a strict application of the system. Mr. Karnovich replied with a firm negative when I asked whether there was any place where the land was actually redistributed annually among commune members. This was confirmed by many other persons to whom I put the same question. There may be a vast number of variations in the different parts of Russia, but the following procedure for redistributing land is followed in Mr. Karnovich's area and probably throughout the entire province of Iaroslavl.

As we know, orders are issued to count the population in Russia every so many years for the purpose of determining the head taxes and mustering recruits. These population counts are called revisions; since the reign of Peter I, or in the past 130 years, there have been eight counts. It is a rule that communal land *must* be redistributed during the census year. If this were not required, the peasants, at least in the Iaroslavl region, would not undertake a reapportionment. Just how inconvenient and disadvantageous this seems to be in their eyes is revealed in the name they have given to the redistribution: *chernyi peredel* — the black or bad redivision. At the time of the last revision the following procedure was employed hereabouts and in a large part of Russia as well.

First of all, the village fields and plowlands are surveyed by the community surveyors and classified according to their quality. . . . In the case of the state communes the approximate number of souls is kept in mind, in the apanage and private communes it is the number of *tiagla*. Since there is a possibility of new members, several more allotments are added as a reserve for the community. The plots whose contours are very irregular because of paths, ditches, river banks, etc., and which are somewhat difficult to survey are divided in such a way that only regularly shaped lots are cut out for distribution. The remaining strips, ends, corners, and so on are also placed in reserve and, if complaints arise, they can be used for making adjustments. These parcels are called *zapoloski*. Each individual is then given the share which he has drawn by lot; the reserve portions are either leased or used in some way by the commune. If a boy is born later or if another *tiaglo* is created, a new share is assigned from the reserve. If someone dies, his parcel reverts to the reserve. However, the commune tries its best to assign the father's share to his son, so that the existing lots are altered as little as possible. [The son can thus reap the fruits of his father's labor.] This is one reason why the families prefer to remain together on the same farm. Indeed, after the father's death, the eldest brother frequently succeeds him as head of the family and is respected and honored accordingly. The entire farm remains undivided.

From this one can see that in practice the method of dividing the land is not as ruinous for the progress of agriculture as it might seem to be in principle. People will argue that if one does not own the land or at least have the assurance of being able to use it for many years, he will not make any improvements or invest any capital to increase crop yields. We have shown that the tenants can be fairly certain of keeping the land from one revision to the next, which is to say for a period of ten to fifteen years. And yet improvements on the land have hitherto been rather insignificant in Russia. In western Europe, for example, and in Germany the plowland usually does not represent more than two-thirds of the value of the entire farm. The farm stock and the improvements comprise the remaining third. Hence in Europe if I were not sure of keeping the land at least for a certain number of years and of receiving compensation for the betterments at the end of the period, I might forfeit one-third of my wealth. I would lose all the money spent for enriching fields, for plowing, and for seed. My livestock might be in great jeopardy; some of my equipment could become superfluous or worthless. If one purchases an estate with 500 morgens of plowland, 100 morgens of meadow land, and 10 morgens of garden land in Germany on 1 June, the breakdown of the price will be approximately as follows:

| | |
|---|---|
| 1. Plowland | 20,000 thalers |
| 2. Meadows | 9,000 |
| 3. Garden | 1,000 |
| 4. Fertilizer, labor, and seed | 3,000 |
| 5. Meadow improvements | 500 |
| 6. Fruit trees, etc., and garden improvements | 500 |
| 7. Cattle and equipment | 6,000 |
| 8. Farm buildings | 6,000 |
| | 46,000 thalers |

If numbers 1, 2, and 3 with a value of 30,000 thalers could be taken away from me at any moment I would risk losing 4, 5, and 6 or 4,000 thalers completely and suffer an incalculabe loss on 7 and 8 which represent a value of 12,000 thalers.

Computations of this nature are not made in Russia. In the central parts of the empire, in the Black Earth region, the soil is so fertile that it is never fertilized. The earth is plowed only once and hardly scratched in some places. Consequently, there are almost no expenditures for fertilizer and labor; the amount spent for seed is insignificant if one considers that a Berlin bushel of grain costs 12 silver *groschen* in cheap years. Meadow improvements and fruit trees are almost nonexistent. Very rarely do the farmers have sheep farms; cattle raising is negligible and horses are cheap. Considering that the usual price for a good workhorse in the province of Iaroslavl is 50 to 60 rubles (15 to 18 thalers), one can roughly estimate how little capital is invested in the stock. The buildings cost the Russian peasant almost nothing, in that he does not have to pay for wood from the communal forest. Since every peasant constructs the entire building by himself, a house costs him less than 5 thalers in hard cash. Whereas one must include, in addition to the land itself, a rather considerable amount for the farm stock and improvements in estimating the value of property in Germany, this is almost never the case in Russia. As opposed to the rest of Europe, it is therefore not nearly so important that the Russian peasant be guaranteed the right to use the land on a somewhat permanent basis.

In most regions of Russia land itself has little value, for the worth of a farm is based on the human labor required to maintain it. Until a few years ago all deeds of sale, gifts, and wills mentioned only the peasant families. . . . The land was simply added as an extra along with the people!

The future will decide whether land in Russia will become more valuable and thus more expensive, or, in other words, whether agriculture will advance and flourish. I am afraid, however, that the answer will not be favorable in the immediate future. I have already mentioned that agriculture and manufacturing conflict in Russia. Agriculture will never thrive as long as it yields so little profit. And it will continue to yield such small profits until the artificially introduced factory system has been brought back within its natural bounds or until the population has increased to such an extent that there is a surplus of workers. In the rest of Europe the factories hire only those workers who can no longer be employed in agriculture and who are superfluous. In Russia the opposite is true: only those workers dedicate themselves to farming who are superfluous in the factories and trades or who are rejected as unfit.

We are convinced that the Russian system of apportioning the land equally among the commune members is wholly appropriate to present-day agricultural and social conditions. Moreover, there is nothing inherent in the system itself that opposes progress. One should simply let the Russian peasants do as they like. They should not even be forced to carry out the "black redivision" in the census year. They themselves know best what is advantageous for them. On their own they have introduced beneficial modifications of the principle, and they will find the necessary changes in the future. If there is any sphere of activity where one would want to caution against too much unnecessary government control, it is undoubtedly here.

With respect to the possession of land we see three coexistent principles in Europe today. These principles are sharply defined in three countries; in the other countries they have been modified and amalgamated with one another.

The following principle predominates in England: the land is divided as little as possible, and only as many people as are absolutely necessary can devote themselves to farming, for only then will it be possible to increase production and keep agriculture flourishing. The whole country is therefore cultivated by large (but not excessively large) farms. The advantage of these extensive manors is that they provide all their employees with work throughout the year. No capital invested in human labor is wasted. Only on larger farms does it pay to make improvements.

The result of this system is that, comparatively speaking, agriculture is more advanced and more productive in England than anywhere else. Nowhere are there more cattle than here, and nowhere can the land thus be enriched to such an extent and nowhere else can the fields be brought to such a high level of productivity. Hardly one-third of England's population is engaged in farming and less than one-tenth of the population owns a plot of land or even a house. Hence nine-tenths of the population are proletarians, even though very wealthy people and even millionaires may be included in their ranks.[10] No one will fail to recognize the dangers which such conditions represent for England's social order.

The second principle of landownership is represented by France. The rise and consolidation of the French system was the product of a vast upheaval there. The French principle establishes that farming is a free trade; all the land must therefore be divisible and everyone must be able to acquire it freely. In other words, land must be a commodity which passes from one hand to another like a small coin. As a result the land is divided up into innumerable small holdings. If one assumes that there are about 400,000 estates in England, France should have, in proportion to its area, about 1,400,000. In 1831, however, there were no less than 10,404,121 farms in France or twenty-six times the number in England! More than two-thirds of the French population is engaged in farming. To show the consequences of this system I want to include an anecdote told by the English traveler Arthur Young.[11] Along a highway in France, he met a peasant carrying four hens. When asked where he was going the peasant replied that he wanted to go to the city four *lieues* away to sell his chickens. Young then asked how much he hoped to get for them. Answer: Maybe 24 sous. Question: How much do you earn if you are working for someone. Answer: 24 sous. Question: Why don't you stay at home instead where you can earn 24 sous, keep your chickens worth 24 sous and even eat them yourself? Answer? It is true that I earn a daily wage of 24 sous when I work, but I am unable to find employment. In my village everyone has a house, a garden, and a strip of land. This hardly occupies us for three months of the year; there are but few outside jobs. Consequently no one needs the help of a worker and is willing to pay him a daily wage! This anecdote provides us with a glimpse into conditions in France. If the people do not find employment on the side, the small amount of farm work by no means

10. For similar views on the proletariat in England by contemporaries of Haxthausen see Eugène Buret, *De la misère des classes laborieuses en Angleterre et France*, 2 vols. (Paris, 1840), and Friedrich Engels, *Die Lage der arbeitenden Klasse in England* (Leipzig, 1845).
11. See chap. 2, n. 3.

suffices to occupy them throughout the year. Hence, there is a great loss in human labor. The farm that is too small also yields too little profit to enable the owner to make important and lasting improvements. Horticulture can flourish but not agriculture. The lack of cattle means a shortage of fertilizer, which is the basis for all agricultural progress. Arthur Young is therefore right when he says that the French cultivate the good land to perfection but seldom bother with mediocre areas and never with the poor land. In comparing France with England one must conclude that even though France on the average has better soil, it cannot measure up to England agriculturally. Whereas almost one-half of the land under cultivation in England is used for supporting cattle, hardly one-tenth is set aside for this purpose in France. It is obvious that such a large number of cattle improves the fertility of the soil. And whereas meat comprises one-half of all the food consumed in England, in France it is only one-fourth According to the ministerial report of 1812 the rural population in France hardly consumed 19 pounds of meat annually per person; in England, however, it is not less than 220 pounds.

Agriculture flourishes much more in England than in France, but France has far fewer proletarians. In France, however, the proletarians are much more active and dangerous than in England. In England there is a barrier which strictly separates the propertied and the unpropertied classes; as long as the authority of law remains intact, the latter cannot lay claim to the ownership of land, nor do they have any hope of acquiring it. Under such circumstances most people become resigned and seldom strive for the unattainable. In France the road to acquiring property is completely free and open; the ownership of property is the prize rewarded for effort, boldness, and luck, a prize which everyone feels impelled to seek. Consequently, a perpetual instability is visible in the entire social structure. In England poverty and wealth coexist rather peacefully, albeit in an atmosphere of tension; in France they are openly opposed to one another.

Germany stands between England and France. Germany has neither the English system of absolute stability in the ownership of land and its indivisibility nor the instability and infinite partition of the land found in France. In Germany the larger estates are usually indivisible, as established in part by law and in part by custom. In the case of small holdings the principle of land tenure varies according to region; in some areas the land can be divided as much as in France; in other areas property can be partitioned but only

88

among the members of a commune. In other regions some of the land can be divided, while peasant farmsteads run solely by the owner's family are indivisible. And again, in other regions all the land is indivisible, although this practice is rare. A number of factors brought about this state of affairs which on the whole can be called favorable: age-old customs, the various principles of government in the different provinces, the nature of the soil, the different methods of cultivation, and natural interests that developed over the years. Agriculture is not on such a uniformly high level as in England, but it is much more advanced than in France. Only in the cities are there proletarians; in the countryside their numbers are few.

The third principle is represented by Russia. France stands for the principle of the divisibility of the land. Russia goes much farther in that the land there is continually divided. France proclaims the principle of free competition and regards all property as a commodity that everyone can acquire for money. Russia grants to each of her children the right to share equally in the use of the commune's land. In France the land is the exclusive property of the individual; in Russia it is owned by the people and its microcosm, the commune; the individual simply has the right to use the land temporarily like everyone else. One must admit that such an advanced level of agriculture as found in England or even in Germany cannot be attained with this system. In our opinion, however, Russia can reach the same level as France, if various requirements in the social sphere are fulfilled and if certain obstacles are removed, as mentioned above.

In considering Russia's social conditions as we have sketched them here, we can only be struck by their remarkable similarity to the utopia which modern political sects, namely, the Saint-Simonians and the communists, have imagined to represent the perfect society. Men of learning with a strictly scholarly point of view despise the philosophical notions on which these doctrines are based as vulgar and superficial. Practical politicians call them immature reveries which would necessarily miscarry if put into practice. According to them these ideas are just perfect for seducing young or ignorant minds and for stirring up discontent among the masses; and for these reasons they are dangerous. Politicians conclude that one can do nothing other than suppress such ideas by force.

We are not of this opinion. The emergence of these notions is absolutely inherent to the natural evolution of the human spirit, the stage of our culture, and our present social institutions. They are the symptoms of an acute malady afflicting our society, but are by no means the disease itself. The corpus of human society is aware of the disease and would like to help itself; it gropes about in search of remedies, and even poison seems to be a heroic and potent medicine. To be sure, ideas usually expressed by these theorists, these wandering political healers, are very vague, vulgar, and superficial and in no way new or striking; they have been expressed since ancient times. The means which they advocate for curing the body politic are violent and yet are inappropriate and contrary to sound reason. Common sense tells us that if one were to follow their advice the result would be anything but a new and healthy society. One can only view the increasingly rapid dissemination of these theories and their overwhelming influence on the masses with anxious astonishment. . . .

At this juncture we want to characterize briefly that doctrine which became the basis of the new ideology and whose philosophical principles pervade all modern doctrines, albeit with many different consequences. We are speaking of Saint-Simon's teaching. . . . According to the Saint-Simonians, the earth should not be divided as private property among individuals enjoying equal rights, as the Jacobins believe; rather, the earth is the communal property of the whole race, and every man has the right during his lifetime to enjoy an unequal share. . . . For the Saint-Simonians God does not exist. They recognize only the *Weltgeist*, which pervades and is one with nature, and the concentrate of the *Weltgeist*, mankind. . . . From the beginning, the Saint-Simonians continue, some people rebelled against this spirit of man. In despotically arrogating the wealth of corporate mankind, they encroached upon the right and claims of every individual which issue from his abilities. They created private property by dividing the wealth of the corporation, and to secure it for all eternity they devised and introduced the right of inheritance. This was the act of tyrants and men of violence. . . . Only after the power of the tyrants had been broken by the march of culture and only when the social institutions created by them had been utterly shattered by the French Revolution could the truth come to light. According to his followers it was left to Saint-Simon to preach unadorned the logical conclusions derived from the obscure teachings of Jesus and other sages of antiquity. He was borne along by the enlightenment of the century which will carry him to victory, albeit not immediately. Since the French Revolution men have gradually begun to undermine and destroy the basis of all private property, namely, the ownership of land. . . . The old rule by the propertied and aristocratic classes has already disappeared; the Saint-Simonian spirit of human reason already reigns in many modern states.

Monarchs who were removed from their princely thrones and placed on the pyramid are now nothing more than the apex, the pyramid's *centrum unitatis*.

The tempting and therefore dangerous aspect of this doctrine is rooted primarily in the many truths it contains, truths derived from a false premise. As we have said, no demon is more dangerous than one that can assume the radiant form of an angel. The Saint-Simonian doctrine does not merely appeal to the passions and inclinations but also to the mind itself; nor do the higher emotions, the sense of justice and love, go away empty handed. This teaching does indeed repeat the age-old proverb of the snake: *Eritis sicuti Dei scientes bonum et malum*. Who can resist reasoning that appeals so strongly both to the mind and the emotions? Indeed, only the individual who has recognized the principle of this demonic teaching in its depth: the spirit of arrogance, the abandonment of God, the idolatry. At bottom the Saint-Simonian believes that as the temporary representative of the universal spirit he is the god who directs world history.

Philosophically speaking the Saint-Simonians are absolutely right in maintaining that private ownership of earthly goods is unacceptable to human reason. No man can call the land he possesses his property, nor can a nation call the territory it inhabits its own. At most both can claim that no other person or people has a better right to it than they. Not once has the entire globe become the property of men or nations. Besides the many regions which man has never set foot upon, vast tracts of land are traversed by nomadic peoples who frown upon the ownership of land. The terrain which is either uninhabited or roamed by nomads may easily amount to more than a quarter of the earth's land surface.

The Saint-Simonians' negation of property is correct; however, their assertion that the goods of the earth and land in particular are the collective property of mankind is false. They offer absolutely no proof of this and answer only with a counter-question: if the earth does not belong to mankind, to whom does it belong? The answer is easy if one views the question from a Christian standpoint: the earth is God's property; God created the earth, He maintains it in its created form and has never ceased to govern and guide it. . . . Since man is God's viceroy on earth, mankind does not possess the earth on the basis of its own right but as a fief granted by the Divine. . . .

It is from a Christian perspective that we have presented this short description of Saint-Simonian teaching, the mother of all the later doctrines of Fourierism, Owenism, and so forth that are included under the general name of communism or socialism. We should like also to add several observations on Russian popular institutions in that they obviously bear an outward similarity to the utopias which those theories seek to create in western Europe.

It will never be possible to realize these dreams on the foundations which those doctrines provide, because they are atheistic, unchristian, and false. It would be a building erected on quicksand. Immediate collapse and boundless anarchy would be the certain consequence of such an attempt.

Disregarding the principles upon which those sectarians would like to institute [their utopias], we must deny the assertion that such an order of things is unchristian, absurd, and thus impossible, as has generally been maintained. We must refer to conditions existing in Russia in order to prove our contention that a [utopian] socio-political order and a Christian monarchy can actually coexist. Saint-Simon's doctrine wants to destroy and abandon the private ownership of property and the right to inheritance, at least the right to inherit land, and substitute for it the right to use the land for one's lifetime. In Russia this system actually exists. Among the majority of the people the individual does not own any private property and does not even occupy a certain piece of land permanently; instead he enjoys the right to use land temporarily; consequently the land cannot be inherited. But the social foundations upon which this arrangement rests are not those which the Saint-Simonians want to lay for their modern state. They are truly national and are also in harmony with the principles of Christian monarchy.

Saint-Simon argues as follows: the land belongs to Humanity, the god of the earth. Since every human being is a temporary emana-tion of this god, he has a right to a certain share of the goods of the earth as long as he lives. This right, however, is purely personal and cannot be bequeathed to his children. Like all preceding and succeeding generations they are nothing more than an emanation of the terrestrial deity and have a personal, rather than an inherited, claim to a share of the earth's fruits.

The Russian people say the earth belongs to God and that Adam and his descendants, or mankind, hold the earth in fee. . . . As their numbers increased, men occupied more of the globe and shared it among themselves according to God's ordering of history. The land which is now called Russia fell to the ancestor of the Russian people and . . . through the dispensation of Providence the land has become their property. As in every organic family the father, the tribal chief, or the tsar is entitled to dispose of the land. The individual has the right to share in the use of the land only as long as he lives in unity with the nation and the tsar. The land is thus the collective property of the national family. . . . Russian family law developed analogously to national law. The familial patrimony belongs equally but undivided to all the members of the family, and the father (alone) is entitled to distribute the rights of usufruct. If a member of the family insists on partition, his share is turned over to him. However, this means that he no longer belongs to the family collective and forfeits all his rights to the communal property as well as the right to any inheritance from the family members who have remained in the community. He has been indemnified in full and ostracized, and henceforth he constitutes a new family. Families thus remained together as a family unit under their leader for many generations, thereby becoming family communes. And it is on these principles that communal law is based. . . .

From this we can see that Russia, displaying a healthy social organism, has no reason to fear the revolutionary forces now threatening Europe — pauperism, the proletariat, and the doctrines of communism and socialism.

The situation is different in the rest of Europe. Pauperism and the proletariat are the festering sores produced by the organism of the modern state. Can they be healed? The communist healers advocate the complete destruction of the existing organism, since one can best build anew on a *tabula rasa*. . . . One thing is certain; if these people acquire the power to act, there will not be a political but a social revolution, a war against all property and total anarchy. Will new national states be created from this, and, if so, on what moral and social foundations will they rest? Who can lift the veil of the future?

Which role will Russia assume? A Russian proverb says, "I am sitting on the bank and waiting for the wind."

After digressing at length to characterize Russia's social institutions and to compare them with European conditions, we shall continue with comments on our travels.

We received some information on agriculture in these regions of the province of Iaroslavl. The farmers employ only the simple three-field system. From the end of June to the beginning of August manure is spread on those fields to be sown with winter wheat. The manure frequently lies on the field for four to six weeks without being plowed under. After the land has been turned up with the heavy plow and harrowed the winter wheat is sown; the land is then turned a second time with a light forked plow (*socha*) and harrowed. In the fall the peasants do not plow over the fields which are to be sown the following spring, although this is done on some estates where agriculture is more advanced. The planting of the spring wheat is completed in the middle of May.

Perfect order, one could almost say military discipline, characterizes the work in the fields. On the same day and at the same hour everyone sets out to plow and harrow and they all return at the same time. The *starosty* or elders issue no set rules and no regulations; the undertaking functions by itself without interference. The influence of Russian social and imitative instincts and the authority of the Russian commune are everywhere evident.

In the village of Velikoe Selo, where the wealthiest inhabitants are linen manufacturers and only the poorer people engage in farming, agriculture is backward. The land is plowed only once immediately after it is fertilized or sometimes before it is planted in order to keep the stubble for pasturage as long as possible and also because of the short summer and weak horses.

People complain here about the lack of meadows, particularly good ones; they are either too dry or marshy and acidic. It has never occurred to anyone to irrigate the meadows even though the terrain would probably present no difficulties. If the owners of the estates were to form associations joined by the crown and its villages for the purpose of connecting the rivers and streams in an irrigation system, they would have one of the few improvements that would definitely pay even here. The necessary cash outlay would be small and the benefits great and lasting, for the quality of the livestock would improve at once and agriculture would advance. At the present time hay is relatively high priced here and is more expensive than other farm products. This year a *pud* (37 pounds) of hay cost 40 kopeks banco (3 silver *groschen* and 7 *pfennig*). In scarce years one pud costs up to 120 kopeks banco (10 silver *groschen* and 9 *pfennig*)

Cattle raising is, of course, very poor, the animals small and inferior; sheep raising is also insignificant. The peasants' horses are small. However, estate owners and wealthy farmers do have a larger breed of good, strong horses, which sell for 180 to 200 rubles banco. On Mr. Karnovich's estate we saw two magnificent stallions which he had bred. Peasants frequently buy the horses they need in the spring and sell them again after the harvest for lack of winter fodder. At this time they are purchased by coachmen, whose services are engaged primarily in winter. The various branches of industry are thus interrelated in every respect and compensate for each other's deficiencies.

In these regions a substantial amount of flax and hemp is raised. In the past several years alone, the quantity of flax grown in the province of Vologda has increased to such an extent that it has caused the price of flax here to drop as much as one-third.

Five years ago the farmers still raised no potatoes, considering it a sin to grow this tuber. Today they are beginning to get accustomed to cultivating them and on the seigneurial estates potatoes are already being used for fodder.

Nowhere can one speak of a systematic management of the forests. Those owned by seigneurs who live on their estates are at least somewhat protected. Forests belonging to villages placed on *obrok* are turned over with the land to the peasants and can be used without restrictions. These woodlands are being devastated in a frightful manner, and shortages have already appeared. The same conditions prevail among the state peasants, and the Ministry of State Domains is now trying to protect the forests to some extent.

Early in the morning of 10 May our excellent host accompanied us to the home of the village priest, who had invited us to coffee. Later I often had occasion to visit village priests; as a rule their apartments were poorly furnished and filthy, and often dirtier than the peasants' living quarters. The wives and children of the priests made an especially unpleasant impression because of their slovenliness and vulgar manners. At this priest's house, though, everything was completely different. The house was, of course, a typically Russian dwelling constructed of logs placed one on top of the other. The apartment was attractive and comfortable and nearly Dutch in its cleanliness; the living room had a well-scrubbed floor, good windows, and contained old-fashioned but well-kept European furniture. The walls had been neatly planed and looked almost as if they were paneled; they had not been papered or whitewashed. All of this lent the entire apartment a certain warmth and comfort. Hanging on the wall were two portraits of his mother and his father, who had also been a priest in this same village. One showed them at the young age of twenty-five and the other as an elderly couple past sixty. In one corner, as is proper, there was an icon of the Virgin, illuminated by a lamp. On the one wall there was a small library which contained, in addition to homiletic volumes and church histories, several French works and a Russian translation of Klopstock's *Messias*. The man had a fine intelligent face with friendly benevolent features. His parted wavy hair and the violet silk vestment which hung down to his feet gave him a dignified appearance, and he resembled a Benedictine scholar. He had had an unusual education; he understood French very well, for example, but in a most peculiar way. He had learned French simply from a grammar and a dictionary as a dead language. He read the books only with his eyes and translated correctly and with facility. However, if one read a passage aloud from the very same book and spoke to him in French he did not understand a word. Likewise, we hardly understood a word when he uttered a sentence in French. His name was Nikolai Ivanovich Rosov, and he had been the village priest for many years and a widower for twenty years. The entire community loved and revered him like a father. There was something touching about this modest, completely unpretentious but rewarding way of life and the inner pleasure it afforded the priest. A sweet peace hovered over the humble house and the friendly servant of God who dwelt there.

Upon returning we noticed a number of children going toward our host's house. We were told that our host had set up a school in his home for the children of his servants and peasants. The modest man had not mentioned this earlier, and we first learned about it at the moment of our departure. There may have been some twenty children there, boys and girls between seven and thirteen years of age. The priest and the blind son of a peasant whom he had instructed taught reading, writing, and arithmetic. My companion, Mr. S., improvised a little exam that proved the children were able to read even his somewhat difficult handwriting. We noticed several maps hanging on the wall. Mr. Karnovich said that he had put them up in order to see if it would occur to some of the children to ask what they signified. Several children did inquire, and he provided them with an explanation. From this experiment he said he could see who had a particular thirst for knowledge and could arrange for the child's further education. How ingenious and sensible an idea this is!

Upon our departure our host accompanied us to another of his estates named Talitsa. He had set up a large croft here for bleaching linen, an enterprise that was already beginning to become important. Last year approximately 70,000 arshins of linen had been bleached. On our visit we found a set of table linens that had been brought from Moscow and fine linens from Velikoe Selo. Among others there was a very fine unbleached piece for 4 rubles banco per arshin which almost equaled good Dutch linen in evenness, strength, fineness, and sheen. On the whole, however, the linen delivered by the individual peasants is said to be stronger than that from Velikoe Selo, where purchased yarn is used in a more factory-like system of production. Two German compatriots from Bielefeld in Westphalia were employed as supervisors at this bleaching croft, and we received much information from them. Here the season for bleaching is about two months shorter than in Bielefeld; the sun and water are excellent. However, the flax does not bleach as well as German flax, since the latter is better retted. The manufacture of linen is expensive here, primarily because of the high wages. The highest wage is earned by the soapers who have to perform very strenuous work. A good worker soaps up to 70 arshins daily and receives 2½ kopeks banco for each arshin. He can thus earn a daily wage of 16 to 17 silver *groschen*. . . . Here we bade farewell to a man, to whom we were indebted for such instructive information. Toward noon we arrived back in Iaroslavl.

We decided to visit the famous commercial city of Rybinsk on the Volga the following day.[12] The head of the local office of the Ministry of State Domains accompanied us there.

We departed early in the morning of 19 May and arrived in the village or city of Romanov-Borisoglebsk around ten o'clock. The community is famous for its forgings. Almost all of the inhabitants are smiths, and they even manufacture the boilers. The village situated on the opposite bank of the Volga, Borisoglebsk, is a wealthy community of tanners. We visited a factory there which produces horsehair cloth. The workers in this factory are serfs, who pay an *obrok* of 60 rubles banco. Depending on their usefulness they earn 70 kopeks to 1½ rubles banco . . . (6 silver *groschen* and 3 *pfennig* to 13 silver *groschen* and 6 *pfennig*). . . .

In the villages where we stopped we were very often plagued by beggars. In private villages this seldom happens, or begging is practiced on the sly, since it is forbidden. Russian nobles consider it disgraceful for their serfs to beg. In the state villages, however, begging is a free profession like all other trades in Russia. There are wealthy villages where all the inhabitants live from alms. Each has his beggar's costume, and in the spring one or several members of the family set out to beg. They formally divide the land into

12. Rybinsk is situated approximately 75 kilometers northwest of Iaroslavl and retains the same name today. Romanov-Borisoglebsk is some 30 kilometers downstream from Rybinsk toward Iaroslavl.

districts and gather at certain places in order to settle these plans. They then return in autumn to consume their profits with their families during the winter.

Rybinsk is located eighty-one versts from Iaroslavl and is the center of Russian domestic trade. All the products and wares which are shipped along the Volga and its tributaries to Petersburg have to be loaded here onto smaller boats in order to pass through the various canals. These products and goods arrive here on seventeen to eighteen hundred large ships and are transferred to six thousand barks and boats and in this manner are sent on to Petersburg. The value of these wares is estimated at 40 to 50 million rubles annually.

Before the construction of the three canal systems connecting Petersburg with the Volga, Rybinsk was an unimportant village (*sloboda*) whose inhabitants payed *obrok* in the form of either fish or cash. The village was then elevated to city status, and the *obrok* dropped. The inhabitants now pay nothing other than the usual head tax to the crown and an additional 50,000 to 60,000 silver rubles in municipal duties. At the present time more than six hundred merchants belong to the three guilds. The retail trade is run by the *meshchane* (the petite bourgeoisie) and the *ranznochintsy* (an intermediate class between the bourgeoisie and the peasantry).[13] As a rule the latter carry on their business in the name of guild merchants. In order to be considered a member of a merchant guild, one simply has to declare one's willingness to pay the public taxes required of that particular guild. A merchant of the first guild pays 2,500 silver rubles annually, a merchant of the second guild 550 rubles, and of the third 200 rubles. The rights of the guilds are different. Only the merchants of the first guild have the right to engage in foreign trade and to sign contracts of an unlimited value. Those of the second guild can only sign contracts worth up to 50,000 rubles, and so on.

The next morning we made the acquaintance of a multimillionaire merchant named Tumanev, a genuine bearded Russian with parted hair and a long blue caftan. His home, however, was furnished in European luxury, and his married son appeared in elegant modern clothes and cleanly shaven, with a toupee and standup collar. Of

13. The *meshchane*, from *mesto* (place, city), were similar to the west European petite bourgeoisie except that they formed a jurdically constituted legal class or estate (*soslovie*) which in each town or city had its own organization (*meshchanskoe obshchestvo*) with an elected head (*starosta*). Sergei G. Pushkarev, *Dictionary of Russian Historical Terms from the 11th Century to 1917* (New Haven, 1970), pp. 59–60.

course, he was not half so handsome as his father. The latter presented me with a copy of a small book he had written on Rybinsk and its commerce. Although it was full of unreliable statistics, it otherwise contained useful information. We went with him to the newly built Exchange but found it very empty. Our old gentleman told us that the genuine Russian merchants could not get accustomed to this new arrangement; the confusion caused by so many people running about and shouting was fatal to the gentle and quiet Russian, who likes to observe and whisper. They were used to gathering at an inn, where they drank their tea, discussed their business affairs, and struck a bargain "from ear to ear, and not publicly." This is the reason why most transactions, including the most important ones, are still made outside the Exchange. We then went to a famous inn near the Exchange and found the great merchants on the Exchange sitting along the walls as motionless as pagodas. Serious and quiet men, they sipped their tea, perspired, and now and again whispered to one another. Even though more than one hundred men were present, there was certainly not as much noise as in a pub in a small German city when ten of the regular guests get together. A music box, which is unavoidable in Russian inns, played *tanti palpiti*, and one might have thought that the good, bearded Russians spoke so softly only so as not to spoil the splendid pleasure afforded by the music. On the days of active trading, fifty pounds of tea are said to be consumed daily in this particular inn.

From here we went to look at various kinds of boats used for navigating the Volga. Since it was early in the year, there were not many vessels on the river, which at this point is wider than the Elbe near Magdeburg. And yet a forest of masts stood before us. In the summer the river is often so crowded that one can go from one ship to the next by way of planks and reach the opposite bank. The White Sea type of boats, which are also called *karbasy*, are distinguished by their extreme neatness and their elegant construction. On other ships we had to admire the unusual carved work with its very attractive arabesques adorning the outer walls. In their leisure time the sailors chipped away with an ax and retouched their work a bit with an ordinary pocket knife or a small chisel. They are not familiar with other tools and never use them. The love for ornamentation, predominant among Great Russians, indicates a great capacity for refinement. Everywhere on the ships we found Bibles, histories of the saints, and prayer books written in Old Slavonic. A sailor gave me one containing prayers. We were told that the sailors were Raskolniki (Old Believers) who could read Old Slavonic but not Russian print. We heard a song coming from a passing ship; the sailors' voices were pure and gentle; the melody in minor key was mournful and melancholy. Situated on the opposite bank of the Volga was a large number of buildings, magazines and sheds for storing produce and wares. All were simply constructed of spars, beams, and posts. The roofs and walls were merely covered with bast mats. A number of carpenters were busily working. In our presence a young fellow used an ax to hollow out a hexagon measuring a half a foot in width and depth. He had not sketched it before but simply measured with his eye. When he finished, we measured the hole; all the sides were equal, and the angles correct. It had turned out to be a symmetrical figure which none of us would have been able to draw freehand without a ruler and compass. Another lad blundered a couple of times. When we laughed at him he replied ironically: "Crown whetstone is always bad." . . .

Rybinsk actually has only about six thousand permanent residents, but in summer the number of transients on business climbs as high as one hundred and thirty thousand; there are never more than thirty-five hundred women here. What strange circumstances and how difficult it is for us western Europeans to understand such a place. Most of the people in this multitude are hired men brought here by the shipping and commercial trade. Among them is a very interesting group, the *burlaki* (barge haulers). They have formally organized themselves into communes and artels; they have their elected leaders, *starosty*, masters, and are a very hard working breed of men. Generally they come from areas along the Volga, but also from as far away as the province of Riazan. For the trip from Samara to Rybinsk, a distance of one thousand versts if measured in a straight line but certainly more than fifteen hundred versts with the meander of the river, the *burlak* receives 70 rubles banco. For the nearly seven-hundred-verst run from Nizhnii Novgorod he earns 50 rubles banco. The time required for the trip is contingent on many factors and varies from fourteen days to six weeks between Nizhni and Rybinsk. If the *burlak* is lucky he can make the trip from Samara to Rybinsk three times during one summer and can save about 60 to 70 rubles. However, if he has to struggle with untoward incidents throughout the trips and can make the run only twice, he usually consumes his entire earnings. The owner of the barge is obligated to provide the *burlaki* with several boats on which they can return to Nizhni Novgorod in three days.

With such vast throngs of people in this rather small village one

*100*

can well imagine that food products immediately become more expensive. As we were told, merchants, ship owners, and grain dealers all take advantage of the situation and fleece the masses of workers and poorer people by giving them usurious loans. Some people here have already felt and expressed the need both for stores where the workers can obtain grain or flour at fixed prices and strict regulation of the wage for the worker and the horse based on the market price of flour and oats. The Russian police are good at maintaining order and at preventing and solving crimes; however, they have hitherto done little to protect the public except in larger cities.

We walked around until late in the evening; there are some attractive promenades, and the quay on the river is luxuriously constructed of magnificent granite and has a cast iron railing. In northern Russia granite and iron grow wild, so to speak.

We met many river pilots and heard that they were natives of the neighboring village of Koprino on the Volga. There, as everywhere in Russia, the entire community was specialized, this one being comprised of nothing but pilots.

Around nine in the evening we left Rybinsk and arrived back in Iaroslavl the next morning. On the way I had noticed that in this area agriculture was more advanced than anywhere else [in the province]. Some of the fields were surrounded with hedges. The proximity to the great river explains this. The villages on this route are generally small; the houses and farmsteads are more exposed and are not as close together as along city streets.

We spent 21 May and the larger part of the next day in Iaroslavl in the company of the governor and head of the local Bureau of State Domains. We also visited some local factories, among them a very old one organized according to principles introduced by Peter I and then a very modern one. The first was the Iakovlev linen factory situated outside the city. Before arriving there, one has to pass a village belonging to the factory. There follows a large open space at the end of which a gate leads to the factory's courtyard. With its long, regular stone buildings, small windows, and an imposing church built after European models, the factory resembles a German cloister or a Benedictine abbey. However, one visit to the factory did not afford us much joy, for it gave the impression of total decline. The workrooms were dirty and dark, the machines old and rundown; the supervisors and workers, both male and female, looked slovenly, lazy, and stunted. This linen factory was established under Peter I in 1720 by the merchant Satrapesnov. In accordance with the economic principles of the time the government assigned twelve hundred crown peasants to the factory on condition that it specialize in the preparation and manufacture of linen and provide nourishment and work for the peasants. The factory prospered and shot into vigor, especially after it was sold in 1768 to a Mr. Iakovlev. Additional peasants were purchased. Many volunteers even enrolled as factory workers during one of the revisions. The factory flourished, dominated by the manufacture of linen. Often the annual sales amounted to more than 2 million silver rubles with a profit of 100 percent. The crown alone usually ordered more than 200,000 silver rubles worth of linen annually. The favorable location near an important city on the Volga and the large number of workers (about three thousand souls belonged to the factory) explain this extraordinary prosperity. A village was built next to the factory for its workers. The peasants were given houses and gardens, but no land. Those who came later were assigned a lot for their house and a loan to build it, which they had to repay with 25 percent of their annual wage. The villagers received provisions from the factory: every month they were given 1½ puds of flour for each adult, male and female, 1 pud of flour for each child and 30 silver kopeks in cash for each infant. They had to work in the factory whenever they were called and there a man earned 100 to 120 rubles, a woman 50 rubles, and children up to 20 rubles. The wage was determined according to the amount of work delivered.

The factory has now gradually gone to ruin. The basic causes for this decline are the failure to introduce modern advances in management and improved machinery and finally the growing competition of thriving cotton factories, which are hurting the linen industry in Russia. Also, the constant increase in wages elsewhere has led the employees to look for work in other industries where higher wages are paid. Through inheritance the factory has come into the hands of thirty-three owners and the law does not permit the factory to be divided. Naturally, such a mammoth administration stifles all initiative. The crown stopped its orders. Even though in 1840 sales still amounted to 600,000 rubles, there had already been a deficit for ten years. Recently there has been an attempt at reorganization. The crown took back those peasants who were becoming a burden to the factory and offered the factory 35,000 silver rubles as compensation. The village has been made a suburb of Iaroslavl whose residents are said to complain a good deal about this gift as being a great burden (the people are believed to be completely uncivilized!). The factory still has the peasants it purchased but has imposed an *obrok* of 8 silver rubles for each *tiaglo* although they have also to work in the factory for the usual wage whenever it is required. Those not called to work can look for employment elsewhere. The entire system of production is now better organized than in other modern Russian factories. Since the workers no longer receive provisions and wood, their earnings have had to be increased by 20 to 30 percent. Instead of the thirteen to fifteen hundred looms formerly in the factory buildings, there are now only two hundred. There are also about three hundred looms in the workers' homes. The work is paid for at a set rate per piece. A woman who weaves linen for shirts receives 6 kopeks per arshin. Since she can easily weave ten to twelve arshins a day, she earns 60 to 80 kopeks banco (6 to 8 silver *groschen*). A man who weaves table cloths is paid 1 ruble 10 kopeks per arshin and can earn 2 rubles a day (18 silver *groschen*). We asked a man who wove napkins how much he earned. He replied that he received 34 kopeks per arshin and that he could weave four to five arshins a day. Consequently he made a daily wage of 136 to 170 kopeks (14 to 17 silver *groschen*). Let us compare these wages with those of the Silesian weavers, taking into consideration the price of the basic necessities of life, for example grain. Here [in Iaroslavl] one pays about 12 to 15 silver *groschen* for a bushel of grain and in Silesia 1 thaler, 20 silver *groschen*. Comparatively speaking, I do not believe there is any country where the average wage is as high as in Russia. . . .

The factory owns outlets in Iaroslavl, Nizhnii Novgorod, and Moscow. In addition to its own church the factory also has a school for the workers' children, a hospital for sick and infirm employees, and a pharmacy.

We then visited a very modern factory located right in Iaroslavl and owned by a Russian tradesman named Olovianishnik. We entered a large courtyard with many buildings. Under a shed there hung a great number of church bells and other kinds of bells; among them was a huge, pretty-sounding one weighing 202 puds (7,676 pounds). They had been produced in the foundry owned by our tradesman. They sell for 42 rubles banco per pud, no matter whether they are large or small. Also in this courtyard were factories which produced white lead, calico, and silk. We took a somewhat closer look at the silk mill. We saw pretty Italian and Armenian silks priced at 2½ to 10 rubles banco per arshin (23 silver *groschen* to 3 thalers). Our attention was caught by a very attractive striped national silk with bold colors worn primarily by Cossack women, who annually purchase thirty thousand arshins of it at 2 rubles and 40 kopeks banco per arshin. It was woven on some twenty looms.

The pay was comparable to that in the other factories. The workers earned a daily wage of 11 to 20 silver *groschen*. A man weaves approximately six to seven arshins of these lighter cloths daily and is paid 20 kopeks banco per arshin. He can weave one and a half to two and an eighth arshins of fine brocaded cloth and earn 1 ruble banco per arshin. . . .

# 4
# *Nizhnii Novgorod*

The road from Iurevets[1] to Nizhnii Novgorod runs along the right bank of the Volga and is lined on both sides with double rows of birch trees.

Around eight o'clock we reached Diakonskii, a small village with a mere nine farmsteads and a village church which belongs to the imperial family.[2] A number of neighboring villages and this hamlet constitute an appanage *volost*, whose *golova* lives here. He accompanied us everywhere and kindly showed us all of the institutions. First, we visited the school, where one of the village priests was instructing. All the peasant lads read very well and the majority wrote in an excellent hand. On the Russian abacus they readily worked out the short problems I gave them. They also receive religious instruction in connection with biblical history. For the three hours of instruction he gives a day, the priest receives an annual salary of 500 rubles from the treasury of the Ministry of State Domains. Then we went to the trade school endowed by this ministry. Here twelve to eighteen youths selected from the better peasant families of the appanage district are instructed in several trades from which they can choose: cabinet maker, smith, tanner, hatter, felt-sock maker, etc. They receive free room and board for three years and for the next couple of years an additional wage of 52½ rubles banco. We saw excellently wrought furniture, articles of iron, and a

1. Iurevets, also called Iurevets Povolzhskii, 120 kilometers north of Nizhnii Novgorod on the Volga.
2. The village of Diakonskii does not appear on contemporary maps of the region.

storehouse for hats, the proceeds from which go to the school treasury. Nevertheless, the school needs, in addition, considerable subsidies.

After this, we visited the churches. One was an old Russian-style wooden church built in 1717, where the summer services are held, and the other a massive church in the modern style, which is heated in winter. The latter was built in 1797 by the entire parish, to which sixty-five surrounding villages belong. The church employs three priests, two deacons, three subdeacons, and three sacristans. The church has also been provided with thirty-eight desiatins of land. The priests hire workers to cultivate their fields and pay each one 30 rubles for each year's work. For a single day's work in the summer they pay a wage of 80 kopeks banco.

This small village has only nine farmsteads and an equal number of families. The population numbers twenty-four male souls or about fifty members.[3] Together they own fifty-nine desiatins of plowland, eleven desiatins of hay fields, and two desiatins of communal pasture land. The three-field system is employed. Since they do not have any forests, they have to buy all their wood. . . . They grow rye, spring wheat, barley, oats, flax, potatoes, cabbage, and peas. . . . Near each house there is a small garden which remains with the house and is not included in the distribution of communal property. With every census the land is reapportioned, although, if there are many newcomers or people leaving the village, the property may also be redistributed earlier. The members of the commune reach an agreement on their own. If there should be a disagreement, which no one, however, can ever remember happening, the *golova* would intervene and decide the matter.

They have a communal granary, to which the head of every family must contribute a small specified amount. In addition, one-sixteenth of the arable land is set aside as communal property; under the supervision of the *starosta* the members of the commune cultivate this land without pay. The seed, however, is supplied from the granary. For fertilizing the land, each household must provide seven cartloads of dung, each weighing fifteen puds [555 pounds]. Their livestock consists of eight horses, seventeen head of cattle, and thirty-six sheep. Of the feathered animals I saw only chickens.

Several inhabitants work as *burlaki* or haulers on the Volga and are given passes for this purpose, which cost 15 silver kopeks a month.

In all of the villages through which we passed we found the

3. See Haxthausen's note on "souls," p. 70 above.

prettiest ornamentation on the houses, carvings and fretwork alike. In particular there were very handsome gable decorations, an example of which I sketched in Lukurki, the second station after Iurevets. Although the ornamentation is unusually pretty, on the whole the houses themselves are not nearly as large and spacious as those in the northern part of the province of Vologda. . . . At dusk we arrived at the bank of the Oka across from Nizhnii Novgorod and were ferried across the river. We found lodging in a rather good hotel in the upper part of the city.

The morning of 7 June was spent paying visits. I made the acquaintance of the municipal chief of police, Count Stenbock, who, during my entire stay in this remarkable city, took the greatest pleasure in showing me all the sights.[4] We then called upon the governor, a Mr. Buturlin,[5] with whom we also ate lunch. For many years he had been an adjutant to Emperor Alexander and had participated in the German and French campaigns. He was well spoken, well informed, polished, and of mild and noble temperament. He is descended from a family whose members were often closely involved in Russian history, and one could detect a slight air of the old boyar class about him.

'In the oldest, larger Russian cities, the former residences of the rulers, there is always a kremlin, a fortified castle on a predominant hilltop, as in Novgorod, Vladimir, and Kazan. Nizhnii Novgorod also has such a citadel surrounded by high walls and set upon a hill, at the foot of which the Oka flows into the Volga. Located here is a newly built imperial palace from whose windows one has a magnificent view of the city, the two merging rivers, and several villages along them. Beyond this beautiful foreground, a vast, flat, wooded plain stretches to the horizon. Such is the nature of all views in Russia: close up — pretty, often picturesque and even idyllic; the background — always an unbounded flat wilderness. Civilization is an oasis here!

After lunch I drove with Count Stenbock to the *guliane*, a large, treeless, shrubless meadow located southeast of the city on the 200-foot-high bank of the Oka. Once a week, when the weather is good, the common people gather here in the afternoon and gaily romp

4. Count Iulii Ivanovich Stenbock (b. 1812) was a Russified Estonian nobleman of Danish extraction. See *Russkii biograficheskii slovar* 19:380–81.

5. A. P. Buturlin (1802–63) was one of the many governors of the era who rose through the military.

around until evening. It was a picturesque sight and just perfect for studying the national dress, character, and customs.

There were rows of tents and arbored huts with refreshments. Over small pit fires the famous Russian patties, *pirogi*, were being baked. For the most part, strong young boys carried around these and other edibles on platters which they balanced on their heads. Everywhere people were standing or lying in compact groups which were divided according to sex. . . . Each group, so to speak, temporarily formed a closed community. Wholly in accordance with the basic principle of the Russian national character, each group was an organic association with its elected leader, its *starosta* or host. Only flirtatious females and people of the middle and upper classes, who were watching more than participating, strolled about. The ordinary Russian never takes a walk. In many of the male groups there was singing, whereas in the groups of women I heard no singing at all. The leader began a plaintive, monotonic melody alone; a chorus answered or repeated the refrain. In one spot a number of soldiers had formed a circle. The leader stood in the center with a tambourine. The songs were for several voices, very regular, often fuguelike and artistically interwoven, and were performed with the greatest precision. The comical songs are accompanied by a complete skit. The leader addresses the circle in song and various people reply; he makes faces, he jumps, he gesticulates wildly and with definite mimic talent. Only among the Italians have I seen anything similar. Yet the Italian clowns, although singly often inimitable in their own way, seldom put on a show in which everyone participates equally.

While strolling about and observing the groups, I also had occasion to study the national costumes. It is remarkable how little variety there is in Russian costumes. Among the Great Russians the men's dress is the same except for slight differences in the head covering; even the women's costume, although of course more varied, nevertheless has the same elements and the same character throughout Great Russia. In Germany each region, often only a couple of villages, has, or rather had its own dress, for with the advancement of modern civilization the various costumes are dying out. There are more than a dozen main differences based on the ancient tribes: the Frisians, the Westphalians of the plain and those of the mountains, the Lower Saxons, the Hessian-Thuringians, the Franconians, the Swabians, the Bavarians, the Alpine tribe, etc. In these provinces there are also many subdivisions, each of which, of course, has the general character of the particular tribe while displaying an endless variety in the style, color, and adornments. Consequently there are several hundred different costumes in Germany. In Great Russia, which is more than six times the size of Germany, there is only one native costume with perhaps no more than several dozen nuances. In Germany there is, moreover, such a great number of dialects that people who live far apart, for example the inhabitants of the area around Lake Constance and the East Frisians or the Dutch, cannot understand each other. In Russia there is only one language, the same for the educated and the common people, and basically only one dialect with very slight differences in single words, accents, and intonations. As a result Great Russia has the most homogeneous population in Europe. Thus, in Russia there is little individual growth of provincial life, little diversity, and little fresh poetic contrast but only monotony. However, the basis and potential for a great and vigorous political power are present.

What vast quantities of pearls and precious stones have been accumulated in Russia and are still being accumulated! All the women I met, even the poorest fishwives, had at least three or four strands of genuine pearls around their necks; wealthier women wore ten to twelve strands and often a pearl-studded cap in the shape of a diadem. At the weddings of the local merchants, the merchants' wives appear covered from head to toe with pearls and jewels. Jewelry valued at 100,000 rubles is considered little at such an occasion!

I heard that there was a theater in the city and that a national Russian piece was being given. Curious to learn about the state of the modern theater in the Russian interior, I drove there that night with Count Stenbock. The building, its furnishings, the boxes, the stalls, etc., were the usual ones, but respectable and good. A Russian opera, *Askoldova*, composed by Verstoskii was being performed.[6] As far as I could judge, the subject seemed a bit confused. It treats an attempted revolution against the tsar, which aims is to place a petty prince from Iaroslavl on the throne. The latter, however, declines to participate in the conspiracy because he is happily in love with the daughter of a poor fisherman. But his sweetheart is kidnapped by a boyar. The prince's favorite servant discovers the place where she is being held captive and draws up a plan to free her. He disguises himself as a storyteller and gathers the entire village before the boyar's castle. He sings the prettiest folk tunes

6. Aleksei Nikolaevich Verstovskii (1799–1862) the most successful Russian secular composer before Glinka, was best known for his *Askold's Tomb* (1835), a *Singspiel* showing strong influence by Weber and also Rossini.

and at the end sings the highly exciting story of a kidnapping, which completely captivates the audience. While he is singing and talking, the guard, who is supposed to be watching the house and the girl, draws near and listens. He becomes so involved in the story that in the meantime the prince can successfully free his beloved and escape with her. The boyar is furious and goes to a *babushka*, a sorceress, who by means of magic is supposed to determine the whereabouts of the girl. A scene of magical incantation follows. As usual, in the end everyone is happy.

The music was reminiscent of *Der Freischütz* and *La Sonnambula* in particular, although all the interpolated songs were composed from national melodies and were most charming. The actors did not perform badly; a couple, especially the storyteller, were superb. The prima donna was excellent; the tenor and bass very good. The impersonation and gestures of the storyteller (the *durak*, a universal comic figure) were genuinely national. His role was obviously the most interesting of the entire piece, for one does not see the same comic characters in other national theaters because each people has its own national comic figure.

In studying a provincial Russian theater and especially the local one, I was fascinated to learn that all the actors, singers, etc., were serfs. The prima donna, a celebrated and greatly applauded singer, was a serf and the daughter of a fisherman. The actors who played tsars, princes, heroes, etc., and who necessarily had to have a certain literary training, were serfs! What a vast conflict in feeling this must evoke. From their earnings in this the freest of all arts, as in the lowliest trade, they have to pay *obrok*, to their masters. Of course, in Petersburg and Moscow there are also cases where even the priestesses of the Venus vulgifaga have to pay their master *obrok* as proof of the ignominy of their gentlemen callers.

The theater in Nizhnii came into being many years ago when a wealthy bachelor landowner built a theater on his estate, trained a select group of his serfs to become musicians and actors, and had them perform plays and operas. Later he moved to Nizhni, built a theater there, and extended invitations to his friends and acquaintances. Extravagance gradually became his ruin; he began charging admission and ended as the concession director of his own company! . . . After his death another man took his place and an impoverished landowner now heads this undertaking.

Despite the fact that the actors performed well for a provincial theater and that a popular opera was being given, the theater was very empty. Except for the eight persons in our party, there were fewer than twenty persons in the boxes and fewer than ten in the last seats. It is said to be this empty every day, and one can see that the Russian people have not yet acquired a love for the theater. The owner would certainly not be able to carry on if he did not take in 24,000 to 30,000 silver rubles during the four weeks of the great fair. At this time the theater is packed daily. However, the performances are then given in a larger theater located on the fair grounds, since the municipal theater is much too small and also too far away. . . . During the rest of the year the director has his people perform so that they do not get out of practice. He hardly covers expenses for the lighting and the music.

The next day I paid several visits. Shortly before I called upon a German gentlemen, a petty theft had occurred in his house. I was told how one goes about discovering the culprit in such a case and how in this instance he was caught immediately. The woman of the house sent for a *babushka*, an old woman reputed to be skilled in the black arts. As soon as she arrived, all the servants were assembled in one room and told that if the thief were among them he should confess, for then he would be punished lightly; otherwise the *babushka* would certainly discover the culprit. Before she could start her trick, the guilty man had already confessed and begged for mercy. The procedure is as follows, however: the *babushka* makes as many little balls of bread as there are persons present, places a container of water in front of her, and has all of the people form a semicircle before her. She then takes one pellet, fixes her eyes on the first man, and says: "Ivan Ivanov, if you are guilty this pellet will fall to the bottom just as your soul will plunge into hell." The pellets of the innocent are supposed to float, the pellet of the culprit to sink to the bottom. No ordinary Russian, however, lets this trial proceed to the point where the pellet with his name is cast into the water. Consequently, it cannot be ascertained whether this magic actually works. Without particularly believing in the *babushka*'s witchcraft, I am of the opinion that this method is highly practical for discovering the thief; it is at least psychologically very well worked out. . . .

In the afternoon [of the next day] we drove to the village of Visena located just before the gate of Arzamas. Visena belongs to Prince Saltykov and is known throughout Russia for its trade and wide-ranging production of boots and shoes.

Mr. Alexei Sergevich Tarchov, the administrator of the estate for the past twelve years, received us most cordially and took the trouble to show and to explain everything to us. First we were taken to the church, a visit which is always unavoidable in the Russian interior. The church was built in the Italian style by an ancestor of the present prince. There were several good paintings which had been collected and willed to the church by a former Prince Saltykov, who for many years had served as ambassador at various courts. Among others we saw an excellent painting of a repentant Magdalene by an unknown French artist. The face was a portrait of the famous La Vallière. A portrait of La Vallière in a Russian village church is one of the curiosities of art history. The Russian people, however, did not venerate these modern western European paintings but preferred an old Russian madonna, a copy of the Virgin of Kazan, which was framed and indeed studded with pearls and jewels.

The village is well built and boasts several modern stone buildings which, if columns and balconies are a criterion, would have to be called palaces. In the last census, 1,820 souls belonged to the village community.[7] There may be about seven hundred houses in the village. The amount of plowland is relatively small and totals only around five hundred desiatins. But there are almost five hundred desiatins of hay fields and meadows which, however, like the forests belonging to the village, are a considerable distance away, namely, on the opposite side of the village.

I have already mentioned that the majority of the inhabitants constitute an association of boot and shoe manufacturers. In addition there are six glue mills, two candle factories, and eight large factories which make rugs and felt boots from cattle- and horsehair. This trade is also carried on in many homes as a secondary occupation. The principal industry is the manufacture of boots and shoes. Footwear valued at more than 50,000 rubles banco is sold annually at the Nizhnii fair and an additional 10,000 to 20,000 rubles banco are earned at smaller fairs in the vicinity. Around five hundred members of the community who hold passports are always absent. They journey about looking for employment as far away as Saratov, Astrakhan, Uralsk, and even in the depths of Siberia. Some stay away for ten to fifteen years; some settle permanently in other cities and never return home. But this does not mean that they are no longer counted as members of this community; they pay their taxes here and retain their houses, their gardens, and their shares of the communal property, all of which they rent or turn over to someone

7. This refers only to taxable serfs, that is, adult males. The population would in fact have been several times this great.

else. Two hundred inhabitants attend the Nizhnii Novgorod fair annually and stay two months, some working, some selling the wares of the village.

Among the inhabitants there is a great disparity in wealth. Formerly one found even greater wealth here; there were two peasants who each had more than 500,000 rubles banco. Even today there are still fifteen houses whose trade is valued between 20,000 and 50,000 rubles.

The prince has imposed a specific collective tax and leaves it to the community to distribute the tax burden among the individual inhabitants. The administrator said that the prince receives 18,000 to 20,000 silver rubles. However, I have reason to believe that he did not tell us the whole truth. I learned the following about the manner in which the taxes were divided. The community elected one "white head" or elder for every hundred souls, for a total of eighteen; they assessed the wealth of all the commune members and taxed them proportionally, in the old Russian manner according to souls. A wealthy man, for instance, had to pay for thirty souls; each of the two candle manufacturers paid for twenty souls, but there were some poor men who paid only for half a soul.

Little agriculture is carried on here and the methods of cultivation are primitive. The rich grow only as much as they need for their households; the poor engage in horticulture which is rather productive. The true farmers cultivate as much as they can. . . . With a light plow they scarcely scratch the earth, which is very fertile. Every other kind of work and industry is more remunerative than agriculture. One has to pay the fieldhand a daily wage of half a silver ruble, and four bushels of rye do not cost much more than 1 silver ruble. Is it at all surprising that Russian agriculture is declining instead of progressing?

I made the following brief notes on the local boot and shoe industry. There are families here with three brothers making forty pairs of high boots in one week, although the women and children may also help. A pair of high waders costs 8 rubles banco and a pair of winter shoes 2 rubles and 40 kopeks banco. The ordinary ones, which are usually made of horsehide, are not very good. If one orders a particularly well-made pair, they are expensive. A pair of locally made felt boots costs 40 kopeks banco.

The administrator Tarchov took us to the home of a peasant, one of the above-mentioned candle manufacturers. The balcony supported by columns was not lacking, nor were the black upholstered sofas and chairs, tables, tapestries, curtains, and, of course, the music box. But all this modern tinsel was merely for the sake of outward appearance. The owner was a genuine bearded Russian in a blue caftan, his wife a *matushka* in peasant dress with a fur-trimmed shawl, the children all in national costumes. They did not live in the modern part of the house but in an adjoining wing in the *izba* built of logs in Russian style. The *izba* was not very different from the ordinary living quarters of the peasants. We were hospitably treated to tea, cakes, a variety of meats, and champagne. I expressed the desire to hear folk songs and to see the peasants' Sunday dress. Within a quarter of an hour a male choir, which sang surprisingly well, had formed in the adjoining room. Though only folk songs, the themes and modulations were very bold and intricate. Among other songs they performed a very beautiful fuguelike piece for five male voices; even the text, as much as was translated for me, seemed to treat a poetic theme, a stormy and sad ballad. Then a young girl appeared in her Sunday dress. It was the same girl whose portrait we had seen in the artist's home in Arzamas. She had a truly delightful expression of youth, fresh charm, innocence, and piety. She was an Eve in Paradise before the Fall! And not only her facial expression but also her speech revealed this same gentle innocence. After I had asked her about the various parts of her dress, praising and admiring many details, I told her she was one of the most beautiful of God's creatures that I had ever seen. She replied, "I am but the child of poor peasants who have not yet been freed." What a pitiful answer to a compliment! What is beauty without freedom, beauty in the face of a master's caprice?

My companion, the adjutant, gave her a small ring. She blushed deeply and replied, "I am a poor girl who can give nothing in return, but I want to pray to the Virgin Mother to bless you." . . .

In the evening the adjutant and I departed by coach and reached the environs of Nizhni Novgorod at seven o'clock the next morning. Half an hour's distance from the city, I noticed tents to the left, a couple of hundred paces from the road. I was told that it was the camp of a regiment which always spends the summer here. I left the coach in order to surprise a Russian regiment *en négligé*. I had often seen Russian regiments in parade and when they were prepared for an outsider's visit. I also found exemplary order here; since breakfast was being prepared, I convinced myself that at least here the people were well nourished.

At first we ambled along the streets of tents, and soon several officers joined us. We came to an area for calisthenics, and to my astonishment I saw all the athletic equipment used in Germany.

After I had changed clothes in Nizhnii Novgorod, I drove with my travel companion to Count Stenbock's and asked him if we might visit the local prisons. He and a Colonel Pochotin took us there. The prisons are large stone buildings with several yards, the whole surrounded by a high wall. The prisons were rather empty, since a large convoy of exiles had left for Siberia the previous day. The local prison is used for two categories of convicts. Various suspects whose trials are pending are kept here. Also, a part of the prison serves as one of the two main depots in Russia for prisoners banished to Siberia, the other being Kazan. Those convicts condemned to Siberian exile are gathered here, and when there is a sufficient number, one to two hundred, they are transported under escort. As a rule this happens once a week.

There is nothing frightful about the buildings; the ceilings are high; there is adequate light; everywhere there are stoves for heating during the winter. As prisons, the buildings, which date from the time of Empress Catherine II, are very ill suited. There are many large rooms but only a few small cells. In each of the large rooms ten to twenty-five convicts were locked up together. They are more or less grouped according to their crimes, so that the murderers and incendiaries share one room, the thieves another, etc. Even those who have already been sentenced to exile in Siberia are not strictly separated from those whose trials are pending. They are completely free to talk to one another. Words of caution and conspiracies cannot be prevented or controlled. This must vastly complicate every normal and reasonable inquiry into a criminal trial. However, here one is not dealing with the clever rogues of western Europe, who often are as familiar with the laws, their subtleties and ambiguities, as are the judges.

In every cell with more than three or four prisoners, a *starosta* is immediately chosen. The order he maintains and the obedience he commands are remarkable. In every social situation the principle of the Russian commune lives before our eyes!

In separate cells, there were two men imprisoned for debts and two aristocrats, who were permitted at their own expense to have somewhat better furniture and beds. The food, however, was the same for all. Twice a day they got *shchi* (cabbage soup), meat or fish, and two and a half pounds of bread. There is plenty and it is good, as I was able to prove to myself by trying it.

The following types of criminals were described to us: murderers, of whom there were quite a few; incendiaries, most of whom were women; deserters; felons and petty thieves. Among the prisoners convicted of a serious crime was a peasant woman who had tried to poison her husband. Certainly no one can say that civilization has not penetrated Russia yet! A child-murderess gave birth in prison. In such cases the law holds that she must nurse the child for one and a half years before the sentence can be carried out.

We also visited the hospital, whose orderliness was exemplary. The beds were good, the rooms bright, very clean, and well ventilated. Among the sick women was an extremely pretty girl who, out of love for another man, had tried to murder her husband but had been unsuccessful. In prison she slit her throat but was not mortally injured. We also found a woman here with four children, aged three to nine, who had obtained permission to follow her banished husband to Siberia. She had taken ill and therefore lay in the hospital.

In front of the prison we found a wagon with all kinds of provisions which had been sent in from the country by a wedding couple for the prisoners. Also, a good *matushka*, a fat peasant woman, was standing before the door with a huge sack of white bread and meat, all of it for the convicts. For no one does the common Russian interest himself more than for the prisoners. On all occasions throughout the year they receive contributions and gifts. No wedding, baptism, or celebration goes by without all of the participants contributing to them, each according to his means. In the local jails the convicts cannot consume all the food brought to them; a part is sold in order to buy clothing for the Siberian exiles. The subaltern officials and prison wardens do not embezzle any of the charitable contributions, as this is considered a very grave misdeed. Moreover, people would quickly stop contributing as soon as they became convinced that the prisoners were not receiving their donations. The fact that I myself saw the generous gifts being delivered at the prison gate was the best proof that the local convicts were treated humanely. It convinced me more than anything I had been told or shown in that the attempt to show foreigners the best side of everything was evident.

Since my *tarantas* had broken down and could not quickly be repaired, I decided to travel by boat down the Volga from Nizhni to Kazan and to buy a new vehicle in Kazan, the true land of the *tarantas*. I went to the shore of the Volga with my companion ר order to hire a skipper. We were immediately surrounded by a crowd of shouting skippers offering us their services. Hardly had we chosen one to bargain with but all the others grew silent, formed a circle around us, and attentively followed the bargaining without interrupting. Unable to reach an agreement with the first candidate, we broke off the negotiations. Immediately, the shouting of offers began anew. After we had selected a new partner to bargain with, everyone was quiet and watched. The common people in Russia are remarkably polite and well mannered.

The majority of the throng which crowded about us was comprised of *burlaki*, the jacks-of-all-trades in the Volga shipping industry. They are an interesting group of men who, as I mentioned above, have very peculiar institutions. I was told here that the *burlaki* are generally serfs belonging to private seigneurs and are seldom state peasants. The reason for this lies in the various methods of taxing the peasants. Disregarding the disparities in the ownership of property, in the wealth, in the intelligence, physical abilities, and skills of the individuals, the state crown has imposed an equally high *obrok* on all its people. The crown is not interested in the individual's occupation and does not tax it. In this respect the state peasants are completely free, for they can pursue the trade of their choice. No one forces or trains them to take up a specific livelihood. Hence the state peasants engage only in those trades which promise the most money with the least amount of effort and avoid every kind of heavy and tedious work. In taxing their peasants, the private masters take their abilities as well as their property and wealth into consideration. Depending on the locality and the peasants' abilities, the masters train them for specific trades, particularly those which promise the most profit. They force a strong and healthy man to do heavy continuous labor, a sickly man to do light work. Whereas the strong state peasants are vendors of baked goods, peddlers, etc., these jobs are done by the weak and poor serfs of private seigneurs. The state taxes each individual equally and does not tax capacities or trades; the private master imposes a graduated tax and taxes the aptitudes and occupations.

The state taxes the soul, the private master the occupation, and this makes a vast difference. The Russian peasants would only very seldom assume the arduous tasks of the *burlaki* voluntarily, which explains why one finds so few state peasants among them. The private seigneur urges the superfluous peasants in his villages to take up this livelihood or forces them indirectly to do so through high taxes. Were it not for this pressure and the high tax burden, there would no longer be any *burlaki*, or only at an exorbitant price.

Without them the most important industry for the Russian interior, the commercial trade along the Volga, would come to a standstill and with it all industrial activity. The results would be incalculable.

The *burlaki* on the bark which we finally hired for the trip to Kazan were serfs belonging to Prince Gagarin from a village located twenty miles from Arzamas. The village, whose population has climbed to 480 souls, does not have an adequate amount of land; there's hardly one-half desiatin of plowland and meadow for each soul. Because all the trees in the village forest have been felled, the peasants have to buy their firewood for the time being; every household spends 10 to 15 rubles banco for wood. Since they are unable to grow enough food on their land, they have to look for work elsewhere. The majority of the strong men leave the village every spring and return in the winter. About one hundred fifty of them work as *burlaki* on the Volga, where they earn up to 100 rubles banco after deductions for personal needs and food. During their absence, the women, the elderly, and the children cultivate the land and tend the households. Whoever does not have a sufficient number of people at home hires a farmhand whom he has to pay a wage of 45 rubles banco. The commune has to pay the seigneur an *obrok* of 50 rubles banco for each *tiaglo*. One can see here that in very many cases the *obrok* is not a tax on the land but a tax imposed on the workers and their trades. Instead of feeding, clothing, and caring for the needs of his people, the master turns over to them as much land as is needed to provide housing and sustenance.

## The Nizhnii Fair

I did not visit Nizhnii Novgorod at its most brilliant time of year, namely, during its world famous fair. However, my travel companion, Dr. Kosegarten, attended the fair. I am therefore including the following description of his trip from Moscow to Nizhnii and his stay there.

At the end of July 1843, I journeyed from Moscow to Nizhnii Novgorod (Lower Novgorod, also shortened to Nizhegorod, or simply called Nizhnii) in order to visit the famous fair or *iarmarka*, as the Russians now say, whose language has borrowed so many German words. The fair begins about the latter half of July and continues until the end of August or into September. As everyone knows, this fair is the center for overland trade between Asia and

Europe, at least along the entire route from the Caspian Sea to the Arctic. Chinese articles destined for all of European Russia, of which tea is foremost, pass through Nizhnii as do the Russian articles exported to China. The most important of these are cotton cloth, especially plush, and furs.

I made the trip in one of the comfortable, privately owned diligences which run between Moscow and Nizhnii during the time of the fair. These coaches are divided into several completely separate rooms in such a way that two persons occupy one compartment with a small table and mirror. German merchants rarely frequent the fair, so I made the trip exclusively with Russians. My vis-à-vis who had visited England and was somewhat Anglicized, drank Madeira wine in good English fashion, but then in fine Russian style ate raw cucumbers. . . .

Along the entire route the landscape made the same impression as the northern part of Great Russia proper. The southern section of Great Russia, or the Black Earth region, is distinguished by its lush vegetation, its rich grain fields and in part by its lack of forests. Everywhere flat or rolling terrain, fields of grain alternating with forests (besides conifers, few tall trees), wide roads which are seldom paved and even more seldom well paved. Great Russian villages, namely, rows or clusters of brownish wooden houses close to one another, often neatly built, treeless and bleak except for farmyards and small kitchen gardens — these are in general the principal features of the northern regions. At a considerable distance from my destination, the high banks of the Oka and the Volga, which join in Nizhnii, provide an unusual sight. The upper part of the city is about 350 feet above the water level. On the jut of land where the Oka flows into the Volga the white walls of the citadel or the kremlin with its towers climb up the steep cliff; at the foot of the cliff is a forest of masts displayed by the barks lying at anchor on the two rivers. On the near side of the hill the rivers and the canals joining them form a spit on which the fair is held. . . .

The fair at Nizhnii Novgorod is still occasionally called the Makariev fair, since it was formerly held near the cloister of Makariev located approximately eleven miles east of Nizhnii. Everything destined to attain permanence in the Russian nation, so it seems, must be associated with the religious element. This was also the case with the numerous fairs. As Storch has observed, they originated with the church festivals held to commemorate the saints from whom the church and cloister derived their names.[8] The fair at Makariev came into being after Tsar Vasilii Ivanovich had forbidden the Russian merchants to visit Kazan in 1524. The cloister was destroyed in 1544 by the Tatars. After it had been rebuilt in 1624, streams of pilgrims revived trade, and the monks did everything to enhance the importance of the fair. In 1817, following the destruction of the bazaar at Makariev by fire in the previous year, the fair was moved to Nizhnii Novgorod, whose location and facilities offered important advantages. The number of persons who gather there during the fair has been estimated to be upward of two hundred thousand at times; one writer gave six hundred thousand as an estimate. I would judge that the crowd assembled there at any one time does not exceed twenty thousand. However, owing to the throngs of people arriving and departing and milling about, a relatively accurate estimate is very difficult.

The long street running in the direction of the Oka bridge and the surrounding area resemble a large second-hand market. Primarily the common people, and the peasants in particular, crowd together here. One sees displays of clothing, various household articles, and jewelry and has occasion to marvel at the sellers' cleverness and sales talk. Several shops especially catch the eyes of passing peasant women with their displays of old and new women's clothes, for example, shiny red silk *dushagraikis* trimmed with fur, silver fringe, and the like, such as one sees on well-to-do peasant women. Other stores attract the men, for instance the hat shops, where felt hats in the style commonly worn by the Russian peasants are sold. Although these round hats with a narrow brim may be very worn, they are freshly blackened. . . .

In one place Tatars stand in the open selling sheepskins, which they have lying about on the ground. A sheepskin is the Russian peasant's most essential piece of clothing. In spite of the scorching sun, a tatar seller often puts on a coat and makes various movements to demonstrate its excellent quality and its beauty to the eager buyers. Of course, among the most important Russian products are the metal wares of brass, tin, iron, and steel such as samovars, candleholders,

8. Heinrich Friedrich von Storch, *Materialen zur Kenntniss des russischen Reichs*, 2 vols. (Riga, 1796–98), vol. 1, pt. 2. Of the several thousand fairs held annually in Russia the major ones were identified by the saint's day on which they opened but many more were identified simply by the town in which they were held. See Cornelius Walford, *Fairs, Past and Present* (London, 1883), pp. 284–307, and A. Murashkintsev, "Iarmarki," in Brockhaus and Efron, *Entsiklopedicheskii slovar*, 41a:811–14.

locks, knives, etc., manufactured in Tula and Pavlovo. Thousands of arshins of coarse linen are sold to the peasants. Nizhnii and its surroundings supply wooden utensils, porcelain stoves, and bells; most of the leather comes from Kazan. The spectator's attention is caught by one row of shops which contain nothing but colorfully painted wooden chests bound with tin plate and black sheet iron. I was told that these chests, which can be used for storing one's effects or as suitcases, are manufactured in villages. A chest approximately four feet long and more than one foot wide sold for 2 silver rubles. At the fair there was a 20,000-silver-ruble supply of such suitcases and chests, almost all of which were sold. In another row of shops one finds domestic wines, namely, Don wines (Sudak and other varieties generally called half-champagne) and Caucasian wines from Kisliar. Even soap' is included among the Russian products.

Especially near the river banks, one saw vast quantities of articles sold in the wholesale trade stored out in the open or in sheds. Of the domestic products there were cattle skins, potash, which usually comes from Orenburg and Kazan, wheel rims from Viatka and other regions, and bast mats, the products of the linden forests in Kostroma. But the most important products found here are the iron and copper stored along the banks of the Oka. The iron supplies and the small shops which the sellers occupy measure approximately a thousand paces in length. We find here iron in various forms as it is produced in the iron foundries of the Urals and other areas rich in this metal: as rods, rails, hoops, and sheets which serve as roofing on the houses in the Russian cities. We also saw steel, as well as bowls, pots, stoves, doors, etc., made of cast iron.

In 1843, 3,500,000 puds of iron (one pud equals 40 Russian or slightly more than 36 English pounds) were brought to the fair in addition to the 150,000 puds of cast iron. From Nizhnii the iron is distributed throughout Russia. Among the merchants who had come to the fair with this product was a former serf of Count Sheremetev who is said to have a fortune of 4 to 5 million rubles.[9] Stored alongside the iron were 48,000 puds of copper, which for the most part had come from the Demidov foundries in the vicinity

9. This was a common phenomenon in the early nineteenth century. See Henry Rosovsky, "The Serf Entrepreneur in Russia," *Explorations in Entrepreneurial History* 6 (1953–54):207–29; and on serfs of the Sheremetevs in particular, Roger Portal, "Origines d'une bourgeoisie industrielle en Russie," *Revue d'histoire moderne et contemporaine* 8 (1961): 35–60.

of Ekaterinoslav. In passing we heard of a 1,200,000-ruble deal in copper that had just been closed.

Of the foreign goods we noticed above all the immense supplies of tea on the shores of the Volga. This year, thirty thousand crates of tea plus nine thousand crates of tea compressed in the form of bricks were brought to market. This is considerably less than last year, when a significant amount was not sold. My attention was caught by many items but particularly by the raw cotton which had been brought from Bukhara via Astrakhan and some of which is said to have come from Khiva and India. Another unusual item was the yellowish palmwood displayed in pieces and blocks which is used for fine furniture.

The entire section of the fair of which we have been speaking thus far can be called the outer part. This year there were 2,333 wooden booths or barracks located in this area. Most of them were used as shops or storehouses and some served other purposes that we shall come to later. It would be impossible to mention all the goods to be seen there. Instead we shall pass on to that part of the fair that, because of its location, can be designated as the inner part. This is the stone bazaar in the shape of a large parallelogram, which is divided into sixty sections. Comprised of 2,521 stone booths and built on timbering, the bazaar is surrounded on three sides by a canal in the shape of a long half-ellipse. In order to protect it from floods, the inner part of the fair grounds was elevated considerably, an expensive but splendid construction. An imposing Orthodox church in the background, the government palace, in which the governor, the fair director, and the police authorities reside during the fair, the post office, and the commercial bank in the foreground and the shops on either side from a large square. Four bridges across the canal provide easy communication between this part of the fair and the other areas. Here one finds primarily manufactured goods and other valuable wares, such as Muscovite fabrics, Russian and foreign cottons and silks, Persian silk articles, tobacco products from Siberia Astrakhan, and Bukhara, and many other articles. Because of their particular style, one row of booths is called Chinese. But one would search in vain for a Chinese, since as a rule they are not permitted to leave the country. These booths are occupied in part by Russian tea merchants, in part by manufacturers and businessmen of different nationalities from Petersburg and other Russian cities, and in particular by Germans dealing in such wares as household goods and clocks.

In the entire stone bazaar there are few crowds. Compared with the other areas of the fair, the pace is rather slow here. The merchants in their various national costumes often sit quietly in front of their shops. Besides the national Russian and modern European dress, one sees in particular Tatar and Armenian, some Persian and less frequently Turkish costumes. Generally, one observes only a few merchants actively selling their goods and engaging in transactions. This is the area where the larger deals are made; thousands and hundreds of thousands of rubles change hands with a few brief words.

Next to the Orthodox church, but beyond the canal, is an Armenian church and on the other side a Tatar mosque. The spiritual needs of the majority of the fair's visitors are thus provided for. Equal care has been taken to meet their physical needs. The pharmacists from Nizhnii Novgorod have their booths at the fair, primarily of course because of the rush of orders for drugs which they receive from Siberia. There was even an apothecary from Irkutsk who was doing business with them. Of course, there are plenty of taverns and restaurants. The latter, so many of which are meant for the common people, permit the passerby to peer deep into their interiors, where one can see fish, mushrooms, cucumbers, potatoes, and other foods being prepared. There are also elegant restaurants for the upper classes in various places on the fair grounds. To be sure, the Russian cuisine, and specifically the use of oil instead of butter, does not always appeal to the non-Russian palate. Despite many a German dish, the Russian menus present problems to the foreigner because of the unfamiliar script. However, a great many polite waiters in rather fine white shirts or smocks (the typical Russian dress of this class) are most eager to fulfill every wish of the guests. After the meal they will even provide the guests with long, lit pipes if desired. Russian custom prevails in all these restaurants. Even the wash basin suspended on a chain at the entrance is not missing, as required by Russian custom. . . .

The usual forms of entertainment can also be found in the market place. Not only are there clowns, carrousels, and wandering musicians, but also a respectable Russian theater, housed in an attractive building. If I am not mistaken, this building is constructed entirely of wood. An elegant concert hall or ballroom is located in the above-mentioned government building. As far as I know it was used only once during my sojourn, when Schubert, the excellent cellist from Petersburg, gave a concert, which, however, was not well attended. In regard to the graphic arts, there were several shops with prints and engravings. But they could make little claim to artistic excellence. A daguerreotypist was also present, although I cannot say whether he was successful in offering his services. I think I saw only a few of the priestesses of Venus, who were said to have been present in great numbers. The baths, without which the Russians cannot survive, are not lacking. Moreover, the cleanliness of the rest rooms is provided for by a unique arrangement. The toilets are located in two subterranean galleries, which are exposed to the fresh air. They are also equipped with a contrivance which permits water from the canal to cleanse them daily. . . .

To help with the business transactions there are no agents under oath at the fair, but only commissioners or agents who, as private individuals, enjoy the confidence of the merchants. One of these agents, who is well known, is an Armenian. In addition, there are notaries who certify the bills of exchange which are to be discounted at the commercial bank. These bills are issued when goods are purchased on time (as is often the case in the wholesale business). The notaries, too, have their booths at the fair.

Not only are the goods transported along the waterways but also overland; hence, the large number of carts and horses standing in long lines at the edge of the fairgrounds. One even sees the ox-drawn carts of the Little Russians. On and near the two rivers there is, of course, a lot of activity. In the vicinity of the fair, the rivers are covered with boats of various sizes and shapes. One sees many persons loading and unloading goods. Some articles, such as talc, are also sold on the ships. The different kinds of vessels, in particular those which travel the Volga, have already been described by others. Many are distinguished by colorful ornaments, especially on the stern. The decks of some of the boats have the shape of houses or pavillions with galleries and the like. Others are simple, flat, very long and broad barges without any kind of covering. I even saw the steamship which makes regular trips to Astrakhan.

In spite of the large crowds of people, there seem to be few violations of the law. There is no special court for the fair. According to common Russian practice, minor controversies are settled verbally before a court which is part of the police department. The Cossack guard, stationed at the market place to keep order, seems to perform its duty as well as its predecessors, the Kalmyk guards. Only once (and I visited the fair every day for nearly two weeks) did I see the guard actively intervene, and even this incident appeared to be very minor. As far as I can remember, the Cossack dealt only one blow with his whip.

At the fair I observed several striking instances of the kindness and gentleness of the Great Russian character. I saw a very lowly man, who may have been just above the level of real poverty, give alms to a beggar. I also had the opportunity to note that a member of the lower class in Russia is humbly polite not only to his superiors but also to his peers. I saw a man lying on the ground before two or three people who, judging by their appearance, did not belong to the upper strata of society, perhaps small merchants. The man looked as if he were about to kiss their feet, probably in order to beg their forgiveness for having offended them. (My command of Russian was not adequate for me to understand what was being said.) The person to whom the apology seemed to have been directed spoke calmly to the prostrate man, appeared to forgive him, and finally departed, removing his hat in a polite gesture.

The estimated annual value of the goods purchased at the fair is an indication of its importance. In the past ten years up to 1842 the value has always been between 40 and 50 million silver rubles.

# 5
# The Sectarians

Upon returning from the banks of the Volga, we entered an open church in which a child was being baptized. It was a Edinovertsy church.[1] After the christening we made the acquaintance of the priest. When I showed interest in their religious life, he offered to visit me the very same day and to answer all my questions. Immediately after dinner he arrived accompanied by another priest of his sect. They did indeed answer all of my questions but what answers they were! Their replies were so evasive, so brief, so forced, and bore so little relation to the sense of my inquiries that I was unable to tell whether they were based on cleverness or profound ignorance; it was probably a combination of both. Their answers, nevertheless, did provide me with clues for further inquiries.

The Russian sects are on the whole a very difficult field for research. From the ecclesiastics of the state church as well as from the government officials one can obtain little or no information. In part they are unwilling to comment on the subject and in part they actually know nothing about the sectarian institutions, since all the Russian sectarians are at great pains to keep their internal affairs as secret as possible.

Since one can never truly know and appreciate the national character, social conditions, and political institutions of a country without

1. A church founded by Marshal Rumiantsev on his estate in the Starodub region of the Ukraine during the late eighteenth century as a means of reuniting the Priestly group of the Old Believers with Orthodoxy. See V. V. Andreev, *Raskol i ego znachenie v narodnoi Russkoi istorii* (St. Petersburg, 1870), chap. 17.

examining its religious life as well, I have endeavored throughout my trip to collect notes on this subject. And even though I can in no way claim to have contributed an exhaustive study, I nevertheless know more than other foreigners and more than even the majority of Russians, including the government officials and authorities.

In several other places, which I do not want to mention by name, I had the opportunity to come into close contact with some of the most forbidden sects, to win their confidence, and to attend their secret religious services. I give here a brief summary and reserve a more detailed and thorough discussion for a separate treatise on religious life in Russia.[2]

After the ninth century, Christianity spread in Russia and the country became a branch of the Eastern church, of the patriarchate of Constantinople. Although the time of the Gnostic heresies had passed, Gnostic ideas and views continued to endure in the Orient. The Crusades brought them to the West. Even today we find Gnostic ideas widely spread among the Mohammedans.

The internal history of the Russian church is still obscure. Hence I cannot actually prove my opinion that Gnostic ideas also found acceptance in Russia in the Middle Ages.[3] I can only point out that unmistakable traces of Gnostic views are still present in some Russian sects. I would not hazard an opinion on whether they were borrowed directly from the Orient during the Middle Ages or whether they came from the West after the seventh century, which, however, is improbable.

Unlike the contemplative peoples of the Orient, the Russians are not given to philosophical musings and subtleties. With the exception of the Dukhobortsy (Spirit Wrestlers) one should not expect to find a complete body of teachings among the modern Russian sects. Generally their teachings center on only a few disconnected ideas, for this reason producing a kind of madness and leading to the most terrible fanaticism.

The most extreme of these sects are the Morelshchiki, who either sacrifice their lives or partially immolate themselves.[4]

2. This treatise was never published, but may be preserved. See above, Introduction, n. 47.

3. Gnostic influences in medieval Russia came not from western Europe but from Dalmatia, particularly during the fourteenth century. See G. Florovskii, *Puti russkogo bogosloviia* (Paris, 1937), pp. 9 ff.

4. The Morelshchiki or Self-Immolators were those Old Believers of northwestern Russia who, during the late seventeenth and early eighteenth centuries, resisted official repression by mass immolation in their wooden churches.

The teachings of the former are completely unknown. Almost annually and in every part of the empire some horrible piece of evidence appears, testifying to their existence, particularly in the north, in Siberia, and in the province of Saratov, etc. Accompanied by special ceremonies, a large deep pit is dug and surrounded with straw, wood, and other combustible materials. A small community of these fanatics, numbering twenty, thirty, fifty, even one hundred individuals, gather in the middle of the pit, ignite the pyre, while breaking into savage song, and cremate themselves with stoic indifference. Sometimes they assemble in a house which they have surrounded with piles of straw and then set fire to it. The neighbors gather around without disturbing them, for they are holy and are "receiving the baptism of fire." The authorities and the police first learn of the incident long after it has taken place and can no longer be prevented.* The ideas attached to this rite are unknown; only the phrase "baptism of fire" stands as an isolated symbol that makes us suspect some dark, occult, and fanatic doctrine. Moreover, there must be some sort of religious belief involved as well as a distinct sect since these self-immolations have been taking place under very similar circumstances almost every year for more than a century in areas far removed from each other!

The Skoptsy (Self-Castrators), who maim themselves, constitute the second category of fanatics. It is not entirely clear whether they, like Origines, derive their teachings from a couple of biblical passages, since they regard the Gospels as well as the entire Bible to be a forgery.[5] They believe that the true Gospel was in their hands, but that Peter III, who is their leader and a new emanation of Christ, immured it in the cupola of Saint Andrei's on Vasilevskii

---

*Earlier travelers, such as Pallas, Gmelin, Georgi, Lopukhin, and others, all mention these facts. I was told that several years ago on the estate of a certain Mr. Gurev located on the left bank of the Volga, a small community of these sectarians decided to sacrifice themselves by killing each other. After making certain preparations, they carried out their horrible resolve. Thirty-six of their members had already been murdered when a young woman, who was seized by the desire to live, fled to a neighboring village. Upon arriving at the scene of carnage, one found two murderers still alive and forty-seven dead. The captured murderers were flogged, but with every lash they rejoiced at having attained martyrdom.

5. The Skoptsy or Castrator movement was founded in the 1760s by Andrei Ivanov, a former Flagellant, and disseminated by Kondratii Selivanov, who in turn was patronized by Prince D. A. Golitsyn at the Petersburg court under Alexander I. Their rites were generally similar to the Flagellants. See K. Grass, *Die russischen Sekten*, 2 vols. (Leipzig, 1907), vol. 2.

Island in Petersburg. In general this fanatic mutilation does not seem to be directly related to the corpus of their theological thought. (It is doubtful if one can properly speak of a system of thought, since they actually seem to have only disconnected, vague beliefs and ideas.)* They teach that in the beginning there was only God the Father, one and indivisible. He then created the world and manifested Himself in various forms: as the Son in the Person of Christ, Who was only "He Who is consecrated by God and Who is full of His grace." Christ taught by divine inspiration but was not a sovereign god. As the Holy Spirit, God manifests Himself eternally and daily in His true children, the Skoptsy. Christ is not dead and never died. He forever wanders the earth in the form of a sexless being and is today incarnate in Peter III, who did not die as is recorded in history. The body placed in the tomb was not his, but that of a soldier who resembled him. Rather at that time he fled to Irkutsk, and henceforth all salvation will come from the East. He will soon return and ring the large bell of the Uspenskii Sobor (Cathedral of the Assumption) on the Kremlin in Moscow so that his true disciples, the Skoptsy, will hear it in all corners of the world and gather around him. This will mark the beginning of the eternal kingdom of the Skoptsy in all the splendor of the world!

They do not believe in the resurrection of the body and do not regard Sunday as a holiday. They do have a kind of mystical communion, whereby a loaf of bread is lowered into the grave of one of their saints and is mystically consecrated in this way. On the first day of Easter, which is their only holy day, everyone partakes of a small piece. They generally gather on Saturday night and perform all kinds of strange and bizarre ceremonies. . . .

The members of this sect have secret symbols for recognizing one another. One of these signs consists of putting a red cloth on one's right knee and striking it with the right hand. Everywhere one finds the portrait of Peter III among them [the Skoptsy]. He is always depicted bareheaded, with a short black beard and a blue caftan trimmed from top to bottom with black fur; also on his right knee is a red cloth upon which his right hand rests.

The Skoptsy are a very widespread sect. A large part of the

*Histoire des sectes religieuses, by M. Gregoire (Paris, 1814), Vol. 2, p. 306: "Le célèbre chirurgien Desfault assurait que dans quelques cantons de la ci-devant Champagne, des femmes pratiquaient sur des enfants une semicastration par des motifs superstitieux. Il n'est idée si folle qu'elle ne trouve accès dans quelques têtes!" In Russia, too, the operation is usually performed by old women.

jewelers and the gold and silver mongers in Petersburg, Moscow, Riga, Odessa, etc., belong to this sect. They are very eager to convert others to their teachings and then to perform the operation on their neophytes. Very often they seek their converts among the soldiers and pay them large sums of money, frequently several thousand rubles. Whoever converts twelve persons attains the dignity of an apostle, a title whose meaning I was unable to ascertain. In some provinces such as Orel the populations of whole villages belong to this sect. At first sight there is nothing about the appearance of these villages that would betray the abnormal condition of the inhabitants. One sees nicely furnished homes, women, children, etc. Here the sectarians actually do marry, and only after they have a son do they undergo the operation. However, the fathers of most of the children are said to be men and young lads from the neighborhood. But this makes no difference. The Skoptsy live most compatibly with their wives and care for their children as only real fathers can.

About two to three thousand Skoptsy are officially known and under police surveillance; in reality there are probably ten times that number. Since they are very wealthy, the police can usually find their money but not the individuals themselves!

The doctrines of the Khlysty or the Flagellants, whom the Skoptsy recognize as their brothers and precursors, seem related to those of the latter.[6] Since they are regarded as being rather harmless and for this reason are not persecuted, one would probably find it easiest to learn more about their philosophical or theological teachings. However, no one has hitherto considered it worth the trouble to investigate these psychologically peculiar aberrations of the human spirit!

No one knows anything specific of their teachings and their faith. Meeting in rooms in which no images are permitted, they jump and stamp about in circles while flagellating each other. A barrel of water stands in the center; at certain intervals they wet their heads or lap the water out of their hands until they finally collapse from exhaustion. Often several of them experience convulsions when the spirit visits them, and they begin to prophesy.

Among the Khlysty and the Skoptsy alike there occasionally are individuals who, in order to mortify the flesh, always wear either old chain mail next to their bare skin or shirts made of horsehair.

6. The Khlysty or Flagellants, a late seventeenth-century sect with legendary connections with medieval groups, organized principally by Ivan Suslov. See Grass, vol. 1; and Konstantin Kutepov, *Sekty Khlystov i Skoptsov* (Kazan, 1882).

I found one man who wore a small metal cross on his chest and a small metal picture on his back, the significance of which was unknown to me. I was told that this is not unusual. The two pictures were suspended around his neck on a leather strap and were also fastened under his arms by two small chains which had been drawn through his skin.

The Besslovesniki are a sect whose teachings and ceremonies are completely unknown.[7] Whoever joins this sect immediately becomes mute, and from that moment on there is no way of forcing him to utter a sound. The government has tried in vain to get information about them. Individual officials who got carried away went so far as to subject these poor souls to many kinds of torture, but without success. At the time of Catherine II, a well-known governor general of Siberia by the name of Pestel forced them to undergo the most cruel torture; he had people tickle the soles of their feet and drop burning wax on their bodies, but they uttered not a sound.

Seemingly related to these sects which subject themselves to a complete or partial martyrdom are several whose faith is based on individual mystical teachings or views, such as the Sect of the Exalted Redeemer. In describing the Trinity-Saint Sergei Monastery, we mentioned the legend of Christ's image. According to Roman Catholic legend, the image is the countenance of the Suffering Savior imprinted on Veronica's handkerchief; according to the Eastern church, it is the image of the Exalted Savior as he ascended into heaven. In the above-mentioned sect, this image constitutes the center of their cult; all other images are banned. Indeed, the initiated abstain from every other form of religious worship. During devotions they are supposed to concentrate their thoughts and become so absorbed in the contemplation of this mysterious image that they are transported to a state of profound rapture and celestial bliss. This is all that I was able to learn about the sect. I heard the names of several sects of this kind but could not obtain any information on their teachings.*

---

*An archbishop of Rostov named Dmitrii wrote a book on the Russian sects at the beginning of the eighteenth century.[8] . . . He is said to have included about two hundred different sects, most of which, however, are extinct. Since then many new sects have emerged.

7. The Besslovesniki or Silent Ones were a latter-day survival of the fourteenth-century ascetics, the Trans-Volga Elders. See Florovskii, pp. 28 ff.

8. Dmitrii, bishop of Rostov (1651–1709), author of *Rozysk o raskolnicheskoi Brynskoi vere, o uchenii ikh, o delakh ikh i iziavlenie, iako vera ikh neprava, uchenie ikh dushevredno, i dela ikh ne bogougodna* (Moscow, 1745).

A curious sect is that of the Subbotniki or Sabbatarians. According to Karamzin, this sect originated in 1470 in Novgorod when a Jew from Kiev named Zacharias persuaded several priests that only the law of Moses was divine.[9] Since then their teachings have spread considerably in spite of several persecutions, including that of 1503 when the government moved against them with fire and sword. Even today their numbers are said to be increasing steadily, especially in Siberia. They neither speak nor learn Hebrew but use the Slavonic translation of the Old Testament. They await the arrival of an earthly Messiah and, like the Sadducees, they do not believe in the resurrection of the dead. Since they practice many cabalistic arts, they are reputed to be soothsayers and sorcerers.

A second category of sects grew out of the schism of the seventeenth century. In the judgment of scholars such as Griesbach, the translation of the Holy Scriptures into Old Slavonic by Saints Cyril and Methodius is excellent. The translation and the liturgical books of the Eastern church were introduced into Russia with Christianity. At that time culture and learning began to flourish there in the cloisters. The theological and liturgical manuscripts up to the end of the thirteenth century are evidence of this; they are beautifully and most accurately written. During Mongol rule, however, all scholarship and culture declined. Because ecclesiastics and monks no longer understood the language of the church, many errors crept into the liturgical manuscripts. In almost every petty principality individual practices, ceremonies, and religious usages arose. The sacred books contained interpretations which were utterly absurd or definitely inaccurate.

When the Grand Duchy of Moscow restored the unity of Russia and particularly when, with the creation of the patriarchate, all ecclesiastical matters were tackled with greater vigor, these errors and abuses became more salient. Encouraged by the tsars, the patriarchs began seriously to set about expunging these errors in the liturgical books and restoring the original text. The patriarchs and their schools, however, were themselves not entirely certain of what they were doing. Even Filaret, the Romanov, failed to correct many errors out of ignorance and, to a certain extent, recognized as authentic

9. The Subbotniki or Sabbatarians have been traced to the so-called Judaizers of fifteenth-century Novgorod. They flourished particularly under Alexander I (see A. Scheikevitch, ''Alexander Ier et l'hérésie sabbatiste,'' *Revue d'histoire moderne et contemporaine* 3 [1956]: 223–35), but as Professor A. I. Klibanov shows, they still exist today (*Istoriia religioznogo sektanstva v Rossii 60 gg. XIX veka – 1917* [Moscow, 1965], p. 40).

passages that had obviously been falsified. The erudite patriarch Nikon was the first to proceed methodically. He sent learned monks to Mount Athos to consult the oldest manuscripts. After long preliminary studies he finally published a reconstruction of the original text and the corrected liturgical books. In 1659 he ordered their general introduction and declared those formerly used to be invalid.*

But Nikon soon met with strong opposition. Instead of acknowledging that Nikon had restored only the oldest, most authentic liturgical texts held in common with the entire Eastern church, many priests and a multitude fanaticized by them accused him of trying to introduce innovations, of leaning toward the Poles, toward Roman Catholicism, etc. Others contended that the German Luther had also claimed he was restoring early Christianity, but that he then overthrew everything, abolished the mass, the five sacraments, and so on. Since the Eastern church recognizes no supreme independent leader whose incontestable authority could have settled the controversy, agreement soon became impossible and the rupture grew even deeper. No alteration, however small, in the most insignificant ceremonies, can be justified in the eyes of the masses. The very essence of the Eastern church is tradition. Everything, including the smallest ornament in the architecture of the church, has been handed down by the fathers, and no one of the living has the right to change or abandon anything; rather, it is his duty to pass it on well secured to future generations. In the Eastern church the hierarchy is merely the bearer of the cult, not the regent and leader and not even the interpreter of dogma and ritual.

Nikon was absolutely right. The other Eastern patriarchs approved his measures. Yet his reforms would not have been accepted by the masses had they not been supported by the secular authority which had an even greater political interest in the absolute uniformity of the rite than the patriarchate itself. In this matter the powerless position of the patriarchate and its shallow roots in the nation became evident. This circumstance alone explains the facility with which Peter I later abolished the patriarchate and completely concentrated the unity of church and state in his person. Even prior to this, however, the secular authority in Russia had always governed the church in its outer form. Only after Peter I did the schism which

---

*After the liturgy had been printed, it was forbidden to use a handwritten copy. To this very day the Old Believers have only handwritten copies and condemn every printed text. Their liturgical books are continually being transcribed in the nunneries.

had begun under Nikon assume definite character.[10] It has not simply remained an ecclesiastical rupture but has become a political schism.

I had a long conversation with a somewhat educated Raskolnik who had an unusually penetrating mind. He showed great trust in me because a German friend to whom he was very attached introduced me to him and also acted as our interpreter. He made the following curious remark: "It was not Nikon who completely alienated us from our Russian brothers, but Peter I with his movement toward Westernization, of which the order to shave off our beards was only an outward sign."

At another place the Raskolniki expressed the most profound hatred for Peter I. I was shown pictures on the walls of Raskolniki whom he was said to have martyred and killed. One sect of the Raskolniki calls him nothing less than the Antichrist. With him the era and the world dominion of the Antichrist began, an era in which there are no longer any true bishops and priests. It is the night before the advent of the Lord. For this reason the sacraments are no longer necessary, except for the rite of baptism which every believing father can administer. Is it not written in the Bible that the Antichrist will change the time, and did Peter I not move the New Year from the first of September to the first of January? Did he not abolish the reckoning of time from the creation of the world and accept the chronology of the Latin heretics, which begins with the birth of Christ? Is it not written that the Antichrist will demand money and taxes from the dead? And did not Peter I introduce this by means of the revisions? Indeed, it is utter blasphemy to have to pay taxes on one's soul (the immortal breath of God) rather than on one's earthly possessions!

Peter I no longer persecuted the true Starovertsy (Old Believers); the usual name, Raskolniki, meaning heretics, is applied to them most inappropriately. When it was proved that they had been deeply involved in the rebellion of the Streltsy, he imposed on them a double head tax which, however, was later forgotten. Ever since Catherine's time, attempts have been made to reconcile them with the church. Under Alexander and the present emperor the government has tried hard to bring them back into the fold by friendly means. It yielded to them completely in the majority of points. It declared that all of their deviations from the liturgy and religious ceremonies

10. This evolution within the Old Believer movement is recounted by Robert O. Crummey, *The Old Believers and the World of Antichrist : The Vyg Community and the Russian State, 1694–1855* (Madison, Wis., 1970), chap. 3–4.

were not at all heretical and solemnly permitted them to keep their rites. They were given the name Edinovertsy. The government promised not to interfere in the education of their clergy and demanded only that they have their priests ordained by bishops of the church; the ordination, however, was to be performed according to their old practices and not according to the modern rite.

Nevertheless, the success has been modest. Relatively few communities have loosely joined the national church and even they quietly remain as aloof as possible. Moreover, the laity regards its priests with suspicion; they are afraid that the ordaining bishops may exercise an objectionable influence on them. The majority of Old Believers prefer to manage with so-called runaways. They are orthodox priests who either were dismissed for some crime and then fled or priests who converted because of the lucrative material advantages which the Old Believers often offer them. Cloisters in which the bishops of the Old Believers lived are said to have existed in the north, in the depths of the forests.[11] But they were discovered and abolished and all the residents were carried off. Their bishops, who for some time provided them with ordained priests, are long dead. As we have said, the Old Believers now get along with apostate priests.

The Old Believers exercise a mysterious and profound moral influence on Russia and her government. In every question concerning legislation, church affairs, and domestic policies, and with every proposal for reforms and alterations, one secretly asks oneself, "What will the Old Believers say to this?" The Old Believers are the embodiment of ancient Russian traditions; in Russia they represent the principle of stability, or rather that of the petrified past. They are the regulators whom one must consult to find out how far one can go with changes.

Whoever wants to learn about the national characteristics of the Great Russians must study the Old Believers. Even for the foreigner this is not as difficult as one might think. The genuine Russian is by nature sociable, talkative, and trusting, particularly toward foreigners. In this respect he is basically different from the Germanic peoples — the Germans, the English, and the Dutch — who, as a rule, are reserved, uncommunicative, and even suspicious of foreigners. The Russian is more like the Frenchman. He is unusually flattered when a foreigner shows an interest in him, his affairs,

11. The reference is to communities such as that at Vyg (see Crummey) and the Monastery of Solovetsk on the White Sea, scene of a great rebellion in the seventeenth century. N. A. Barsukov, *Solovetskoe vosstanie 1668 g.* (Petrazavodsk, 1954).

national customs, and usages. Even though I had no command of the language and conversed with them through an interpreter, they not only gave open and confiding answers about their family and community affairs, their relationship to their masters, etc., but also, without being in the least bit shy, enthusiastically showed me their household furnishings and their fields. They had their wives and daughters dress up in their Sunday apparel; they sang their folk songs, told their legends, etc. In brief, if I had had the time and had been able to speak their language, I could have observed and collected more information among them than among any other people.

The Old Believers are in general much more simple, moral, sober, and reliable than the other Russian peasants. Indeed, one can say that the more closely the Russian peasants resemble the Old Believers in customs, dress, and habits, the better they are. On the other hand, when the Russian peasant becomes Europeanized, shaves off his beard, discards his native dress, and builds a modern house, he is no longer to be trusted; he has, as a rule, become a rogue!

The Old Believers are usually somewhat educated and in this respect are far superior to the other Russians. Most of them can read and write, although they generally know and use only the Old Slavonic letters. (They consider the modern Russian alphabet to be heretical.) All of them have a thorough knowledge of the Bible and can almost recite it by heart. They sharpen their minds with theological subtleties. I can include several examples which testify to the dialectical skill of these peasants.

I told the above-mentioned Old Believer that I found it quite right and good to uphold the customs of their fathers and not to shave their beards. I continued by saying that a beard looked masculine and attractive and that I would certainly keep mine if this were the custom in my country. I added, however, that I could not see why it was a sin to shave off one's beard and that I would be happy to hear his opinion on the subject. He then replied:

*He*: Are you a Christian?
*I*: Yes, indeed.
*He*: Do you believe that Christ is the Son of God and that we must do everything He commanded?
*I*: Certainly.
*He*: Do you believe that the Bible and the four Gospels in particular are really the word of God and that we are duty bound to uphold what Christ commands us therein?
*I*: Yes, I do indeed believe this.
*He*: Did Christ not say, "I have come not to abolish the law

but to fulfill it"'? Is not the law of which He is speaking
the law of Moses? Did not Christ Himself often refer to
the law and command us to obey it?

I could only respond in the affirmative to all of these and to similar
questions.

*He*: Is it not quite clear in the New Testament that the precepts
of Mosaic law which Christ did not specifically abolish should
also hold for Christians?

*I*: I quite agree.

*He*: Now, without a doubt the Ten Commandments are among
those laws which have been retained. In the nineteenth chapter
of the third book of Moses, in which the Ten Commandments
are explained, it explicitly says, "Ye shall not round the
corners of your head, neither shalt thou mar the corners of
thy beard."

He had me there, and I did not know what to say.

*He*: We have thus the biblical commandments and the tradition
of the church on our side. Our fathers and forefathers always
wore beards and as long as we Russians are Christians we
shall teach generation upon generation that that is a law.
The images of Christ and the saints, whom the church commands us to venerate and whose example we are to follow,
are always portrayed with beards.

I had been thoroughly beaten and assured the good man that as
soon as I returned to my country I would publicize his convincing
arguments for keeping one's beard. . . .

In Moscow I took down almost verbatim a second discussion
from an account given to me by one of the participants. The discussion
together with all the circumstances involved provides deep insight
into the character and the customs of the Russian people. Since
time immemorial it has been the unusual custom in Moscow for
crowds to gather every morning during the week following Easter
in the Kremlin on the square before the famous Uspenskii Sobor
(Cathedral of the Assumption) in order to hold religious discussions
and disputations. Only the common people are present; neither the
clergy nor government officials nor the aristocracy take part. The
police ignore these gatherings, and one notices no officers at them.
The presence of the police is, moreover, completely unnecessary,
since the gathering is perfectly peaceful and orderly; there has never
been any disorder. The people themselves maintain order and even
reprimand a person for speaking too loudly.

# Chapter Five

The followers of the Orthodox church assemble on one side; across from them are the Raskolniki from all the sects and in particular Old Believers of different shadings. Various groups form, each of which has several apologists who defend or attack some religious doctrine. Both sides display the greatest courtesy and composure; one tips his hat, makes a deep bow before his opponent, and asks him for permission to reply to his statements or questions. No one interrupts the speaker. The debate is characterized by highly logical argumentation. If someone cannot continue, one of his supporters will step forward at once and help him out or take over the discussion on his own. If someone loses his temper and shouts or simply cries out, "That isn't true," the members of his group will immediately admonish him by saying, "*poshlo na da i nyet,*" "This is no longer a dialogue!" Indeed, if he should fail to keep quiet, they would at once pull him back into their group.

The upper or educated classes formerly took little notice of this interesting popular custom. In the past decade, however, there has been a growing interest in the research and study of national life throughout Europe and Russia alike. Five young men of the upper class decided to attend this unusual disputation. They were five of the most intelligent and talented men in Moscow, including Mr. K., an excellent poet, endowed with a great gift of eloquence.[12]

All five dressed as peasants and on Easter, 1841, went to the Kremlin in order to watch the entire proceedings and, if possible, to participate. They found a great throng and pushed their way forward to get close to the disputants standing in the center.

Mr. K. was the first to join in the discussion. At first he was ignored, probably because he interrupted without being called upon. However, when the champion of the Orthodox church got stuck and Mr. K. provided a very convincing argument on his behalf, he attracted everyone's attention. Gradually they permitted him and his companions to lead the entire disputation.

Stepping forward to represent the sectarians was one of their most experienced leaders, an Old Believer belonging to the sect of the Pomorane or Bespopovtsy (the Priestless). He had a fine expressive face and a magnificent long, white beard. The discussion had reached the point where the Raskolnik advanced the following argument:

*The Raskolnik*: There is no outward church. Christ taught that his disciples were the churches. However, because they were

12. The reference here is to the Slavophile Aleksei Khomiakov, with whom Haxthausen later corresponded for many years.

138

persecuted, they fled to the mountains and into the forests. Can the stone church do likewise?

*Mr. K.*: Brother, you misquote the biblical text. The Bible does not say: You (disciples) are the *churches*, but the *church*. The apostle says, "Whoever does not listen to the church," "whoever does not obey the church," and so on. Hence it is the *community* of believers together with the bishops in the houses of worship which is given the name *church*.

*The Raskolnik (switching to another topic)*: But what about the sacraments? How can one administer and receive them since it is written, "Whoever is in a state of sin receives in the sacrament eternal death"? But who is without sin? Even if a man has just confessed, he has already sinned again by the time he receives communion! There is only one instant when a man is free of sin and that is the moment of death. Then his guardian angel invisibly administers the sacrament to him.

*Mr. K.*: What are you saying, Brother? It was Christ, of course, who instituted the sacrament. He says, "Eat, drink, this is my body and my blood." Christ also says, "I am a God of the living!" But you would make him a god of the dead. Furthermore, he installed the bishops and priests to administer the sacraments.

*The Raskolnik*: What are you trying to tell me about the bishops? They are human beings, sinners like us! Take away their vestments and you will see that they are no different from us.

*Mr. K.*: What you say is true; they are human beings. The tsar is also a human being, and nevertheless you obey him! However, you do not obey him but rather the office and the power which he represents. So it is with the bishops and priests; the church speaks through them.

*The Raskolnik*: You always speak of the church, but where is the church in times of misery and suffering? If I am on a desert island or in the land of the heathens, I am outside the church! I don't know the church!

*Mr. K.*: You may not know the church, Brother, but the church knows you! Every day, during every mass, the church prays for you! Hence, you are in the church, even if you are physically far away from her!

*The Raskolnik (changing the subject after a moment of silence)*: What about the cross? There is only one way of making the sign of the cross, and nevertheless you do it differently than Christ did. Simply look at all the old images of Him; He joins His thumb, the little finger, and the ring finger and holds up the others to give the blessing. But you join the first three fingers to make the sign of the cross.*

*Mr. K.:* The sign of the cross with which Christ blessed us is a sign of benediction only, which He alone is permitted to make. This is why the bishops and priests make this sign when they bless the people in His name, for the hand of God blesses the multitude through them! But we are all sinful men and cannot bless ourselves. To show this we cross ourselves with three fingers, thereby imploring the Holy Trinity to bless us. For this reason our bishops and priests, poor sinners like ourselves, also make the sign of the cross in this way when they cross themselves.

The Raskolnik obviously did not know what to say. He theretofore launched a personal attack against his adversary, who was better dressed than the other Russians present and who, above all, did not wear a beard. In this way, he could count on the sympathy of all the bearded Russians.

*The Raskolnik:* Why do many of you shave your beards? It's a sin! You are disfiguring the image of God. You are rejecting something that God has let grow. Christ wore a beard as did the saints, and we certainly want to be like them!

*Mr. K.:* It is good to wear a beard and not to shave one's chin, and I commend this. But to shave is no sin. Does God have a body? Is your body an image of Him? No, it is your spirit, your soul. Isn't this so?

*The Raskolnik:* Yes, but what about Christ?

*Mr. K.:* Did Christ have a beard as a boy? You are supposed to become Christlike, but which Christ should be your model? The young boy who taught in the temple or the man who suffered for us? How can you demand physical resemblance

---

*I cannot refrain from mentioning a conversation here which a Catholic friend of mine had with an Old Believer. My friend had asked him if he knew that in olden times all Christians, including the forefathers of the Old Believers, recognized the pope in Rome as the head of all Christendom. He answered that he had heard this. But, he continued, he had also heard that there once was a pope named Formosus who had introduced the practice of making the sign of the cross with the first three fingers. All of the orthodox turned away from him, declared him to be a heretic, and refused to recognize his authority as head of all Christendom. After his death, Formosus was exhumed and his fingers cut off. What a strange legend! How amazingly traditions are spread and perpetuated! Baronius also mentions that in the ninth century Pope Stephen VI had his predecessor, Pope Formosus, exhumed and beheaded. Baronius does not mention that his fingers were also cut off, but it is quite possible!

to Christ? And the Mother of God and all the female saints and all women in general, are they not also created in the image of God? And, after all, they do not have beards.

*The Raskolnik:* But we are supposed to emulate the male saints as far as possible, and you can see that they all have beards!

*Mr. K.:* Saint George didn't have one, as you can see from the pictures of him.

*The Raskolnik:* He was a warrior and probably had to follow the orders of his superiors.

*Mr. K.:* Saint Lawrence, too, did not have a beard.

*The Raskolnik:* He most certainly did.

*Mr. K.:* No, he didn't.

*The Raskolnik:* Yes, he did. We can't continue arguing, "*poshlo na da i nyet.*" The books must decide the matter. But you have spoken well and intelligently. Let us now break off the debate.

*Mr. K.:* Farewell. But before we depart, all of you listen to this: when the multitude crucified Christ, they tore his clothes and distributed them. Was this right?

*The Raskolnik:* Certainly not.

*Mr. K.:* But you, Brothers, you Old Believers, you continue to do this every day! You do more than this! The church is not the vestment of Christ; it is His body, His bride, and you are dismembering her.

Mr. K. and his companions bade them farewell and departed. The entire group of Orthodox Russians, however, followed them to the great square before the Kremlin. There one man stepped forward and addressed Mr. K.: "You spoke so well! Come again, as often as you can, and help us. And now give all of us the Easter kiss of peace."

Several of them pulled one of Mr. K's companions off to the side and asked him, "Brother, tell us, who is this man, who spoke so especially well?" He replied, "He is a nobleman, and we are all aristocrats." In astonishment they called out, "How can that be? An aristocrat and he knows all this?"

The Great Russian is lively, alert, and cheerful, but he is fickle and light-hearted. The liveliest and boldest of all the Great Russians is the Cossack. The Little Russians, on the other hand, are contemplative and imaginative; they tend to be melancholy and are quiet and slow in their movements. One would think that Old Believerism, the earnest, brooding, and exclusive doctrine of sectarianism, would have the greatest appeal among the Little Russians. On the contrary!

One finds not a trace of it among them.[13] All the Old Believers who live among the Little Russians, that is, in several villages between Kiev and Chernigov, are Great Russians. They are unable to convert the Little Russians, whereas sectarianism is spreading more and more among the Great Russians. It is precisely among the lively and bold Cossacks that the sects have gained the most ground!

In both intensity and numbers, sectarianism in Russia is strongest in Siberia, along the Ural River, in the northern regions, in the province of Saratov, and among all the Cossack tribes. For many years there was a kind of center on Lake Irgis in the province of Saratov. Located there were four large Old Believer monasteries whose members were recruited mainly from the so-called runaways, for example military deserters, escaped criminals from Siberia, and priests and monks who had been expelled from the church. In 1838 the government dispatched troops there, took them by surprise, and banished all of them to Siberia.

One finds Old Believers only among the peasants and among the merchants and manufacturers of peasant background. Nowhere did sectarianism gain a following among the aristocracy. They have absolutely no scholars and no real theologians. Their teachings and views are passed on solely by tradition and their liturgical books are copied only in their nunneries. I was unable to learn, however, whether they had written any new books in the past century.

The Russian Orthodox church has hitherto been unable to subdue the Old Believers. This will only be possible if the church makes greater headway in the religious education of the masses and if the clergy takes greater interest in the ministry and in preaching. Archbishop Innokentii of Kharkov, a gifted preacher, has brought several thousand Old Believers back into the fold of the church!

Modern European culture and its leveling influence are gradually succeeding where the church has hitherto failed. In the large cities, in Moscow, in Petersburg, in Riga, only the first generation of Old Believers who have become wealthy merchants and manufacturers remains steadfast to its faith. The following generation shaves off its beards and doffs the caftan for a frock coat. With the passing of old practices and national costumes, religious ideas also lose

13. Though Old Believers were on all border regions of the empire, most other sectarians were concentrated on the southern periphery of Great Russia on account of immigration and colonization policy. See Grass, 2:91–135.

their value. One cannot maintain, however, that these people distinguish themselves by rectitude and true refinement!

Among the Old Believers one can study the original national views of the Russians toward other peoples. These old Russians recognize, as it were, only three nations. *Slaviane* (those who speak, those who understand one another) is the name they give to themselves and those peoples related to them by race — the Serbs, Poles, Bohemians, etc. They designate all the peoples of the Occident as *Nemtsy* (the Mutes) — Germans, English, etc. They call all Orientals *Musulmane* (Muslims). The Old Believers do not even recognize the peoples of the West as Christians, since they are not really baptized because they are not immersed. Up to the reign of Peter I this was, moreover, a common opinion in all Russia. Most of the Old Believers do not even recognize the baptismal rite of the Orthodox church as valid but rather rebaptize their converts.

As evidence of their ancestral national views, we include the following anecdote. A member of a sect which repudiates the taking of oaths is inducted into the military and refuses to take the oath of loyalty. "Why don't you want to swear allegiance?" "My religion forbids it. But even if I were allowed to, I would not pledge my allegiance to the man whom you call emperor (*imperator*). I would only swear allegiance to the real tsar, the white tsar. Our books and images depict him as he really looks; he has a crown on his head, the scepter and imperial orb in his hands, and is wrapped in a long golden robe. But this emperor is wearing a hat and uniform and carries a sword at his side like all the soldiers that I've seen. He is one of us rather than the real tsar." I was told that these people were later freed from taking the oath.

One may distinguish three main divisions of sects, the second of which grew out of the first and the third out of the second. The last category has broken up into innumerable splinter-sects.

I. The *Edinovertsy* or *Blagosloveniia* (the Unitarians or the Blessed Ones). The first name was given them by the government and the Russian church, but they designate themselves by the second. There are absolutely no essential differences between their teachings and those of the Russian Orthodox church. The only differences concern ceremonies and symbolic usages. Whereas the Old Believers cross themselves by joining the thumb, the small finger, and the ring finger, the Orthodox use the thumb, index, and middle finger. The Old Believers consider it a sin to shave off one's beard, as does the ordinary Orthodox Russian at the bottom of his heart. The Old

Believers contend that Jesus' name must be pronounced in three syllables. In processions the Old Believers walk around the church clockwise, although the patriarch Nikon established the rule of proceeding counterclockwise. All the Old Believers carry prayer beads and say the rosary, whereas in the Orthodox church this is done only by the monks. During the Easter service the Old Believers sing the Hallelujah only twice; the Orthodox, however, sing it three times. . . . One can hardly conceive how all of this could cause a schism! But this part of the seventeenth century was a time of keen religious hairsplitting. A similar atmosphere prevailed throughout Europe, as is evidenced in the casuistic disputations of the Jesuits and the Protestant theologians. . . .

II. The *Staroobriadtsy*[14] represent the second category. Their teachings are exactly the same as those of the former, but they renounce every tie with the Russian Orthodox church. Hence, rather than permit their members to be ordained by the Russian bishops, they manage with runaway priests who either have been expelled from the church or have deserted. Before they accept these priests, they make them renounce all their ties to the church, whereupon they pray for them. They call this ceremony the *rectification*. The sect is numerous.

III. The *Pomorane*[15] (Dwellers by the Sea) or the *Bespopovtsy* (the Priestless) constitute the third group. Since they no longer have any priests and also no longer consider priests to be necessary, they have split into innumerable small sects which are usually named after their leaders: Filippov, Feodosii, Avvakum; hence, Filippovtsy, Feodosiane, Avvakume, etc. However, they do have definite and close ties to one another and even to the other two divisions of the Old Believers, It is also not improbable that several of the older sects, some of which I consider to be remnants of Gnostic sects, joined with them.

Originally the Bespopovtsy belonged to the second category. These sects came into being either because they were unable, despite their efforts, to find apostate priests or because they doubted the validity of the ordination performed by heretical bishops, even though these priests had deserted the Russian church and had joined them.

According to the Bespopovtsy it is through no fault of their own

14. The reference here is to the Old Believers, that is, followers of Avvakum.

15. The Pomorane or Dwellers by the Sea were named for the Old Believers in the Vyg region whose leader, Andrei Denisov, wrote the *Pomorskie otvety* in 1723 to refute Orthodox missionaries.

that they must do without true priests and consequently without the sacraments which priests alone can administer. Two different theological systems then evolved among them. Some of them regard themselves as Catholics cast upon a desert island. Since they cannot receive the sacraments, they seek to partake spiritually of the blessings of the sacraments through complete submission to God's will, through prayer and piety. They cling firmly to the hope that the other Russians will someday join them, renounce Nikon's errors, and reestablish a true church through a new order of priests and bishops to be ordained and consecrated by the other Eastern Orthodox churches.

The others believe that the reign of the Antichrist began with Nikon and the gradual extinction of the true Orthodox priesthood. The Orthodox Christians must therefore roam about like stray sheep and await the coming of the Lord to deliver them from the Antichrist. One individual expressed this as follows: "The world had four epochs: a spring or a morning, from Adam to the construction of Solomon's temple; a summer or noon, which lasted from then until the time of Christ; an autumn or evening, extending from Christ to Nikon or the Antichrist; now it is winter and night, and this epoch will last until the Lord appears and destroys the kingdom of the Antichrist. We try as best we can to live according to the commandments of Christ and the church. We believe in all seven sacraments but, except for baptism, we do not consider them necessary since it has become impossible to receive them."

As we have said above, these two major sects have split into innumerable subdivisions,* which differ from one another in minor

---

*In one of the small sects the communal ownership of all property has been introduced.[16] They have no permanent marriages but instead they conclude marriage contracts for a certain numbers of years. Since there is no right of inheritance, the children do not belong to the parents but to the community. (Our modern Saint-Simonians, the communists, etc., would do well to attend the practical school of these people.) In the province of Orel a Russian woman owns an estate to which a village with members of this sect belonged. When she tried to convert them, a peasant woman began to debate with her. Since the peasant knew the New Testament by heart, her arguments were so superior that her owner was at a loss for words. And the peasant woman could neither read nor write. The owner ordered her administrator to make further attempts to convert them. He replied, however, that this would run completely against her material interests. Now, he continued, these people are the most industrious and orderly workers and are never drinkers, thieves, liars, or swindlers. Whether they would remain this way if converted is more than doubtful!

16. Communal ownership of property was advocated by a Trans-Volga branch of the Molokane whose members followed the teachings of Akinthiev

details, in usages, nonessential ceremonies, and in the interpretation of the liturgical books. These subdivisions may have had their origin in the divergent practices and the various versions of the liturgical books which grew up in the petty principalities and which Nikon opposed. I had the opportunity to study rather closely two of the splinter sects, the Filippovtsy and the Feodosiane.

In 1837 I became acquainted with the *Filippone* in East Prussia to which approximately four or five hundred of them had emigrated from Poland in 1825. . . . The Filippovtsy, as I have already mentioned, do not have any priests, but instead have church servants or elders (*stariki*).[17] A father singles out one of his sons for the ministry when still a child. The youth is allowed one warm meal a day and can never eat meat, drink alcohol, or marry. As soon as he reaches an appropriate age, a *starik* from the vicinity introduces him to his new congregation; kneeling he recites several prayers with him and then embraces him. With this the *starik* has installed him in office. During the ceremony the *starik* is not permitted to make the sign of the cross over him, since this would resemble an ordination which they do not allow. All the *stariki* have the same rank. There is no differentiation among them, there being no hierarchy. They wear long black woolen robes similar to monks' habits and black caps with red borders. They live solely from alms. The congregation can dismiss them for misconduct, but only after the neighboring *stariki* have closely investigated the matter. Their duties consist of reading, singing the psalms, and praying during divine worship. . . .

Every Filippovets must have a number of sacred images before which he recites his prayers, especially the Lord's Prayer, three times daily. They devoutly observe the fasts of the Greek church: every Wednesday, because Christ was betrayed on Wednesday; every Friday, in memory of His crucifixion; the entire seven weeks before Easter; two weeks before Peter and Paul; two weeks at the end of August; six weeks before Christmas. The drinking of liquor and beer is strictly forbidden. Wine is allowed only if it has been pressed by their co-religionists (all Old Believers). Although forbidden to take oaths, those Filippovtsy who emigrated to Poland and thence to Prussia do submit to a kind of oath. They place the fingers

---

Popov, a Samara peasant. The rite of marriage was restricted by certain Priestless groups and abolished by the Skoptsy.

17. A purely Russian sect named for Daniel Filippov, a mid-seventeenth-century founder of the Skoptsy from the Riazan region whose life is so wrapped in obscurity that his existence has recently been denied by Klibanov (p. 43).

of the right hand in the same position used for making the sign of the cross; they extend their index and middle fingers (symbol of the dual nature of Christ) and join their thumb, ring, and little fingers (symbol of the Trinity). Stepping before a cross, they utter the words, "Zhe, zhe, zhe pravda!" ("It is, it is, it is true!")

I add the following notes on their civil constitution. They have no family names but rather only baptismal names. Nor do they have a real civil code. In general they submit to the laws of the countries where they happen to live. They order their family and communal affairs according to old customs and practices. With the assistance of the heads of several families, their *starik* settles their disputes. Among the spouses there is joint ownership of property, although only the husband has the right of disposition. The surviving partner retains the possession of all the property. Illegitimate children have the right only to their mother's property. Although these children bear no stigma, the fallen woman has to wear a specific type of clothing and must let two braids hang down on her breast. A married woman, on the other hand, wears only one hanging down her back.

The legal concepts of child inheritance, inalienable inheritance, legal majority and legal minority, and trusteeship are alien to them. After the death of their parents, the sons take all the property. Division of property is against custom; rather, it remains a common possession under the control of the eldest. Often this prevails through the next generation. When the property is divided, however, all the brothers receive equal shares and arbitrarily settle with the sisters. If there are no sons, the daughters inherit; if there are no children at all, the near and then distant relatives inherit. If there are no relatives at all, the property reverts to the community. Among the Filippovtsy, as among all Russians, the land cannot be inherited, since it belongs to the community and is divided to the equal benefit of all the male villagers. If the legal arrangements which I have mentioned here prevail among the Filippovtsy in Russia proper or if they first originated in Poland to which the Filippovtsy emigrated many years ago, I do not know. Since their marriages are not recognized in Russia, the children obviously cannot inherit from the fathers. They help each other through legal fictions, donations, and transfers of property before death.

In Russia I got to know the Feodosiane first hand.[18] Through

18. The Feodosiane were named for the Moscow clerk Feodosii Vasiliev, who died in 1711. They were the most puritanical of the Old Believers and distinguished themselves in industrial endeavor. See W. Blackwell, *The Beginnings of Russian Industrialization, 1800–1860* (Princeton, 1969), pp. 215 ff.

the intervention of my above-mentioned friend, a doctor who was on friendly terms with them, I was invited to attend their Sunday morning worship service. We drove to an isolated farmstead and were received at the entrance by the elders. They led us across a wide courtyard to a large one-story building whose exterior was no different from an ordinary house belonging to a Russian aristocrat or manufacturer. We passed through several rooms filled with members of the community, who solemnly greeted us with a deep bow, and then entered a large hall, furnished like a church. . . .

Little by little all the rooms were filled, but only with men, since we had first entered the men's prayer room. (Later we also saw the completely separate women's prayer room and attended their worship service.) The service began when one of the readers stepped up to the pulpit at the right and read in a monotone a long prayer, at the end of which *Gospodi pomilui* ("Lord, have mercy upon us") was repeated forty times. After the prayer the elder of the congregation, who had magnificent long white locks and a beard, stepped before the center pulpit and bowed several times before the iconostasis. He uttered several words to which the chorus at the right and that at the left sang alternate responses. It was a simple chant, sung in unison. Then a reader standing before the pulpit at the left read the Gospel of the day, another reader at the right read the creed. The singing of the *Te Deum* by the choir followed, and the service was concluded with a hymn in praise of Mary. Deep silence, great reverence, and a melancholy solemnity reigned in the congregation.

We were then led through several rooms and across another courtyard to the equally large women's prayer room. This room was arranged in the same way as the men's prayer room; the iconostasis, however, had several different icons. . . . The service in the women's church was essentially the same. Except for us strangers there was only one male in the entire church, who read the Gospel of the day. All of the other readings were given by women, or rather old spinsters who enjoy special respect among the Old Believers. Among the Ural Cossack Old Believers an old unmarried woman is called *Khristova Nevesta*, a bride of Christ. This is certainly more noble and polite than the name "old maids" given them in western Europe, which is an expression of social ridicule. . . . Quite similar to the Muslim women, they wore a long white cloth down their backs which covered the head, forehead, and even the lower part of the face.

After the service, the elders of the community led us into a room with rather modern furnishings and, to make the contrast between old Russian traditions and modern European life complete, they served us champagne and oranges!

In Moscow I became acquainted with the charitable institutions run by these Bespopovtsy. A learned man procured a letter of introduction for me, addressed to one of their elders. . . . After breakfast our host took us to their hospitals which are listed only by their cemeteries in the police registries. Located on a vast site were two huge quadrangles resembling fortresses. High walls with towers and large arched gates stood before us; rising above them were the numerous cupolas of several churches within. The view of the entire complex was impressive. Individual aspects of the architecture were interesting and very original, particularly a magnificent sandstone portal with unusual bas-reliefs. Obviously part of a much older building in Moscow, perhaps an old imperial palace, it was used here as an entrance gate to the women's hospital. Within, the quadrangles were surrounded by a large number of buildings, most of which were adjoining. They served as living quarters for the poor, the elderly, and the sick, as stalls, magazines, kitchens, etc. Standing in the center of the quadrangles were two magnificent churches with numerous cupolas and the same furnishings I described above, namely, an iconostasis but no altar.

First of all we were taken to the gatehouse in which a complete chancery was housed. Such an office is undoubtedly necessary if one considers that there may be more than one thousand persons living in one quadrangle. Generally fifty to sixty individuals, separated according to sex, dwell together in the large halls. An equal number shares a dormitory where each has his own bed, straw mattresses, pillows, and a woolen blanket. The rooms are connected by an open passageway, on either side of which are small separate cells for the gravely ill. A similar passage with cells to the right and left leads to a large prayer room which is furnished exactly like those in the churches described above. In addition to the two churches in the center there were six to eight of these prayer rooms in each quadrangle.

The sick, aged, and infirm without means are fed and cared for at the expense of the community; the more robust have to work a bit for their keep. In general, everyone must attend the worship service in the prayer rooms for ten hours each day; only those who are obliged to work are exempt. The service, which is conducted in the manner described above, continues day and night without interruption; the readers and singers are relieved every two hours.

In the women's quadrangle the readers are, of course, female. Around two hundred men and seven to eight hundred women were cared for in these homes. I did not see any children. All the people here belong to the sect. The poor who stop by and are not members are fed, but they are not permitted to spend the night.

All the facilities may be inferior and crude and cannot be compared in detail with the better organized European hospitals. But one must keep in mind that these basically excellent institutions were organized by people whose cultural level is nowhere near that of the German peasants. They received neither support nor guidance from the government and they have no contact at all with foreigners and the educated classes of other nations. Although they encountered obstacles everywhere, they nevertheless acted on their own initiative and succeeded in founding an institution which in size and wealth surpasses most of the private institutions of this kind. And who are these people? Uncultured Russian peasants without priests, without an aristocracy, without a European education, full of distrust and prejudice against every form of progress! . . . Only the unusually strong associative spirit and the incomparable communal institution of the Great Russian tribe which is an outgrowth of this spirit can explain this organization.

The third category of Russian sects is comprised of those which, obviously influenced by Western religious views, have separated from the Russian church since the reign of Peter I. However, remnants of older Russian sects may also have joined this group and fallen under the new name. Although there may be a large number of sects and subdivisions in this third category, one groups them under the names *Molokane* and *Dukhobortsy*.

These sects do not have a closed ecclesiastical organization and do not even constitute compact social organisms. But they do have a more developed theological and philosophical system than any of the other Russian sects. These systems, however, are capable of such amplification and deviation that one can list a large number of fundamental doctrines found in one community but not in another nearby. . . .

Whereas we could observe among the Old Believers the strictest and most scrupulous adherence to old traditions and the reaction of conservative (although misunderstood) primitive Catholicism, we see among the modern sects reform elements which tend to contradict the fundamental principles of the church. The former stand for a complete petrification of ritual, whereas the latter represent a complete spiritualization of ceremony. . . .

The origin of these Russian sects and their evolution is completely unknown.[19] Traces of individual teachings seem to appear at the beginning of the eighteenth century, although completely developed theological systems cannot be recognized at this time. In 1734 an investigation was conducted in Moscow of an emerging sect which believed in a direct, inner revelation and recognized the sacraments of baptism, Holy Communion, and marriage only in a symbolic sense. While jumping about wildly, the followers of this sect summoned the Holy Ghost which supposedly then dwelt in their limbs; they frequently experienced convulsions and a state of ecstasy and began to prophesy. I suspect that these people belonged to those older sects described above. However, their teachings, though fragmentary, prepared the ground upon which the Molokane and Dukhobortsy constructed their theological system with the help of western European ideas and teachings. The Molokane may well be the older sect. The Dukhobortsy are either a direct outgrowth of the latter or the doctrines of the Molokane provide at least the inspiration for the Dukhobortsy's own teachings. There is, moreover, absolutely no connection between the two. Rather, if they happen to live near each other, they are constantly at odds. Whereas the Old Believers exercise a very considerable political influence in Russia, this is certainly not yet true of these sects. . . .

Up to this day no member of the educated classes has ever belonged to these sects.[20] No Russian clergyman has ever joined or led them. No aristocrat or government official is to be found among them. They are simply ordinary Russian peasants. Not one in a hundred can read, and not one in a thousand can write. Their penetrating logic and their rich imagination are thus all the more remarkable. They testify to the great intellectual abilities which still lie dormant in the common Russian people. Perhaps with the exception of two extremely rare works, they have absolutely no books which contain and present their teachings. Although all is tradition, they are said to have two books. The one is entitled *Keys to Understanding or*

19. Both groups were indirectly descended from the Flagellants (P. Miliukov, *Ocherki po istorii russkoi kultury* [Paris, 1931], p. 122) but did not crystallize until the 1760s in the Tambov and Kozel districts of Tambov province. The social background for both movements is provided by P. G. Ryndziunskii, "Antitserkovnoe dvizhenie v Tambovskom krae v 60-kh godakh XVIII veka," *Voprosy istorii religii i ateizma* (Moscow, 1954), vol. 2.

20. In fact, the Castrator Selivanov attracted many noble adherents during the "golden age" of the sect in Petersburg in the early nineteenth century. See Grass, 1:167–269.

*Mystery*. The other is a kind of compendium of all their teachings. However, hitherto neither the government nor the friends of the Dukhobortsy have succeeded in obtaining them. Members of the sect are extremely secretive about them. Even Mr. Kornies,[21] whom they honor as their benefactor, was unable to see these books, although he offered a considerable sum of money. . . .[22]

The sect of the Molokane proper is small in number. Their theological system is incomplete. Even among themselves there is no unity of opinion on dogma. Very frequently the more zealous Molokane join the Dukhobortsy, who likewise are not in complete agreement but who generally carry their teachings to their logical conclusions.

The Molokane appeared for the first time around the middle of the eighteenth century in the province of Tambov. The people gave them the name *Molokane* (Milk Drinkers) because they drank milk on the holy days. They called themselves *Istinye Khristiane* (True Christians). Soon thereafter they were also discovered in the province of Kharkov. Shortly after the Seven Years' War, there lived in the village of Oshokh in the province of Kharkov a foreigner who, according to some, was a petty Prussian officer who had been taken captive during the war, had learned Russian, and did not want to return home. In a curious way he won the confidence and affection of the people. He became their friend, their advisor, their helper in every need, and their judge in disagreements. Soon he also became their religious teacher. He seems to have found the theological foundations already present in a sect which he joined; otherwise the Russian clergy would certainly not have permitted him to teach without interference. He had neither a house nor desire for one, but rather went from one neighbor to another. Every evening, throughout his life, he gathered the members of the household about him, read to them from the Bible, and interpreted the text. It cannot be ascertained if he was a Quaker as some believe, since even his name is unknown. However, it seems certain that the more logically developed system of the sect stems from him.

On my trip I found members of this sect in the district of Melitopel on the Molochnaia River, located in Tauride province. They had settled in three villages between the Mennonite colonies and the Nogai. The names of the villages were Novo-Vasilevka, Astrakhanka, and Novo-Spasskoe and there were about three thousand members of this sect living there. The villages were pic-

21. On Kornies see below, chap. 6, n. 4.
22. The five preceding sentences have been moved from the original volume 2, p. 400, the remainder of which is not translated here.

turesque and the inhabitants looked prosperous and respectable. I heard them praised as good and sober people, but also as cunning and reserved. Agriculture and cattle raising thrive among them. . . .

Their view of the sacrament of baptism is as follows: "Although we know that Christ was baptized by John in the River Jordan and also that the apostles baptized others with water, notably Philip the Circumcised, nevertheless we do not understand by baptism terrestrial water which merely cleanses the body and not the soul. Rather, we understand by baptism the living, spiritual water which is the belief in the triune God and the complete submission to His holy words. The Redeemer said, 'Streams of living water will flow from the body of him who believeth in me.' John the Baptist said, 'A man can take nothing that is not given him by heaven.' Paul also said, 'Christ did not send me to baptize but to preach.' For this reason we understand by the sacrament of baptism the spiritual cleansing of the sins of our spirit through faith and the death of the old man with his works, so that we are clothed anew through a loyal, irreproachable life. Although we wash a child's bodily impurities with terrestrial water following his birth, we do not recognize this as baptism. We name the child after the calendar day."

They explain the other six sacraments in a similar manner. They do not recognize extreme unction or confirmation in the resolute conviction that according to Christ's teaching they receive a spiritual anointing from above. They maintain that the Eucharist was only a celebration commemorating Christ but that the Gospel is the true spiritual bread of life. "Man does not live by bread, but rather by the eternal word of God." "It is only the spirit which gives life; the flesh is of use to no man." Hence it is not necessary to partake of terrestrial bread and wine. With respect to the sacrament of penance, they observe the words of Paul: "Confess your sins to one another and pray for each other." "This is all that we recognize."

Concerning the sacrament of ordination, they maintain: "We have the bishop and high priest alone in the person of Christ, Who summoned all of us equally. In accordance with the apostolic command we have selected worthy men from our midst, who lead God-fearing lives and whom we call elders. They have been entrusted with reading the word of God and tending to our other needs. We honor and obey them as the apostle Peter instructed."

The sacrament of marriage is received and concluded before the congregation in whose presence the engaged couple expresses their mutual consent to wed. The marriage cannot be dissolved. With respect to the sacrament of unction, they teach: "We do not perform the sacrament of unction, although we know from the Word of God that the apostles healed the sick with oil. We interpret the sacrament of unction as a magnificent and fervent prayer of the faithful for the sick. This is the reason why several of our members always go to the sick and pray."

From all of this one can see that the western European spiritualistic views on the sacraments have infiltrated here. We even find the distinctly Protestant expressions "the death of the old Adam with his works in us, in order to be clothed anew, etc.," phrases which would never have grown up independently on Russian soil and which would never have found expression in the Russian language. Nevertheless, one can see that the entire spiritualistic edifice is constructed on the foundations of the Eastern Catholic church. They still have the seven old sacraments, whereas the Quakers, who emerged from an already established Protestantism, recognize only two sacraments which are interpreted symbolically.

They observe the fasts before Christmas and Easter and also during the week, as often as the individual feels the need and for as long as he can hold out. But it is real fasting and not simply abstinence from meat, as is the custom in the Russian church.

In conclusion, they discuss their concept of the church which they recognize solely as an assembly of true believers according to the words of Christ: "Where two or three are gathered in my name, I am present among them." They do not approve of material churches, buildings made of stone or wood. "Solomon built a House of God, but the Almighty does not live in temples made by human hands, etc." . . . The conclusion of their confession has a distinctly old Protestant ring, and almost appears to be a translation from the German. "In addition to the Holy Sacraments we recognize the word of God and the inner faith. We do not consider ourselves to be without sin or to be saints. We work toward our redemption with fear and trembling in the hope of attaining salvation only through our belief in Jesus Christ, only begotten son of God, and the fulfillment of the Lord's commandments. We cannot attain salvation through our own efforts, but we receive our strength only from the living faith in our intercessor and Savior, Jesus Christ."

Curiously enough, I found among these Molokane a translation of Jung-Stilling's writings.[23] I was told that the passages dealing

23. The translation to which Haxthausen refers is Heinrich Jung-Stilling, *Toska po otchizne*, 5 vols. (Moscow, 1817–18). At the end of volume 5

with a thousand-year reign of peace on earth are of particular interest to them. They interpret these passages as a reference to themselves, the chosen people, who will rule together with Jesus Christ. As a result, it seems that in 1833 a certain Terentii Belizhorev felt a call to appear as a prophet, to teach repentance to the Molokane and to announce the dawn of the millennium, which was to begin when two and a half years had passed. He ordered them to stop all business and labor except for that which was absolutely necessary and to devote themselves exclusively to singing and prayer. When asked to identify himself, he declared that he was the prophet Elijah, who preceded the coming of the Lord, and that his companion Enoch was presently in the Occident also preaching repentance. He even designated the day when he would reascend into heaven before their very eyes. The day of his ascension arrived. Several thousand Molokane, some of whom had even come from other parts of Russia, had assembled. Terentii appeared on a cart and commanded everyone to kneel and pray. But when, after praying, with outstretched arms he tried to ascend into heaven, he fell pitiably into the multitude, injuring a woman. Great tumult broke out; the Molokane, who by now had come to their senses, accused him of being an impostor, tied him up, and took him to the district court. Up to this point he continued to insist that he really was the prophet Elijah. The chains with which he was bound were, according to him, the best proof of this. However, after having reflected for a time in prison, he forgot completely that he was Elijah. After his release, though, he preached on the millennium until his death. He left a rather large number of followers who often assembled for several consecutive days and nights to sing and pray. Frequently some of them received an inspiration, stamped their feet, gasped for breath, fell into convulsions, and prophesied. They introduced communal ownership of property. After some years, however, they emigrated to Georgia, with the government's permission. There, with the rainbow surrounding Noah's ark on majestic Mount Ararat in view, they met the Würtemberg Lutherans, who were also awaiting the millennium!

The Molokane living on the Molochanaia are accused of regarding their three villages as an inviolable refuge based on the fourth book of Moses, chapter 35:6, and of granting asylum to every escaped criminal. One has found counterfeiters, passport forgers, monks

---

is a list of subscribers to the publication in which are to be found the names of a number of peasants.

escaped from their cloisters, etc., among them. For this reason the police search them now and again.

In general the Molokane are peaceful and quiet, although occasionally there are still outbreaks of fanaticism. In the vicinity of Nikolaev shortly before I was in the province of Saratov, a Molokan had leapt into the ranks of a procession, snatched the sacred image, thrown it to the ground, and trampled it with his feet. After the initial shock, the people quickly overpowered him and without hesitation put him to death.

Among the Molokane the vague legends of the extraordinary exploits of a Western hero continue to live on. When Napoleon embarked upon his Russian campaign, they believed that he was the Lion of the Valley of Josaphat mentioned in their old psalms. He was to come to overthrow the false emperor and to restore the throne of the white tsar. The Molokane from the province of Tambov selected a deputation which, dressed in white robes, was sent out to greet him. In 1812 these people pushed southward through Little Russia and Poland as far as the Vistula, where they were captured. One of them escaped and returned to his people. Nothing was ever heard of the others.

Whereas one must certainly recognize the Molokane as a Christian sect, this is no longer true of the extreme groups among the Dukhobortsy. The origin of the Dukhobortsy is even more obscure than that of the Molokane.* It seems, however, that the Dukhobortsy are the more recent sect and that they emerged separately from the Molokane in various places and with different teachings, which merely have a common point of view. Only because of the latter circumstance were they given the same name.

The name *Dukhobortsy* is said to have been given them by Archbishop Ambrosius of Ekaterinoslav, who conducted research on their teachings around 1785. *Dukh* means spirit or light, *bor*, to struggle or to fight. The name can have a double meaning: fighter against or for the spirit, fighter against or for the light. The archbishop probably meant it in the first sense; the sectarians themselves adopted it with its second meaning and since then have liked to call themselves fighters for the spirit. The Russian people, however, call them

---

*The Dukhobortsy themselves know nothing of their origin and history. They simply claim to be descended from three youths who were burned in a furnace because they did not want to worship Nebuchadnezzar's image. Hitherto no written documents, chronicles, etc., have ever been found in their possession.

Freemasons.* Formerly they were occasionally called *Shchelniki*
and *Ikonobortsy* (Iconoclasts).

The Dukhobortsy seem to have been discovered for the first time
in the province of Ekaterinoslav. But soon thereafter they appeared
in every part of Russia, in Old Finland, on the island of Ösel,
in Moscow, in Kaluga, in Kursk, in Voronezh, in Kharkov, in
Tambov, in Saratov, among the Don Cossacks, in the Caucasian
provinces, in Irkutsk in Siberia, and even on Kamchatka. It is highly
curious that a number of Mordvines, a Finnish tribe, converted
to this sect. They left their fellow tribesmen and moved to the
Molochnaia to join the other Dukhobortsy.[24] (See von Köppen, *Über
einige Landesverhältnisse zwischen dem untern Dnjepr und dem
Asowschen Meere*, Petersburg, 1845, p. 56.) . . .

With respect to their entire way of life, the teachings of the
Dukhobortsy assume two distinct directions, depending upon whether
they attach greater importance to the recovery from original sin
and a life of expiation or to the belief in the inner Christ. The
former is the dark, mystic, and ascetic tendency, the second the
joyful tendency based on the peace and tranquility of God's presence
within us. The moral code of the first is the stricter. According
to them the passions are the basic source of evil in man. Since
this world is the place where the soul is punished for the first fall,
and since the body is the prison of the soul, the world and all
its joys are to be despised; all the pleasures of the flesh are useless
and to be avoided. All passions are to be condemned, including
expressions of those which are not criminal but commendable and
beneficial in society. Hence the striving for fame and honor, for
example, is strictly forbidden, because it has its roots in pride, the
cause of the first fall. They condemn all sensual pleasures, "even
the pure joys of nature, the flowers of the earth, the song of the
birds, as beautiful and innocent as their enjoyment may be, so as

*How remarkable! At the same time the Illuminati were haunting western
Europe! What a mysterious instinct the people possessed to call these
Dukhobortsy ("fighters for light" or "illuminati") Freemasons! A book
by Saint Martin, recognized as a classic by the French Freemasons, *Des
erreurs et de la vérité*, develops the fundamental teaching of the fall of
the soul before the creation of the present world almost exactly as did
the Dukhobortsy. . . .

24. The Molochnaia River area, north of the Sea of Azov, became a
center of the Dukhobor group because many were attracted there by Moravian
settlers, to whose religion their own bore a strong resemblance.

not to attract and to occupy our spirit. Seduced and inflamed by them, our spirit would remain tied to the earth and could not soar."

The adherents of the second tendency, which they designate as a higher development, do not at all approve of this austere, somber, moral philosophy. They do not deny the truth of this moral code, but they maintain that it applies only to those who have not reached the level of inner faith. "If our faith is truly alive in us, we receive Christ. He is awakened in us, and we become Christ, we become God. Sin is then an impossibility. Everything we do is good because God does it in us. Even if it should have the outward appearance of vice, it becomes a good work as soon as we do it. However, everything which others, nonbelievers or heretics, do is a sin, even that which appears to be good." . . .

It is obvious that they do not recognize the external sacraments. They give their inner sacraments a far more mystical and symbolical meaning than do the Molokane. In the confession of 1791 the sacrament of marriage is taken very seriously, even though the ceremony is rejected as being nonessential. The Dukhobortsy living on the Molochnaia expressed a very frivolous opinion on the subject. "Marriage is based on the consent of the engaged couple; the basis for its perpetuation is love, whose nature is divine. It must be possible to dissolve the marriage if the married couple consents, or if they no longer love each other. If the love ceases, the divine foundation of the marriage has crumbled and the continuation of the purely sexual relationship would be sinful."

Of course, the Dukhobortsy do not recognize the sacrament of ordination or a special priesthood. "Everyone who is truly enlightened by the Word can and must pray to God for himself." At the conclusion of the confession of 1791, there is this significant verse. . . .

> What am I finally? A temple to honor God,
> Building and priest, and also the offering should I be.
> Let our heart be the altar, our will the offering,
> Our spirit the priest, in fulfillment of the commandments.

It is clear from this that the Dukhobortsy do not have any churches and actually are not allowed to have them. Also they do not have a congregational worship service, since everyone is completely alone in his relationship to God. (At their meetings, they can instruct each other, but in principle there can be no common prayer.) Nevertheless, the natural instinct toward sociability is stronger than principles, and they actually do have a common worship service. Here and there they have prayer rooms, which, however, are completely bare. There is no decoration or image and not even a cross or symbol. In the center stands a table with bread and salt. The Dukhobortsy in the province of Tambov assembled on certain days in a room such as this. The men stood on one side, the women on the other, in rows according to age. They began singing a hymn which was pieced together from various fragments borrowed mostly from the Book of the Prophets. (All of their hymns, psalms, and prayers are taken from the Bible, but they always piece them together in the most unique way from single sentences. They never use an entire psalm of David, for example.) After the hymn, the second oldest man approaches the first oldest; both bow to each other twice, kiss each other, and bow a third time. The third man bows to the first two, kisses them, whereupon the fourth does likewise and so on down to the last man. The women then repeat the same ceremony among themselves. According to the Dukhobortsy, this ceremony is supposed to contain a confession of the Trinity and its presence in each of them. When they visit each other, they also greet one another in this way and recite the words, "I am the Lord Thy God; Thou shalt have no other gods beside me!" . . .

# 6
# The Mennonites

Early on the morning of the twenty-third, we reached the Dnieper and crossed it on a German ferry. Instead of being placed crosswise on the ferry as is the Russian custom, a procedure involving untold effort, the carriage drove slowly straight onto the boat. I do not understand why the Russians, who are so practical in handling everything, cling to their absurd practice. Here German colonists tended the ferry, and we soon reached the colony of Rosenthal, which belongs to the large German Mennonite settlement in the district of Khortitsa. So very German were all the surroundings that at once we felt that we were back on the West Prussian lowlands along the Vistula. Not only were the people, their character, their language, their dress, their dwellings and household furnishings German, but every dish and container, and even the domestic animals, the Pomeranian and the poodle, the cow and the goat as well. The colonists even know how to give nature itself a German appearance. The artist who paints local landscapes here would easily be able to pass them off as German. The fields are laid out and cultivated in the German manner; the farmlands and meadows are enclosed with German fences. Everything is German: the villages with all their individual farmsteads, the gardens and their arrangement, the plants, the vegetables, and above all the potatoes. This was not at all the case in the German colony on the Volga, where the people had remained German only in language, dress, and customs. Everything about them had a much more Russian character but with the addition of German comforts.

# The Mennonites

This flourishing German colony of seventeen villages was founded by and is inhabited by Mennonites exclusively. The Mennonites are a sect that originated during the Reformation. In setting forth the principle that the written word or the Bible alone could be the basis of the Christian faith and Christian doctrine, Luther repudiated the tradition and the authority of the church and its living representatives, the pope and the bishops or councils. Very soon many of his former followers challenged his conception of faith and dogma, used the principle of free inquiry which he advocated against him, and dissociated themselves from him. The most extreme of these sectarians, as they were called, were the Anabaptists, so named because, among other things, they did not recognize the validity of infant baptism. If one did not recognize the authority of tradition and the practices sanctioned by the church, so they contended, then infant baptism could not be justified according to the letter of the Bible and was actually inefficacious. According to them the words, "Whoever does not believe although he be baptized," etc., presuppose that one must first believe before one can receive the sacrament of baptism. With the words, "Suffer the little children to come unto me," and "If you are not as little children, you will not attain eternal life," Christ said that it was not necessary for children to be baptized to attain salvation. And they were unbaptized children! These sectarians were soon persecuted, and there grew up among them the teachings of a Kingdom of Christ here on earth, of Christian freedom, and so on. In the city of Münster in Westphalia they won the upper hand over the Lutherans and actually began to organize this so-called Kingdom of Christ. Their leaders were fanatics, and atrocities soon caused the temporal authorities to march against them. After offering desperate resistance, they were defeated. Their leaders succumbed to the temporal sword.

Soon thereafter a cleric in Friesland, Menno Simons,[1] revived the religious teachings of the Anabaptists in a more spiritual, milder, and, indeed, more Christian form. He rejected above all the doctrine of the temporal Kingdom of Christ. Indeed, he set forth the very opposite principle of complete passivity. Not only did he declare it erroneous to want to usher in the Kingdom of Christ by force and violence, but he taught that the Kingdom of Christ was a kingdom of suffering. Not only should one not bear arms, but one must

1. Menno Simons (1496–1561) was a Dutch priest from Friesland who in 1536 renounced his vows, joined the already flourishing Anabaptist movement, and gradually assumed leadership of it. See *The Mennonite Encyclopedia* 3: 577–84 for biographical sketch and bibliography.

also remain passive if attacked, bear every insult, pain, injury, and even death without resistance.

Despite tribulation and persecution, Menno Simons found many followers, particularly in Friesland and Holland. Harassment caused a large number of them to emigrate between 1540 and 1550 from Friesland and Holland to West Prussia, where they settled on the lowlands along the Vistula. At first the Polish kings issued several decrees against them, but later they received privileges. (One privilege which they still enjoy dates back to 1642, although it is based on even earlier ones.) Prussia's warlike kings were most irritated by the fact that the Mennonites, for religious reasons, did not want to serve in the military.* In those areas where they lived, they were, of course, tolerated and protected, but they had to buy their exemption from military service with a separate tax paid to the military schools. Also, they were not permitted to acquire more property than they already possessed. Otherwise, given their diligence and love of order, they could be expected to spread out far too much. Whoever was willing to renounce the principle of refusing military service, however, was freed from all these restrictions.

Among the strict Mennonites, farming is a religious duty which no one can shirk without cause, for the Bible says, "In the sweat of thy face shalt thou eat bread." There were several reasons why the Mennonites agreed to let those emigrate who were unable to find a suitable place to settle in their native land. First of all, as a result of the above-mentioned restrictions, it had become extremely difficult to acquire property; second, because of their scattered location, the Mennonite farms could not be conveniently divided; moreover, a division was inconsistent with their customs and practices. Third, there had been a considerable increase in the population. By paying the emigration tax, they received permission to leave from the Prussian government and turned to the Russian government, which readily accepted them.

The first emigration took place in 1783. It is not certain where they went at first.[2] They probably settled in the Russian part of

---

*Based on strict rite, the catechumens must promise before being baptized, "in accordance with Christian duty, not to rule and not to bear arms." In conformity with the lax observance now generally accepted, only the following declaration is required: "It is better to obey than to rule and better to suffer than to defend oneself." In North America they have abandoned this principle and have entered the military. Since then their humility has disappeared and they have become more boisterous and licentious than other communities. See *Evangelisches Magazin*, Philadelphia, 1812.

2. In the early 1780s Catherine opened her southern border to foreign

Poland where a Mennonite colony of two villages still exists near Ostroga. From here the majority of these settlers, after having been joined by many from West Prussia, seem to have moved to the Dnieper, 60 versts south of Ekaterinoslav. Here the government allotted the newcomers, who numbered 330 families or approximately 1,650 individuals, 32,648 desiatins, or almost 105 square miles. Every family was to receive 65 desiatins with the rest held in reserve for new families. These Mennonites were by no means poor; nevertheless, to help them establish themselves, the government loaned them the considerable sum of 341,800 silver rubles (1,196,300 rubles banco), of which 30,000 silver rubles still have to be repaid. . . .

Owing to its proximity to the Dnieper, the terrain of the colonies is not flat but hilly. All the villages lie in the small valleys and glens, since there is absolutely no water on the high ground. The villages Kronsweide and Einlage are very attractively situated among high rocky hills close to the Dnieper.[3] Although the soil is very fertile and requires but little tilling, the climate and weather, especially drought, often dash all hopes for a good harvest. . . . Wheat seldom does well, but a good deal is grown nevertheless because it guarantees relatively high prices, often three times more than rye. . . . The cheapness of grain induces the settlers to keep a huge stock of poultry. Because of the shoals the navigation of the Dnieper upstream is impractical; downstream the river silts up more and more. Only cattle raising is profitable. Dairy and meat products find such a ready market because the Russians and Tatars living nearby prefer the German preparation of meat, butter, and cheese to any other but do not imitate it themselves.

The colony does not own its own forests, but they do have an island in the Dnieper with a good stand of timber. In addition they grow as many trees as they can in the valleys and gorges, so that they have the necessary amount of timber and some firewood. They

---

colonists and sent recruiters abroad to attract them. In October 1786 the first Mennonite legates arrived, Jakob Hoeppner and Johann Bartsch. The first charter to the Mennonites was issued in 1788 and Hoeppner and a group of Danzig Mennonites left for Russia in March of that year. See Adolph Ehrt, *Das Mennonitentum in Russland* (Langensalza, 1932), chaps. 1 and 2; P.M. Friesen, *Die Alt-Evangelische Mennonitische Brüderschaft in Russland, 1789–1910* (Halbstadt, 1911).

3. Kronsweide and Einlage were two small villages in the Khortitsa settlement, whose capital was Neu Kronsweide. Other villages included Schönweise, Kronsgarten, Insel Khortitsa, Neu Schönweise, and Iakovlevo. All were broken up and renamed during World War II.

now have fine orchards; formerly the melon had to serve as a substitute for all other fruit. . . .

The seventeen villages constitute one community under a common administration. The earnings from the communal sheep farm, the Dnieper ferry, the tax on the brewery and the distillery constitute common income. They have a communal granary, a fire insurance company, two churches, and a school in each village. The community house, the seat of the communal office, which is presided over by a director, is located in the village of Khortitsa. A colony clerk, who knows German and Russian, assists him.

After a sojourn of several hours we left this settlement in order to visit the newer Mennonite colonies on the Molochnaia. They are located about eighty to ninety versts to the south. Toward evening we reached a village of this group named Halbstadt, where a rich Mennonite accorded us a friendly and hospitable reception. Early the next morning, Sunday, the twenty-fourth of July, we drove to Orlov, the seat of the district office, which is an hour's distance from Halbstadt. We were given a friendly welcome in an attractive, neat farmhouse. Since the worship service was just about to begin, we entered the church or rather the great prayer room. This was the first time I had attended a Mennonite service. The prayer room was completely bare. It had no altar but only a raised platform for the preacher as well as ordinary pews. The service began with a hymn (they borrowed the early Lutheran hymns), which was followed by the sermon. The Mennonites have no educated preachers. Rather the community selects one of its members for this position and he has to accept. He receives no salary unless he is very poor or unless this position would keep him from earning a livelihood. This was one reason that I was all the more astonished at the sermon. The speaker had obviously not memorized it, nor had he worked it out completely, for at a most suitable point he directed his attention to us. . . . The sermon was intelligent, logical, natural, simple, free of any inanity and in good, correct German. How is it possible for a simple, uneducated peasant to give such a grammatically flawless sermon, surpassing those of hundreds of "learned" preachers whom I have heard? The answer lies in the force of traditional Christianity, in which the older generation instructed the younger among people who otherwise reject the tradition of the church! All the sects that have broken with the church can never completely free themselves of the essence of Catholicism, which is tradition.

Upon returning home, we met a man who without a doubt is one of the most interesting personalities now living among the Germans in Russia. As a very young lad, Johann Kornies,[4] a native of West Prussia, moved to the Molochnaia with his parents at the beginning of the century. He received no schooling in his youth, but he had a clear, unprejudiced mind, a keen practical intelligence, a loving heart, and deep emotions. He educated himself to such a degree that one must recognize him as a man of the highest culture. And while he became one of the most influential personalities of southern Russia solely through his intellectual superiority, his rectitude, and his reliability, he has remained in his entire being, in his family, and in his way of life the homely, simple, and unassuming peasant. At any moment the Russian emperor could appoint him governor of the province and he would be the right man for the job. But Kornies himself wants to be nothing more than a Mennonite peasant, who at his baptism promised "in accordance with Christian duty not to rule and not to bear arms." He has no rank or order. To live up to his religious duty, he would have to reject both, even though he might well deserve them more than many a starred official in Russia! Just how powerful his personality must be, can nowhere be more clearly seen than in Russia, where no one is of consequence without rank and order. Even the governor of all southern Russia, the noble Prince Vorontsov, would not be likely to take measures concerning the internal administration of this region without asking the advice of J. Kornies.

We spent the day thoroughly inspecting the local colony. We examined almost every house and farmstead, the farm implements, the cattle, the garden, and the crops, etc.

The next day, the twenty-fifth of July, I drove with Mr. Kornies to Akeima, a neighboring Nogai Tatar village. I was not a little surprised to see a completely German village after the Mennonite model. Mr. Kornies had trained the Tatars in laying out their villages in this manner and had helped them in every way. The Tatars had already built a large number of villages according to his instructions. Other persons, not Mr. Kornies himself, told me that he had already

---

4. Johann Kornies (1789–1848) was brought to the Molochnaia River settlement in 1804 by his parents and eventually became the chief mediator between the community and the Russian government. He was a corresponding member of the Scientific Committee of the Ministry of State Domains and Russified his name to Ivan Ivanovich Kornis. See *Zhurnal ministerstva gosudarstvennykh imushchestv*, 1848, chap. 29, pp. 220–31.

settled seventeen thousand Tatars in this manner. Again in this village we saw a deputation from a large number of nomadic Tatars who came to him and said, "You are the father of our people. Be our father, too, and help us, as you have helped the others."

All the houses in the village were completely alike and sturdily built. They had chimneys and stood in enclosed yards. Before the house door there were usually a couple of poplars and to the right and left small flower beds. In the gardens we found a large number of grafted fruit trees; in the yard there were plows, harrows, and carts like those of the Mennonites. In one corner of the yard there was a large pile of very neatly stacked manure bricks which are used as fuel.

The owner of the farm, a handsome, husky Tatar who was the head of the village, received Mr. Kornies cordially and respectfully and led us into the house. The furnishings were also modeled after those of the Mennonites; the kitchenware and living room furniture were not plentiful and old-fashioned as among the Mennonites but yet not particularly mean. There were tables and chairs, pots and pails, and even a pancake pan. Our host complied with my wish to see the women in their native attire which, requested of a Moslem, is actually most improper. He left the house and returned in a quarter of an hour with his three women dressed in their best. As with all Moslem women, all but the eyes was closely concealed. They were young, but short, fat, and unattractive.

From here we drove to a large dairy farm established and owned by Mr. Kornies. Along the way we passed some flourishing forests and nurseries laid out by him. Plantings of oaks and elms, on and around a high kurgan,[5] were doing excellently, which was all the more astonishing since they were particularly exposed to the steppe winds. The dairy farm built by him measured several thousand desiatins. The buildings, which were constructed of brick, were all new; there was an excellent stock of West Prussian cattle and an improved breed of sheep. Beginning on one side of the farm were his seedlings and tree plantings. One could find here every possible variety of tree; each had its field where it was seeded, another where it was seeded, another where it was first planted out, and a third where the largest trees were permanently planted. The young plants from the first two fields were sold. Almost all the chief varieties of trees appeared to thrive splendidly, although

5. *Kurgan* is a Turkic word for the large burial tumuli which dot the landscape of the southern Ukraine.

it seemed to me that the deciduous trees did better than the conifers. Mr. Kornies's brother administered this estate.

The longer one stays among the Mennonites, the more impressed one must be by their confiding, fraternal relationships. It is not that ceremonious politeness common among the Russian peasants, nor is it that tenderness expressed with kisses and embraces which manifests itself among the Russian peasants as soon as whiskey has gone to their heads. They are genuine German peasants who are stiff and awkward in their movements, taciturn and independent. But when it comes to doing something, one sees them willing at any moment to help and support each other.

Nowhere is the complete equality of men, based on a principle (in this case a religious principle) more evident than among the Mennonites. Since farming is a religious duty for them, no one can be more or less than a farmer. Every trade, craft, and business is included in this term and is related to farming. Their governing and administrative officials and even their preachers are not only of peasant background, they are themselves peasants.

The existing equality is most clearly expressed in the relationship between masters and servants. I became particularly aware of this as I observed the relationship between Mr. Kornies and the farmhand who was our driver. In the outward forms of politeness it was very like the relationship of a son to his father rather than that of a servant to his master.

When I mentioned this to Mr. Kornies, he replied, "Among us it is the rule that everyone, including the son of the wealthiest farmer, works for a couple of years as a farmhand for his neighbor. Being a farm laborer is not a social class among us, but a school, a period which prepares one for life. A younger brother of mine worked for me as a farmhand for several years and is now my administrator. We pay our farmhands, both male and female, a very high wage of 30 to 70 silver rubles and uphold this as a custom; no one is then at a disadvantage. In this way even a poor man has the opportunity to accumulate a small fortune, to set up a small farm here, where there is still vacant, fertile land everywhere, and often to become an owner himself. It is, moreover, common for the daughters of wealthy farmers to marry a servant of the farm, even a poor one, if he is upright and industrious. My daughter can also marry whomever she wants, even a servant provided she likes him and he is upright."

Mr. Kornies had only one son and one daughter, a pretty eighteen-year-old girl who was not yet baptized. It is said that he is worth well over a million rubles! This is not to say that wealth and poverty do not often act as a barrier even among the Mennonites and that some individuals are not arrogant because of their wealth and are also guilty of other vices. I was told, for example, of all kinds of evils that existed among the Mennonites in the district of Khortitsa. But at least these attitudes do not meet with approval in the public morality and customs of the people. They are exceptions rather than the rule.

We ate lunch at Mr. Kornies's; the meal was very tasty, genuine home cooking. Everything put on the table, even the wine, was a product of his own farm. The kitchenware and furniture were old-fashioned and sturdy. His wife and daughter did not eat with us. Rather, his wife remained in the kitchen and arranged the meal while his daughter, following an age-old German custom, waited on the guests.

On the twenty-sixth of July, I drove with Mr. Kornies to the other German colonies, which were inhabited mostly by Württembergian peasants, etc. Here there is neither the order and discipline nor the wealth and comfort found among the Mennonites. These colonies were very stunted for a long time. However, recently they have recovered somewhat and in several villages there are the beginnings of prosperity. . . .

From Mr. Kornies I received very detailed statistics on the local Mennonite colony which I shall include here only as they provide insight into the economic conditions of this interesting settlement.

Encouraged by the successful settlement in the district of Khortitsa another 347 Mennonite families in West Prussia decided in 1803 to emigrate to Russia.[6] The Russian government assigned to them for settlement a district on the Molochnaia. These first immigrants founded seventeen villages in 1804 and 1805. Sixteen villages were established and from that time to the present another eleven, the last of which was founded just several years ago.

Over the years, the Russian government granted these forty-four villages the right to use a territory of 96,812 desiatins. But the industrious colonists were not satisfied with this. From their neighbors, the Tatars, the German colonies, the Molokane, and

6. This first migration to the Molochnaia River area north of the Sea of Azov consisted of families from Rosenort and was led by Elder Cornelius Warkentin; initially they settled the towns of Halbstadt and Gnadenfeld. See Ehrt, chaps. 1 and 2; Friesen; and *The Mennonite Encyclopedia* under village names.

the Dukhobortsy they bought an additional 48,446 desiatins. Lastly, the emperor gave them another 3,500 desiatins to be used for a special purpose. The entire territory now measures 148,767 desiatins or about 628 square miles. In 1838 the male inhabitants numbered 5,521. In 1842, however, there were 2,517 families with 6,334 males and 6,227 females. Of these families, 1,041 were farmers, 938 day laborers, and 538 merchant and artisan families. Eighty-four children of colonists served as farmhands as did 242 Russian workers. . . .

Since they were aware of the fortune and the entire situation of their brothers in the district of Khortitsa they had prepared themselves thoroughly for their move. They brought along cattle, sheep, horses, and wagons which they had loaded with beds, all kinds of kitchenware, and furniture. In order to find sufficient forage, they had to split up into several convoys as they moved on through Poland. They did not need any loans from the government to establish themselves. Some had 10,000 to 20,000 ducats in cash with them. The first 347 families to immigrate had all together 150,000 ducats.

The villages were laid out very regularly; each farm was given a forty-fathom frontage [about 230 feet] and between two farms there was always a space of fourteen fathoms [about 77 feet]. From the government they received a ten-year tax exemption and the promise never to be forced to serve in the military. Every family engaged in farming received the use of 65 desiatins. Up to now 68,052 desiatins of the 96,812 granted by the government have been distributed among the families already living here, and 28,769 are being reserved for future settlement. Of those 68,052 desiatins, 26,018 are under cultivation and the rest are used for growing hay and grazing.

The taxes paid by the Mennonites amount to: (1) in lieu of *obrok*, 4 2/7 silver kopeks on every desiatin of land as well as special land taxes of 3/4 silver kopek per desiatin; (2) a head tax of 60 silver kopeks paid by every able-bodied male and female between the ages of fourteen and sixty.

One can see that the system of taxation here is set up completely differently from that in the rest of Russia. I suspect, however, that the crown imposes the head tax and *obrok* in the usual way based on the number of Revision "souls" but that it has permitted the Mennonites to pay the amount owed in a lump sum and to divide the tax burden among themselves in the above manner. The district office annually determines the amount of tax, collects it, and turns it over to the crown treasury. In 1842, of the 6,434 male souls only 4,976 between the ages of fourteen and sixty had to pay taxes; 314 were not required to pay because they still enjoyed the ten-year tax exemption.

A tax of 30 silver kopeks was imposed on every hearth to cover the salary of the district elder, the scribe, etc., and 14 silver kopeks was levied on every able-bodied soul for upkeep of the communal possessions.

There were 1,779 houses, or rather farmsteads, for the Mennonites brought along from West Prussia the custom of constructing the living quarters, the barn, and the stables under one roof. Such a farmstead is usually built in such a way that two wings meet at a right angle. Located in one wing are the living quarters and some of the stables and in the other the barn. . . .

The following plan has been established for farming the land. The private property (48,446 desiatins) purchased by individual colonists can be used for growing crops or other purposes as the owners choose. The 65 desiatins assigned to each farmstead by the crown (68,052 desiatins in total) belong permanently to the community, which determines their agricultural disposition. The four-course method, which had already existed, has been systematized since 1838. Twenty-five of the 65 desiatins belonging to each farmer are set aside as plowland, three parts of which are used annually for growing grain while one part lies fallow; about one-sixth of the fallow land is planted with potatoes. In the fall of 1842, 1,599 measures of winter wheat were sown and in the spring of 1843, 13,402 measures of spring wheat. The extent of the meadows varies greatly in the different villages, depending on the nature of the soil. Every farm has between 6 and 10 desiatins of meadow land. Every farmer is free, however, to use the hay fields as meadow land, as private pasture, or as plowland. The rest of the territory is set aside as common grazing land for each village, whereby the number of cattle which each farmer can drive to pasture is fixed. The number varies between twenty-five and thirty full-grown cattle for every farmer; two foals or heifers, four pigs or calves, or six sheep count as one cow.

In 1842 the following implements were on hand in the colonies: 1,518 plows, 2,314 harrows, 2,775 carts, and, as an indication of progressive economic efforts, 89 threshers driven by horses and 42 machines for harvesting flax, 38 of which were driven by horses and 4 by manpower.

These Mennonites display a great deal of intelligence and judgment in farming their land. In no way do they cling to old practices but instead, after careful consideration, they keep pace with all improvements.

When they first arrived here forty years ago, there was not a tree to be seen in the entire area. At that time they used straw, rush, burgan (a huge plant that grows on the steppes), and manure bricks for fuel. Today their woodlands and saplings provide them with some firewood. In the past several years they have begun to use the dung as fertilizer rather than for making manure bricks. In this way they have succeeded in increasing the fertility of the soil and in reducing significantly the amount of fallow land. Kornies declared that in 1843 the fields of the colonists which had been fertilized and carefully cultivated produced four, five, and six times more than those which had been worked only according to the former, established methods. Crop failures, which were formerly very common, occur seldom on carefully cultivated fields; in the past ten years there has been no crop failure. As I have mentioned in the case of Khortitsa, there used to be an especially frequent failure of the wheat crop. Now the amount of wheat grown is increasing each year; in 1842 nearly 1,547 more desiatins were planted than three years previously. This year an additional 2,000 desiatins were used as plowland. To protect the fields against storms and the inclement climate, some trees have been planted on the fields, especially mulberry trees, and in some places also as hedges. . . . The Mennonites grow a lot of potatoes, even as fodder. The Russians living nearby have gradually adopted from them the practice of raising potatoes. Mr. Kornies, above all, deserves the credit for having introduced the potato to the Nogai Tatars. As late as 1838 the Nogai hardly knew potatoes by name. With the exception of Ackerman, the village nearest the Mennonites, not a single potato was planted in any of the seventy-five Nogai villages located here. But in 1843, when they had a bad grain harvest, their diet already consisted almost entirely of potatoes.

A sufficient amount of flax is grown to satisfy their needs. In the winter of 1842, about 2,571 persons were engaged in spinning the flax and weaving linen. . . .

The Mennonites have begun to improve their meadows through irrigation. Theirs were the only irrigated fields that I saw in Russia. I am firmly convinced that through irrigation Russian agriculture would make the most promising and, for the present time, the only possible profitable progress. In the spring 1,384 desiatins of meadow land had already been irrigated by means of banks of earth, and the yield of hay doubled.

*171*

The Mennonites also grow some tobacco. Count Vorontsov had sent them Albanian tobacco seeds, which thrived there. For the so-called little people, who have only garden plots which they work by hand, the raising of tobacco could be very important.

The growing of fruit is beginning to become very significant. Each of the 1,041 great farmers has been allowed to take one desiatin of his land out of the agricultural plan and to use it as a fruit and vegetable garden. It has been estimated that each one could have 500 fruit trees. (The owners of the older gardens now sell fresh fruit for 200 to 300 rubles banco annually.) . . . The Russians living nearby were inspired by their example and also began to take up growing fruit. . . .

Most important, however, for the future of southern Russia are the woodlands belonging to these colonies, since they offer practical proof of the feasibility of turning certain areas of the steppes into forests. After isolated attempts had been made to plant all kinds of small seedlings, regular plantings started in 1834. Each of 857 farmers living in thirty-nine colonies set aside half a desiatin as woodland, of which one-third was to be planted with mulberry trees and the rest with other varieties. In 1842, 163 of the 428½ desiatins had already been planted with twenty-nine different kinds of trees. In 1843 more than 2,300,000 trees had been planted, excluding the private woodlands belonging to Mr. Kornies. . . .

For the support of their community the Mennonites pay both taxes and certain usufructuary fees. It has already been mentioned that every hearth pays 1 ruble and 5 kopeks banco for the salary of the district elder and the scribe and that every able-bodied person between fourteen and sixty years of age is taxed 49 kopeks banco for other community needs. There is a communal granary to which everyone must contribute a certain amount of grain annually. On 1 January 1843 there was a supply of 5,212 measures of winter wheat and 833 measures of spring wheat. On that day the communal sheep farm had a stock of 8,220, including the lambs. In 1842 the sheep farm supplied 437 puds and 15 pounds of wool, which were sold for 11,025 rubles banco. Lastly, the liquor tax provided the community with an annual income of 15,316 rubles banco. The total income amounted to about 30,000 rubles banco.

I have described the agricultural conditions of the Mennonite colony on the Molochnaia in such great detail firstly because it offers incontestable proof of German diligence, the German love of order, their advanced culture and morality. Second, their significance for Russia has in no way been sufficiently recognized. In all of Russia there is no region where, on the whole, there exists such a uniformly high level of agricultural and social development as here. These Mennonite colonies can serve as a standard for the government and as a model for all the Russian peoples as to what one can achieve through diligence, integrity, and order. Above all, they provide the government with the certain measure of how much could be accomplished in the area of cultivating and particularly of converting the steppes and all of southern Russia into forests. This point is most vital for Russia's power and domestic politics. If all of southern Russia were as advanced agriculturally and socially as this region, Moscow and Petersburg would no longer be the focal points and hubs of the empire; rather, these functions would pass to Kharkov or Ekaterinoslav and Odessa.

On the twenty-seventh I drove with Mr. Kornies to another of his large plantations which his only married son manages. On the territory bordering directly on this farm a new colony is springing up, whose members were brought here by a most strange fate. At the time of the Reformation a cleric in Zwickau named Hutter developed basically the same system of religious teachings that Menno Simons later set forth.[7] However, it cannot be proved that they had the slightest contact with each other. Hutter did correspond with Thomas Münzer, though, and also met with him once; they were unable to agree, however, since Hutter rejected the notion of a temporal Kingdom of Christ and His chosen people to be established and consolidated by fire and the sword if need be. Like Menno, he taught that no one should use force. He does not seem to have had the least contact with the other reformers of the time but rather to have been completely isolated. He gathered a small following and in 1540 we find him with his community in northern Bohemia. Expelled shortly thereafter, he settled with them in the vicinity of Innsbruck. It is said that he was later burned in Innsbruck.

Persecuted anew at the time of the Thirty Years' War, they moved to Hungary and Transylvania. For a long time they lived there in peace and were joined at the beginning of the eighteenth century

7. Jakob Hutter, or Huter, was an Anabaptist minister from the Tyrol who in 1533 joined a group of Tyrolean Anabaptists who had migrated to Austerlitz in Moravia at the invitation of the Counts Kaunitz in 1528. Assuming the leadership of the group, Hutter pressed for full communality of goods and by 1547 achieved it in ninety village communities (*Brüderhöfe*) of "Hutterites." See Dr. Hans Fischer, *Jakob Huter, Leben, Froemmigkeit, Briefe* (Newton, Kans., 1956).

by coreligionists from Carinthia. Around 1752 the Jesuits succeeded with their sermons in bringing fourteen hundred, or approximately half of them, back into the Catholic fold. Recognizing the danger, the rest emigrated again and settled in Walachia near Bucharest. During the Turkish War from 1770 to 1775 their villages were plundered and burned. Then they turned to the Russian field marshal, Count Rumiantsev, and asked to be moved to Russia. He actually did settle them on his estates in Podolia.[8] As long as the count was alive and even after his death they fared well. Recently, however, the estates changed hands and the people felt oppressed. They asked the Minister of State Domains to assign them crown land for cultivation. Mr. Kornies was then commissioned to investigate their circumstances and needs and to supervise their settlement in the vicinity of the Mennonite colony on the Molochnaia. It is certainly a curious fate that after three long centuries of roaming about they are now settling in a foreign land near fellow countrymen and coreligionists who had probably never heard of their existence! They have been here for only two years and already have had a good harvest.

When I visited these so-called Hutterite Brethren, they were still living in earthen huts. However, they were busily carting stones, slaking lime, preparing clay, etc., in order to construct homes exactly like those of the Mennonites. One could tell from their appearance that they were good, respectable people. Their neighbors, the Mennonites, helped them as much as possible. How different and stable the national characteristics are! While one can still recognize the Old Frisians in the Mennonites, the Hutterite Brethren have completely preserved the national traits of the southern Germans even though they left Germany entirely two hundred years ago. Their dialect, dress, and temperament distinguish them very definitely from the Mennonites.

With Mr. Kornies I climbed down into the earthen hut belonging to the elder of the community. It was spacious and contained several divisions or chambers and a kitchen. It looked very neat and clean throughout. The elder of the community showed me a most remarkable manuscript. It was started by their founder, Hutter. Part of the folio volume contains his teachings, followed by a description of his fate and that of his community. Since his death the book has always been continued by the eldest member of the community. Unfortunately, I had too little time and could only skim the pages.

8. Field Marshal Count P. A. Rumiantsev (1725–95) was the leader of the Russian forces in Rumania and Moldavia in the Turkish War of 1769–70.

In addition to the theological discussions, it contained a great number of the most interesting historical notes, particularly on the early movements of the Reformation and on the Thirty Years' War. Of course the people regard this book as a sacred relic and would never let it out of their hands. However, they would be glad to provide a copy if a public library were thinking of spending a couple of hundred thalers.

In spite of their long wanderings far and wide, these Baptists (the actual name they adopted for the sect), these Mennonites and Hutterite Brethren, have fully preserved their national qualities. They owe this primarily to the circumstance that they never intermarried with other peoples as a consequence of their religious convictions. Since they do not recognize infant baptism as true baptism, they must necessarily regard all other Christian relatives as not being baptized. Every Christian religious sect, of course, forbids marriage with the unbaptized.

Upon returning I found the ispravnik of the district, who had heard of my arrival and wanted to introduce himself. He was a Russian through and through, and I could only communicate with him through my companion. He seemed to be a good man. I asked him how he felt about the Mennonites and he replied that he had never heard a complaint about them; as long as he could remember they had never violated the law. He continued by saying that they lived in perfect peace with all their neighbors and helped them wherever possible. This was truly a complimentary and reliable report! . . .

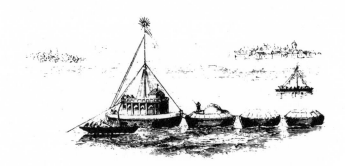

# 7
# *Colonization*

History shows us no people which from its first appearance has manifested as persistent and indestructible a drive to colonize as the Russians. Starting from a relatively small region south of the Valdai Hills, the Russian people gradually spread out over one-seventh of the globe during the course of a thousand years. The Germanic peoples expanded over all of Europe, between the second and fifth centuries, but these were collective migratory movements whose goal was conquest. Entire tribes abandoned their homes for lands already inhabited, but not in order to colonize peacefully. They conquered these territories, subjugated the native population, and took from them a part of the land which they had been cultivating for many years.

The Portuguese and Spanish colonization enterprises of three centuries ago were also more like conquests. Those who left their homes were adventurers in search of treasure; the founding of colonies which followed later was of secondary importance. At first the English simply established trading colonies along the coasts of every country. Only after religious strife and internal unrest had forced many Englishmen to leave their native land did agricultural colonies such as Pennsylvania emerge. . . . However, the purpose and nature of the settlement of North America is the cultivation of virgin lands by peoples from every nation on earth and not the expansion of a homogeneous people, as characterizes the Russian colonization movement.

With no pressure from other peoples and without government guidance the Russian people, primarily the Great Russians, began very early to found colonies in all directions. Individual bands of settlers set out in search of favorable places on the vast plains of Russia at which to establish communes. As soon as the members of the community became too numerous the parent hive sent forth young swarms to found new communities in the vicinity. Their relationship to the former was that of daughter communes to the mother commune. Even after the actual bond between the mother and daughter communes had long ceased to exist, this relationship lived on in the memory of the people until modern times. Historical documents always speak of Mother Novgorod, of Mother Suzdal, or Mother Moscow. Together the mother and daughter communities constituted a kind of political unit known as a land (territory). Documents from the seventeenth century still mention the Land of Nizhnii Novgorod, the Land of Suzdal, and the Land of Rostov. The colonization movements primarily followed the course of the rivers. In the twelfth century, we already find settlements along the rivers of present-day Russia: the Volga, the Don, and the Dnieper in the south, as well as the Duna, the Sukhona, and the Dvina in the north. The interior of the country either remained vacant for a long time or was inhabited by other tribes or traversed by hunters and nomads.

This colonization drive is deeply rooted in the national character of the Russian people. The Russians are the most sociable people I have met. The German is strongly attached to his place of birth. The village where he was born and spent his childhood, the forest, the meadow, and the mountains where he played, his ancestral house and the field he inherited constitute the many indissoluble bonds which chain him to his home. Not so the Russian! He has little feeling of allegiance to his place of birth, but an extraordinary love for his country. He is deeply attached to all his kinfolk, to his community, and to his compatriots. Neither the village of his birth nor the field which he has cultivated in the sweat of his brow binds him the most, but rather the people, his neighbors and relatives. When he is among them he is happy, even though he may be far away from home.

This alone explains the facility with which colonies formed in Russia. The history of the people has hardly dawned when we find isolated settlements spread over nearly the entire vast plain between the Polar and Caspian Seas, between the Ural Mountains and Hungary. Everywhere they settled peacefully among other peoples, the Finns and Scythians, though not in individual families. Unlike the Germanic peoples they did not assimilate with the foreign nationalities

*177*

and were not absorbed by them. Instead they always settled in tightly knit communities which preserved their national identity and always remained in close community with the entire powerful tribe of Russians.

So strong and so dominant was this Russian nationality that it gradually caused the disintegration of the national character of the aboriginal inhabitants and completely Russified them. We are still witnessing this process today. Without pressure the remaining Finnish tribes — the Karelians, the Ingrians, and the Mordvines — are becoming more Russified with each passing day. Even the most uncompromising tribes such as the Sirianians and the Cheremiss will not escape their fate. As we see in the case of so many aristocratic Tatar families, even the Tatars become unmistakably Russian when they convert to the Russian church. Historical studies offer adequate evidence that on the whole the original inhabitants were by no means driven out or annihilated by the Russians. Rather, they gradually assimilated with the Russians and adopted their language and customs. Their nationality was absorbed by that of the Russians.

The Great Russians are not, as their entire habitude reveals, a racially pure tribe. Although basically and originally a Slavic people, they are a strongly mixed race, having amalgamated with the Finns in the north and the Tatar, Caucasian, and even Mongol tribes in the south. Precisely this fusion imparts to them the fortunate blend of characteristics which qualifies them to play a major role in the history of the world.

In the Middle Ages, when Tatar rule halted the migration toward the south, Russian colonization with Novgorod as the starting point primarily assumed a north and northeastward direction, toward the old Biarmerland (Perm). In the past two centuries, however, the South has been colonized. This has occurred on such a large scale that more than half of the steppe region extending as far north as Tula and Penza is under cultivation and populated, albeit sparsely.

Most of the colonies which originated in the center and extended like radii to the periphery of the empire were formerly spontaneous undertakings brought about by the natural instincts of the people and the interests of the seigneurs. They were carried out privately and the government simply allowed them. . . . But by no means did the government plan or supervise the entire enterprise. Prior to Peter I the government was, moreover, not organized in such a manner that it could have carried out a large and systematic economic project of this nature. Only with some of the Cossack settlements did the government exercise its direct influence, at least with respect to directions and the choice of regions. Since Peter I, however, the government itself has organized the new colonies on the Black Sea and on the Caucasian line wonderfully well.[1]

Peter began to make presents of land to such luminaries of his court as Apraksin. They were even granted extensive tracts of land in the newly acquired but desolate southern and southeastern regions for the purpose of having their serfs cultivate the land. The giving away of increasingly large territories was continued by the next government. Under Catherine II this practice assumed such extravagant proportions that it led to great evils. The *otchët* or *compte rendu* of 1803 published by the Ministry of Internal Affairs (see Storch, *Russland unter Alexander I*, vol. 6, p. 35) deplores the fact that the goal of these grants, namely, the cultivation and populating of the newly acquired regions, was too often missed. According to the report, the crown gave away so much territory in New Russia that the government now frequently lacks land there for projected colonies that are an economic necessity. The most fertile land was long ago assigned to private individuals and then lay fallow for many years despite the fact that it had been granted for the purpose of colonization and cultivation. These gifts of land were therefore greatly restricted under Emperor Alexander, and I believe that they have been virtually discontinued under the present government.

For the most part the government allowed this peaceful but powerful colonization movement from the interior to the extremities of the empire to take its own course for over two centuries, only now and then checking glaring abuses. However, it has given very close attention to several other colonization enterprises. We are speaking of the Cossack colonization, the military colonization, the Siberian colonization, and the colonization of territories by foreigners called in for this purpose.

## The Colonization of the Cossacks

The Cossack military organization is one of the most interesting phenomena in the entire Slavic world. The Cossacks represent, as it were, a modern and democratic Slavic knighthood. . . .

The civil constitution of all the Cossack tribes is based on the Russian communal institution which the government has left completely intact. They were granted the privilege that no Russian aristocrat could possess property in Cossack territory. Nor is the crown

1. For the most intensive period of colonization activity in the South see Hans Auerbach, *Die Besiedelung der Südukraine in den Jahren 1774–1787* (Wiesbaden, 1965).

allowed to own land there; it has only the right to construct roads, canals, and fortresses there. The essential foundations of the military organization have been preserved in their traditional form. Only the great independence of the *ataman* and the supreme assembly which assisted him has been abolished, since it appeared dangerous in a monarchical state.[2] Cossack leaders have been placed under the government's direction and authority. I cannot decide whether the modern military discipline recently introduced threatens to alter the character of the popular institution. However, the constitution granted to the Don Cossacks in 1775 forms the basis for all the others.

The territory of the Don Cossacks may have 600,000 to 700,000 inhabitants. In time of emergency every Cossack is duty bound to serve in the military from the age of fifteen to sixty. The regular army, however, is comprised of fifty-four cavalry regiments of 1,044 men each or a total of 56,376 troops.

[Table 1 gives] estimates of the various Cossack tribes, in round figures.

[TABLE 1]
[COSSACK TRIBES]

| | Inhabitants | Soldiers on Active Duty |
|---|---|---|
| Little Russian Cossacks at the Black Sea | 125,000 | 18,000 |
| Great Russian Cossacks on the Caucasian line | 150,000 | 18,000 |
| Don Cossacks | 440,000 | 60,000 |
| Ural Cossacks | 50,000 | 8,000 |
| Orenburg Cossacks | 60,000 | 10,000 |
| Siberian Cossacks | 50,000 | 9,000 |
| | 875,000 | 123,000 |

These figures give us some idea of the importance of the Cossack military. They are, to be sure, rather unreliable, although they are probably below the effective number. What other country has such a competent light cavalry with 120,000 well-armed, militant, and well-disciplined men?

The Cossacks are freemen. Serfdom or tenancy in any form is

2. The powers of the Cossack *ataman* were curbed in the wake of the Pugachev rebellion, which strongly affected Cossack territories in the Volga basin. See John T. Alexander, *Autocratic Politics in a National Crisis* (Bloomington, Ind., 1969.)

unknown among them. Rather, the entire territory belongs to the Cossack commune as such, and every individual has an equal right to use the plowlands as well as the pastures, hunting and fishing grounds, etc. The Cossacks do not pay any taxes whatever to the government. Instead they are obligated to serve in the military. For this purpose the males are divided into three categories:

1. *Maloletnye* — Minors up to the age of sixteen.
2. *Sluzhilie* — Those who are serving for twenty-five years, which is to say until they have reached the age of forty-two.
3. *Otstavnye* — Those who have been discharged and remain in the reserves for five years or until they are forty-seven years of age.

They are then discharged permanently and regarded as invalids. In case of a national emergency, however, every healthy Cossack between the ages of fifteen and sixty would have to mount.

Each Cossack must equip himself completely at his own expense; he has to provide his own clothing and weapons and keep his horse. During a tour of duty outside the Cossack territory he receives rations and forage, a small amount of pay and 15 rubles for a packhorse. The government supplies artillery, ammunition, and transport.

To make it easier for the Don Cossacks to sell their products, a trading company of five hundred men was established in 1834. The members of the company are exempted from active military duty but have to pay 200 rubles to the military treasury. Instead of collecting a tax from the Don Cossacks, the crown pays the Cossack administration 21,310 rubles banco for salaries, 20,000 rubles banco for the widows and orphans of those who died in battle, and in lieu of 10,000 measures of grain it pays 30,000 rubles banco, 247 puds of gunpowder, and 150 puds of lead.

## The Military Colonization

The Cossack settlements are military colonies originated by the people themselves. Since 1820, however, the government has also begun to organize military colonies along economic lines.[3] I myself

3. A considerable literature exists on the military colonies, among which the following should be consulted: A. K. Gribbe, "Novgorodskie voennye poseleniia," *Russkaia starina* 45 (1885): 127–52; A. N. Petrov, *Graf Arakcheev i voennye poseleniia, 1809–31* (St. Petersburg, 1871); and Richard Pipes, "The Russian Military Colonies, 1810–1831," *Journal of Modern History* 22 (1950): 205–19; Alan D. Ferguson, "The Russian Military

visited one of these colonies, at Chuiugev in the province of Kharkov. . . . Here I want to give only a brief summary of all the
military colonies hitherto established in the Russian Empire.

In the Middle Ages Russia was nearly subjugated by the Mongols
and scarcely preserved a semblance of national unity. Even after
securing her autonomy Russia was at first in a position to wage
only defensive wars. At that time the Cossack defense system was
organized spontaneously by the people. This system closely resembles the military colonies on the Turkish-Austrian frontier. In time,
however, the Cossacks grew so bellicose and bold that in addition
to defending the motherland they carried out incessant raids and
small expeditions against its enemies on the latter's own territory.

When Russia became a modern state and began to assume her
natural political position in the great European family of nations,
a large standing army became a necessity. In addition to a defensive
force to protect the country, she needed an active force to wage
an offensive war. For no state is it more difficult and more expensive
to maintain a large standing army than for Russia. In the adequately
but not overpopulated countries of western Europe where on the
whole there is a surplus of workers, the maintenance of a large
army deprives neither agriculture nor industry of the necessary hands.
Indeed, the army there appears to be a true blessing in that it partially
absorbs the misery of the proletariat. Russian agriculture does not
have sufficient laborers, and up to now there has been almost no
proletariat. As rich as Russia is in natural resources, though, agriculture, industry, and commerce were still quite underdeveloped thirty
years ago. Consequently, her national revenues were relatively small.
Even though the soldiers' pay was low and rations inexpensive,
the army nevertheless cost enormous sums of money, much of which
was lost through dishonesty and embezzlement. The huge army shattered the finances.[4] The tremendous expansion of the empire, the
deployment of the army over this immense territory, and the poor
means of transportation made it impossible to concentrate a substantial
force quickly at one spot at the right moment. Despite the fact
that Russia had anticipated the war three years in advance and had

Settlements, 1825–1866,'' *Essays in Russian History: A Collection
Dedicated to George Vernadsky*, ed. Alan D. Ferguson and Alfred Levin
(Hamden, Conn., 1964).

4. Large military expenditures continued to pose a major problem to
the Ministry of Finances long after the establishment of military colonies.
See Curtiss, *The Russian Army*, p. 100; Walter M. Pintner, *Russian
Economic Policy under Nicholas I* (Ithaca, N.Y., 1967), pp. 31 ff.

armed herself, at the outbreak of the War of 1812 she could send barely 200,000 men into battle against an approaching enemy of twice that number. *Cundo crescit* can serve as Russia's motto. At the end of the war in 1815 the available troops numbered 300,000.

This entire experience necessarily forced the government to ponder the possibility of establishing a colony of active forces similar to the defensive forces of the Cossack colonies. Sweden and the Prussian *Landwehr* could serve as models for this; also the Austrian border militia, an excellently organized military settlement, furnished an example worthy of imitation.[5]

One can be confident that every idea that proved to be beneficial for Russia originated with Peter I. Herein lies his real greatness. With him Russia's entire future was actually born. It was Peter I's idea to concentrate the population and to organize a system of military settlements, although he himself did not make any real attempts to carry it out. But the idea had been born, and soon after his death his successors began to make this idea reality. In 1727, Empress Anna settled in the Ukraine a regiment of hussars comprised of Serbian immigrants. In 1737 an entire line of military colonies was organized in the Ukraine, and Catherine II had nine colonies of hussar regiments in southern Russia alone. However, all these settlements quickly deteriorated and collapsed during Catherine's own reign. Only the Cossack colonies founded by Catherine on the Black Sea still exist. . . .

Emperor Alexander took up the idea again on a larger scale. A first attempt was made in 1810 with a battalion but failed. Later, in 1814, after he had learned of the Austrian border militia, his intention to found similar colonies was rekindled. The abortive attempt of 1810 had shown that one could not very well settle soldiers alone. The decision was now made to amalgamate soldiers and country folk, and through common institutions and constant togetherness to make the soldiers farmers and the farmers soldiers. With this new method of colonization, the original inhabitants were not to be moved into other regions. Rather, every farmer was to be given one or two soldiers whom he was obligated to provide for on his farm in return for exemption from all taxes and other privileges. The soldier was supposed to help him on his farm.

The first such attempt was made in 1816 with a battalion in the province of Novgorod and was soon followed by two infantry and

5. Haxthausen's source is C. Freiherr von Pidoll zu Quintenbach, *Einige Worte über die russischen Militaircolonien im Vergleiche mit der k. k. österreichischen Militairgrenze* (Vienna, 1847).

two cavalry divisions in southern Russia. The soldiers were assigned to villages which had to quarter permanently an entire, a half, or a quarter of a company or squadron. The farmsteads in the villages were arranged in a regular pattern; all the buildings were constructed according to a definite plan at the expense of the crown. The soldiers and peasants alike were given all the farm equipment and household furnishings, and the required number of livestock was made complete. On a complete farm, to which sixty desiatins of land were assigned in the infantry districts and ninety desiatins in the cavalry districts, three pair of oxen, one pair of reserve oxen, two horses, two cows, and twelve sheep were considered necessary. Half and quarter peasants were also assessed; they together with others constituted complete farms and were supposed to bear a proportionate amount of the quartering expenses.

A comprehensive order was issued for all the military colonies under the date of 11 December 1826. However, with respect to the infantry colonies in the north it was significantly modified by the *ukaz* of 20 November 1831.

The colonization of the cavalry began in 1818. The steppe between the Dniester and the Dnieper was inhabited and traversed by hordes of bandits, only a very few of whom had permanent homes. Some of them who dwelled on the river Bug had Cossack privileges and were called the Cossacks on the Bug. Under their aegis a rabble roamed about, committing the most wicked acts of brigandage. The privileges, however, had been granted only for a specified term which expired at the beginning of the century; these were not renewed, and an *ukaz* reduced all these Cossacks and the other inhabitants as well to the status of crown peasants. This was actually accomplished, though, only after they had formally been settled in specific districts and forced to quarter troops of the regular cavalry on a permanent basis. General Count Witt deserves the credit for having solved the problem with great perseverance and circumspection.

At the present time a total of 82,260 men have been settled in four large groups in the western parts of the Russian Empire, that is, in the provinces of Novgorod, Kharkov, Kherson, Kiev, and Podolia.[6] The troops are comprised of nine regiments and three battalions of infantry with a peacetime force of 29,950 men; four regiments of cuirassiers with 4,600 men; the second division of light horse guards comprised of three regiments with 3,450 men;

6. The figures presented total 64,690 rather than 82,260. As was customary, the figure includes only adult males.

ten regiments of lancers with 13,810 men; six regiments of hussars with 9,210 men; ten batteries of mounted artillery numbering 2,760 men; two battalions of cavalry supply-troops of 1,000 men. These figures do not include the working companies and the mobile working battalions.

From a political and military perspective the Russian military colonies must be considered a complete success.[7] With them and the 70,000 guards in Petersburg, Russia possesses an army prepared for an offensive attack at any moment; previous experience taught that it was hardly possible for Russia to mobilize her troops within a year and a day. There supposedly exists a plan to colonize the entire army over a period of years in a line extending from the Baltic to the Black Sea. This is a most ambitious plan fraught with great obstacles. But what is impossible in Russia?

From a financial standpoint, the advantages are not as great as one might expect. If one were to calculate the interest on the vast sums that it cost to establish the military colonies, there would be no profit to speak of. It is said to have cost 5 million silver rubles to set up a single regiment. . . .*

## The Colonization of Siberia

I myself did not see the Siberian colonies. Furthermore, I do not have detailed and clear reports on them. However, for the sake

*The dangers which Baron Pidoll enumerates in his book [see n. 5, above — Ed.] should be given very careful attention. I would like to refute only one point, namely, that the peasants in the colonies are worse off than the other state peasants. It is very difficult to calculate material advantages and expenses. However, I ask the reader to bear one fact in mind. In most provinces the state peasant has only three to four desiatins of land, and nowhere does he have more than ten. The colonist, however, has sixty to ninety desiatins of land. The state peasant does not pay 10 rubles in taxes, as Baron Pidoll states, but 15 rubles. The colonist is constantly supervised and regimented. This would be intolerable for other peoples, but the Russian is accustomed to it and does not feel oppressed. In every respect the colonist is secure; he is protected against poverty, hunger, etc. This cannot be said of the state peasant. In my opinion the colonists are being trained to become a very competent peasantry for Russia. Whether greater freedom would be beneficial after their education has been completed is another question.

7. Contradictory evidence on the supposed political success of the military colonies may be found in G. A. Vereshchagin, ed., "Materialy po istorii buntov v voennykh poseleniyakh pri Aleksandre I," *Dela i Dni* 3 (Petrograd, 1922): 118–65; and A. Slezhkinskii, *Bunt voennykh poselian v kholeru 1831* (Novgorod, 1894).

of completeness I must mention the colonization of Siberia. I am including some information given to me and notes I collected as well as several studies on the subject.

Siberia is one of the territories or rather one part of the globe whose destiny is boundless and wholly uncertain. This statement, when made in reference to North America, is self-evident. However, few people know that this also applies to Siberia. The very mention of Siberia conjures up a foreboding image. And yet this territory is probably as important as North America for the study of the world's great social issues.

Nothing will have a greater influence on Europe's future than its relations with the great empires and countries of the Asian interior from Asia Minor to China. Today Europe is trying to open up the Asian interior from two sides. The English possess one key in East India. For many years they have been very actively advancing by way of land toward Bukhara and Tibet, while at the same time seeking to force open the door to China and Persia by means of their fleets. Russia, which is in possession of the other key — Siberia — has just begun to open up the Asian interior. Russia is still too occupied with western Europe and with its own internal consolidation to try to exercise a great influence on the Asian interior. Recently, however, Russia's developing industrial and commercial activities have pointed the country somewhat in these directions. From the Caucasus and Siberia, Russia is beginning to compete with England on the market in Persia, Bukhara, and China.

Far too occupied and engaged in other directions, Russia would have allowed many years to pass before placing the main emphasis on Asia and setting about to develop Siberia, had it not been for the discovery of immense gold reserves there. If it does not turn out to be a mare's nest, the results of the discovery must necessarily elevate Siberia, within ten to twenty years, to the center of attention not only for its ruler, Russia, but also for the entire civilized world. The legends of griffins guarding an immense treasure of gold which Herodotus preserved for us are not fairy tales but a prophecy which is now being fulfilled. Herodotus correctly locates the region in the northeast. Has the Slavic race not always displayed the griffin as a mystical symbol on their coats of arms?

The original old Finnic inhabitants had already worked mines in Siberia. One finds their old pits and waste heaps everywhere. Thereafter, mining remained at a standstill until the Russians conquered Siberia. It was above all Peter I who revived mining. He primarily used Swedish prisoners for resuming operations at the mines. Since this time, mining has been actively carried on, particularly in the Urals and several other regions such as Nerchinsk.

For centuries it was more legend than fact that gold could be found in Siberia. The first important gold-bearing quartz veins were discovered in 1745 in the vicinity of Basovsk. All the gold produced by the mines in the Urals and Siberia amounted annually only to somewhat more than sixteen puds (about 460 [Russian] pounds). But that amount is very insignificant compared to what has recently been found by panning.

Golovin, the governor general of Siberia, brought sand rich in gold to Peter I.[8] At that time, however, the place where it was found was kept secret. In 1774 areas of debris containing gold were discovered in the Urals. But the amount of gold discovered has increased significantly only since 1820, when private persons also went out to seek grains and leaves of gold in the debris. In 1814 16 puds of gold were obtained in the Urals and in 1820 more than 27 puds, of which somewhat more than 7 puds had been washed by private persons. The year 1830 yielded 352 puds of which 204½ puds were extracted by private individuals. This amount was slightly exceeded in the following two years and then dropped to around 300 puds.

In addition to the gold in the Urals, private individuals, who swarmed in great numbers over all of Siberia, had by this time found veins on most of the eastern slopes of the mountain ranges as far as Kamchatka and began setting up gold washes. The government followed, but only on a small scale. In 1828 there was a small yield of only 25 pounds. However, four years later more than thirty times that amount was extracted. Six puds had been obtained in the crown washes and around 16 puds in the private washes. Nine years later, in 1841, the yield increased to 355 puds, only 37 of which were produced in the crown washes.

According to official information the following amounts of gold were obtained in 1843: in the Urals, 140 puds in the crown mines and 199 puds in private washes; in Siberia, 78 puds in the crown mines and 925 puds in private washes or 1,342 puds in all. The gold officially produced in Russia from 1814 to 1842 is valued at more than 25 million *Friedrichsdor*. According to the 18 February 1847 issue of the *Augsburger Abendzeitung* the 1846 yield amounted to 1,722 puds. But the actual amount is far greater still. Much

8. Avtomon Mikhailovich Golovin had begun his career as a military aide to Peter I and was sent to rule Siberia only at the completion of the wars with Sweden and Turkey.

of the gold found by private persons has not been reported. Who could control this in Siberia! Private individuals who register are assigned districts where they can set up gold washes. From the gross yield they have to pay the crown a tax of 15 percent in some regions and in others 20 and even 24 percent. In 1843 the crown received in taxes from private persons about 176 puds valued at 2 million silver rubles. However, it is more than likely that a good deal of fraud is committed in these private washes and that much of the gold is made away with. How many adventurers are wandering about in the Siberian wilderness, searching for and finding gold, without the government's learning of it? According to a note given to me, approximately 2,000 puds of gold valued at more than 30 million thalers were discovered in the Russian Empire in 1842.

At the present time about twice the amount of gold is obtained annually in Siberia as in the mines and the gold washes of the entire world.[9] Besides gold other metals are also present in great abundance. The platinum yield which in the Urals was hardly 2 puds in 1824 amounted to nearly 122 puds in 1838 or sixty-one times the original quantity. The platinum extracted here now exceeds the total production of the rest of the world by four to five times. The silver yield is also enormous. Count Demidov is said to own a mountain of pure malachite whose copper value is estimated at phenomenal sums.

If this vast production of metal and particularly of gold continues to increase as is to be expected, it will necessarily have an incalculable influence on the Russian Empire and the entire world as well. Certainly its impact will be as great as once was the opening up of the mineral resources in America.

For the present the Russian government is allowing these prospectors to do as they please. It lacks a sufficient number of trained officials, miners, and laborers to take the matter completely into its own hands. Even the greatest number of available government experts would not be able to locate the innumerable gold-bearing river beds and canyons as quickly as these gold-hungry adventurers. However, when fortune hunters discover areas rich in gold, the government too finds out about them. Through the tax on gold the government receives a pure profit without much effort and at no expense. . . . But the government cannot delay for many more years in assuming the direction and control of this enormously impor-

9. Russia's preponderance in the world gold market was to be curtailed drastically with the discovery of gold in California in 1848. See Tengoborski, *Commentaries on the Productive Forces of Russia* 1:203–8.

tant enterprise. The rapid increase in the amount of gold must necessarily lead to a depreciation in the value of this precious metal which could have unforeseen consequences. Moreover, the morality of the people and the Siberians in particular is being undermined in a war hardly imaginable by this vagabond life and the lure of gold. . . .

The first settlers in Siberia were Cossack conquerors. Births and newcomers increased the population considerably. The inhabitants are scattered everywhere, although they primarily constitute a frontier force against incursions. For many years Siberians have no longer had to fear large-scale attacks from foreign armies. As a reward for excellent and difficult service, they enjoy great privileges and constitute a kind of lower military aristocracy.

Over the years many state peasants moved to Siberia, above all a large number of Old Believers and other Raskolniki who felt ill at ease or oppressed in their native provinces. At late as 1803 an entire village of 132 families, Petrovsk in the Caucasian province, requested permission to emigrate at their own expense to the province of Irkutsk on the Chinese border.

In every war Russia transported a great many of its prisoners-of-war to Siberia. Immediately following the battle of Poltava, for example, Peter I deported nine thousand Swedes. If the war lasted many years, the prisoners would establish colonies, which, moreover, was made very easy for them, and a large number never returned to their homes. They wanted to stay!

The most important aspect of the Siberian colonization is the settlement there of criminals and exiles from Russia. I was unable to learn who first conceived of this method of settlement and when it began. I believe that the enterprise was entirely spontaneous and did not follow a predetermined plan, although it was always controlled by edicts as circumstances required. At the present time this colonization enterprise is undeniably very thoroughly and carefully regulated.

In Moscow I visited the jails on the Sparrow Hills where the prisoners are kept before being sent to Siberia. I can only confirm what Cottrell has said about the gentle treatment the convicts receive.[10] Their food is wholesome. The prisons are high, airy, and warm in the winter; the chains they wear during the march weigh only four pounds. (They can choose whether they want to wear the fetters on their hands or feet, although they generally prefer

10. Charles Cottrell, *Recollections of Siberia in the Years 1840 and 1841* (London, 1842).

to have one foot bound to that of another prisoner.) They cover only two to three miles a day, and the stations are well equipped. . . . The convicts from twenty-six provinces who have been sentenced to Siberian exile are assembled in Moscow, and twice a week a transport leaves for its destination.

I have taken the following information from an official list printed for the ministries containing statistics on the prisoners banished to Siberia from 1823 to 1832. Included are the exiles from the forty-eight European and two Caucasian provinces. During those ten years a total of 83,699 individuals, 72,904 men and 10,795 women, or an annual average of 8,000, were banished. However, since both men and women have the right to accompany their spouses and under certain circumstances to take along their children the average number who migrate to Siberia each year can be estimated at around 10,000. Despite all the humane precautions the mortality rate during the transport is, of course, very high. Also, many die before they become accustomed to the climate and the way of life. One can assume that at least one-fifth of the prisoners perish during the two years of the march and the first years of acclimation. The effective annual increase in Siberia's population is thus 8,000 persons, of whom there may be 6,000 men and 2,000 women.

Those 83,699 exiles fell into five categories:

1. *Criminals:* 37,736 men and 5,259 women. All the provinces with the exception of Finland contributed to this group, albeit in greatly varying degrees. Georgia supplies the least number of exiles with one for every 91,320 inhabitants, probably not because fewer crimes occur there but because the police and criminal courts are very remiss in the performance of their duties. After Georgia, Iaroslavl had the least number of criminals; the annual average is only one exile for every 35,520 inhabitants. In the province of Grodno there is one exile for every 29,760 inhabitants, in Vologda and Vitebsk one for 28,970, in Estonia one for 28,220, in Bialostok one for 20,740, and in Olonets one for 20,270. In the provinces of Tver, Minsk, Mogilev, Podolia, Volhynia, Poltava, Livonia, and Courland one out of every 15,000 to 20,000 persons is exiled. The provinces of Archangel, Pskov, Viatka, Vilno, Smolensk, Kiev, Kharkov, Bessarabia, Saratov, Nizhnii Novgorod, Vladimir, Tula, Kaluga, Kostroma, Riazan, Simbirsk, Tambov, Voronezh, Kursk, Penza, Novgorod, and Ekaterinoslav have one exile for every 10,000 to 15,000 inhabitants. In the provinces of Moscow, Chernigov, Orenburg, Tauride, Perm, Astrakhan, and Kazan the estimate is one for every 5,600 to 9,970 inhabitants. In the province of Petersburg,

there is one exile for 4,020 inhabitants and in the province of Kherson one for every 3,840.

2. *Vagabonds:* 30,703 men and 4,605 women. The following provinces contributed the smallest number to this category, i.e., one for every 30,000 to 100,000 inhabitants: Archangel, Vologda, Viatka, Kazan, Kostroma, Kursk, Moscow, Olonets, Orel, Orenburg, Poltava, Pskov, Penza, Riazan, Simbirsk, Petersburg, Tula, Tambov, Tver, Georgia, and Bessarabia. However, the number of vagabonds apprehended and sent to Siberia was very high in the provinces of Ekaterinoslav, Kiev, Minsk, Podolia, Tauride, Chernigov, Kherson, Iaroslavl, and the two Cossack provinces on the Don and the Black Sea. In some provinces one of every 5,000 inhabitants is a tramp.

3. *Condemned for misconduct and licentiousness:* 2,798 men and 579 women. In this regard the provinces of Petersburg and Moscow distinguish themselves in an unfavorable sense, in that one of every 30,000 to 40,000 inhabitants is banished.

4. *Convicted by village courts for poor conduct:* 716 men and 20 women. Only in the provinces of Perm, Tauride, and Kherson is this practice common. They alone contributed six-sevenths of the total number. I did not learn the reason for this.

5. *Exiled to Siberia for misconduct at the request of their seigneurs in accordance with a government regulation:* 931 men and 300 women. The government has granted the seigneur the right to remove his serfs from his estate "for impudent offenses and intolerable conduct" and to turn them over to the government for exile to Siberia. Legal sentencing is not required. It suffices for the seigneur alone to be convinced by the evidence of the crime. However, such formalities, conditions, expenses, and losses of property are involved in carrying out this arbitrary decision that these cases are very rare. The serf has to carry on to extremes before the seigneur decides on a step so detrimental to his real interests.

As a rule the serf with a strict master does not consider it a punishment but a blessing to be sent to Siberia. As I know from my own experience there are many who tramp about and actually try to get picked up or who commit a minor offense such as petty theft in order to have the good fortune of being banished to Siberia.*

In the above case the serf has the right to take along his wife

*Charles Cottrell, in his book on Siberia [see n. 10, above] [German translation, Dresden, 1846] p. 8, reports having seen an old man in the prisons of Moscow fall on his knees before the warden and beg the official to arrange to have him sent to Siberia.

and his children under legal age. As soon as they set foot on Siberian soil they become free men. They are settled and, if they work hard, they become wealthy in a few years.

. . . If out of the 24 million serfs in Russia 95 men and 33 women are annually banished to Siberia by their masters, one cannot consider the consequences of this privilege to be very dangerous and far-reaching, although I certainly hesitate to acknowledge the justness of this particular law.

Upon arriving in Siberia the exiles are distributed in various regions. The majority is now sent to East Siberia since the better areas of West Siberia are already fairly well cultivated.

As soon as the exiles reach the Siberian border they have left their former life behind and are no longer regarded as criminals. They are referred to as the unfortunates (*neschastnye liudi*) both by the people and in the official language of the authorities. The exiles fall into three categories: (1) *katorzhniki* or felons who have been sentenced to hard labor, sometimes in the mines, for life or for an indefinite period: (2) *poslannye na rabotu*, exiles employed for a number of years in public works projects before they are colonized; (3) *poslannye na poselenie*, exiles who are settled immediately. This last group is comprised of vagabonds and those persons banished by the villages and seigneurs. The criminals in the first category, who are guilty of the most serious crimes and are regarded as morally dead, are employed in the mines at Nerchinsk. Formerly their lot was supposed to have been very pitiful. Upon arrival they descended into the mines and never again saw daylight, since provisions were made to house and feed them underground. Today they are required to work only eight hours in the mines. The rest of the time, as well as on Sundays and holidays, they are above ground in their own quarters. Some have been accompanied by their families and their lot is not completely unbearable. One must not confuse the criminals working in the mines with the true local miners. A number of peasant colonies settled in villages near the mines have been assigned to work in the mines for a wage.

The second category is employed for a set time by the government for public works projects, that is, in the salt works, the lime kilns, etc. In 1804 they received an annual wage of 36 silver rubles. Food is very inexpensive and since they barely need half of their earnings the remainder is set aside for them. After working for four to six years and provided that they have conducted themselves well, the *poslannye na rabotu* are settled. They receive land and timber but have to construct their houses themselves. The small amount of capital that has accumulated is then used for purchasing household effects and farm stock, though they also receive some assistance, such as seed, provisions for the first year, etc.

The third category is destined for immediate settlement. Some are colonized in existing villages and others in villages founded for them. Everyone receives his own house, land, a share of the communal meadows and forest, one horse, a cow, two sheep, one plow, a harrow, a cart, a sickle, an ax, etc. In seed they are given nine puds of rye, one pud each of barley, oats, and hemp. In addition, everyone receives a soldier's rations for three years, 1 silver kopek per day for himself and ½ silver kopek for his wife and each child. During the first three years he is exempted from taxes. Henceforth, however, he pays the usual crown duties. The layout of the villages and each individual farmstead is prescribed and very regular. All the colonists including those of the second and third categories are *glebae adscripti*. They cannot leave the village overnight without permission nor can they choose another vocation, etc. A soldier, usually a Cossack, is placed at the head of each new village. He maintains order and justice and also settles their minor disputes, most of the time, of course, with a rod. If real crimes are committed, he arrests the culprits and turns them over to the authorities. However, martial rule lasts only one generation and is then replaced by the leadership of the elected *starosta*.

The experience of the past century has taught that a large part of these new colonists very soon become peaceful, hard-working, and respectable people. The second generation grows prosperous and often rich.

## [*The Colonization of Foreigners*]

Like the military colonization, the colonization of foreigners was planned, initiated, and directed by the government. Given the vast expanse of excellent vacant land and the sparse population in every part of the empire, the government could not entertain the idea of colonizing native Russians. These circumstances necessarily led it to consider the possibility of calling in foreign colonists to subdue the wilderness. As early as the sixteenth century Ivan Vasilevich settled Polish prisoners and summoned Germans to Moscow, an event to which the German *sloboda* still bears witness.[11] In 1617 Mikhail Fedorovich carried off several thousand Finns and Karelians and settled them between Tver and Moscow. Peter I colonized many

11. See below, chap. 10, n. 11.

Swedish and Finnish captives. In 1705, after the conquest of Narva and Dorpat, he marched off around six thousand local residents and set up colonies scattered through the empire. At the beginning of her reign Catherine II seized upon the idea of "populating the uninhabited and uncultivated southern provinces of the empire by calling in foreign colonists who would disseminate modern farming techniques and industry among her Russian subjects," as it is stated in the *ukaz* of 1763.

The first large colony of this kind was founded soon thereafter at Saratov on the Volga. This colony, which I visited and described above, was comprised exclusively of Germans. For many years the colonies languished, and they would have deteriorated completely had the government not come to their aid in 1801. Only in the past twenty to thirty years have they begun to prosper, and today they are in excellent condition. However, they have fulfilled the expectations of the *ukaz* of 1763 only in part. To be sure, the settlers populated and began tilling this formerly uncultivated and uninhabited region to the best of their ability, but their farms are not very outstanding. Even though they are superior to the Russian farms, they simply cannot serve as a model for Russian agriculture. These Germans have spread little "modern agronomic knowledge and industry among their Russian neighbors."

The conditions and privileges which Catherine II granted these settlers were also accorded all later immigrants. Since they constitute a kind of general law for foreign colonists throughout Russia, I want to enumerate them here. (1) Freedom of worship and state support of their ecclesiastical institutions. (2) Exemption from military and state service for all time. (3) Exemption from all taxes for a specified number of years, and thereafter the usual duties imposed on every Russian state peasant. (4) Autonomy in administrative and police matters, and the subordination of their self-government to a department especially created for the foreign colonies. Their autonomy even includes the right to negotiate loans for the colony's benefit under certain restrictions and contingent upon the permission of those higher authorities. (5) Jurisdiction in controversies among themselves.

The first colonists received travel expenses from their homeland to their destination and duty-free importation of their effects up to 300 silver rubles. They were also given homes built at the expense of the crown, rations and money for the first year, as well as a considerable sum as a loan given without interest for a certain number of years. These last benefits were not granted to all the later colonies, nor were they as generous.

These German settlements were soon succeeded in southern Russia and the Crimea by colonies of Greeks who had sided with the Russians in the Russo-Turkish War. Settlements of Germans, Swedes, Armenians, Bulgarians, Serbs, Walachians, and Moldavians followed later. Finally, some other colonies of Polish Jews were established.

According to official sources available from the last or eighth revision in 1835 the data on the foreign colonies in Russia can be summarized as [in table 2].

[TABLE 2]
[FOREIGN COLONIES IN RUSSIA, 1835]

| Names of the Provinces in Which the Colonies Are Located | Number of Colonies or Villages | Population | | |
|---|---|---|---|---|
| | | Male | Female | Total |
| 1. Bessarabia | 105 | 38,995 | 35,478 | 74,473 |
| 2. Kherson | 55 | 20,796 | 19,795 | 40,591 |
| 3. Cis-Caucasia | 3 | 236 | 245 | 481 |
| 4. Georgia | 7 | 1,201 | 1,187 | 2,388 |
| 5. Ekaterinoslav | 47 | 6,750 | 6,547 | 13,297 |
| 6. St. Petersburg | 13 | 1,522 | 1,513 | 3,035 |
| 7. Saratov | 102 | 63,717 | 63,311 | 127,028 |
| 8. Tauride | 80 | 12,237 | 11,323 | 23,560 |
| 9. Chernigov | 8 | 862 | 890 | 1,752 |
| 10. Voronezh | 1 | 631 | 600 | 1,231 |
| | 421 | 146,947 | 140,889 | 287,836 |

In round figures the population at the present time can be estimated at about 330,000.

The colonies in Bessarabia were founded and populated by Bulgarians (60,701). There are also 7,832 Bulgarians in the province of Kherson. In all it can be estimated today that there are 70,000-75,000 Bulgarians, 6,000 Moldavians and Walachians, and around 5,000 Serbs, almost all of whom are in Bessarabia and Kherson. Fourteen hundred Bulgarians and several thousand Greeks also live in Tauride province. The number of Armenians is unknown although it probably does not exceed 1,000.* In the province of

*We are speaking here only of those Armenians engaged in agriculture. All the southern cities swarm with Armenian merchants, whose numbers are estimated at 70,000.

Kherson there are nine colonies of Jews with about 7,500 inhabitants. The four colonies of Swedes have a population of around 800. All the remaining colonists or more than 230,000 individuals are Germans from various regions: Switzerland, Baden, Württemberg, Nassau, the Rhineland, and West Prussia.

Regarding the religious confession of the 330,000 colonists, 80,000 belong to the Greek church and 1,000 are members of the Armenian church; the Protestants, including the Herrenhuters in Sarepta, number 181,000. There are also 21,000 Mennonites, including the Hutterite Brethren, 40,000 Catholics, and 7,500 Jews. . . .

In 1843 there were 2,846,300 fruit trees, 700,000 mulberry trees, and 12,455,000 grape vines in the southern Russian colonies. This year 775,865 barrels of wine were pressed. Much has been done for cattle raising. In all of the colonies there are very good communally owned bulls, horses, and sheep kept for breeding. The livestock total in the southern Russian colonies in 1843 was 78,600 horses, 207,500 horned cattle, 735,180 Spanish sheep, and 150,810 ordinary sheep. To facilitate the sale of produce four fairs are held annually; in twelve colonies bazaars were permitted. In time small cities will probably grow up around them. In 1843 wares valued at 737,790 silver rubles were displayed for sale at these four fairs. The following industries were located in the southern Russian colonies: 1 textile mill, 6 vinegar factories, 1 distillery, 5 breweries, 2 cheese factories, 22 brick works, 4 roof-tile works, 18 potter's shops, 1 soap factory, 98 oil mills, 9 fulling mills, 31 dying works, and 7,230 linen looms.

Twenty-two inns, 17 restaurants, and 68 wine cellars indicate the beginning of European luxury and comfort in the colonies. In all there were 78 churches, 53 of which belonged to the Greek church, 107 prayer houses, and 871 sacristans. There was one church for every 895 souls and one clergyman for 762 souls. The 279 elementary schools with 283 teachers served 20,532 pupils. In addition, schools of higher learning were founded. The school in Bolgrad in Bessarabia also had a department for training surveyors and architects.

The preceding facts can give us an idea of the great importance of these colonies of foreigners in Russia. And yet they have by no means fulfilled the somewhat exaggerated expectations of Catherine II's manifesto of 1763. Their influence on agricultural and industrial advancement in Russia has not been nearly as significant as had been hoped. . . .

These colonies have cost Russia millions, though only as invested capital. The settlers have repaid the loans over a period of years or are still paying the balance. The government merely lost some of the interest.

The majority of the colonies are flourishing. After years of hardship and oppressive poverty, the settlers have become prosperous, and some have grown rich. Over the years they have found a home in a foreign country. I cannot say that I met anyone who wished he were back in Germany, as was said to have frequently been the case in the beginning. The government treats the colonies benevolently and is very concerned about their welfare.

In recent times the government has taken no measures to attract new settlers to Russia. Today it would probably exercise great caution in accepting new colonists, taking only those who bring a knowledge of agriculture and experience, diligence, and capital. If the government could obtain another 100,000 people like the Mennonites, it certainly would spare neither effort nor money.

# 8
## *Kiev*

Around eight o'clock on the morning of the thirteenth, a magnificent October day, we caught sight of Kiev, the old Metropolis and mother of Russian cities. A half-mile from Kiev we saw to the left and right of the road important old circumvallations, moats, and remains of bulwarks, etc.

After settling down in a rather good inn, we made the necessary calls. The governor general, Mr. Bibikov,[1] a man of the finest manners and also very energetic and versatile, we were told, instructed a Mr. Chadois to show us around and give us the essential information on everything. Mr. Chadois, who is the son of a very rich landowner and a very well-informed young autodidact, took us first of all to the famous Monastery of the Caves.

The cloister and church are new and are constructed in the same style as all such institutions in Russia. The older buildings burned down several times; the last fire was in 1728. In the sanctuary of the church we were handed wax candles; the archpriest opened a side door and led us down a long flight of stairs into the subterranean passages. These roughly resemble mine shafts; the passages are seldom more than seven feet high and four to five feet wide and are

1. General-Adjutant Dmitrii Gavrilovich Bibikov (1792–1870) distinguished himself as a field commander during the last phase of the Napoleonic campaigns; subsequently he headed the Department of Foreign Trade before being appointed military governor of Kiev in 1840, in which post he worked to unite the former Polish areas to Russia and to assure their loyalty by protecting the local peasantry against exploitation by Polish *szlachta*. *Russkii biograficheskii slovar* 3:23–26.

comprised of two labyrinthian corridors extending for more than half an hour's walk into the mountain cliff. Every twenty to fifty steps, to the left and right, a niche has been carved out of the rock and fashioned into a stone coffin. The old hermits, all of whom are venerated as saints, lie buried here. The bodies do not decay in these caves, but simply shrivel up. In these stone coffins all of the bodies lie exposed in their monastic vestments. A magnificent multicolored, gold-embroidered silk cloth covers each corpse. The archpriest removed the cover from several coffins and showed us the nondecomposed corpses. A horrible sight! One of the saints had himself buried alive in the earth up to his shoulders, so that only his head protruded, and he died in this position. He too was covered with a gold-embroidered cloth. Here and there small cells inhabited by the hermits were carved into the cliffs adjacent to the passages. Food was handed to them through a small window. They never left their cells and never spoke to anyone. We were shown the cell of Saint Antonii, the founder of the Monastery of the Caves, and the stone bench hewn into the cliffs where he sat and taught the brethren. Above the tomb of Nestor, the famous chronicler of Russian history, was hung a metal votive tablet bearing a commemorative inscription. . . .

[Returning to the city,] we saw a beautiful garden which was laid out by Potemkin for Empress Catherine and which now contains an artificial spa built according to Struve's system. One certainly cannot ask for more! I also saw a large and most elegant boarding school for aristocratic young ladies which was founded by the nobility of the province. Here as in all the Russian boarding schools the girls are educated to become salon ladies rather than housewives. I then drove to the university. Situated in a large square on a hilltop, the university is a colossal and excellently built palace. I made the acquaintance of several professors. The library has a rich collection. Much has been transferred here from Vilno, including an entire faculty. In the natural history office I saw a revolting collection of hair infected with plica. Professor Ivanishev,[2] a very learned and most amiable man, showed me around and in the course of our conversation gave me some information on local rural institutions.

The aristocracy in the provinces around Kiev is of Polish origin. Only a few Great Russian families have settled here. Among the Little and Red Russians (Ruthenians) there was never an indigenous

2. Nikolai Dmitrevich Ivanishev (1811–74) was appointed professor of state laws at Saint Vladimir University in Kiev after study in Berlin under Savigny and at Prague under Palacky. *Russkii biograficheskii slovar* 8:4.

aristocracy. According to Procopius this was originally true of all the Slavic peoples. Only after the grand dukes of Lithuania had conquered these territories and Lithuania united with Poland did a Polish and Lithuanian nobility enter these lands. History has yet to explain when and how this took place. The immigration and settlement of the Polish and Lithuanian aristocracy can perhaps best be accounted for by the fact these these fertile regions, having been ravaged by the Mongols and Tatars, lay fallow and deserted for the most part. This was the reason why the *szlachta* or lower nobility immigrated; they tilled the land with their own hands and usually settled in communities. However, it remains more difficult to explain the origin of serfdom among the formerly free Ruthenians and the manner in which the landed upper aristocracy was able to establish large domains here and make the Ruthenian villages tributary to their estates. Neither history nor Polish law sheds light on this.

Very few Polish noblemen moved into Little Russia on the left bank of the Dnieper and none entered the Cossack territories. Here Empress Catherine gave many of her courtiers grants of peasants. Formerly freemen, these peasants fell victim to Russian serfdom. In these regions the lands of the Russian and Polish aristocrats meet, and they frequently live one next to the other. In the Cossack territories, many former Cossack officers who achieved a Russian rank also acquired hereditary nobility and now constitute a landed gentry.

In Podolia and Volhynia the Polish aristocracy had the same position as in eastern Galicia, where the native population is likewise comprised of Ruthenians. However, Russia and Austria treated their territories differently. Austria did not show partiality to the Polish landed aristocracy, especially regarding its relations to the peasantry. The Austrian government did not recognize the peasants as serfs but simply acknowledged and regulated by legislation their obligation to remain on their seigneur's estate. To be sure, not all the laws have been enforced, but still the aristocracy there has supposedly to pay very high taxes.

In the Russian territories of the former Polish Empire inhabited by Ruthenians, the government continues to treat the landed Polish aristocracy very leniently with respect to its property. Because Russian legislation was introduced here, the local aristocracy is in the same favorable position as the Russian nobility. The serfdom of the aristocracy's subjects is unconditionally recognized. Even though the law limits the number of days the serf has to work for his master to three per week, the seigneur basically has not been denied any of his rights. It is virtually impossible to require the peasant to perform more work on the lord's estate if he is not to let his own land lie fallow and thus starve.

Patrimonial jurisdiction can still be found in Austrian Galicia; it does not exist in the Russian territories, although its most important aspect in regard to material interests, namely, police authority, is left to the aristocracy. Patrimonial jurisdiction is of no real value to the landowners in Galicia though, since it is exercised by their representatives and agents. This gives these despicable bloodsuckers of the province new opportunity to oppress and harass the peasants for their own profit and at the same time provides the peasants with new reason to hate the aristocracy. . . .

The local aristocracy [of Kiev province] has by no means forgotten old Poland, but the memory of the past is more alive among the [Polish] nobility of Galicia. This explains why the aristocracy in the Russian parts of Poland was little involved in the revolution of 1831.[3]

About twenty-seven to thirty thousand peasants may have been confiscated in these formerly Polish territories, which implies that only a small number of the aristocracy supported the revolution. Those noblemen who have estates in both [Austrian] Galicia and in the Russian-ruled part of Poland usually reside in the Russian-held territory, where they feel [more secure].[4] Furthermore the financial situation of the local aristocracy has improved greatly under Russian administration, particularly through the rise of Odessa and its flourishing grain trade. As a result, the nobility much prefers the Russian to the Austrian government. This observation, which I had occasion to make in 1843, proved to be amazingly true in 1846.[5]

The *szlachta* or lower Polish nobility presents a different case.[6] The *szlachta* is imbued with a much deeper national sentiment than the refined, French-educated upper aristocracy. The former is com-

3. By 1830 many Polish aristocrats, especially those of the older generation, had come to accept as a fact the concentration of the Polish economy on the eastern market and viewed hostility with Russia as an economic disaster. Their position was not shared by the younger *szlachta*, many of whom dreamed of a new Polish republic. See R. F. Leslie, *Polish Politics and the Revolution of November, 1830* (London, 1956), pp. 78–95.

4. Haxthausen's expression here is literally "feel less oppressed."

5. For the obligations of lord and peasant in Austria in Vormärz see Jerome Blum, *Noble Landowners and Agriculture in Austria, 1815–1848,* The Johns Hopkins University Studies in Historical and Political Sciences, series 65, no. 2 (Baltimore, 1948), pp. 45–90 and 447 ff.

6. On the *szlachta* see A. Bruce Boswell, "Poland," *The European Nobility in the Eighteenth Century*, ed. A. Goodwin (New York, 1967), pp. 154–72.

pletely uncultured, even less so than the German peasantry, for example. Although poor and vulgar, the *szlachta* is as proud and courageous as one can be. In all the old Polish provinces they became deeply implicated in the revolution of 1831, which, of course, led to a change in their circumstances. The *szlachta* was required to prove its nobiliary status by means of documents or other official forms of recognition. Since they were naturally unable to do this, the majority of them lost their rank. They were given the position of *odnodvortsy* as based on Russian laws.[7] If the former petty aristocrats owned their own land, they were called *volnye liudi*, or freemen; they did not have to pay *obrok* but they paid the head tax and were also subject to military duty. If they happened to be on crown land, they were treated exactly like the other crown peasants, who are personally free but have to serve in the military and pay the head tax and *obrok*. Those on seigneurial lands had to pay only the head tax and rent and were thus free tenants. . . .

The system of land tenure among the aristocrats in the former Polish territories is different from that in Great Russia. In Great Russia a nobleman possesses land and peasants who cultivate it and pay him rent in return. Here, however, the aristocracy has large, fully equipped estates with separate plowlands, meadows, and pastures. They are partitioned into small indivisible units with their own stock. On the lord's estate, the tenants have to perform specified services which are based on the size of their farms. In brief, the system of land cultivation corresponds to that found in most of Germany as well as in a large part of the rest of Europe.

It seems that when the land was taken possession of for the first time by the Poles and Lithuanians, it was divided . . . into a large number of small territories which were then granted to aristocratic Polish families. These territories are known here as *klucza* (castles or domains). Besides the lord's mansion with its park, etc., a *klucz* is comprised of a number of *vollwarks* (obviously a corruption of the German *Vorwerk*, farm). In a broad sense the *vollwark* is an estate with its plowlands, meadows, and pastures and includes the village belonging to the domain; the peasants from the village are required to render certain services on the estate. In a narrower sense a *vollwark* is the demesne or the steward's house, together with the cowsheds, barns, and granaries. The arable land of a *vollwark* is divided into three fields. In very productive regions one-half of each field, and in less fertile areas one-third belongs to the demesne.

7. On the *odnodvortsy*, see p. 286, n. 10.

The other half or two-thirds is parceled out among the peasants. We have already mentioned that the peasants are divided into different categories according to the amount of land they occupy and the work they have to perform on the demesne. On small *vollwark*s the peasants are generally divided into only two groups: *tiagla* (those who are required to work with teams) and the manual laborers, or *peshtsy*.[8] Now and again one also finds a third category, the *galupniki*, who merely have a house but no garden.

If one wanted to study the rural institutions of these territories in their entirety, one could greatly facilitate one's work by examining and comparing a number of so-called inventories from each district.

In this connection an inventory is the detailed account of a *klucz* or simply of a single *vollwark*. . . . Such an inventory includes an exact description of a *klucz* or *vollwark*, an enumeration of the lands and their area, the number of peasants and other inhabitants of the village, their services and payments, the proportionment of the latter and the land which is turned over to the peasants in return, etc. In brief, such an inventory provides a clear picture of the rural life of a region.

Every landowner has inventories of his estates. The custom of taking inventory probably came from Germany, although it is a very old practice in Poland. Sixteenth-century documents from the imperial diets mention their existence. However, the custom did not cross the border of the old Polish Empire, and in Russia it is nowhere to be found. . . .

On 17 October we left Kiev. The view of the city from the hills on the opposite bank of the Dnieper is truly majestic and there are but a few cities in Russia — perhaps Nizhnii Novgorod — which can compare with Kiev in this respect. The landscape and the villages on the left bank of the Dnieper gradually assume a different appearance. On the right bank the farms in the villages lie close together in irregular clusters as in northern Germany, whereas the left bank begins to display the regularity of the Russian villages with their long, straight roads, etc. The farm buildings are not situated in a row alongside the road, as in the Great Russian villages. The villages on the right bank usually have three gateways leading to

8. Haxthausen uses the word *piesché* here, which does not exist in Polish, Ukrainian, or Russian. The term *peshtsy*, to which it has been changed, refers to the medieval foot soldier, hence manual laborer. The source of the term *galupniki* is not clear, for no similar expression exists in Polish, Ukrainian, or Russian.

their three fields. Only the gateway to the fallow field is open; the other two are closed by barriers so that the cattle cannot break into the winter and summer fields.

On the right bank of the Dnieper the village inns, all of which are run by Jews, are built exactly like those in Prussia, Lithuania, Courland, and Livonia. In their entire construction they resemble the old Westphalian farmhouse. The Teutonic Knights probably introduced this style of construction into the northern regions, and from there the Jews carried it as far as Bessarabia! On the left bank one no longer sees inns like these, but rather a building with a passageway leading toward the yard, such as one finds in the March of Brandenburg. This arrangement appears to me to have been borrowed from foreigners and not to have grown out of Russian customs. The exterior of these houses, excluding the inner walls of the gateway, is whitewashed, as is customary throughout Little Russia. In a variety of minor things one sees that the Little Russians have more taste than the Great Russians. Everywhere they have small flowerbeds enclosed by a fence in front of their homes; they do more gardening and have an excellent fruit culture. The fences around the gardens are very elegantly interlaced. . . . In the direction of the province of Orel we again find the villages laid out in the Great Russian manner, usually along a long, wide street. However, the houses are not crowded closely together in citylike fashion as among the Great Russians; rather one finds large farmsteads situated in a row. The Little Russians are not as sociable as the Great Russians. In general the Little Russian women appear to me to be prettier and better proportioned than their Great Russian counterparts, who are short and fat. However, the Great Russian men are obviously more handsome. The cattle here are small and either black or red. One does not find the large, silver-gray Podolian breed common throughout southern Russia. Fine pigs are bred here, and the raising of geese is extensive.

On 18 October we arrived in the city of Nezhin, which is said to have around eighteen thousand inhabitants, about eight thousand of whom belong to the middle class and four thousand to the *odnodvortsy* or the Cossack class.[9] The rest of the population is comprised

9. The town of Nezhin, 125 kilometers northeast of Kiev, is an ancient settlement united with Russia only in 1664 and from then until the opening of the Black Sea ports the scene of the most important fair for international produce in Russia. Quantities of goods from Germany, Turkey, and Italy, entered Russia through this fair. See Semenov-Tian-Shanskii, *Rossiia*, 7:320–73.

of aristocrats, civil servants, a rather large number of Greeks, and an even greater number of Jews. Formerly Nezhin was an important commercial center, which explains why so many Greeks moved here. A large, famous fair, frequented especially by Ukrainian merchants, is still held here at Shrovetide.

Much tobacco is grown in the environs of Nezhin. In December and January it is driven by sled to Riga, where the price is determined by demand. If the tobacco cannot be disposed of there, it goes to Moscow or Odessa, though at far lower prices. There are two kinds of tobacco here. The better and stronger variety is called *makhorski*. This year it cost only 2½ rubles banco per pud; in other years the price climbed as high as 7 to 8 rubles banco. The local peasants smoke the tobacco before it has been treated; in Riga, however, it is specially prepared. The second variety, which is called *papusha*, costs now only 80 kopeks banco per pud and in other years as much as 4 rubles banco.

The field on which tobacco is raised is heavily fertilized every two years and then planted annually with tobacco. After a number of years, when the field is no longer productive, it is planted with summer wheat for two years in succession and then again with tobacco. Formerly the growing of tobacco was left almost exclusively to crown peasants; now, however, the landowners also raise tobacco and in such vast quantities that the surplus has created a shortage of markets. The Jews are the middlemen. They are actually tolerated only in the cities; they are not accepted in the state villages and can reside in the seigneurial villages only with the master's special permission, which, however, is usually denied. Most of the local state peasants are called Cossacks; since they own the land outright they pay only the head tax and no *obrok*. There are but a small number of *obrok*-paying peasants here. One village of *obrok* peasants, Losenska, is said to be distinguished by its wealth. The seigneurial peasants in the province of Chernigov are generally required to work on the master's land three days a week; they employ the Great Russian system of land apportionment based on *tiagla*.

We were told that thirty to forty versts from here there was a very old German colony of approximately three hundred souls, which was said to have been founded by Peter I. Although they retained the German style in the construction of their farmsteads as well as German household customs, they were nearly completely Russified in every other respect. The extensive raising of tobacco in this region is supposed to have originated with them. They also were the first to introduce the raising of potatoes, which is now rather widespread. . . .

We reached the border of the province of Orel, which roughly forms the boundary between the Little and the Great Russians. The physiognomy, physique, beard, and dress showed this, although gradual transitions were, of course, still noticeable. Here and there the dress is a combination of both nationalities. The layout and construction of the farmsteads and houses are still predominantly Little Russian. There is an arbor before the house, the broad side of the houses face the street, and the walls are whitewashed. However, the villages with their long, wide streets and the farmsteads arranged closely together in a row are Great Russian in their layout. The village of Sevka, where we changed horses, was completely Great Russian; the houses were situated with their gable sides toward the street, and they had the customary three windows in a row. On some of the houses the center window was lacking, having been replaced by a simulated one. The window frames were painted in oil colors, and the exterior of the house was not whitewashed.

In determining the border of the provinces, both real and national boundaries seem to have been considered to some extent. At least the more important differences between the Great Russians, Little Russians, and White Russians appear to have been kept in mind.

We arrived at Sevsk, the southernmost major city in the province of Orel.[10] On the southern border of this province most of the population is an amalgam of Little and Great Russians. The latter seem to have been the first colonists, the majority being retired soldiers. The names show this: *Peshtsy* (footsoldiers), *Mushketery* (musketeers), *Pushkaria* (cannoneers), *Reitary* (horsemen), and *Streltsy* (bowmen). In addition there are peasants attached to cloisters, demesnes, etc. However, none of these names constitutes any real distinction, in that all of them have state land; they are in the same circumstances and pay the same taxes as the state peasants. Only the Little Russians with the title of Cossacks own their land outright and pay no *obrok*. All of the local private peasants are required to perform services on their master's demesne.

Only the poor petty aristocrats live in the countryside; the prosperous noblemen reside in the cities and the wealthy in Moscow. The latter usually have peasant *starosty* or, less often, trained administrators to manage their estates. I received some notes on the adminis-

10. The town of Sevsk was a center of settlement for Streltsy punished in 1683. See Semenov-Tian-Shanskii, *Rossiia*, 2:559–60.

tration of such an estate in the neighboring district of Dmitriev in the province of Kursk. The estate has approximately one thousand desiatins of plowland, meadows, pastures, and sparse woodlands. Six villages are situated on the estate. The largest is Prelep, and the entire estate derives its name from this village. Fourteen to fifteen hundred male souls live in the six villages. Located in the main village of Prelep are the seigneurial demesne, a large textile mill, and a beet-sugar factory. Half of all the plowlands and meadows are set aside as the lord's land. The population of all six villages is comprised of eight hundred *tiagla*. They till the lord's field, in addition to their own, plant it, harvest and thresh the grain, and drive it to the markets. Each *tiaglo* is responsible for nearly all the work on two desiatins of the seigneur's land in each field. The soil here in the Black Earth region is excellent and among the most fertile land in Russia. Little wheat and barley are grown, the most important crop being rye. A *starosta* supervises the seigneurial farm in each village. Located in each village are a seigneurial drying room, a barn, and a granary. On the whole, the three-field system is employed, although the master has set up a kind of eight-field system as a model in one village. The lord keeps about three thousand sheep. The wool is taken to the annual fair in Kharkov; in 1842 it cost 12 to 14 rubles banco per pud. A *starosta*, a simple peasant, took the wool there and directed the sale of the local products, which amounted to approximately 60,000 rubles banco! Fields for growing flax and hemp, which are not included in the distribution of the communal land, are assigned on a permanent basis to every peasant household. Some of the beets for the beet-sugar factory are raised on the seigneurial fields and some are bought from the peasants, who now like to grow them.[11] Both the beet-sugar factory and the textile mill, which supplies 100,000 arshins of cloth annually to the crown alone for the army, are managed and supervised by local peasants. Formerly the lord employed foreigners as factory managers, who then trained the local peasants to become their most able and reliable successors. Four hundred souls have been assigned to the factories. Homes where four to five families dwell together

11. The extent to which the beets themselves were raised by peasants or by the seigneur varied from province to province. In Tula it was done largely by the peasants and in Kiev by the seigneur. See Tengoborski, *Commentaries*, 1:463–93; also M. A. Tolpygin, *Sakharnaia promyshlennost ot osnovaniia eë do nastoiashchego vremeni* (Kiev, 1894); and B. V. Tikhanov, "Razvitie sveklosakharnoi promyshlennosti vo vtoroi polovine 40-kh i v 50-kh godakh XIX," *Istoricheskie zapiski*, vol. 62 (1958).

under one roof have been built for the peasants near these factories; they are given housing and gardens without charge. For the work in the factories they are paid according to fixed rates; they receive a specified amount for every arshin of woven cloth, for every pud of spun wool and so forth. Every male can easily earn 10 to 15 rubles banco monthly; some industrious men earn as much as 20 rubles banco; the women earn 6 to 8 rubles banco and the children 2 to 3 rubles banco. The essential foodstuffs, namely, 2 puds of rye flour, 2 puds of oat meal, 3/16 chetverts of wheat, 5 puds of meat, 3 puds of salt, and 1½ puds of oil monthly per person, are supplied to them by their master; 2 rubles banco per person are then deducted from their monthly earnings.[12] It is clear from the above, that these factory workers are better off than their counterparts in the rest of Europe. In addition, the lord must feed them, when they are old or take ill. There is a hospital established by the seigneur for all the sick in the villages.

The city of Sevsk has around five thousand inhabitants. In the environs abundant flax is raised, which requires spreading with manure, whereas the grain fields are not fertilized. Much oil is pressed from the flax and hemp seeds. Neither flax nor hemp is spun or woven here, but each is sold raw instead. The daily wage here now stands at 60 to 80 kopeks banco and for masons and carpenters at 1 ruble banco. At the moment the price of grain was 3 rubles, 50 kopeks banco for a measure of rye and 3 rubles, 45 kopeks banco or only 5 kopeks less than rye, for one of oats. I did not learn the reason for the high price of oats. It must be constant, though, since it seems to have established the rule of planting only oats and no barley on the summer field in these regions. In Orel the price of rye was 4 rubles banco, although it had been 38 rubles banco two years ago!

Most of the villages that we now passed through were small, with ten to twenty houses. However, there were also some very large villages with stone churches, one of which had three thousand inhabitants.

On the morning of 22 October we reached Orel, a provincial

---

12. If the figures cited by Tengoborski, *Commentaries*, 1:486 ff., for Count Bobrinskoi's estate in Kiev province are accurate, then Haxthausen has greatly exaggerated his figures. Tengoborski claims that wages in the late 1840s were 15 kopeks for a twelve-hour day, plus food. Women received 8 kopeks per diem and horses and oxen were hired at the rate of 30 kopeks. In Chernigov province the rate was 4 rubles a month with food or 6 rubles without, while in Tula it was from 3 to 3½ rubles per month.

capital like most in Russia, with several very modern streets, multidomed churches, palaces with balconies and pillars, as well as entire quarters where only genuine Russian block houses with three windows are to be found. Most of the residents in these sections are coachmen and vegetable farmers. Like the burghers and local merchants, they have gardens next to their homes. At the entrance to the city one never finds gardens as is customary in Germany. I paid the necessary visits to the governor, Prince Trubetskoi, whose German wife is a Princess Wittgenstein by birth, to the president of the Bureau of State Domains and several others. . . .

The province of Orel is located along the old steppe frontier. The southern and southeastern regions are still called the land of the steppes. There are few woodlands, whereas the northern and northwestern districts are abundant in forests. On the whole the province is among the nation's most fertile regions. However, narrow strips of barren sandy soil intersect the province like tongues from north to south, for here we find the transition from the sandy soil, with its granite pebbles, to the soil of the Black Earth. When this fertile land is divided among heirs or sold, its value is not determined according to the number of peasants but according to the number of desiatins. I was told, to give a comparison, that in this province the value of 150 to 200 peasants including the land turned over with them is estimated to be the same as that of 100 peasants in the province in Pskov.

In the south there is a shortage of woodland. Nevertheless the villages are attractive, the houses well built and clean, and the people prosperous. In the north everything looks much poorer. Furthermore, the forests there are threatened with total ruin. The Russian peasant never protects them. In order to obtain money and to feed their peasants in lean years, the landowners sold entire stretches of woodland to speculators and townspeople for the purpose of deforestation; the buyer usually imposed the condition that he be allowed to let the wood lie about for years. The new seedlings were smothered, and the forest could not restore itself. As it is, no one thinks about conservation. Consequently there are no longer any forests near the city of Orel and the price of wood has increased substantially within five years from 12½ to 15 rubles banco per cord. The state forests were said to have been utterly neglected in former years. Their management was turned over to any chinovnik for the asking; corruption and knavery were the order of the day. They sold the wood at a ridiculously low price and accepted "special fees" in return. When the forest was devastated and they feared an investigation, they set fire to the rest and burned everything to the ground so as to destroy the evidence. The new Ministry of State Domains introduced some order, brought several culprits to trial, and so forth.[13]

In regard to the relations of the seigneurs to their serfs in these regions one seldom hears complaints about great oppression. The majority of peasants are required to perform services on the lord's demesne. In selecting his three days of the week the master can claim the more favorable time for himself and in this way impose some hardship. On the whole, however, the Russian peasant does not let himself be taken advantage of, since he has before his eyes the free *odnodvortsy* and the Cossacks. The undivided villages in particular offer stubborn opposition to every form of oppression. Since every extraordinary or unusual task is performed with distrust, any improvement in agriculture is nearly impossible. If the master were simply to order them to plow an inch deeper, they would immediately say, "The master is not good; he treats us cruelly." And then woe to him, if he resides in the countryside. In general, the peasants who are required to work on the lord's estate put up with less than the peasants who must pay *obrok*.

I had the opportunity here to make the acquaintance of a man who gave me some notes about the spirit trade. I am not in a position to judge the value and authenticity of his information. One hears only unfavorable remarks, and it is only natural for exaggeration to enter into an account of the situation.

There are two sets of legislation governing the distillation of spirits in the Russian Empire.[14] In Finland, the Baltic provinces, the Polish territories, and Little Russia the distillation of liquor is turned over for a fee to the landowners, Cossacks, etc., whereas in Russia proper it is a crown monopoly. The government leases both the right to distill and the right to sell the finished product. In the spring, and always before harvest, the government, through the office of the Ministry of Finances, puts up for bid the right to produce alcohol on condition that distilled spirits be delivered to it for a fixed price. The undertaking always involves a risk, since one can hardly guess what the price of grain will be after the harvest. The minister of finances fixes the maximum price for a *vedro* (barrel) of alcohol, and no offer above the maximum is accepted. Of course, the price

13. On forests and forest legislation see Tengoborski, *Commentaries*, 1:409–29.

14. On brandy distilling see Tengoborski, *Commentaries*, 1:454–60; a detailed treatment of the subject is to be found in Ivan Pryzhov, *Istoriia kabakov v Rossii v sviazi s istoriei russkogo naroda* (St. Petersburg, 1862).

is kept very secret. The revenue office then informs the landed proprietors and distillery owners of the appointed date for the bidding and requires the bidder to supply a specific quantity of liquor at a specified price. On the day set for the submission of bids (*torg*) the proprietors of the distilleries offer to deliver set quantities of alcohol of a specified quality and at specified prices, and the lowest bidders are awarded the contract. If on the first *torg* no suitable bids are submitted, a second date or *peretorg* is set. One can see that it is a venture and a dangerous one at that, but the Russians like to speculate! Some landowners undertake to supply one million vedros of alcohol, which often leads to the ruining of the forests. As soon as the commission has been awarded, the bidders receive written contracts, in which the time and place of delivery is specified. If they desire, they can obtain advances on the liquor to be delivered, to as much as half of the bid.

The second manipulation then begins for the government. It negotiates the right to sell the spirits in the various provinces. For this purpose dates are also set and competition begins anew, but this time more among the merchants and urban speculators. In this case the highest rather than the lowest bidder is the recipient of the contract. One buys the alcohol from the government for the maximum price, which often exceeds by four to six times the price at which the distillery owners sell it. In return one receives for a substantial offer the right and the monopoly to sell it at wholesale or retail for fixed prices, in a specific province. The contract-holder (*otkupchik*) then sells the liquor in sealed casks and bottles both to subcontractors and innkeepers. As a rule the liquor sold over the counter is still good, though expensive. In the *kabak*s [taverns], however, it is horribly adulterated, especially that in casks, and to a lesser degree that which is in sealed bottles. Occasionally it is diluted to 50 percent with water but, to make it intoxicating, narcotic herbs, tobacco, belladonna, etc., are added. If the drinkers could always buy whole bottles or casks, they would, of course, be cheated less.

Intemperance is one of the greatest evils, indeed the true plague, of the Russian Empire. One of the greatest and most salutary measures on the part of the government would be to combat it. However, great obstacles stand in the way of reform, since the granting of contracts for the sale of alcohol yields enormous sums, which are absolutely essential and which can hardly be made up for by other means. Moreover, the situation is not better and may be even worse in those provinces where the crown has no monopoly.

There are national differences where intemperance is concerned. The most inveterate drinkers are the White Russians, who as a result are the most debilitated. The Great Russian does not drink constantly or daily. There are many who do not touch a glass for months and who refuse a dram when it is offered them. But then there are times and temptations when, if he tastes one drop, he is seized by a fit of drunkenness; he drinks without cease for days or even weeks. He squanders everything he owns for drink, and this is the time when the innkeeper makes his real profit. As long as the drinker has his senses, he is given unadulterated brandy, but later the innkeeper gives him inferior liquor and charges him for more than he has actually had. The price for a dram is, of course, fixed everywhere. However, natural products such as grain, bread, talc, and flax are accepted as payment at arbitrary low prices. The peasants are less addicted than the artisans, which explains why the latter seldom get ahead. The Little Russians drink regularly, though usually in moderation. Among them drunkenness is rare, and they do not drink themselves insensible.

Since there is no monopoly among the Little Russians, the liquor is, of course, superior. Here along the border the Great Russians frequently try to smuggle the better liquor over to their side, although the punishment is most severe: exile to Siberia and induction into the army! This peculiar situation in the same country and among the same people obviously must arouse a feeling of injustice.

The traveler is seized with horror when he sees these miserable state *kabaks* with the double eagle overhead. We passed through a village of *odnodvortsy*; the houses and farmsteads were attractive, and the entire village looked prosperous. However, when we asked our coachman about conditions there he replied, "Yes, it was in former times a wealthy *odnodvortsy* village, but do you see that small house with the eagle? It has been there for only ten years, and it has already devoured all the large wealthy homes!"

The owners of private estates do not have to tolerate the *kabaks* in their villages. However, the holders of liquor contracts far too often seduce them to sell the rights. And once there is a *kabak* in the village, it can never be got rid of.

In Orel a vedro of ordinary brandy cost at that time 10½ rubles banco, and a vedro of better brandy 17 rubles banco. At the same time a vedro of so-called Greek wine from the Crimea, Bessarabia, or Podolia cost only 9 rubles banco.

An intelligent Livonian doctor took me around the city. We visited in particular those parts of the city where the Russian artisans live.

As in many provinces the local artisans are for the most part seigneur-ial serfs and less often state peasants. . . .

As a rule the nobleman selects young boys among his people and sends them to the city to learn a trade. Upon completing their apprenticeship, they return. The nobleman keeps the best among them, those whom he needs for his own purposes, and sends the others back to the cities, charging them to establish themselves there and to pay him an annual *obrok*. To establish themselves, they have to do nothing more than enroll in a guild, pay 10 rubles banco to the city council as a kind of license tax, and hang out a sign. There are no conditions for acceptance into the guild: no years of apprenticeship, no years of travel as a journeyman to acquire greater skill, no sample of work to be submitted, and no ceremony whereby one is declared qualified to follow his trade independently. There is complete freedom in the trades, which explains why all the artisans in Russia are such poor workers. . . .

In regard to the institution of the guild, Russia did not pass through the Middle Ages and in this respect did not acquire an education for modern times. Through the institution of the guild the Germanic and Romanic Middle Ages gave rise to the artisan class, with its own individual culture, its class pride, its ceremonial customs, its industry, reliability, and honesty. When the modern era tore down the restrictive barriers, abolished the privileges of the guild, and introduced freedom in the trades, the lack of restraint did not have such detrimental effects as some people prophesied. The customs had become firmly established, the old traditions lived on, and a social class with its own distinctive character emerged. The artisan class had come of age and could endure freedom in the trades without injury to itself or to the public. In Russia, however, this freedom in the trades is a great evil.[15]

If the Russian tradesman is a good worker and acquires some money, he has self-esteem and attempts to gain his freedom. He takes advantage of the benevolence of his master or the latter's need for money and purchases his freedom. In the second case the two parties generally haggle for hours and even days about one kopek. The price of freedom usually fluctuates between 200 and

15. Catherine II had as a policy the division of Russian local society into self-governing corporations, one of which was to be the artisan guild. This principle, embodied in the 1785 Charter of the Cities, had no precedent in Russian experience and the guilds were stillborn. See Iu. R. Klokman, *Sotzialno-ekonomicheskaia istoriia russkogo goroda, vtoraia polovina XVIII veka* (Moscow, 1967), pp. 109 ff.

2,000 rubles banco. I was told that the lowest annual *obrok* rate paid by the artisans in Orel was 30 rubles banco and the highest 200 rubles banco.

In every Russian city there are foreign tradesmen, chiefly Germans. They have a long-standing reputation for better craftsmanship, which they frequently have not lived up to in recent times. The foreign artisan, if he is not a Russian subject, pays 20 rubles banco annually [for his registration]. Foreigners in Russia enjoy such a privileged position that they often remain in the country until they die, and several generations live there without becoming Russian subjects. Only when they enter into marriages with Russians or when they seek a rank in the government service (*chin*) for their sons, do they generally become naturalized.

The merchants in the Russian cities, except in the capital cities, are as a rule Russians and the majority are bearded. Instead of wearing a suit they keep the caftan and do not shave. Everywhere they are divided into three guilds. These guilds are not corporations which independently receive members. Rather, everyone who pays the prescribed fees for any guild is accepted *ipso jure*. In the Russian cities the merchants nearly constitute a hereditary social class, and their sons always become merchants. A father brings his son into the business at the age of twelve; consequently they have no schooling. Only a few learn to read and write, but they can all calculate with the Russian abacus. It is a principle that a son should not know more than his father. Among the merchants there is a large number of Old Believers, who are very religious and who cling firmly to the old customs. But, nevertheless, they are usually completely unreliable and often fraudulent in their business dealings, except with one another. They often remain together in the same business and live in the same household for several generations. In one house in Orel I found four families, the parents and three married sons with their children. The sons almost always marry within their social class. Everywhere in Russia gatherings are held on Pentecost (or in May). All the merchant families meet at a public place, the daughters laden with ornaments and jewels. People pass one another without uttering a word. Marriages are arranged there, but the young people have little to say in this matter. The parents make the choice amidst vehement bargaining back and forth about the dowry etc., which, however, almost never includes money as long as the parents are alive, but rather movables, jewels, etc.

There is a basic difference between the merchants and artisans. When the artisans become well to do and have purchased their freedom, they adopt modern ways. They shave off their beards and exchange the caftan for the frock coat. They try to give their sons an education in order to get them into the class of government officials, if possible. Their sons never become tradesmen if it can be at all avoided. The artisans are therefore always recruited among the serfs, whereas the merchants are always enlisted from the ranks of the sons of the merchants themselves. In recent times, however, the merchants have also begun to permit their daughters at least to marry into *chinovnik* families, just as the latter, of course, are very eager to marry the daughters of wealthy merchants. Consequently, the daughters now often receive more education than the sons. In some homes of genuine bearded Russian merchants I found pianofortes, which the daughters played quite well. In Kursk there is supposedly even a school for the daughters of merchants where they receive a superficial training in French conversation, music making, and dancing without being educated to be efficient housewives. The true old-Russian merchant wives likewise do almost nothing the livelong day. They virtually neglect the household and perform no woman's work; they munch on sunflower seeds all day. This boredom far too often leads them to all kinds of excesses; love affairs and debauchery are more than common. Nowhere in Russia did I see women and girls in bourgeois homes work or wait on the guests and customers in the inns and stores. A French confectioner whose shop I entered said to me in this connection, "I would not want to marry a Russian woman for anything in the world, even if she were rich and had 100,000 rubles banco! She would deem herself too high-class to sell a pound of bonbons; she would not be domestic or industrious, but rather extravagant, fond of luxury, and unfaithful. I would prefer to marry a poor German woman, since I would get an honest, hardworking housewife."

Some of the squares and streets in Orel are very elegant and attractive in their modern way. Seldom do the houses in the Russian cities have more than two stories. Every building plan for even the most modest house in a provincial city must be approved in Petersburg. Everywhere there are modern, trained architects, but they are endowed with little originality and creative genius. They follow the existing models to which the inhabitants of the city have also grown accustomed, and the greatest monotony and uniformity are evident.

Some of the aristocrats residing in the environs of Orel own their homes, which they have built or purchased, while others rent an entire house. It is considered improper to rent the upper floor if the lower story contains shops. So as to live alone, the less wealthy nobleman therefore prefers to rent a one-story Russian block house, which also has the advantage of being more comfortable and more compatible with Russian customs. Even the merchants build modern houses, partly as an investment, with a view to setting up restaurants there, and partly for their own use, in which case they have their business in part of the ground floor, rent the rest for shops, and live on the second floor. Upstairs there are no entrances or hallways. Rather the rooms all open into one another.

Bachelors are in the worst situation, since it is very difficult for them to find an apartment. Furnished apartments are nonexistent, and it is not proper to rent several rooms. Since there is no table d'hôte anywhere, they are forced to set up their own small household. Because no one can live without an equipage, the coachman and his wife help out in the household. Generally one enters into a formal contract with them regarding food, drink, fodder for the horses, etc. This is not a bad arrangement; given the inexpensiveness of foodstuffs, with the exception of wine, sugar, and tea, one needs to pay only about 30 to 40 rubles banco for a year's board in such a small individual household. The same meals, not nearly so well prepared, would cost 60 to 80 rubles banco at a restaurant.

Toward evening on 24 October we left Orel. The weather had already begun to get bad; the roads were miserable, We drove slowly, and without stopping anywhere along the way we reached Tula on 26 October. All of us were out of sorts, and we did not stay here for any time, but rather hurried on to Moscow, where we arrived on 29 October.

The essay on Tula which follows was written by my travel companion, Dr. Kosegarten, who had the opportunity to see more of this interesting city than I. For the greater part of the summer he was in Moscow. I shall now include a description of what he saw in Tula before speaking of my own three-month sojourn in Moscow.

# 9
## *Tula*

On 29 June (Old Style) I traveled from Moscow to Tula in the company of Pastor S., whose *tarantas* we used; we arrived the following day. Pastor S., a friendly gentleman, is a very well-known writer in Germany. He resides in Moscow and ministers to a number of German Lutheran congregations scattered in several provinces of central European Russia. He visits them at set intervals, usually twice a year. At this time he was taking one of these trips to Tula, Orel, and some other places. The highway between Moscow and Tula is paved; however, we traveled considerable distances alongside the road, since the pavement was in poor condition and under repair in parts. At the last stop before Tula, where the repair zone ended, we discovered that there are good highways even in Russia; at that point the road was excellent.

Here, south of Moscow, more agriculture was evident than to the north of the capital. Except for wooded areas, I saw almost nothing but cultivated land, extensive grain fields, and grazing herds of cattle. Villages with pretty farmhouses were numerous; here and there I also noticed separate farmsteads. The road passes through two cities, Podolsk and Serpukhov, a well-known industrial city. Here, too, one finds the large squares and broad avenues which characterize the cities of Russia, where there is no need to economize on space. Spreading far out into the plain, Tula with its largely new, white buildings (the city suffered the ravages of fire several times), its kremlin as well as thirty churches and cloisters, provides an impressive view even from a distance. On the basis of the last official count, the population is estimated at about fifty-one thousand, which no doubt includes the suburbs. One inhabitant gave me a figure of fifty-five thousand.[1] The city is situated on the bank of the small Upa River, which is dammed up here so that the rifle factory owned by the crown can utilize the water. . . .

All of Tula can be regarded as a factory, and in this respect it resembles Liége. The principal occupation of the inhabitants is the manufacture of numerous metal objects, most of which are produced in the homes. The work is divided into various operations so that many persons work on any one object, such as a gun. However, each individual performs a special task, usually in his home and for his own profit. Whoever gives the final touches puts his stamp on the finished product. However, in the case of some important articles, samovars for example, the entire object is produced in one factory. This also applies to the well-known musical instruments called harmoniums, which consist of a small bellows with several keys such as one occasionally sees in Germany. I was told that fifty to sixty thousand harmoniums are produced each year in Tula; depending on the quality, they sell for 1 to 15 rubles each. Most find their way to the fair held in the Siberian city of Irbit and from there to China. As I was told, about one hundred youths are employed in one factory that manufactures these instruments. They have divided the various tones to be produced in the harmonium among themselves, so that each one tests only one tone. The bazaar and other stores offer a great many products of local industry.

The Imperial Rifle Factory is located in the suburb on the right bank of the Upa across from the city. The workers attached to the armory live near the factory buildings, the majority in the suburb with wooden dwellings called Shulkina, and they perform single operations, such as welding barrels, in their homes. There are six thousand workers, and it may be estimated that including their families twenty thousand persons are attached to the factory. The factory was established through an *ukaz* issued by Peter I in the year 1712. However, even prior to this time there were already imperial blacksmiths there, who at the order of the tsars Fedor Ivanovich and Boris Godunov built for themselves a separate suburb, probably Shulkina.

The factory buildings are for the most part new and at the time I was there they were still in the process of being erected. One of the gentlemen in charge of construction, a colonel in the engineers,

1. Haxthausen's figure is correct; the population of Tula in 1816 was estimated at 52,100 and in 1863 at 56,800. See Rashin, *Naselenie*, p. 104.

von Sch., was kind enough to show and explain everything to me. An old building housed a steam engine, which in the future is supposed to serve only as a reserve, since steam power is impractical owing to the appreciable rise in the cost of wood. The new works are designed entirely for water power, which is produced by damming up the Upa. The water, conducted under a road into the building through a strong vaulted structure made of iron and stonework, sets large iron undershot wheels into motion. A separate device regulates the volume of water to be let in. Completely new to me were the vaulted structures built of earthen vessels in a certain convenient shape to make them light and nevertheless safe. To prevent fires, which have destroyed Tula several times in the past, the new buildings have been constructed almost entirely of stone and iron, so that wood has been completely eliminated except for the flooring in some rooms. Even the attractive staircases are wrought iron.

We viewed the various buildings which were for the most part completed. One building, designated for the preparatory operations, contained the machines for expanding and contracting the iron, the cutting of the rods, the manufacture of steel, etc. Second and third buildings housed the equipment for the finer operations, which included the forge and related machinery. There one can see the shaping, smoothing, and drilling of the rifle barrels, the handwork on the locks and screws, the hammering into shape of the lock plates and cocks by stampers, the construction of the stocks and ramrods, etc. In the polishing of the bayonets I noticed a new device that by means of an air current removes the metal dust, which is injurious to the workers' health. I was told in this connection that the laborers engaged in this work had not lived beyond the age of forty in former times. The bellows has been replaced by a large ventilator, which is more practical in that it does not require frequent repair. I also saw the workers deliver the finished products to one another at special places, where their older, experienced colleagues examine them and detect possible defects. For the purpose of control the finished pieces are stamped with the name of the worker who produced them. Lastly, I was shown a collection of rifle locks as they had been perfected over the years since the founding of the factory. Percussion locks were not yet made. A finished rifle weighs eighteen pounds. Pistols and other such weapons are also manufactured. An attractive iron suspension bridge, built by the abovementioned Colonel von Sch. spans the Upa. Located beneath the bridge is the dam, which is designed in such a way that it can be lowered when the ice breaks up, thereby permitting the ice to pass over it. As he remarked, this arrangement is to be found nowhere else.

There are different estimates of the number of rifles that are or can be produced each year in the Tula armory. According to Colonel von Sch. the new installation is designed to manufacture one hundred thousand muskets annually, assuming that the employees work only during the day, which is supposed to be the rule. An ordinary musket designed for the infantry of the line costs 18 rubles, if one counts only the metal and the labor. However, if all the other expenses are taken into consideration, presumably including the interest on the capital investment, the cost is 28 rubles. The basic material, namely, iron, comes from the area. The workers are state peasants who have been assigned to the factory; they stay on as long as they are able and do not have the right to buy their freedom. They are paid for each piece and can also work for their own profit. Consequently there are wealthy laborers among them, some of whom hire laborers to work in their place while they engage in other pursuits, especially commerce.

My attention was called to the handsome, expressive faces of several factory workers; their features, like those of the Great Russian men in general, strongly reminded me of the physiognomy of the ancient Greeks.

From Tula we drove to Mikhailovskoe, an estate owned by Count Alexei Bobrinskoi.[2] It is located about twelve to fifteen German miles southeast of Tula, not far from the city of Bogorodsk and the border of the province of Riazan. The luxuriant vegetation that we found along the way, the rich grain fields in particular, with their colorful borders of field flowers, and the soil which in the rain presented many difficulties for our vehicle reminded us that we had reached the Black Earth zone (*chernozem*). The estate, to which ten thousand persons belong, is pleasantly situated in a broad hollow that forms a large, flat basin in the hilly landscape. The seigneur, who to my knowledge usually resides in Petersburg, was not at home. Near his modest dwelling one finds the buildings of

2. Count Aleksei Alekseevich Bobrinskoi (1800–1868) began his career in the military but retired in 1828 in order to manage his estate at Mikhailovskoe, Bogorodskoe district. In the course of four years spent there he built one of the first beet-sugar factories in Russia, importing equipment from Paris. During his subsequent work in the Ministry of Finances he convinced that organ of the importance of his experiments, and the ministry consequently did much to stimulate this activity. *Russkii biograficheskii slovar* 3:112–13.

the large beet-sugar factory, perhaps the largest in Russia, which the owner built. The valley is dotted in part with peasant dwellings. An attractive park, together with the homes of the persons employed in the management of the factory and the house of a German doctor, lends a more varied view to the valley. I was cordially received by a compatriot and school friend, Mr. M., who is the refiner of the factory. Mr. M. is a native of Hamburg and has found a rewarding sphere of activity here. He spoke enthusiastically of his employer, the above-mentioned count, who lavished kindness on him, no doubt in consideration of the services that Mr. M. rendered to him. After Mr. M. had worked twelve years for him and had also instructed apprentices, the count promised him, among other things, a pension for the rest of his life and provision for his children. Mr. M. took me to his garden where, as is common throughout this region, the humus causes the plants to luxuriate without fertilizer.

The Germans living here and in the vicinity comprise a small Lutheran congregation. Owing to the lack of an organ and preceptor, Pastor S. had to hold quiet services for them in a room in the seigneur's home. I was told by M. that there used to be a greater number of Germans here. Pastor S. also had to perform a marriage ceremony, during which the couple stood on a beautiful, multicolored wool carpet. Such carpets, so I was told, are made by peasant girls in a local village and cost 45 rubles if they are of the same size as the one I mentioned.

M. showed me the installations of the plant, in which modern inventions are employed, for example, a machine to cut up the beets, a series of kettles in which they are macerated, the aerometer, etc. The juice is filtered with animal charcoal, which can be used again several times for the same purpose after it has been purified. The powdered and lump sugar is made in metal forms. Direct examination confirmed the assurance given me that the refined sugar produced only from beets is equal to that made from sugarcane. The water necessary for the operation of the plant is brought from neighboring springs, which are situated at a higher elevation than the factory. The water can therefore be raised without a special mechanism. The supply of wood (oak) is brought here from a place thirty versts away and costs 13 rubles per cord in addition to the 10 rubles for shipping, which the count's peasants earn. Peat can also be obtained and will replace the wood in the future. The beet roots are raised on the estate itself; the wives of the peasants grow the roots in their gardens in lieu of the vegetables and hemp formerly planted. The count pays them 1½ rubles (banco, or assignat) for every *chetvert*, which is somewhat more than 3 4/5 Prussian bushels. One *chetvert* yields seventeen to eighteen pounds of sugar. Since 7 rubles banco are added as production costs to the 1½ rubles, and since one pud (40 Russian or 35 Prussian pounds) is sold for 30 to 35 rubles, one can calculate a net profit of 50 percent. However, in the long run such profitable circumstances can be taken for granted only if the factory is large and the capital substantial, since the beet root does not thrive every year. Forty-two to forty-five thousand *chetvert* are processed there annually. Only volunteer workers are employed in the factory. The count does not require his serfs to perform services on his demesne, but simply takes a modest tax (*obrok*). There are wealthy peasants among them. When one of the count's factories in Kiev province was destroyed by fire and they thought he was in need of money, the peasants collected among themselves 80,000 rubles, which, however, he did not accept.

Since my obliging companion left me in order to travel on, I had to take the coach service run by peasants and permit myself to be mercilessly tossed about in a *telega* as far as Tula. A *telega* is an ordinary peasant conveyance, which is called a *kibitka* if it has a roof made of linen or interwoven strips of wood; *kibitka* also signifies a nomad's tent. In Tula I joined a traveling *chinovnik* (civil servant) for the trip to Moscow. Of course, he employed the same means of transportation, although in keeping with Russian custom, he prepared a comfortable seat in the *telega* with sofa and bed pillows for himself and me. Now the journey was bearable.

The coach service run by the peasants is an example of the associative spirit of the Russians. A route such as the entire seventy-five-verst stretch between Tula and Moscow, is divided into relays, which are generally longer than the relays of the government-operated coach service. There are, of course, stopping places in the villages. Peasants from all these villages are united in a company (*artel*), which transports the traveler in accordance with the conditions agreed upon at the start of the journey. The *artel* provides him with fresh horses and if need be with wagons at the relay stations. For the trip to Iaroslavl a peasant in Moscow gave me a ticket, on which all the stations were listed with the distance and the price of each. Whoever belongs to the company and signs a contract with a traveler must notify the *artel*. I was told that it is not uncommon for transport to be turned over to the least expensive member of the *artel*, so that any profit benefits the entire company. However, the *artel* may spend it for drink.

Since I passed through villages in the evening, I had the opportunity on the return trip between Tula and Moscow to see how the young villagers of both sexes amuse themselves with merry games under the open sky. In one village I saw a unique dance skillfully performed by two lads in a circle of spectators. This merrymaking by no means made the impression on me that a traveler describes on a similar occasion: "Le silence préside à toutes les fêtes des villageois russes."

# 10
# *Return to Moscow*

On 29 October 1843 (New Style) or the seventeenth (Old Style) we returned to the starting point of our trip, Moscow. Until the twenty-sixth we had dismal, rainy autumn weather, which turned to frost in Tula. Moscow was in the depth of winter and yet it was only the end of October. From then until my departure from Russia in April 1844, winter continued without interruption. But the winters are much more pleasant in Russia than in Germany. As soon as a sufficient amount of snow has fallen, the weather is continually beautiful, clear, and usually still. In dead calm, even the most severe cold of −22°F to −40°F is not very penetrating, whereas a temperature of 19°F to 21°F, combined with a snowstorm as frequently occurs in the steppes, threatens man and beast with almost inescapable death.

I settled, as foreigners usually do, in a boardinghouse. For the first fourteen days I was confined by an attack of intermittent fever, which I had contracted four weeks earlier in the Crimea, as is not uncommon in that climate. (At that time it was checked after two attacks.) I then began paying visits everywhere and making the necessary acquaintances, in order to see and hear what could be useful for my travel puposes.

It was primarily Baron Alexander von Meyendorff who looked after me and introduced me everywhere.[1] Several years ago Baron

1. Baron Alexander von Meyendorff (1798–1865) was president of the Moscow Manufacturing Council, author of numerous studies of the Russian economy and, in 1842, of a manufacturing map of Russia used by Haxthausen, and leader of an expedition through Russia in 1840–41 in which Keiserling, Murchison, de Verneil, and Blasius participated.

von Meyendorff headed an expedition which, under the auspices of the finance minister Count Kankrin, had undertaken a trip through all the regions of Russia in order to assess the resources which nature could offer industry. The excellent travelogue of one of the participants, Professor Blasius of Brunswick, which appeared in 1844, is one of the literary fruits of this important scientific journey.[2] The little that Baron von Meyendorff has published so far from his rich treasure of experiences and impressions has been excellent.

I made the most varied and, in part, interesting acquaintances in Moscow. The governor general, Prince Golitsyn, a dignified figure of the old boyar class whom I had met in the spring before setting out on my journey, had died in the meantime.[3] Prince Trubetskoi succeeded him. I was most cordially received by him and his wife, one of the most charitable women in Moscow, and I found at their large circles and social gatherings nearly everyone who belongs to Moscow's *haut monde*. In the Kremlin I visited its governor, General and Senator von Stahl, an able old soldier whose keen gift of observation has taught me much. Of the higher officials, I met the deputy governor, Novosiltsev, who has a completely German education, Senators Kinfief and Vasilchikov, who has a very amiable family, the chief of police, the marshal of the nobility, Nebalsin, and others.[4] I made the acquaintance of Moscow's leading scholars and professors, almost all of whom received their scholarly education at German universities: Professor Kriukov, an archaeologist; the Messrs. Shevyrev and Bodianskii, an excellent Slavist and pupil of Šafařik; Shevelov and Maroshkin at the Armenian Institute; Granovskii, Pogodin, one of the most eminent historians; and lastly Professor Snegirev, whose field is historical linguistics and folklore and who is undoubtedly one of the most important authorities in Russia.[5]

2. Professor Johann Heinrich Blasius (1809–70) was a zoologist and author of *Puteshestvie po Evropeiskoi Rossii* (Brunswick, 1844).

3. Prince Dmitrii Vladimirovich Golitsyn (1771–1844) was governor general of Moscow from 1820 to 1843.

4. Karl Gustafovich von Stahl (Staal) (1778–1853) was commandant of the Moscow garrison. Senator Count Ilarion Vasilevich Vasilchikov (1777–1847) was inspector-general of the cavalry and president of the State Council and the Council of Ministers; Nikolai Andreevich Nebalsin (1785–1846) was civil governor of Moscow and later marshal of the Moscow nobility.

5. Dmitrii Lvovich Kriukov was a leading classical archaeologist; Stepan Petrovich Shevyrev (1806–54), poet and historian, had returned in 1843 from an extensive German tour; Osip Maksimovich Bodianskii (1808–77) had just returned from five years in eastern Europe; Fedor Lukich Maroshkin (1804–57) was a historian of civil law; Timofei Nikolaevich Granovskii

Most instructive and interesting for me, however, was my association with the aspiring younger minds among the Russian nobility; almost all of them are passionate Russian patriots, to whom my conception of Russian national life had an appeal and among whom I consequently found the most hospitable and benevolent reception: the Messrs. Melgunov, Koshelev, Saverbeev, Chaadaev, Kireev, Samarin, Kireevskii, the poet Khomiakov, and others. I came into the closest contact, however, with Mr. Aksakov, one of the most brilliant men whose acquaintance I made in Russia, the poet Pavlov, who is well known and recognized in all of Europe, and his gracious German wife, an excellent poetess, who is also recognized and has written many pieces in both German and Russian.[6]

I have included these names so that the reader may see that I associated primarily with Russians in Moscow. In contrast to my stay in Petersburg, where, except for some Russian scholars, I had close contact almost exclusively with Germans residing there, in Moscow I met hardly any Germans with the exception of the remarkable and interesting Dr. Haas.[7] In both cases it lay entirely in the nature of the circumstances and the purposes which I was pursuing.

---

(1813–55) was a historian and jurist who was currently giving popular public lectures on medieval Russia; Mikhail Petrovich Pogodin, by origin a serf, was a professor of history and a leading critic of Schlözer's "Normanist" theory of the origin of the Russian state and was currently editing the journal *Moskvitianin* (founded 1841); Ivan Mikhailovich Snegirev (1793–1868) published collections of Russian proverbs and the first work on *lubki*, the seventeenth-and eighteenth-century wood engravings.

6. Nikolai Aleksandrovich Melgunov (d. 1867) was a historian and author of a polemic with the German scholar König on Russian literature; Alexander Ivanovich Koshelev (1806–83), publicist, acquaintance of Goethe, and student of Schleiermacher and Savigny, spent years after Haxthausen's visit in freeing his own serfs; Peter Iakovlevich Chaadaev (1794–1856), *saloniere* and author of *Philosophical Letters, Apology of a Madman*; Iurii Fedorovich Samarin (1819–76), publicist, in 1840–43 was working on a doctoral dissertation in Moscow; Ivan Vasilevich Kireevskii (1806–56) was a philosopher, publicist, and follower of Schelling; Peter Vasilevich Kireevskii (1808–57), brother of the above, was a collector of folk songs, which he published at Haxthausen's urging; Aleksei Stepanovich Khomiakov (1804–60) was a poet, theologian, philosopher, and leading critic of Hegelianism in Russia; Konstantin Sergeevich Aksakov was a historian who wrote a master's thesis on Lomonosov and traveled in Germany in the late 1830s; Nikolai Filipovich Pavlov (1805–64) was a poet and journalist who in 1841–42 was on the Moscow Jails Committee, where he defended the interests of poorer classes.

7. Dr. Fedor Petrovich Haas (Gaaz) (1780–1853) immigrated to Russia in 1802 and thereafter pioneered in public health. See A. F. Koni, *Fedor Petrovich Gaaz: biograficheskii ocherk* (St. Petersburg, 1897).

I do not know whether the public will look upon the following with praise or censure, but I must confess that I was unable to discover any essential difference in the physiognomy of the so-called high society in Moscow and that of other large European cities: Berlin, Vienna, Paris, etc. Upon walking through the elegant drawing rooms of the governor general on the evening of a large soirée or ball, I could easily imagine that I was in Paris, even more so as almost nothing but French conversation struck my ears. Beginning with the physical appearance, one could by no means recognize a sharply pronounced national type in the builds and faces. *Tout comme chez nous*! Tall, medium height, short; slim, scrawny, fat, corpulent; black, brown, and blond hair; black, hazel, and blue eyes; expressive, sharply chiseled, but also Mongoloid, mulatto-like, or vague and inexpressive features; a great variety of uniforms, the finest Parisian toilettes, the mannerisms, the dances, the card parties, the conversations — nowhere any difference from the elegant world in the rest of Europe.

With great predilection for the prehistory of Russia, the younger, rising generation of Russians has turned to the customs, practices, and views of the common people. What we witnessed in all of Europe and in part still have before our eyes is being repeated here. During the period of French oppression we saw the most noble minds in Germany dedicate themselves to loving and painstaking research on the history and prehistory of the German people, to the collection, recording, and recognition of national poetry and the customs and usages of our ancestors, to the purgation of superfluous foreign elements from the language and to its genuinely national development. After the Wars of Liberation in 1815, the younger generation ardently strove to revive older ways of life; that this was an abortive attempt is clear. At that time this effort degenerated partly into a game of wearing older fashions, swords, disheveled hair, and beards. This did not lead to the establishment of a standard of dress but was simply a passing fad. In part it soon took a ruinous political turn, to the Germanomania so commonly found in the student associations, and ultimately resulted in the very antithesis of everything national, the most vulgar, atheistic demagoguery.

Inasmuch as the endeavors of these younger Russians, of the *Young Russia*, are directed toward scholarly research on the prehistory and history of Russia as well as the poetry, customs, and practices of the common people, they are excellent and most commendable. Likewise, one must praise their efforts to preserve antiquities, old customs, and practices as much as possible. But that must be the

227

ultimate objective and the limit. Anything beyond that is folly or childish naïveté. Modern civilization is a tree of knowledge; whoever has once eaten of it cannot return to the innocence of older national customs and the patriarchal way of life!

The educated classes in Russia are separated from the populace by a much greater gulf than exists in the rest of Europe. . . . Throughout the rest of Europe the common people have the same culture as the educated, albeit less sophisticated and to a lesser degree. In Russia, however, the upper classes have adopted the foreign European culture, whereas the populace possesses a very old, although rather unsophisticated and inferior, national culture basically different from that of Europe.* These two peoples have only their language and religion in common. The real task of those men standing on the crest of this present national movement should be to see that these bridges are further extended by mutual effort, through the intelligence and creativity of the cultured people, and through the receptivity and pious devotion of the patriarchal *Volk*.

At the imperial court the headdress of the Russian peasant women has been elevated to the official dress at gala affairs. Even the portraits of the empress show her in this habit, which is as beautiful and picturesque as it is stately. We hope that this is not a craze, but that it will be kept as standard dress. It must make a friendly impression on the common Russian, the muzhik, when he sees his empress adorned with the same headdress as he is accustomed to seeing on his fiancée or wife on formal occasions, in church, and so on. Several years ago, however, young people began wearing not the dress of the present-day muzhik but old Russian court fashions from past centuries, a practice that one can only designate as an innocent, naïve game. They were also punished for this and what is more by the people themselves, the muzhiks, who regarded this as a new fashion borrowed from the Nemtsy, or Germans.[8]

---

*When the traveler journeys from the highest points of European culture, London, Paris, and the Rhine, toward the East, he detects a gradual decrease in this culture among the lower classes, until it completely disappears in Lithuania and White Russia. Then the beginning of another culture gradually dawns before his eyes, a culture specifically different from the former and increasingly more developed in Moscow, Iaroslavl, Vladimir, and Nizhnii Novgorod. It has borrowed nothing from the West; rather, it has traces of old Oriental coloration. Whatever has recently infiltrated or been introduced of Western culture has not yet taken root, although it may gradually become amalgamated with the older culture.

8. *Nemtsy* referred at first to all west Europeans; gradually it came to apply only to north Europeans and then only to Germans. Pushkarev, *Dictionary of Russian Historical Terms*, p. 68.

Out of this just predilection for ancient national institutions and old traditions developed simultaneously an unjust hatred for all foreign intrusions and importations. There prevails in this more passion than reason or profound insight into the true state of affairs. These experts and architects who want to build a new social and political system out of purely indigenous and ancient national elements would be highly embarrassed at the amount of available material. At home they would not find the materials for the essential foundations and requirements of this social and political order.

The careful preservation, further development, and improvement of national institutions which are actually alive among the people is possible and commendable. A revival and reintroduction of older, now extinct institutions would appear in the eyes of the people to be a foolish and arbitrary innovation. Just try to tell the people: "Discard the caftan; it is of Tatar origin; go back to the old Slavic dress of the twelfth century!" The people would ridicule you or not understand your intentions. Civilization has introduced a great many things from the West, which in part replaced unsuitable indigenous institutions and in part represent and fulfill an older, or new but now vital need. In both cases, these innovations have become an integral part of your national life, as well as a necessity.

These devotees of national antiquities also formed a political school. This school condemns the entire policy which the government has been pursuing for three centuries, but particularly since Peter I, a policy of introducing the political institutions, the customs, the culture, in short, the whole of Western civilization. It urges a departure from these false pursuits and a return to national paths, the eradication as far as possible of foreign elements everywhere, the cultivation, development, and revival of national institutions and the enhancement of their importance. . . .

For a correct appraisal of the true state of affairs, it is imperative that we consider these general statements as they apply to each individual aspect and direction of the Russian political and social order. We see then that the premise, as well as the conclusion in the [historical] generalization expressed above is indeed totally false. It is wholly inaccurate to suppose that the governments of the tsars and emperors from Ivan Vasilevich arbitrarily desired to draw near to the West and to introduce its culture into Russia only for their own pleasure and because of their false preconceptions. Rather, it was an inner necessity, a *conditio sine qua non* of life, a gradual, though sometimes obscure, drive on the part of the Russian people themselves, to which those rulers simply yielded and gave form.

Russia has always belonged to Europe; the Russians are a European people and, to be sure, the most powerful of the Slavic tribes, which comprise a good third of the European population. After the consciousness of self and drive for unity had awakened in the Russian people, they accepted Christianity and the rudiments of Christian culture from Grecian Rome, from Constantinople. Up to the time of the Mongol rule, Russians were at approximately the same cultural level as the rest of the Slavic and Scandinavian North. There followed, however, a couple of centuries of Mongol suppression, during which the existing culture was almost destroyed. But then the people arose and cast off the foreign yoke. The drive for progress grew strong, the indigenous means for improvement, however, proved everywhere insufficient.

All cultivation is, of course, traditional and no people has produced it exclusively by means of its own indigenous resources; instead, each people has learned from the other. To whom could Russia possibly turn to acquire learning and the means for improvement? The Mongols, Tatars, Persians, and Turks could offer Russia nothing.* The Greeks, with whom Russia was closely bound by religious ties, had themselves been cast into harsh slavery and lacked all strength for self-improvement. Hence there remained only Occidental Europe to which Russia could turn in order to acquire learning and the means for progress. Russia held herself aloof from her closest [European] neighbors, the Poles and the Swedes, for national antipathies and constant wars formed a barrier between them. Thus it was natural that Russia should turn to those peoples who were cultural leaders: the Germans, Dutch, English, and French.

As early as the sixteenth century, foreigners from these countries were invited to Russia to engage in crafts, commerce, and industry.[10] These "guests" were accorded extensive privileges. At that time the English settled in Archangel, and Moscow acquired its own

---

*Nevertheless, Russia did borrow many important things from these peoples: customs, clothing, dwellings, and implements. She even borrowed from the Chinese, for example, the excellent abacus and perhaps the samovar.[9]

9. Compare Chaadaev's statement in *The Major Works of Peter Chaadaev*, ed. Raymond T. McNally (Notre Dame, 1969), p. 38: "Nothing from the first moment of our social existence has emanated from us for man's common good; not one useful idea has germinated in the sterile soil of our fatherland."

10. The sixteenth-century influx was preceded by a substantial group of Italians in the fifteenth century. See G. Barbieri, *Milano i Mosca nella politika del Rinascimento* (Bari, 1957).

German suburb.[11] For a century and a half, Russia gradually prepared herself for her position in the world. The contacts with the West were at that time still superficial. At first only the material and mechanical arts of the West penetrated Russia; Occidental thought failed to gain access. Then came Peter I, who aroused and established the political greatness of Russia. Hitherto a landlocked country, Russia through his efforts reached the seas. From this time forward the atmosphere of culture poured in over Russia from the Baltic Sea. First of all an army based on the European model was organized, followed by the creation of a comprehensive political organism, which is hierarchically ordered down to the lowest levels of popular life.

I have never been a warm friend, let alone a partisan, of the modern European bureaucracy. I have always regarded it as a necessary evil. In part it has led Europe to that modern form of idolatry, the omnipotent state. However, if I imagine the total abolition of the bureaucracy even in the rest of Europe, obviously nothing would remain but naked anarchy, floundering about in socialist and communist activity. Does Russia possess adequate national elements out of which a healthy political organism, subscribing to the principle of self-government, could be developed if, on some blessed day, the modern European bureaucratic system and the military organization were done away with? Should the copies of the old official records of service and titles, which Fedor Alekseevich had burned, be sought out from the musty archives, the boyar constitution reintroduced, and the old disorganized summons to arms be reestablished? No one could take such nonsense seriously! Or should one contemplate the organization of a representative government in accordance with the ideas of the revolutionaries of 1825?[12] This form of government, which is the craze throughout Europe, is for Russia an insane notion, totally antinational in theory as well as in practice.

A reform of the political sciences along Russian national lines is, without a doubt, a great task, a problem for the future republic

11. The "nemetskaia sloboda," situated three miles from the Kremlin, housed all foreigners except diplomats. In 1700 it was one of thirty-six *slobody* and had a population of approximately seventeen hundred. Similar quarters existed in Nizhnii Novgorod, Vologda, and elsewhere. Akademiia Nauk, *Istoriia Moskvy*, 6 vols. (1953–56), 1:58; also, Samuel H. Baron, "The Origins of Seventeenth Century Moscow's Nemeckaja Sloboda," *California Slavic Studies*, vol. 5 (Berkeley, 1970).

12. On representative government as an ideal of the Decembrists see V. I. Semevskii, *Politicheskie i obshchestvennye idei Dekabristov* (St. Petersburg, 1909), chap. 2, 4, 6.

of Russian scholars to solve. No Russian political scientist or jurist has hitherto succeeded in freeing himself from the fetters of western European doctrines. The same thing is happening to them as happened to the French and to a greater extent to the Germans from the fifteenth century on with respect to the renewed study of Roman law. Among German jurists and legislators Roman law gained such an intellectual preponderance that all Germanic legal institutions were treated according to Roman legal principles. Purely superficial resemblance was sufficient reason to classify a thoroughly Germanic institution, of which the Romans were totally ignorant, in the same category as a remotely similar Roman institution, to confuse the two, and to deal with them accordingly! Thus, the German peasant was regarded as a Roman *colonus*; the relationship of the German serf to his master was treated according to the principles of Roman slavery and German collective property according to the principles of the Roman *condominii* and so on. This created vast confusion and legal incertitude. A despotic, equalizing legislation resulted, which undermined the morality and the legal sense of the people and finally contributed greatly to the dissemination of revolutionary views and to the outbreak of revolutions themselves.

We are witnessing the same phenomenon in Russia. Like the Germanic tribes, the Russians, too, had no primordial national jurisprudence. Such uncomplicated social relations as exist among primitive peoples were adequately ordered by age-old customs and practices and by religious prescripts. As political and social relationships became more complex, laws were enacted. These laws, which nearly always dealt with one specific case and which were often in the form of a verdict, multiplied endlessly, contradicted each other frequently, were often obscure, and provided great latitude for arbitrariness. Catherine II conceived the idea of a general code of laws. All the extant ukases and decrees were to be collected, extracted, and published as a whole. This tremendous task was completed under the present emperor.[13]

Because of its very nature, this code could not contain a perfect legal system, complete in itself. Nevertheless, the promulgation of the code has undeniably succeeded in putting an end to the vast confusion with regard to the applicability and nonapplicability of old ukases and decrees. In two respects, however, the results were

13. This effort was preceded by calls in 1700, 1714, 1720, 1730, 1754, 1762, and 1767 to codify the law and to replace the *ulozhenie* of 1649. See S. V. Pakhman, *Istoriia kodifikatsiia grazhdanskogo prava* (St. Petersburg, 1876).

the same as those which followed codification in other countries. First, many old juridical customs and practices which were still alive in the legal consciousness of the people were suppressed. Generally in those regions and localities where old legal practices were employed, they were decidedly effective and at least peacefully ordered those relations which have now been abandoned to an emotional egoism and to an awakening disposition toward litigation.* Second, the terminology of the *Svod* [Digest of Laws][14] was borrowed from Roman and German law. Furthermore, all Russian jurists have either been trained at German universities or by German jurists.[15] It is quite obvious that they tend to view all Russian social institutions through Roman and German juridical glasses and to deal with them accordingly, even more so as there scarcely exist the rudiments for a purely national Russian jurisprudence which could correct their views. With difficulty it could probably be proved that the draftsmen of this code interpreted and formulated the most important institutions of Russian national life, that is, inheritance law, serfdom, and so on, in contradiction to Russian national legal concepts and that their application by judges and officials contravenes the principles of these purely Russian institutions.

Roman and hence German jurisprudence contains a great many general principles, a universal law of reason, which subscribes literally to the timeless laws of ethics and religion. The universal law of reason is the fruit of the most profound human research and experience of all times; it has become the common heritage of mankind, which every generation passes on to the following and every

---

*In many regions and towns in Russia, for example, special inheritance laws existed which were very well suited to local economic conditions. For instance, property was not divided on certain occasions; rather, the youngest son received it and paid a certain amount of compensation to the others. There is even a Russian proverb which expresses this: "The youngest son remains at the root." The entire agricultural system was based on this principle. Since the publication of the *Svod zakonov*, this is no longer accepted as valid. Nevertheless, the *starosty* and lesser judges proceed on occasion according to the old practices. Should there be complaints, however, their procedure is then invalidated and they are ordered to proceed according to the principles of the *Svod*.

14. Although Mikhail Speranskii was influenced by French, Austrian, and Prussian models in his preparation of the *Digest*, his greatest debt was to the German historical school of jurisprudence. See Marc Raeff. *Speransky, Statesman of Imperial Russia*, 2d ed. (The Hague, 1969), pp. 321–22, 334–35 n.

15. As Haxthausen wrote, this situation was rapidly changing owing to the foundation in 1835 of the Imperial School of Law in St. Petersburg.

people to its neighbor. That this had to become the basis for all legal training even for Russia, as soon as she had reached the proper stage in her development and culture, is self-evident.

Faced with conditions which first arose with the growth of the state and civilization and which were thus totally unknown to ancient Russian national life, it was right and natural that Russia should simply borrow the legal concepts of other peoples, of course with local and national modifications. This is the case, for example, with international law, maritime law, international commercial law, the law of exchange, and so on. All these laws could be borrowed from other peoples without injuring national pride. But I again return to the conclusion that Young Russia can in no way prove itself more patriotic in the true sense of the word than by furthering and cultivating national jurisprudence with all the powers of the intellect and by excluding, if possible, all foreign elements through scholarship or by reducing them to proportions dictated by utilitarian considerations.

Politically it would be desirable if Russian political scientists would enlighten the rest of Europe as to the structure and legal nature of Russian governmental institutions and their political foundations. One can read in innumerable German, French, and English books and even in so-called scholarly works that the Russian Empire is an absolute autocracy, that it is not a monarchy but a despotism, similar to the Asiatic despotisms, that the Russian peasants are like the Roman *servi*, slaves without rights, etc. One author piously copies the other. I have tried in an earlier chapter to indicate briefly the general principles regarding the nature of authority, tsarism, the composition of the commune, and the conditions of the peasantry, but it would be desirable if accomplished Russian scholars were to enlarge upon and substantiate these comments systematically and in a scholarly manner.[16]

On another occasion we praised the noble, almost religious patriotism of Russians of all classes; we can therefore do nothing other than extol the patriotism of Young Russia, its predilection for national institutions, and its efforts to preserve them. The attempts to extirpate those foreign intrusions which are not essential to the improvement of the nation and the state should be encouraged. However, Young Russia also transfers its aversion to foreign elements to the persons

16. N. Polevoi anticipated Haxthausen's call with the publication in 1829–33 of his six-volume *History of the Russian People (Istoriia russkogo naroda)*, which he intended as a rebuttal to Karamzin's *History of the Russian State*.

of foreigners living in the Russian Empire. This dislike frequently degenerates into resentment and hatred which is neither fair nor beneficial to Russia.

There undoubtedly exists a profound sense of common identity among the various Slavic peoples, greater than among the different Germanic tribes or the Romanic peoples. The endeavors of so-called Pan-Slavism may appear either as youthful poetic enthusiasm or, more seriously, as a political faction spreading revolutionary propaganda, which at present penetrates and poisons every emotion, even the most noble. But the very background of this movement possesses an unmistakable reality: first, in the general sympathy all Slavs have for each other, to which the Polish nobility (not the common Pole) represents no exception in its attitude toward Russia, and, second, to an even greater extent in a common dislike for the Nemtsy, the Germans. On the borders and in those regions with a large mixed population this dislike becomes distinct antipathy.

But this dislike is not reciprocal. Not even the slightest antipathy toward the Slavic peoples can be found among the Germans. On the contrary, now and again there is even an unmistakable sympathy toward them. When German governments perpetrated political injustices against the Republic of Poland, Germans as such have, in truth, never been involved. The general incitement against Russia, which earlier ran through Germany, and particularly since 1848, was merely an artificial short-lived outbreak of fanaticism kindled by demagoguery among the so-called educated classes. The populace knew nothing of this; in the German armies there even existed a decided sympathy toward Russia. In a controversy, Czech scholars have long reproached the Germans for offenses committed against the Slavs six centuries ago, offenses which were, moreover, merely reported by history. Although this accusation met with sharp rebuttal in the German press, those Germans living near or among the Czechs were hardly aware of the dispute. Even in 1848, when all magisterial protection was nil and anarchy close at hand, one heard nothing of an actual conflict between the nationalities in those regions with a mixed population. The bloody conflict in Posen in 1848 would hardly have erupted had there not been intense religious antipathies;[17] Pole and Catholic, German and Protestant have been synonymous in Posen for ages. . . .

17. The Poznan uprising of 1848 followed closely on the heels of the Berlin uprising: modern scholars, particularly Marxists, stress the social conflicts underlying the uprising rather than the Catholic-Lutheran issue. Stefan Kieniewicz, *Rok 1848 w Polsce* (Wroclaw, 1948), pp. 3–166.

As far as Russia is concerned, there are no ancient historical injustices of the Germans to avenge. Russia's relations with the Germans are not yet very old. The German colony, which inhabited a suburb of Moscow as early as the sixteenth century, seems to have been comprised chiefly of artisans. The recognition of the value of German handicrafts in Russia appears to date from this time. Even today the Russian merchant knows no higher praise for his handicraft wares than the guarantee that they are German-made, that is, good, reliable, and solid. . . .

Whereas the French disseminated throughout Russia their false and superficial learning, Russia is indebted to German education for the majority of her scholars. German scholars like Pallas, Schlözer, Ewers, and others first transmitted the impulse of scholarship to Russia.[18] . . . The Russian universities and all the schools were fashioned according to German models.[19] At present a large part of the teachers at these institutions are Germans.

Whenever I pointed out this fact to those Russians who so candidly expressed their dislike for Germans, they acknowledged it to be absolutely accurate, but then added that they did not dislike Germans in or from Germany, but only the Germans in Russia, the Livonians, Courlanders, and Estonians.[20] These people forced their way into military and civilian positions, crowded out the Russians, and offended them by their insolence and arrogance. These reproaches may be justified in single cases but for the most part they are unfair.

The conquest of the Baltic provinces was Russia's greatest political necessity, for only in this way did she become a *European* state. The retention and flowering of these territories is both commercially and politically of immeasurable importance to the Russian Empire. The territory of Great Russia is the ancestral domain of the monarchy, and all the other provinces were gradually acquired or conquered. But today they constitute one large empire. The tsar of Great Russia rules the entire vast empire; it is his duty to treat all his subjects with equity and love. Disregarding the fact that special peace treaties granting privileges permit an especially lenient treatment of the Baltic

18. Peter Simon Pallas (1741–1811) was a Berlin zoologist and botanist and author of *Reise durch verscheidene Provinzen des Russischen Reichs in den Jahren 1768–1773* (St. Petersburg, 1871–76).

19. The Russian school statute of 1804 developed by V. N. Karazin and Academician Nikolai Fus was modeled consciously on the German system of autonomy, although S. Uvarov's 1835 reforms were intended to achieve a more truly Russian system.

20. The reference here is to the Baltic German population of these areas rather than to the native Estonians, Latvians, and Lithuanians.

provinces to appear just, prudence and equity alone require every territory to cultivate and encourage primarily that which can become most beneficial to the whole state. These territories are the only old civilized lands of western Europe which the empire possesses. Since Russia, by virtue of her way of life, her organism, and her geographical position, had to acquire Western culture, it seemed logical and expedient to employ primarily native energies in this endeavor, in other words to draw upon the Germans from the Baltic provinces to disseminate European political institutions throughout Russia.*

When this organization has been completed and when . . . there is a sufficient number of Russians to satisfy the professional needs of the civil service in all of Russia, but particularly in the old provinces, it is self-evident that the summoning of Germans from the Baltic provinces and their employment in Russia proper must gradually cease. Daily experience teaches us, however, that this is not yet possible in all cases.

Anyone who is familiar with the present government must wholly deny that at the present time ministers or other leading higher officials pass over a native Russian for a German with the same qualifications.[21] In such a case the scale would sooner tip in favor of the Russian.

However, in filling positions in certain branches of the public service, the determining factor must be the different natural temperaments of those two peoples. Positions which require uniform calm and unceasing diligence as well as pedantic discretion, free of all frivolity, will be better filled by Germans, even in the case of equal

---

*One of the most profound experts and distinguished public servants in Russia, Count Kankrin, used to say that it was the special grace of Providence that Russia, which was organized in a completely mechanical fashion, acquired the German territories on the Baltic Sea with their politically vital and organic structure. Only in this way was she provided with the means for the gradual development of a political organism. The Baltic provinces have always served as a model in this respect; all of the organizational institutions in Russia, the constitution of the provinces and of the aristocracy, the municipal organization, etc., originated there. For all the important legislative questions, the peasant question for example, the Baltic provinces represent the probationary region. In legal questions dealing with land registry, credit systems, and settlements between peasants, they have had fifty years of experience which the rest of Russia can consult and evaluate.

21. Walter Pintner has demonstrated that Baltic Germans played a relatively minor role in the Russian civil service in this period. "The Social Characteristics of the Early Nineteenth Century Russian Bureaucracy," *Slavic Review* 29, no. 3 (September, 1970): 429–43.

qualifications.* The German will always be the best bureaucrat; the Russian is much too flighty, too lively, and too pleasure-seeking to bear the yoke of service as calmly and patiently as the German. In this respect he is much more like the French. For this reason, the true bureaucrats, the *faiseurs* in the ministries and courts will probably always remain German. The fact that the chivalrous nobility of the Baltic provinces particularly likes to serve in the army and does so with recognized bravery, loyalty, and energy hardly needs mention.

The Baltic provinces transmitted to the Russian Empire the ideas, principles, and models for the institutions most essential to the national welfare, progress, and political strengthening of Russia. At the same time they furnished the men for the civil service who prepared the way for the introduction and adaptation of these institutions and who then consolidated them. The intermediate classes of European society were completely lacking in Russia's social structure at an earlier time and are still lacking, at least in the proportionate number of individuals. There were formerly in Russia (and the ratio has in no way been sufficiently balanced) a wealthy, a highly educated aristocracy and a poor petty gentry, which was usually very vulgar, or, even worse, had a veneer of urbanity. The intermediate class, an educated, independent landed gentry, was almost totally absent, and only now are the seeds of a competent, educated bourgeoisie beginning to mature. Not only for the introduction of new institutions but also for their administration and prepetuation Russia still needs the Germans from the Baltic provinces.

The educated upper class of the Russian aristocracy is well qualified for the higher posts in the civil service but very poorly qualified for the intermediate offices, for which, as a rule, it lacks the inclination, zeal, and the proper professional attitude. They view these positions as stepping-stones, which they seek to leap over as quickly as possible in order to acquire a higher office.

Likewise, these aristocrats are never suited for the lower offices, and even today they are much too proud to accept them. The rank of an *ispravnik* corresponds approximately to that of a Prussian *Landrat* [district president], the most respected and influential position in Prussia. Even men of princely rank have never been ashamed to accept it. Both the governing Count of Stolberg and Prince Karolath

---

*The decree of Peter I, which permitted only Germans to serve as pharmacists in the entire Russian Empire, indicates a noteworthy recognition of this fact.

were at one time *Landräte*. For the most part, the superior statesmen and officials rose from this position. By contrast, what a miserable and undignified social standing a Russian *ispravnik* has! No educated and well-to-do Russian aristocrat from the interior would accept such a post. In Moscow, educated gentlemen who in no sense belonged to the most eminent and wealthy nobility commented to me when the topic of discussion dealt with the *ispravniki* of their districts: "We never accept them into our society; we would be ashamed to see such common chaps at our table!" The lower positions in the interior of Russia are usually occupied by members of the poor, uneducated petty nobility with a modicum of external refinement, which is often combined with an utterly depraved character.

In addition to a large, highly educated bourgeoisie, the Baltic provinces have numerous educated aristocrats who, however, are not wealthy. As has always been characteristic of the Germans, the younger scions of aristocratic families and the ambitious, educated sons of burghers seek positions in foreign countries. (The Courlanders formerly served in Poland, Saxony, and Prussia.) Encouraged by Russia, all of them, of course, presently enter the Russian military or civil service. They fill openings everywhere which otherwise could hardly be filled, since no Russians with such modest demands can be found to undertake the sober administration of the offices with such perseverance and dedication.

The fact that these Germans in Russia do not disavow their nationality and their character by becoming Russified is their most praiseworthy and noble trait and is also in harmony with Russia's higher interest.[22] Moderation and perseverance, qualities which even in Russia are generally accorded just recognition, derive from these Germans! . . .

May the Russians therefore, who live together with the Germans in the most powerful empire on earth, always remember the verse of the psalmist: *Ecce quam bonum atque jucundum habitare fratres in unum!*[23]

22. Those Germans living in closed communities in the Volga and Dnieper basins, both Volga Germans and Pietist immigrants, were particularly resistant to Russification until World War II.
23. "Behold how good and how pleasant it is for brethren to dwell together in unity!" Psalm 133:1.

# 11
# The Aristocracy

Moscow was formerly the city of princes and boyars, the city of the Russian aristocracy. During the four or five summer months, when the nobility left Moscow with their entourages in order to visit their villages and estates, Moscow had one hundred thousand fewer inhabitants. Today this is no longer the case. Moscow has become the industrial center of Russia. Those eighty to ninety thousand indolent courtiers have been converted into an equal number of factory workers who, like their predecessors, are not among Moscow's permanent residents.[1] They are not burghers of Moscow but rather legitimate members of specific villages, where their families usually live and to which they generally return at harvest time. Formerly confined to Moscow, virtually the only powerful city in Russia proper, the Russian aristocracy is now distributed in a number of provincial capitals. Initially half-coerced, a part of the nobility has removed to Petersburg since the reign of Peter I. Nevertheless, Moscow is still the main domicile of the wealthier, independent Russian nobility.[2] Whereas one hardly finds an aristocrat in Petersburg who is not in the service of the court, the military, or the government, I believe that the majority of those in Moscow are

1. In fact, the gentry population of Moscow between 1788 and 1794 and 1902 remained at an almost constant percent of the total, varying only from 4.7 percent to 5 percent; in absolute terms the gentry population grew from 8,600 to 59,600 during the same period. Rashin, *Naselenie*, pp. 124–25.

2. In 1834–40 the gentry population of Moscow numbered 15,700 or 4.7 percent of the total; together with their retainers and servants they comprised 24.7 percent of the total population of 334,700. Ibid., p. 124.

not serving, although everyone has served. Without having been in the service or without having an administrative rank, one simply has no standing in Russian society.

Outwardly the Russian aristocracy appears to have approximately the same social and legal status as its counterpart in the other European countries enjoyed before 1789. They have the same education, the same culture and way of life, the same outward customs, manners, mode of dress, as those of the western European aristocracy. Even the expression of external characteristics and sentiments seems to be alike. Only upon closer scrutiny and more pointed inquiry do very fundamental differences, indeed, contrasts, emerge. We believe that they cannot be explained except by drawing attention to the original differences in the Germanic and Slavic races.

The western European or Germanic aristocracy represents a basic, primordial element of the people; in the Romanic countries this institution was introduced with the Germanic peoples. It is not a privileged caste which, in the course of history, gradually rose above the other classes through the usurpation of power or so-called meritorious services. At the dawn of history we see the nobility here as a separate class, calmly enjoying the recognition of the other classes. Even in prehistoric times folk legend and myth acknowledge the aristocracy. Both testify that the primitive aristocracy, that is, the princes and noble families, have a different origin from the populace; they are the direct descendants of the gods. This is most clearly expressed in the Scandinavian sagas, where all of the princely families, the Aesir, are descended from Odin. It was also frequently alleged that distinguishing physical features revealed their divine origin. The race of the Niflung, for instance, bore the reflection of a serpent in their eyes. All of them, however, were said to have manifested their ancestry by their superior brawn and the most valiant heroism. Nobility, *Od,* means *race*, thus signifying someone of definite, special, and known lineage, in contrast to the common people, whose ancestry is unknown. To understand the character and the nature of the Germanic nobility, one must keep in mind this prevailing belief or superstition among the earliest Germanic peoples. Those princely houses descended from the gods, the Niflung, the Amaler, the Merovingians, etc., are long since extinct. Other noble families whose divine lineage was not as famed took their place and acquired princely power. Even among the populace Christianity long ago obliterated the nimbus of descent from the ancient gods. Out of the remainder of this ancient aristocracy and a large number of free families and retainers and out of the system of vassalage based on services and benefices there developed in the Middle Ages the modern European or feudal aristocracy, a nobility of service. But those basic conceptions of the character and nature of the nobility, that high esteem of immemorial ancestry, held more or less in contempt or never recognized as equals those aristocrats whose titles date back to a specific point in history, be they purchased from or granted by the monarch or even acquired for distinguished services. This idea has survived until today as class-consciousness among the western European aristocracy, which has preserved its exclusive quality. . . .

The basic concepts of nobility and their evolution in the different periods and among the various peoples are unquestionably the nucleus of western European social and political history. Closely linked and in part developing analogously to and out of this core are the remaining factors of political life, the bourgeoisie, the organization of the peasantry, the corporations, etc. The spirit of obedience, submission, and sacrifice [to one's leader] is the true bond in the social and political life of all the Germanic peoples. In antiquity, however, loyalty to one's country was the unifying force. The individual thought of himself as a member of a nation living in a specific country, protected by national divinities, and compelled by instinct, upbringing, and custom to obey and to sacrifice.

Patriotic sentiment was actually unknown in the Germanic-Romanic world, or it constituted only a weak social bond. Until modern times, fealty held peoples and states together. Patriotism is attachment to the soil, the country, the city, and their inhabitants as a whole, to a reality. Fealty is allegiance to a person. In primitive pagan times the Germanic peoples had already submitted themselves to the nobility, which, in turn, was subordinate to the princes. . . .

The primordial conditions of the Slavic peoples were entirely different. Among the primitive Slavs one does not find a nobility as a separate group or class. Procopius claims that this was true even in his time, the sixth century. . . .

When the Great Russians made their first appearance in history, we discover no trace of an indigenous aristocracy. One sees heads of families, tribal princes, and small republican communities under their elder (*starosta*) with no social or political ties to each other. Thus isolated, the Varangians first subjugated the northern communities and forced them to pay tribute. These communities eventually united and expelled their oppressors. "However," the chronicler Nestor reports, "they began to war one against another. There was no law among them, but tribe rose against tribe. . . . They said to themselves, 'Let us seek a prince who can rule over us and judge us according to the law.' They went overseas to the Varangian-Rus . . . and said to [them], 'Our whole land is great and rich, but there is not order in it. Come to rule and reign over us.' They thus selected three brothers with their kinfolk, who took with them all the Rus and migrated.''[3]

The arrival of Riurik together with his brothers and his retinue marks the beginning of the monarchy and the first aristocracy, for Riurik distributed the land among the Varangians who had accompanied him. . . . Foreign immigrants thus comprised Russia's first aristocracy. However, it is likely that Slavic tribal leaders soon entered the ranks of the vassals or boyars. A part of these vassals always attended the princes as their retinue and were known as the *druzhina*.[4] Originally the *druzhina* occupied a lower rank than the boyars. They were free warriors who submitted themselves to the prince for a certain period of time or for life in exchange for their support and personal needs; ultimately this relationship became hereditary. In ancient times, the boyars, on the other hand, were probably immigrant Russo-Varangian nobles to whom the princes had granted land with its inhabitants in order to secure their dependence and assistance. Initially one can distinguish two peoples: the Russo-Varangians who ruled and the Slavs who were ruled. The former comprised the aristocracy, the latter the common people. Proof of this division is offered by the fact that at a later time the former were entitled to a much greater amount of compensation for bodily injuries. The price for a nobleman's blood was 80 *grivny* and for the latter downward to 5 *grivny*. In earlier times, the amount was the same for everyone, namely, 40 *grivny*. . . .

In the following period when through the influence of Mongol rule the authority of the grand princes was gradually transformed into the specifically Slavic monarchy, tsarism, the institutions of the aristocracy also underwent significant changes.

The name *druzhina* disappeared and was replaced in part by the term *dvor* or court. The members of the *dvor* were called *gridny* and later *dvoriane* or court officials. On the whole the organization of the court was borrowed from Byzantium. It was natural that

3. Haxthausen's loose translation of the *Primary Chronicle* entry for the years 6368–6370 (A.D. 860–862) has been replaced here with that of Serge A. Zenkovsky, *Medieval Russia's Epics, Chronicles and Tales* (New York, 1963), p. 50.

4. The term *druzhina* derives from the word *drug*, friend. Pushkarev, *Dictionary of Russian Historical Terms*, p. 13.

a kind of feudal system should develop out of the Germanic element. The practice of granting land and revenues in return for military services became more and more common. This caste of warriors stepped to the head of the feudal army, which, however, was seldom mustered. . . .

In the era of the petty princes, these feudal practices favored the great freedom and independence, even the license, of the aristocracy, which arrogated the right to transfer from the service of one prince to that of another. The noble simply returned his fief and accepted another. Regarding his patrimony, he could be the subject of one prince, while his fief might make him the vassal of another. Gradually these forms of feudalism were abolished. As soon as Slavic tsarism and the political unity of the state had been firmly established, the vassals increasingly returned to the rule of general submission. . . .

As early as the fifteenth century, quarrels over precedence arose among the Russian aristocracy. But the nobility did not have actual legal prerogatives. In reality it did receive preferential treatment, but at that time the warrior caste was not entitled by law to the exclusive ownership of land, nor was it exempt from taxation. The Tatars even taxed the boyars and princes, exempting only the clergy.

Under the Romanovs, the institution of the aristocracy developed wholly in accordance with the principles inherent therein. In every respect the Russian aristocracy had become a nobility of service. It was divided into two classes: the aristocracy of Moscow, which served at the court (*dvoriane*), and that of the interior, the urban nobility, which was joined by the scions of the courtiers of the petty princes. Within these main groups, however, there were many subdivisions. The descendants of a higher court official were given precedence over someone whose ancestor was a lower court functionary. The former did not want to serve under the latter. To deal with these questions there were registers listing service and rank, as well as an official department, the *rosriad*, which kept these records and issued testimonials. The fact that one's ancestors had been members of the ancient aristocracy (the mark of the Germanic nobility!), indeed, descent from a princely family, did not confer the slightest amount of influence. Rank was determined exclusively by the position one held in the service of the court or the government, which, in the military as well as the civil administration, was always performed by courtiers. . . .

At that time the right to own property was restricted primarily, but not exclusively, to the aristocracy. They possessed rural and urban properties but were permitted to settle peasants only on the former. They were now tax-exempt. The tsar frequently presented the nobles with land or occasionally sold estates to them, both of which were nontaxable.

In exchange for military services, the Tatar princes or *mursen* were endowed with fiefs and were then considered to be members of the Russian aristocracy. Even foreigners who entered the Russian military received such fiefs. These constituted a special category of estates and could be regranted only to foreigners. A formal right of inheritance, excluding only those unfit for military service, evolved for these fiefs. Widows and daughters had limited rights of inheritance and use.

The above is a general outline of the Russian aristocracy's political position up to the time of Peter I. Thereafter a significant change gradually came about. During the minority of Peter I, his brother, Tsar Feodor, prepared the ground for the abolition of the hitherto existing institution of the nobility. The distinctions in rank and class and the resultant continual quarrels and bickering over precedence sapped the energy of the state in an incredible way. At the suggestion of Prince Vasilii Golitsyn, the tsar convoked the nobility in Moscow.[5] He elucidated the great disadvantages of these distinctions and the chaos which was threatening the state. Recognizing the peril, everyone voluntarily renounced these earlier differences of rank. All the lists of rank and the extant registries of service were then publicly burned in the assembly, whereby complete equality was established among the aristocracy. Every nobleman was ordered, on pain of severe punishment, to serve unhesitatingly at whichever place and under whomever the tsar designated after evaluating their various capabilities and talents. . . .

One frequently hears the assertion that Peter I completely destroyed the old institution of the nobility in Russia, or at least struck at its roots, transformed it, and replaced it with the *chin* system, a hierarchy of officials with noble rights. I cannot agree. With unprecedented vigor Peter I promptly and ruthlessly executed what had been inherent and inevitable in the development of Russia into a European political power since the reign of Ivan the Terrible and

5. Vasilii Vasilevich Golitsyn (1643–1714) was a leading statesman under Sofia and a prominent westernizer of the late seventeenth century. See N. Ustrialov, *Istoriia tsarstvovaniia Petra Velikogo*, 6 vols. (St. Petersburg, 1858–59), vols. 1 and 2. The proposal to systematize the civil service was acted upon in 1722 with the promulgation of the *Table of Ranks (Tabel o Rangakh)*, often attributed to Leibnitz.

most definitely since the first Romanov. The general *arrière-ban*, the levy of the entire nobility in time of war, no longer met the needs of the state. In the organization of the Streltsy the transition to a standing army had already been undertaken. Peter and his successors fashioned the latter on a purely European footing. Whereas formerly the entire civil government had been, so to speak, merely a delegation of the court, Peter's successors, especially Catherine II, Alexander, and Nicholas, organized the civil institutions after European, chiefly German, models.

Peter I abolished compulsory military service and attendance at court for the nobility. In reality, however, nothing was altered by this measure in that the nobility continued to perform every aspect of service to the state. Whoever did not serve was considered by the law to be a minor, so to speak, although he was not deprived of the rights and privileges of his estate. If a family did not serve for two generations, they lost their noble prerogatives. Throughout Russia public opinion holds that only a person who is presently serving or who has served enjoys social standing. It is a recognized fact that in Russia proper there seldom is or will seldom be an aristocrat who is not or has not been in the military or civil service. Considering the above facts, I cannot share the opinion that the legislation since the time of Peter I has brought about a profound transformation in the political character and position of the Russian aristocracy. The *chin* institutions are actually only simplified European forms of those older, more Oriental distinctions in rank. But Peter I constructed a wall around the court and left the gate open. . . .

Like the princes of Brandenburg, Peter I converted into alodiums those fiefs which the aristocracy had hitherto held. In general the material advantages which accrued to the Russian nobility after its reorganization most likely far outweighed the disadvantages.

The Russian code of laws, the *Svod zakonov*, gives the following definition of the Russian aristocracy:

> Chapter I, paragraph 14. "The nobility is the outgrowth of the attributes and virtues possessed by those men, who in antiquity were invested with political offices and who distinguished themselves by meritorious service. By transforming service into distinguished service, they acquired the title of 'well-born' for their descendants. Everyone whose ancestors were well-born or upon whom the monarch bestowed this title is designated as well-born."
>
> Paragraph 15. "The nobility, is divided into (1) hereditary and (2) personal noblemen."

This definition actually offers full proof for the preceding description of the origin, nature, and character of the Russian nobility.

By special documents the emperor confers the title of prince, count, and baron upon present aristocrats. However, actual patents of nobility are indeed a great rarity in Russia, since noble status is acquired by the rank one holds in the civil or military administration.

In Russia rank is based on the gradations in the officer class, which are similar throughout Europe. There are fourteen grades from ensign to field marshal, the fourteenth being the lowest. The gradations in the civil service correspond to this scale.

Peter I determined that the rights of hereditary nobility should be granted to those who had attained the lowest military rank, that of ensign, or the first eight grades in the civil service. With the extraordinary growth in the required number of officers and officials, the number of families among the hereditary nobility increased greatly. As a result the manifesto of 11 June 1845, limited this right. Thereafter, the acquisition of the rank of officer (ensign) entitled one only to personal nobility, whereas the promotion to staff officer conferred hereditary nobility. In the civil service the attainment of the fourteenth grade (corresponding to that of ensign) merely provided the status of an honorary citizen; the ninth grade granted personal nobility, and only with the attainment of the fifth grade did one receive hereditary nobility.

Catherine II sought to instill corporative sentiments and tendencies into the Russian nobility by ceding it political rights. She divided the empire into provinces and on 21 April 1785 gave them an organic constitution based on German models (which for the most part were adopted from the Baltic countries). According to this the rural aristocracy formed a corporation under an elected marshal of the nobility and under as many district marshals as there were districts in the province. Every three years the members of the corporation convene. This assembly deliberates freely, and the governor is never permitted to be present. The assembly has its seal, its own archives, chancery, and treasury. As an assembly it can neither be brought to trial nor arrested. It can impose penalties on its members and exclude criminals and ignominious persons; it keeps the genealogical registries and patents of nobility. The corporation has a permanent deputation which meets together with the delegation of the cities to examine the proposals for the budget and the repartition of local taxes. In addition, the corporation examines the nobility credentials and checks up on manorial lords and their treatment of their serfs. If necessary, as in the case of notorious squanderers, it can put the seigneur under trusteeship. Almost all of the administrative functions of the province as well as law enforcement are in the hands of the various organs of the corporation: the assemblies, the marshals, and the deputations. The corporation elects the majority of the officials in the administration and in the judiciary; it is in charge of recruitment and local law enforcement, levies federal taxes, supervises the magazines, and accepts orders for supplies.

The Russian nobleman can lose his life, his wealth, and his honor only by legal sentence. He can be judged only by his peers, and the verdict must have the special sanction of the emperor. He cannot be dealt corporal punishment. The Russian aristocrat is exempt from personal taxes and recruitment and does not have to quarter soldiers. On his estates he is free to establish factories and industries of any kind, but in the cities he must enter the appropriate guilds. He can freely sell his own products.

In Europe there is no aristocracy that possesses such extensive property and personal privileges and freedoms, such broad political rights in the internal administration of the empire, and such vast material power as the Russian nobility. More than half of all the land under cultivation belongs to the aristocracy as fee simple. Over half the population of Russia proper . . . is not merely their subjects but their serfs.

I have already mentioned the essential points concerning the personal freedoms and privileges and political rights of the aristocracy. From our European point of view, however, one cannot maintain that the Russian nobility constitutes a powerful aristocracy. It shows little *esprit de corps*, no definite corporate tendencies, and no cooperation in working toward specific goals. In spite of its enormous material power, its moral influence on the thought, the culture, and the character of the serfs and the mass of the people is quite insignificant. With respect to the government or the tsar, the aristocracy as a body exercises only the influence which the government desires, elicits, and, to a certain extent, constrains. One could almost claim that the corporation exists only as a favor to the ideas and intentions of the state. The corporations would disband immediately and with almost no resistance, if such were the government's slightest desire or if it were ordered. . . .[6]

Catherine II and her statesmen evidently sensed, if only instinc-

6. Evidence for the validity of Haxthausen's contention here is provided by Robert Edward Jones, "The Russian Gentry and the Provincial Reform of 1778," Ph.D. diss., Cornell University, 1968.

tively, the dangers of the bureaucracy. The Russian bureaucratic hierarchy, which Peter I in general fashioned after western European models, was better organized and far ahead of its time. Catherine seems to have realized that the gradual decline of the original character of the old Russian tsarist monarchy and the patriarchal order was imminent. The transformation of the entire government into a lifeless, formalistic, bureaucratic absolutism appeared inevitable.

The danger seemed to be even greater inasmuch as the Russian bureaucracy was unable to secure the ethical foundations which the German bureaucracy in particular possesses: soundness of work, exemplary diligence, a high degree of technical knowledge, moderation in its mode of living, and, above all, personal integrity and incorruptibility.

Whereas Peter abolished the old forms of military and civil service, thrust aside the castelike Russian nobility, and forced it to submit to the newly created forms of service, Catherine II sought to reorganize the Russian nobility as a new aristocracy and to establish it as a counterbalance to the absolutism of the bureaucracy. In the Baltic provinces, Russia had territories organized entirely on the Germanic system, territories which were admirably ordered. The models were thus available. All the advantages of this system could be weighed against centuries of experience and the shortcomings compensated for. It is noteworthy that the Christian, Germanic monarchy with its estates was being organized in Russia at the same time that it was being undermined and destroyed in the rest of Europe. In western Europe the entire organization of the estates and corporations of the Christian Germanic state were gradually abolished and the monarchy itself transformed into the modern atheistic state, founded on the absolutism of the bureaucracy. The transition through revolution to a republic based on so-called popular sovereignty was easily accomplished and almost appeared to be the logical outcome. . . .

We have already stated that the Russian nobility is not an aristocracy in the European sense. A true aristocracy, which is useful in modern political life, must, in our opinion, have as its basis a numerous, educated, and wealthy rural nobility. Rural life alone imparts and preserves that vitality of spirit, that practical conception of life, and that ability to judge the needs of the people which a genuine aristocracy should possess. Nowhere are these qualities represented to a greater degree than among that most excellent of all aristocracies, the English. King James once said: "When a nobleman is here in London, he carries no weight, but in the country he is a powerful lord. Similarly, a ship on the sea is only a little dot, but on a river it is a large object.''

The Russian aristocracy, that is, the aristocracy of Great Russia, is not and probably never was a rural nobility. It had no fortresses and experienced no age of chivalry and feudal warfare. Instead, it has always been a nobility of service, living at the courts of the grand dukes and petty princes and in the cities and rendering military, court, and government service. Those nobles who resided in the country and engaged in agriculture were actually of very low rank or incapable of serving. This was also true until very recently. Even today the majority of the Great Russian aristocrats do not possess any country estates such as we see in the rest of Europe. All of the land belonging to the nobleman, the fields, the meadows, and the forests, is turned over to a peasant commune which cultivates the land and in return pays taxes to the lord. Even if he should reside in the country, he is still not a farmer, but lives more like a *rentier*. Most of the noblemen have country homes but dwell in the city, visiting their rural residences only for a few weeks or months. That is an old custom of the Russian aristocracy! As a result the nobleman does not regard his estate as his homestead, nor does he have a sense of belonging to a certain region. He will dispose of his inheritance immediately if he sees an advantage in doing so. The Russian knows little of that deep attachment to one's patrimony which is as strong among the Germanic aristocracy as among the Germanic peasantry. With indifference he sees it pass into the hands of strangers. In Moscow a Mr. S., an intelligent man of excellent character, explained to me that he had sold an estate which bore his name and (what is highly uncommon in Russia) the estate had been in the family for two hundred years. In reply to my reproach, he said, "We do not have a western European attachment to our heritage!"

The relationship between a master and his serfs is frequently very intimate and patriarchal, but it is readily terminated by sale and separation. The lord looks for new serfs, the serf acquires a new master, and the patriarchal relationship is secured anew on an equally intimate footing.

The basic prerequisite for a true rural aristocracy is not simply property but also stability in its ownership. I do not believe, however, that there is a larger country in Europe where this stability is more lacking than in Great Russia. The equal division [of property] among all the sons breaks up the estate enormously, since as a rule the land itself is divided instead of some of the heirs being offered pecuniary compensation for their shares; particularly in the interior there is an acute shortage of capital. One can hardly conceive of the volume of sales in property and in the peasants attached to this land. The market has increased considerably since 1812. At that time the Russians came into direct contact with western European comforts. Because everything was much more expensive in Russia, they had to spend a good deal of money to obtain these items. Since that time luxury has increased enormously. Burdened with debts, they sold their estates, mostly to parvenus. One can thus maintain that in Russia the third generation seldom inherits a large fortune. Only a few of the great families of historical renown, such as the Sheremetevs, Stroganovs, Golitsyns, Vorontsovs, Panins, etc., have retained their old patrimonies.

It would be very interesting to collect and interpret the data on the transfer of property and the debts with which it is encumbered. I was promised these data but as yet have not received them. A privy councillor, J., is said to have attempted such a compilation years ago, but it was never made public. In the absence of something better, I offer the following notes, which were given me orally by a reliable source.

The crown receives 4 percent of the sales price for all realty in the form of a stamp tax. Hence it would be easy to keep a record of the turnover in sales. I saw a kind of commercial newspaper for the province of Moscow, in one issue of which no fewer than sixty-three estates were advertised for sale!

Property encumbered with debts is generally mortgaged to the two credit institutions or to the Imperial Loan Bank. According to the census of 1834, there were 11,365,793 male serfs in all of Russia. The value of privately owned property under cultivation was estimated at 1,932,184,810 silver rubles. On the average a loan of 60 rubles was granted for one serf. On 1 January 1842, the two Lombards held 4,718,142 male serfs in pledge. On the same day the mortgages held by the Imperial Loan Bank amounted to 52,603,000 silver rubles, which meant that around 876,716 serfs had been assigned as security. The total number engaged was 5,594,858 or seven-fifteenths of all the Russian serfs.

From what has been said it is easy to understand why we cannot call the Russian aristocracy a rural nobility. Residing on his ancestral domain, the English or German nobleman considers himself, as it were, to be a sovereign, albeit petty, prince. He will jealously protect the borders and the rights of his patrimony. He feels a right and a duty to represent his estate in the great fatherland. In a majority of the Russian aristocracy, hardly a trace of this sentiment can be found.

If all these points are kept clearly in mind, it is not surprising to learn that the organization of the provincial estates in Russia is not nearly as effective as that of the German Baltic provinces, on which the former is modeled. The shortcomings, which are evident in so many localities, can in general be attributed to the following: (1) the failure of the greater part of the better educated and wealthier aristocracy in Russia to exercise the rights and duties assigned to the corporative institution; (2) consequently, the placing of the corporative rights and in particular the election of the estates' officers in the hands of the unrefined, uneducated, and, for the most part, corrupt nobles; (3) as a result, the worst subjects are frequently, or perhaps generally, chosen for positions in the estates and entrusted with the local administration of the police and justice. . . . The meetings, and especially the elections, of the aristocracy are as a rule held in the winter, when the educated families are in Petersburg and Moscow. Those wealthier aristocrats who dwell in the countryside usually have particular reasons for this, which are often not the most honorable. Nevertheless, because of the circumstances, these very people are the most influential at the meetings and in the elections. In addition, a considerable number of the poorer and, for the most part, uneducated nobility live in the provinces. They are a wretched lot! Lacking a genuine education, they generally have a certain outward polish. They are shaven and wear swallowtails; they have the greatest penchant for luxury and the greatest inclination to imitate the airs and mannerisms of their superiors and those more cultured than themselves. Because their legitimate income is inadequate, they squeeze their serfs whenever possible. Or they seek a position through election by the provincial aristocracy. Formerly every noble who lived in the province was entitled to vote, even if he owned only four or five serfs. With gifts and favors, some worthless, intriguing, and cunning subjects purchased the votes of the electors. To help remedy this abuse, the government recently limited the franchise to those owning a rather respectable amount of property.

I have already mentioned the position of *ispravnik*, the most important and influential office. . . . In commenting on this post, a highly educated aristocrat in Moscow said to me: "Whenever an *ispravnik* is to be elected, a miserable and somewhat cunning property owner with official rank in the district applies. He used to obtain the votes of the small property owners in return for small gifts.

Now he turns to one or a few of the richest landowners who actually reside in the district and who are often persons of dubious character. He flatters them and promises full compliance and official favor. They then invite the electors to dinner, propose the candidate, and secure the votes for him through their influence. Once elected, the *ispravnik* uses his position to procure money and other advantages, knowing that he will lose his office after six years (formerly three years) and that he hardly stands a chance of being re-elected. His patrons and their peasants are shown consideration, but he torments, tricks, and fleeces his peers, the small proprietors and their peasants, especially the very small landowners who do not have the right to vote and whom he therefore does not have to fear. For instance, in ordering the construction of roads and bridges, he may summon the people in the middle of the harvest. If they cannot come, he punishes them or demands payment for a postponement. The *ispravnik*, wielding such great authority, is the most hated and despised official in Russia. No intelligent landowner would condescend to associate with him or would ever invite him to dinner.[7] Whenever the governor travels in the district, he allows the *ispravnik* to ride before his carriage, as if he were a gendarme. Should the *ispravnik* come to see him, he has to wait for hours in the antechamber. In the event that he is granted an audience, the governor treats him like a scoundrel, making him stand while he remains seated, etc. In brief, as the matter stands today, it would be better for Russia's internal administration if the emperor were to abolish the entire organization of the provincial estates with the assemblies of the nobles, elections, etc., and if he were to transfer its functions to officials of the central government. The *chinovniki* are (as a rule) bad enough, although not as depraved as the majority of the officials elected by the aristocracy! The present system merely has the appearance of a corporative institution.''

Contrary to our customary manner, we have presented this point of view as forcefully as it was related to us for two reasons. First, it represents a widely held opinion among the better and more knowledgeable men in Russia. Second, the danger exists that through their influence the corporative organization might very well be abolished or modified in its essential elements. We are convinced that this would be the gravest error, a true calamity!

If it were now a question *de lege ferenda*, if this corporative

7. V. Sollogub wrote an amusing comedy around this theme shortly after Haxthausen's book appeared: "Chinovnik," *Russkii vestnik*, vol. 3, no. 1 (1856).

organization were to be introduced at the present time, it could be the subject of serious consideration. But the institution has existed for nearly seventy years. Even if it is in principle unsuitable and in practice so imperfect, one must ask, above all, what should and what could replace it? This organization was firmly established at one time, and the people are accustomed to it. The more primitive social conditions are, the easier it is to introduce innovations, but the more civilization advances, the more difficult this becomes. Although the introduction of this institution was not very difficult in 1785, its abolition today would be much harder. No one would seriously think of adding a new link to the chain of officials, of increasing the number of Russian *chinovniki*, and of doubling their political power and influence. The greater their numbers, the more difficult it will be to control them and the more corrupt they will become. For this very reason they would become more dangerous to the crown itself, entangling it in new problems and ultimately surrendering it to the forces of revolution, as the German bureaucracy did most recently.

We have repeatedly sought to point out that the Germanic corporate system is alien to the Russian national character. However, as a result of her historical development, Russia necessarily had to adopt western European institutions. Her bureaucracy, army, navy, police, factory system, schools, etc., are borrowed from western Europe. As imperfect as these institutions may be, can they be disposed of? What would replace them? The old Russian institutions, perhaps? No sensible person would even consider this alternative.

Nations have always borrowed institutions, legal and otherwise, from other peoples and must adopt them as they advance culturally. Did the Germans not introduce Roman institutions into their municipal structures and even into their rural organization? And did they not ultimately adopt Roman law in its entirety? Roman legislation had a foreign and often antinational quality. Its introduction resulted in great abuses and hardship, and it destroyed much in the German national character. But its reception as a whole lay in Germany's natural development, and we are deeply indebted to it. Gradually the foreign elements fused with the national institutions, forming a homogeneous whole.

This is also generally true in Russia. . . . Because the estates did not supplant a genuine national institution, they could more readily take root. . . . It is not the institution itself or its principle which is criticized, but the manner in which it is administered. However, one can argue that if the Russian aristocracy were what it ought to be, if it understood its mission and position and acted accordingly, the corporate institution would at once have the most beneficial influence on the entire political organism.

An important change is already apparent in the way of life and thinking of the younger Russian aristocracy which must necessarily affect the conception, development, and efficacy of the corporate institutions. They system of education for the Russian nobility is very different from what it used to be. Whereas the preceding generation was raised almost exclusively on the ideas of the French encyclopedists and the young nobility entrusted to French governesses and tutors and later to émigrés of all types, one now finds in the interior many German teachers and tutors as well as Russian governesses who were reared in Moscow's foundling hospital. Almost all the Russian professors and teachers have studied at German universities and thus acquired a more profound sense of scholarship and dedication. Formerly every young man of seventeen rushed to enter public service or the military and continued to serve as long as possible. At the present time they enter the service at twenty. However, the majority is beginning to regard the service more as a period of transition and only those with a particular ambition or talent and those who expect to find powerful patrons remain in the service. Many resign after several years and move to the country, where they engage in agriculture or manufacturing. Whereas formerly there were almost no [scientific] farms in Great Russia, a large number of educated landowners of moderate means have begun in the past fifteen years to establish them and to employ former *obrok* peasants on them. The presence and personal supervision of the owner are thereby made essential. Modern factories above all compel a great part of the nobility, who used to reside only in the major cities, to live in the country and to acquire the necessary training for these enterprises.[8] Only after the majority of the educated and well-to-do aristocracy have taken up residence in the rural areas, will they automatically begin to appreciate the importance of the corporate institutions, the elections, etc. They will realize, for example, how influential the position of *ispravnik* is, and the better citizens will assume the various offices. If persons of excellent character occupy these posts, everyone will accord them the greatest respect.

The government is also making serious attempts to fortify and

8. These were primarily sugar-beet processing plants, linen mills, and distilleries. See Tengoborski, *Commentaries on the Productive Forces of Russia*, vol. 1, chap. 2; also A. Rgozhev, "Votchinye fabriki i ikh fabrichnye," *Vestnik evropy* 138 (1889):5–43.

to develop these institutions. In order to take the election of the *ispravnik* out of the hands of the ignorant and poor nobles, for example, it has limited the franchise to those who own one hundred male serfs or one thousand desiatins of land. On the other hand, even the smallest property owner can be elected. To avoid a too frequent change in officials, which would impair the efficiency of the administration, the present emperor has decreed that an *ispravnik* be elected for a six-year period instead of the previous three-year term. (A well-intentioned and informed gentleman who was opposed to this measure suggested that the *ispravnik* be elected for a two-year period. The object is not the constant replacement of officials, but rather that those incompetent persons and rogues could be voted out of office more frequently and the good *ispravniki* re-elected.)

Recently the rights and duties of the rural aristocracy have been augmented. It is now entrusted with the election of the very important members of the civil and criminal court for the entire province, the members of the mortgage bureau (*grazhdanskaia palata*) and the tribunal of conscience.[9] The provincial court is composed of the *ispravnik*, who acts as president, two proprietors elected by the nobility, and two peasant freeholders appointed by the governor at the suggestion of the *ispravnik*. As a collegiate body, the provincial court is responsible only for the management of affairs, the equalization and distribution of taxes, with all of the executive functions being vested in the *ispravnik*. Owing to the size of the districts, he was recently given two assistants, the *stanovye pristavy*, who are in charge of the district subdivisions.

Rather than abolish the organization of the provinces or diminishing its effectiveness, the government seems to be interested in strengthening and further developing its potential. In our opinion this represents a sound policy. The development of this organization could be accomplished in two steps, the first of which would be to consolidate the aristocracy as much as possible. When this objective has been sufficiently realized, the noblemen could be entrusted with the positions for which they qualify and from which they could personally benefit.

By "consolidation of the aristocracy" we mean that every possible effort be made to convert the nobility of Russia into a strong and active rural gentry, for the nobility is indeed numerous enough. Everything must be done to keep the aristocracy in the rural areas

9. For a complete listing of these measures to enhance the gentry see A. Romanovich-Slavatinskii, *Dvorianstvo v Rossii ot nachala XVIII veka do otmeny krepostnogo prava*, 2d ed. (Kiev, 1912), pp. 477 ff.

and nothing to attract them to the cities. In this respect, the more recent trends in the education and way of life of the aristocracy, which we have commented upon above, are an adequate beginning. One should further develop the principles laid down in the Charter of 1785, for many aspects of this document will serve to instill a sense of honor, such as those which pertain to the exclusive nature of the corporation and determine rank in the state and social standing, as well as those dealing with uniforms (a very important question in Russia!). Within the corporation the marshal of the nobility exercises the right of censorship; he can place squanderers and persons who mistreat their peasants under trusteeship. This right could be extended. Presently, this official may not intervene without being invited to do so; but it should be his duty to take the initiative, and he should be held personally responsible for his actions. At specified times he should be required to give an account of his actions to the highest authorities or to the emperor himself. However, these proposals cannot be executed as long as the corporation does not have the right to exclude undesirable members. At the present time every aristocrat who owns a piece of property in the province belongs to the corporation. Consequently, a host of poor, ignorant, and generally despicable men are members, *ipso jure*.

To remedy this problem, the government has restricted the franchise to those who possess a somewhat respectable amount of property, but hitherto nothing has been done to eliminate the very small estate. These estates originate mainly in two ways: in part through the principle of equal division of the inheritance and in part because of the intrusion of *chinovnik* nobles who cannot afford to purchase large estates. The right to an equal share of the inheritance generally results in the division of the land itself, since the capital for compensation is usually lacking. One frequently finds villages with 400 to 500 male serfs who are distributed among 30 to 40 masters. I was told of one village of 260 peasants which belonged to 83 proprietors! If the further division of a community were prohibited, if the banks were authorized to furnish the corporation with the necessary capital for compensation, if those persons who own a part of a village were given the right of preemption, or if the corporation were conceded this right and bound by duty to buy up the very small estates and to unite the villages if possible under one owner — if all these measures were enacted, one would soon see a great improvement. It is much more difficult, however, to prevent the *chinovniki* from purchasing small estates. Nevertheless, the government has taken preliminary steps in this direction.

## Chapter Eleven

It is a known fact that in Russia the attainment of a certain official rank first confers personal and then hereditary nobility. To the latter is attached the right to acquire seignorial estates. Formerly the bureaucratic aristocracy was composed primarily of foreign adventurers and parvenus who sought their fortune in Russia. For the most part this is no longer the case. Today there is a considerable number of administrative families among whom service to the state has become almost hereditary and who invest their savings in the purchase of peasants. Their numbers are augmented by rising *chin* families, the following groups of which compete with each other: (1) the sons of priests and widower-priests who return to the secular estate and usually seek positions in the chancery; (2) the sons of subaltern officials and clerks or frequently those persons themselves, should they succeed in working their way up; (3) the sons of shopkeepers, well-to-do merchants, and manufacturers. All these officials, most of whom remain in the lower ranks, seek to purchase peasants with their small communal shares, since they cannot afford large estates. Furthermore, it would be too difficult for them to manage the latter in that their jobs require them to be elsewhere. Hence, they buy five to twenty peasants with their communal allotments and put them on *obrok*. Should this occur in an industrial region, for example, in the provinces of Iaroslavl or Vladimir, a true system of exploitation is then introduced, as we have already mentioned. A Saint-Simonian evaluation of the peasant's capacities is made, but the peasant is not remunerated according to the amount he produces, but rather he pays for the fruits of his labor through taxation!

The corporation must be permitted to refuse membership to these intruders, who pose such a formidable threat to the commonweal. In conferring personal and hereditary nobility only upon those holding higher ranks, the government has already met this problem to a certain extent. But it would be desirable if the corporation were authorized to prevent them from buying property and to deny them membership. They would have to have been accepted in the corporation *before* being allowed to purchase estates. If, for example, a prospective buyer is unable to afford an entire village, the corporation should be permitted to refuse him admittance.

Lastly, the authority of the corporation to supervise the morality of its members could be enhanced. In accordance with definite rules it should be possible to exclude those persons from the corporation who are guilty of dishonorable conduct. In such a case, they should be forced to transfer their property to their immediate heirs or to

258

sell it. Although legal regulations pertaining to these contingencies do exist, they are too lenient and very seldom enforced.

Were the aristocracy fully consolidated in this manner, it could then be entrusted with additional rights and responsibilities. The nobility is already permitted to found banks, but it could be authorized to establish credit funds to set up warehouses and to finance various improvements, the construction of roads, canals, etc.

Russia has gradually adopted the institutions of the estates as they developed in western Europe from Germanic ideas and traditions and sensibly modified them to conform to Russian popular life without essentially altering the character of the autocratic or patriarchal monarchy. These estates, though solidly organized, have not been conceded even a minimal amount of direct influence on the policy making of the state, the economy, the administration of its finances or the military, or imperial legislation. In their own internal affairs, they have been accorded the greatest autonomy. Extensive administrative duties and the responsibility of law enforcement and public safety have been entrusted to them. But imperial estates with the power to levy taxes and with a voice in legislation, rights which the German estates generally had, have not been introduced into Russia. From the sixteenth century onward the larger European states — Spain, France, Austria, and Prussia — gradually freed themselves from these institutions. Hitherto the attempts to restore the old estates to fit the times, as it is expressed, have always resulted in efforts to create their very antithesis, namely, modern representative chambers. Notwithstanding the fact that the elements for so-called representative institutions are totally lacking and that they would find little support among the common people, Russia will certainly never embark upon this path.

# 12
# *Religion in Russia*

It is a well-known fact that the Russians are unusually religious. The religiosity of the common people issues primarily from a profound and instinctive feeling which pervades the whole man, his thoughts, his opinions, his emotions. It is the air, without which he cannot breathe. Every aspect of life is endowed with religious emotions. The natural instinct of filial devotion is heightened to religious veneration and absolute obedience, which is transferred to all his superiors up to and including the tsar. In the Russian's eyes the tsar represents a father raised to the highest power. Similarly, the Russian's expansive love for his brothers, his kin, and all of his compatriots, whom he always addresses in daily life as "brothers" *(brate)*, is an instinctive feeling, rooted in religious communion. Lastly, there is the land, Russia, which God granted to him, his brothers, and his forefathers. His ancestors are buried there; he lives on the hallowed ground which will someday cover him and which contains all the objects of his adoration and love. This religious patriotism regards God Himself as possessing national character; He is the "Russian God" *(Russkii Bog)*. The country, the people, the church, and the "white tsar," whom God has sanctified and entrusted with his office, have become a perfect whole, embracing the individual in all his thoughts and emotions. This religious patriotism is the source and foundation of Russia's unity and of her moral and physical strength.

Religion and its bearer, the church, constitute the true power, the spiritual and mysterious force, which has fused this country and its people into an indivisible whole. So dominant and powerful is this historical fact that even the Old Believers, who broke with the church, never could or wanted to withdraw from this unifying bond. There is absolutely no division between them and the rest of the population. Even though they believe that the church deviated from the true path, their love for their fellow Russians, for the common motherland and its shrines, is wholly religious in nature.

In spite of their great piety, devoutness, and their absolute submission to the precepts of the church, the majority of Russians possess only a very superficial knowledge of dogma. Because they receive little instruction in church doctrine, their faith is in this respect as naïve as that of a child. . . .

Nor have the upper classes, the European-educated Russians, dissociated themselves at all from this great religious bond of national life. To be sure, one frequently encounters very frivolous attitudes among the educated; particularly among the older, French-educated generation, there is a spirit of irreligion ranging from mild skepticism to atheism. But no one outwardly severs his ties to the church or fails to observe the rituals; no one shows disrespect or contempt for the church or its ceremonies, for this would mean a renunciation of one's country and one's membership in the national community. This represents an essential difference between the educated classes in Russia and those of other nations.

Through the church Russia exercises an unusually great and secret political influence on all Eastern Orthodox Slavic peoples. They regard the Russian church as the mother church. In truth, the Russian church does stand at the head of Eastern Christendom. Although the patriarch of Constantinople continues to enjoy honorary precedence, his influence and that of his clergy is insignificant. The spiritual and material preponderance is on the side of the Russian church.

Even in Russia it is frequently alleged that the common man does not have the slightest love or respect for his clergy and that he is superstitious of encountering a priest first thing in the morning, for this would bring him bad luck all day. On such an occasion, so it is said, he would spit in the priest's presence. On the other hand, when a Russian does meet a priest, one always sees him humbly kiss his hand. From this it is inferred that the Russian shows outward respect for the priest only as an administrat of the sacraments, but that inwardly he despises or even loathes him. But this is one of those half-truths which always lead to false conclusions.

The Russian has the greatest religious respect for the holy office of the clergyman. If the cleric is also an honest man who leads a religious and irreproachable life, if he endeavors as pastor to bring to his congregation the consolations of religion, to give instruction, and to look after the children, etc., then he is greatly loved and revered. . . . But excellent clergymen are indeed a rarity in rural areas. The majority of the older priests are exceedingly unrefined, ignorant, and self-seeking. In performing the ceremonies, reading the liturgy, and administering the sacraments, they frequently use their office to procure gifts and favors. They utterly neglect their ministry in failing to provide solace and instruction. It is altogether natural that such priests are not personally loved or respected and that only their sacerdotal dignity is honored. Within the past fifteen years, however, much has changed. The younger clergy is better educated and more devoted to their office. In general it should be noted that the Russians have a much greater respect for the black or monastic clergy than for the married secular priests.

The secular clergy in Russia forms an exclusive, almost castelike group. It is considered improper for a priest to marry any woman other than the daughter of a priest. (He must, of course, marry before his ordination.) Only the sons of priests can become priests or deacons, although in White Russia aristocrats may also join their ranks. The cloisters, on the other hand, are open to members of every class. Serfs, however, are admitted only as novices[1] and can never become monastic priests. At the present time many noblemen enter monasteries. Dmitrii, the archbishop of Kishinev in Bessarabia, is an aristocrat.

Recently much has been done to improve the education of the Russian clergy, to elevate its moral character and to encourage scholarship. In discussing this point, let us take a brief look at the past. Christianity came to Russia from Constantinople, and it assumed the form of the Old Slavonic rite as established in Moravia by Saints Cyril and Methodius. Up to the Mongol invasion Kiev was the center of Russian Christianity and the seat of the metropolitan. Conquered first by the Mongols, Kiev later came under Lithuanian rule. The center of the secular authority as well as the center of the church of Russia proper were transferred to Vladimir and later to Moscow. The flowering of Christian culture and scholarship, which had begun to develop in Kiev, as seen in the example of the old chronicler Nestor from the Monastery of the Caves, was blighted under Mongol-Tatar rule. Only the seed, Christianity, endured. The Tatars did not wage a religious war to convert the

1. *Dienende Brüder*, referring to *poslushniki*, slightly different from novices in that theirs could be a permanent position and not merely a temporary state on the way to full entry into the brotherhood.

Russians to Islam. They were satisfied with affixing the crescent above the cross on the churches. This oppression and misery awakened in the Russians a profound feeling of oneness. In this regard the church rendered an important service to the country, for the monasteries in particular brought aid and comfort to the people.

With this turn toward practical activity it was inevitable that learning and scholarship should decline among the Russian clergy. Even after the Tatar yoke had been cast off, the situation was in this respect deplorable. Owing to the ignorance of the monks and priests a great number of mistakes and erroneous variants crept into the liturgical books. These errors could lead to inaccurate interpretations and thereby to schisms. With the division of the country into petty principalities these variants received geographical boundaries, one province accepting this interpretation, another adopting a different reading. Only after the whole of Russia had attained political unity did this become evident. The attempts to strengthen the religious unity of the country by bolstering the central power of the church resulted in the creation of the Russian patriarchate, to which the patriarch of Constantinople and the other Eastern patriarchs reluctantly agreed.

For the preservation of her autonomy at the time of the Polish invasion Russia is indebted to the church,[2] which the partiarchate had so firmly consolidated. There was no tsar, and the country lacked a political center. At that time, however, the church fulfilled this role. The monasteries, Trinity–Saint Sergei for example, were in the forefront of the liberation movement, and after a bloody struggle Russia threw off the Polish yoke.

The patriarchate also succeeded in standardizing the liturgy and ceremonies, but at the cost of an initially insignificant rupture which ultimately, however, led to the separation of the Old Believers from the church.

While the church of Great Russia had taken this course, the old mother church of Russia in Kiev stood under Lithuanian and later Polish domination. However, a vestige of pre-Tatar culture and learning did survive. Here the church was not confronted with a worldly, anti-Christian form of suppression but rather with the superior culture of the Catholic Occident as represented in the Polish tradition.

2. Haxthausen refers here to the Polish invasion following the Bolotnikov rebellion and fall of Tsar Vasilii Shiuskii in 1606–9. The Soviet interpretation of these events stresses the role of the lower classes and especially Kuzma Minin rather than the church.

The conflict which ensued was spiritual in nature, producing much greater intellectual stimulation in Kiev. The weapons for this struggle were sought among the adversaries themselves. Scholastic philosophy and studies in ecclesiastical history were introduced into the church of Kiev. Even the form of study and the organization of the schools were borrowed from the Occident and later especially from the Jesuits.[3]

When Peter I took possession of Kiev, closer ties were established between the clergy in this city and in Moscow. The hieromonk Simeon Polotskii, a very erudite and strong-willed man, was summoned by Peter I to Moscow where he won considerable influence.[4] He was also the first to resume preaching in the Russian churches, a practice which had fallen out of use under Tatar rule. Thereafter learning improved and spread among the Great Russian clergy, although initially, of course, only among the monastic clergy.

After the death of the last patriarch, Peter I did not appoint a successor.[5] Rather, he transferred the functions of the patriarch to the Most Holy Synod, an ecclesiastical college created and appointed by him. In the following excerpt taken from the Regulation of 1720, the reasons for its establishment are clearly stated: "Government represented by a college will never be capable of agitating as successfully as a (personal) leader of the ecclesiastical order. The common man does not understand the difference between spiritual and sovereign, secular authority. He is so impressed by the great honors and dignity conferred upon the Supreme Shepherd that he considers such a leader to be another sovereign, whose dignity is equal to or even greater than that of the monarch. In his eyes the ecclesiastical order would constitute a preferable form of monarchy. Since the common man generally reasons in this manner, what might happen if the unsound discourses of ambitious ecclesiastics were to fan the flames?" It is clear that Peter I was willing at all costs to prevent the unity of power from being split or even questioned. . . .

Three periods can be distinguished in the leadership of the Russian church. Initially, the church had a foreign head, the patriarch of

3. For the impact of Jesuit ideas on education see I. Zabelin,"Pervoe vodvorenie v Moskve greko-latinskoi i zapadnoevropeiskoi nauki," *Chtenie*, vol. 4 (1886); and Florovskii, *Puti russkogo bogosloviia*, chap. 3.

4. Simeon Polotskii (1629–80) actually came to Moscow as early as 1664. See Florovskii, pp. 75 ff.

5. The last patriarch, Adrian, was in office from 1690 to 1700. See Igor Smolitsch, *Geschichte der russischen Kirche, 1700–1917* (Leiden, 1964), 1:59 ff.

Constantinople, who appointed the metropolitan of Kiev and later of Moscow. In the second period, beginning in 1589, the church was governed by a patriarch who, although designated by the tsar, was otherwise independent. Finally, in the third period the fundamental direction of the church was transferred to the tsar.

Nevertheless, it would be incorrect to designate the emperor as the head of the Russian church in the same sense that the pope is rightly called the supreme leader of the Roman Catholic church. To an even greater extent than the pope, the emperor executes the external functions of governing the church. He arbitrarily appoints the incumbents to all the ecclesiastical offices. However, in permitting the Synod, the bishops, etc., to suggest the candidates, he merely imposes a restriction upon himself. The emperor can transfer and dismiss ecclesiastics as the occasion warrants, but he has never arrogated the right to decide theological and doctrinal questions. Let us imagine that a new heresy cropped up in Russia and that it was necessary to reach a decision on this question. It would not occur to anyone, and least of all to the emperor, for the ruler to pass judgment in this matter. This would be the responsibility of the Synod. If the issue was critical, inquiries would be addressed to the other four Eastern patriarchs, and ultimately a council would be convoked. Once an ecclesiastical verdict has been pronounced, however, the emperor decrees its execution. Also, in official documents the emperor never designates himself as the head but rather as the protector of the church.

The entire empire is divided into 52 eparchies, in which are located 34,899 cathedrals and parish churches and 9,654 chapels and houses of prayer. These various churches are served by 36,701 priests, 15,682 deacons, and 64,863 sacristans. In addition,

1. under the administration of the synodal office of Moscow there are: 78 cathedrals and churches, 7 chapels with 7 priests, 6 deacons, and 78 sacristans;
2. the imperial court has: 20 cathedrals and churches with 25 priests, 22 deacons, and 40 sacristans;
3. the Guards and Grenadier Corps have: 44 cathedrals and churches with 45 priests, 5 deacons, and 12 sacristans;
4. the army and navy have: 236 cathedrals and churches with 362 priests, 19 deacons, and 60 sacristans.

The total is 35,277 cathedrals and churches, 9,661 chapels, served by 37,140 priests, 15,734 deacons, and 65,053 sacristans.

In 1839 there were only 33,271 cathedrals and churches and 9,429 chapels, with 35,617 priests, 15,770 deacons, and 63,108 sacristans.

The black or monastic clergy owns 462 monasteries and 118 convents, in which there are 5,148 monks and 3,960 male novices, 2,250 nuns, and 5,169 female novices.

The secular clergy includes a total of 117,927 individuals, the monastic clergy a total of 16,527. [The entire clergy therefore numbers] 134,454 individuals.

In 1842 there were 439 monasteries and 113 convents. A certain number of the former received support from the state by categories: 28 of the first class, 57 of the second, and 106 of the third class. The remainder were neither recognized nor supported by the state. Of the convents, the government recognized 86, and 27 were not recognized. Thirty-four cloisters operated hospitals in which 241 patients were cared for at the expense of the cloisters, as well as 22 poorhouses, which accepted 260 paupers and elderly persons.

Most of the cloisters are located in the district of former crown land of Great Russia, in the vicinity of Moscow and in the provinces of Moscow, Novgorod, Iaroslavl, Tver, Chernigov, Kostroma, Tambov, Orel, and lastly in old Kiev. In these thirteen eparchies, which comprise one-fourth of the total number [in the empire], there are 198 monasteries with 2,199 monks and 2,062 novices, and 60 convents with 1,255 nuns and 3,207 female novices in all, 9,257 members or more than half of the total number [of monastic clergy]. There are few cloisters in southern Russia and among the Cossacks, particularly among the Don Cossacks, either because of their bellicose temperament or because they are for the most part Old Believers.

Formerly, some of the cloisters were extremely wealthy. The patriarch supervised the management of their property. After the patriarchate had been abolished, Peter I added an economic board to the Senate to administer the monastic estates. The cloisters received only what they required. The Synod later took over the administration, but Catherine II then confiscated most of the monastic wealth for the national treasury. The monasteries, which are divided into three categories, are in part given government support, but only a small number of the convents receive assistance. Most of them exist almost exclusively through alms and from the sale of handicrafts produced by the nuns. In recent times the cloisters and churches have again begun to receive many legacies; in the province of Moscow these bequests amounted to approximately 100,000 silver rubles for the year 1840 alone. Gifts of property, however, can be accepted only with the permission of the government.

Like the rest of Europe, Russia is deeply indebted to its cloisters, which have been the bearers and propagators of national culture.

Because the monasteries were places of pilgrimage, markets grew up in their vicinity. They attracted not only settlers interested in agriculture but also persons engaged in urban trades. For this reason one finds market quarters (*sloboda*) near almost all of the cloisters. Catherine II conferred urban status on 200 of these communities. . . .[6]

Formerly there were no real public schools in Russia. Under the present emperor much has been done to establish them, particularly in the villages located on the imperial domains and appanages. . . . Schools are the exception on private estates, many masters being opposed to them on principle. However, there are a few seigneurs, like Mr. Karnovich in the province of Iaroslavl, who have worked hard and made sacrifices to found elementary schools on their estates, and they have done so with great success.

Previously, only the cloisters maintained schools, for the scanty instruction of the clergy. Under the present emperor considerable effort has been made to increase their number and to improve their standards. In general, the old Jesuit schools and gymnasia have served as models. Presumably these institutions had formerly been adopted in Kiev and were introduced from there into Great Russia as well.

There are official data on the ecclesiastical academic institutions for the year 1846, which we shall summarize here [see table 3]. We note that, in regard to the supervision of these institutions, Russia is divided into four districts: this district of Petersburg in the north, the central district of Moscow, the district of Kiev in the southwest, and the district of Kazan in the east.

All together there are 419 ecclesiastical schools with 60,635 students. The crown assumed the costs for the education of all 414 students at the academies, 7,347 students in the seminaries, 7,595 students in the district schools, and 3,187 students in the parochial schools. Thus, 18,543 students were supported at the expense of the crown and 42,092 at their own expense. In 1839 there were only 3 academies with 51 professors, 45 seminaries with 415 teachers, 173 district schools with a staff of 818, and 193 parochial schools with 367 teachers.

In the century preceding the Mongol invasion, religious instruction and theological literature flourished in comparison to the following period. A great wealth of theological and historical manuscripts,

6. For a somewhat cynical analysis of her motives in doing this see Iu. R. Klokman, *Sotsialno–ekonomicheskaia, istoriia russkogo goroda, vtoraia polovina XVIII v.* (Moscow, 1967), pp. 100–109.

[TABLE 3]
[ECCLESIASTICAL ACADEMIC INSTITUTIONS IN RUSSIA, 1846]

| | District of Petersburg | District of Kiev | District of Moscow | District of Kasan | Total |
|---|---|---|---|---|---|
| Number of academies | 1 | 1 | 1 | 1 | 4 |
| Number of students at academies | 120 | 114 | 118 | 62 | 414 |
| Number of seminaries | 10 | 14 | 9 | 14 | 47 |
| Number of students at seminaries | 2,943 | 4,715 | 5,462 | 4,279 | 17,399 |
| Number of district schools | 43 | 52 | 40 | 43 | 178 |
| Number of students at district schools | 4,294 | 7,394 | 7,606 | 5,948 | 25,242 |
| Number of parochial schools | 44 | 60 | 40 | 46 | 190 |
| Number of students at parochial schools | 3,400 | 6,384 | 3,866 | 3,930 | 17,580 |

some of which are in private hands, date from this period. (In Professor Pogodin's home in Moscow I saw an entire room filled with these manuscripts in folio.) The quantity at any rate testifies to intellectual activity. Only after they have been thoroughly researched, however, will one be able to judge their value. But this will probably take a long time.

After Kiev, the center of this movement, had been conquered, everything lapsed into barbarism. In Little Russia and in Red Russia, however, a seed was preserved, which owed its revival toward the end of the fifteenth century primarily to the vigorous struggle with Polish Catholic theology. Not only did the clergy of Kiev receive intellectual stimulation from this conflict, but their adversaries taught them how to employ dialectical forms and forced them to concern themselves with Occidental thought. In the sixteenth century, the struggle against Protestantism was added to this conflict with Catholic theology. In this period the theological school of Kiev distinguished itself by its dialectical acumen which, however, often degenerated into hair-splitting semantics.[7]

In Muscovite Russia everything lay in profound darkness at this time. During the dismal period of Mongol rule, the clergy was happy with the bare preservation of Christianity among the people. Only with the establishment of the patriarchate did some theological activity resume, which at the beginning was directed exclusively toward an essential and practical goal, namely, the suppression of errors and abuses and the standardization of all liturgical forms. These reforms, however, led to the schism of the Old Believers.

Only after Peter I had reconquered Kiev did theological studies in Russia proper experience a revival. Out of the contacts with Kiev's theologians and the studies pursued there developed the Moscow school which, however, for a long time did not rival the Kiev school in scholarship and intellectual prowess.[8]

Presently both schools are at approximately the same level. In regard to their relationship with foreign countries, however, they still represent different positions. The Kiev school has very close ties with Polish literature and gets its knowledge of the Occident from this source, whereas the Moscow school, when it occupies itself with foreign countries and their theologians, is concerned primarily with German thought. I met Russian theologians who demonstrated a precise knowledge of German theological literature and who had studied Neander's and Schleiermacher's writings in depth. Unfortunately they were unfamiliar with German Catholic theology and wholly ignorant of French theology. A knowledge of French theology would seem to be particularly important though, since the upper classes in Russia are for the most part French-educated and must necessarily therefore assimilate the ideas of French theology.

Today's bishops and monks are not only erudite but also well rounded and refined. Intellectual activity and the beginnings of a spirit of dedication to the ministry are evident. This spirit has also

7. Haxthausen's antirationalism leads him to judge the Kiev schools too severely. See M. Linchevskii, *Pedagogiia drevnikh bratskikh shkol i preimushchestvenno drevnei Kievskoi Akademii* (Moscow, 1870).

8. Florovskii warns against exaggerating the ignorance of Moscow at this period (p. 80); see S. K. Smirnov, *Istoriia Moskovskoi Slaviano-Greko-Latinskoi Akademii* (Moscow, 1855).

begun to spread among the younger generation of priests. It would be advisable for the government to give serious attention to this overzealous dedication of the younger clergy which supersedes the indifference of former times, for it could easily lead to fanaticism and a persecution mania.

The practice of sermonizing in the churches, in public places, out of doors, and on pilgrimages fell into complete disuse among the Muscovite clergy. During the period of Tatar rule it may have been regarded with suspicion or even forbidden. In the church of Kiev, however, the practice was preserved. We have already mentioned above that the hieromonk Polotskii, who was called from Kiev, was the first to begin preaching again in Moscow. Today the majority of bishops and ecclesiastics of higher rank have adopted this practice, although it has not become a general custom, a prescribed duty or an essential part of the divine service. I was told that the Synod has reservations about granting every priest the right to preach and that special permission of his bishop was required. Specifically the church is afraid of the possible dissemination of heterodox teachings and ideas. The reading of printed homilies and approved sermons is permitted.

Among the bishops and higher clergy one finds excellent predicants with eminent oratorical gifts. Some of their sermons have been printed. An intelligent young monk in Kharkov, a Livonian by birth, showed us a large number of sermons which he had translated into German and which substantiated the opinion we expressed above. The very best sermons are by the metropolitan Philaret of Moscow, Archbishop Vladimir of Kostroma, and Innokentii, the metropolitan-vicar of Kiev. As a sample we are including a very brief Good Friday sermon by the latter, a sermon whose depth of feeling and noble, truly sublime simplicity we believe has few equals.

### Sermon for Good Friday

One day the pious Patriarch Antonii was called upon to offer his brothers a word of instruction. Deeply imbued with the feeling of human frailty, Antonii simply replied, "Brethren, let us weep," and they fell to the ground and wept.

I know, dearly Beloved, that you too, are awaiting words of instruction from me, but my mouth is struck dumb at the sight of the Master lying in the tomb. And who would dare to speak when the Lord is silent? And what could one say about God and His justice, about man and his iniquity, that these wounds do not express more forcefully? Will he, who is unmoved by these wounds, be stirred by a weak human voice? Sermons were not delivered on Golgotha; there men only sobbed and beat their breasts. And this grave, too, is not the place for sermons, but a place for repentance and tears! My Brothers! Our Lord and Savior is lying in the tomb. Let us pray and weep! Amen![9]

The Russian church shares with the entire Catholic church of the West and East the doctrines of the veneration, invocation, and intervention of the saints. In regard to the images of the saints and their worship, the Greek church excludes sculpture, which, however, the Roman church permits. The Greek church has only icons.[10]

Both churches adopted the principle of allowing the faithful to venerate only those images which were believed to bear a true resemblance to the object portrayed. Particularly in regard to the pictures of Mary, it was assumed that they had to be copies of a portrait which, according to tradition, had been painted by Saint Luke, the Evangelist. For the representation of Christ one had the ancient image of the Savior imprinted on Saint Veronica's handkerchief, which is designated by the Greek church as the "image of the Savior, which was not produced by human hands." In the course of time, various legends grew up around the images of Mary which, having come directly from heaven, were discovered somewhere and then attested to their divine origin by miracles. The Roman Catholic church restricted the worship of images to those so-called miraculous images. Nevertheless, it did permit other pictures with religious significance, which are only the compositions of artistic genius, to embellish the churches and to stir the religious emotions of the faithful. The Eastern church, however, has remained more rigid in that it does not allow works of art in its churches.

This principle was often articulated in Russia in earlier times. In a circular from the year 1669, Tsar Aleksei Mikhailovich ordered "that the holy images of God should be painted according to the

9. Ivan Alekseevich Borisov (Innokentii), (1800–1857) was rector of the Kiev Seminary and one of the most renowned preachers and scholars of nineteenth-century Orthodoxy. See N. I. Barsov, ed., *Materialy dlia biografie Innokentiia, arkhiepiskopa khersonskogo*, 2 vols. (Moscow, 1883).

10. Primitive wooden sculpture was not unusual in village churches of the north, and Ermolin's one surviving work, a fragment of an equestrian statue of Saint George, now in the Tretiakov, attests to the existence of a developed tradition of sculpture in fifteenth-century Moscow. See Georgii Karlovich Vagner, *Skulptura Vladimiro-Suzdalskoi Rusi, g. Iuriev-Polskoi* (Moscow, 1964).

tradition of the most Holy Fathers who were inspired by the Lord, according to the immutable custom of the Holy Eastern church, and that they should resemble the objects and persons portrayed.''

But modern art was also introduced into Russia with Western civilization. Consequently one frequently finds in Russian churches religious paintings by modern Russian artists who have followed their artistic intuition. As a rule these pictures hang in the nave on the side walls. The iconostasis, a partition which stands before the altar and on which only prescribed images may be hung, generally contains only ancient pictures painted after traditional models in the old Byzantine style. Nevertheless, art has found its way into some compositions; in general the posture and costume are in the old style, but the costume is more idealized and the facial expression bears the imprint of the individual artist's imagination. The static serenity, the rigid austerity and the expressionless divine tranquillity found in the old models has yielded to expressions of human emotion.

Of course, only the old icons can be found in the houses of worship of the Old Believers. They reproach the Russian church for tolerating heretical images. In this respect, however, a reaction has begun to set in. The partisans of Young Russia, whom we mentioned above, are decidedly opposed to the introduction of modern painting into the church. The excellent and convincingly written article entitled "Iconography in the Russian Church" which appeared in the January 1845 issue of the *Journal for Popular Enlightenment* offers sufficient proof of this movement.[11]

In the booths on the market places, where popular books, tales, and jokes are sold, one also finds a large number of black or colored xylographs depicting the saints. Among them is a very large sheet containing seventy-two pictures of the Virgin with the Christ Child, which are reproductions of all the pictures of Mary recognized by the church as miraculous. The name is indicated above each little picture. Included are the Virgins of Kazan, Vladimir, Moscow, Kiev, etc. However, one finds pictures not only of Russian origin but also from all the other Christian countries, for example, a German picture which appears to be a copy of the Mariahilf in Styria and a Roman print which is probably from Loretto. I was told that these xylographs are printed mainly in Moscow and Vladimir.[12]

11. ''S.D.'' (author), ''Ob ikonopisi,'' *Zhurnal narodnogo prosveshcheniia*, January 1845, pp. 29–39.

12. In the early nineteenth century the *Lubok* woodcuts gave way to xylographic reproductions but even in the new medium the influence of

Initially the art of xylography, which seems to have been introduced from Germany, was regarded with suspicion by the ecclesiastical censorship. The patriarch Ioakhim was violently opposed to this form of art and in 1674 explicitly forbade "the printing of the images of the saints and the sale of such prints from Germany, for many artists execute these paintings in an inappropriate and perverse manner; the Lutherans and Calvinists paint them in an absurd and incorrect fashion, by giving the saints German costumes and the features of their own countrymen rather than representing them according to the old originals found among the Orthodox."

We have already mentioned the artist villages in the interior of Russia, which have been painting the images of the saints since time immemorial. All of the village inhabitants, the men, the women, and the children, are engaged in this activity. They have models of all the recognized and approved images, in which the mouth, nose, eyes, etc., have been engraved; one person completes the mouth, the second the nose, and the third person the eyes, etc. These pictures are sold throughout Russia as well as in all the Oriental and Slavic countries. I found them among the Croatians on the military frontier of Austria. In the acquisition of these pictures, the term "purchase" is considered inappropriate; rather, one "exchanges."

Upon entering even a rural church in Russia during divine worship, every unprejudiced person with a sense of melody and harmony will be struck by the impressive and deeply moving liturgical chant of the Russian priests. But whoever has heard the choir of the Russian imperial church will admit never having heard anything so beautiful and sublime. . . .

In the Old Believer churches and prayer houses I was not at all surprised to hear a chant sung in unison and in sharp nasal tones according to the Oriental tradition. To be sure, I recognized the great beauty of the motifs and modulations, but the execution grated on the European ear and was unbearable for a longer period of time. Since the excellent liturgical chant mentioned above is unknown among the Old Believers, I realized that it must be a product of modern times and cannot belong to the old church. . . .

German sources, especially Dürer, Aldegrever, and Piscator, is evident. See *Lubok, i russkie narodnye kartiny XVII–XVIII vv.* (Moscow, 1968), pp. 5–8.

# 13

## *Communes*

. . . When we western Europeans attempt to represent in our languages the characteristics of a totally alien nationality, for example the culture of the Turks or Persians, the concepts and views which we acquired from our education act as obstacles. . . . To be sure, we can understand the common human elements in these foreign cultures, but this is hardly adequate for a comprehensive description. In their attempt to understand the Slavic nations, the Germanic and Romanic peoples are confronted with similar difficulties.

A part of the Slavic race, the Bohemians, the Poles, the remnants of the Wends, etc., have the same history, religious institutions, and the same general culture as western Europe. Consequently, the other Europeans, and Germans in particular, easily understand the social and legal institutions of these peoples. Of great importance regarding legal institutions is the fact that their languages developed in a manner so similar to those of the other European peoples that Slavic and German terms have the same meaning. Indeed, the concepts of German and Roman law have permeated the Slavic social structure to such a degree that, for example, rural and municipal institutions are identical from the Elbe in Germany to the Dnieper on the Polish frontier. Sixty years ago the municipal law of Magdeburg was still in force in Kiev![1]

1. Magdeburg law was introduced into the cities of western Russia during the fifteenth century when Kiev, Smolensk, Polotsk, Minsk, etc., were ruled by Poland. This was done ostensibly to curb Russian political influence in these areas, but the laws stayed in force until long after reunification with Russia. See George Vernadsky, *Russia at the Dawn of the Modern Age* (New Haven, 1959), pp. 210 ff.

Nevertheless, at the core of Polish and Bohemian national life are social and legal institutions which scholars must struggle to describe in their idioms. An indigenous jurisprudence hardly developed at all, nor did it enjoy official recognition, as did national law among the Germans despite the preponderance and intrusion of Roman law. Rather, Bohemian and Polish jurisprudence were altered to fit the Procrustean bed of the dominant foreign law. Consequently, their languages either lack the necessary expressions or these words have so lost or modified their original meaning that they no longer accurately connote the original nature of their national institutions.

Let us take as an example the concept of communal property. Roman law employs the term *condominismus* and German law the concept of *Sammteigenthum*. Because they issued from specifically indigenous conditions, both expressions are so clearly delineated that juridically they can easily be distinguished. The Slavs also have communal property which, having developed out of the organization of the family, constitutes the basis of the entire social structure. But because their languages simply appropriated Roman and German concepts for analogous institutions, the vocabulary necessary to represent these indigenous conditions precisely is lacking.

We are confronted with a much greater task in trying to characterize the peculiarities of the social and legal institutions of the other Slavic peoples, the Russians, Bulgarians, Serbs, etc., whose culture developed independently of Occidental influence. The Russians first entered the great European family of nations in the eighteenth century and the admission of the other Slavic tribes is only now beginning! The very fact that they belong to the Eastern church separated them more sharply from the West than one would imagine, since there is no essential difference in the teachings of Roman and Greek Catholicism. More important in isolating them from European cultural development was the Tatar and Turkish rule, which lasted for so many centuries. However, this did help to preserve the original quality of their social organization; almost no foreign elements penetrated the social institutions, particularly to the level of the populace. To our modern conception of things, they thus appear underdeveloped and in many respects rude. Yet these institutions are better suited to the character of these peoples than are those of the western Slavs.

Within the past 150 years the Russians have begun to adopt the civilization of the Occident. Although this endeavor has been successful among the upper classes and in the governmental institutions, Western culture has hitherto failed to penetrate to the populace.

The Russian church and the rigidity of Russian popular institutions have offered unusually strong resistance. Recently, however, a significant change has come about in this respect, above all in the church. The rapid advancement of industry has also begun to corrode the core of Russian national life, the customs, practices, and conceptions of the people. Whether this impulse was a natural outgrowth of the internal development of the nation, whether it was encouraged or merely guided by the government, whether it will redound to the advantage or detriment of the people — these are frivolous questions at the present time, for this movement is a *fait accompli*, and no human power can arrest its progress. We can only urge an understanding government to endeavor to preserve the nobility and beauty of the national character, customs, and institutions. . . .

Like their Polish and Bohemian colleagues, the Russians, too, must cope with their language. Until 150 years ago Western culture, thought, and legal concepts had little influence on Russia, so that the inner core of the entire social order could evolve almost independently. In the past 150 years, however, when culture [in Russia] has been exclusively foreign, the language, in particular, adopted a great many alien concepts, and words took on new meanings. Since the educated classes departed from national customs and viewed them instead through foreign glasses, they confused their indigenous institutions with analogous foreign ones. Furthermore, because the language of the educated in everyday life as well as in scholarly studies and in commerce is imbued with foreign concepts, the vocabulary necessary to express genuinely national conditions is often wanting. To restore the original meaning of those words relating to indigenous institutions by divesting them of the secondary meanings which crept in with foreign concepts is one of the greatest tasks confronting Russian scholars.

To clarify our point, let us take as an example the Russian word *mir*. Out of the Latin word *communitas* and the German term *Gemeinde* there developed a specific legal concept, which in all the western European countries has only slightly different nuances of meaning. In each of these languages the corresponding term has a specific juridical and constitutional meaning which is wholly comprehensible to the educated and the uneducated. The Russian word *mir*, on the other hand, as it is used in commercial and legal language or in the colloquial speech of the educated, differs from its meaning in the language of the common people. Among the former this term is synonymous with the French *commune*; it designates a group of people who simply happen to live in the same place, or the administrative district of a city, a borough, or a village. Among the populace its connotation is totally different. Literally the word *mir* implies something sacred; it means both *commune* and *universe* and is best translated by the Greek *cosmos*. We recall no proverb in the German or Romance languages in which the authority, the law, and the sanctity of the commune are recognized. Russian, however, contains a vast number of these:

> God alone directs the *mir*.
> The *mir* is something vast.
> The *mir* is a surging wave.
> The *mir* has a broad neck and nape.
> Cast everything on the *mir*, for the *mir* will carry it away.
> The tear of the *mir* is liquid, but caustic.
> The *mir* sighs, and the cliff explodes.
> The *mir* simply sighs, and it echoes in the forest.
> One chops wood in the forest, and the chips fly about in the *mir*.
> A thread from the *mir* will make a shirt for a naked man.
> No one on earth can dissociate himself from the *mir*.
> What belongs to the *mir* belongs also to the mother's darling.
> Whatever the *mir* decides must come to pass.
> When the entire *mir* sighs, the contemporary generation suffers a miserable death.
> The *mir* is the nation's rampart.

. . . Because the Russian commune or *mir* constitutes in our opinion the real foundation of the entire social order, we should like to sketch its principal features and then to add as an example a description of a single large commune, that of the Ural Cossacks.

To understand the nature of the *mir*, one must carefully examine the fundamental character of the Slavs in general and the Russians in particular. . . . Nowhere are the ties of the blood relationship, the unity of the family and its natural extension, the commune, so clearly revealed as in the Russian people. Family unity and the common ownership of property represented the original character of Slavic society. Among the western Slavs, however, this feature is not as well developed or as strictly preserved as among the Russians.

The family found its unity in its head, the father. Without a father, the family simply could not exist. Because absolute equality prevailed in the family, anarchy would have broken out immediately had there been no common leader. If the father died, his eldest brother or son took his place, assuming absolute paternal authority. Indeed, if the natural succession of paternal authority was interrupted by the insanity of the eldest or his entrance into a religious order, the remaining members of the family elected a leader. Even if the youngest was chosen, he nevertheless became the senior, the father, who was obeyed without question. This custom, which acquired the force of law, has found expression in many proverbs. For example, "The opinion of the eldest is always right." "Where there is age, there is also law." "The younger brothers must respect the eldest like a father." The Russian princes also followed this principle. The grand duke was always called the eldest even if he was younger than the petty princes. . . . In his will Grand Duke Vladimir Monomakh bequeathed to his children this precept: "Respect the eldest brother like a father, the younger brothers like a brother." In Slavic families organized in this manner, no member possessed an individual fortune; rather, everything was considered to be common property which each adult member would have been entitled to dispose of freely had he not been subordinated to the absolute authority of his natural or elected father. Whoever wanted to withdraw from the unity of the family with its collective ownership of property in order to establish his own independent family (which, however, has always been considered to be a calamity, a *chernyi peredel*), forfeited his share of the communal property and consequently his right of inheritance.

In the course of time the members of the family became so numerous that it was no longer possible to maintain the unity of the communal household. Several members, together with their wives and children, began to establish individual households. They built separate homes and farmsteads but preserved the communal organization with its patriarchal rule. This represents the original Slavic village-community (a family commune) under the authority of its elder (*starik, starshii, starshina, starosta*). The property was not divided into private holdings, but the land was cultivated in common and the harvest equally distributed among all the households. The very same conditions are said to exist today in many regions of Serbia, Bosnia, and Bulgaria. Even in Russia, in the depths of the forest, one finds similar communes among the Raskolniki, which are known as *skity*.[2]

It is clear that these social conditions are incompatible with cultural and in particular agricultural advancement. Throughout Russia proper

2. The *skit* was a very small and isolated monastic retreat popular in Russia from the fourteenth century on; the form was introduced to Russia from Byzantium by Nil Sorskii and was later adopted by Old Believers as well.

there nevertheless has developed out of these social conditions a rural organization in which the principle of communal property has been fully retained. The forests and pasture land always remain undivided; the plowlands and meadows are apportioned to the various families in the commune, who, however, do not own the land but have only the right to use it temporarily. Formerly the lots may have been redistributed annually among the married couples of the community, each receiving a share equal to all the others in terms of quality. Today, however, in order to avoid expenses and great inconveniences the land is reapportioned after a certain number of years. If, for example, a father should die and leave six sons who are not of age, the widow generally continues to manage the farm until her sons marry. Then, however, they do not divide among themselves the plot which their father had cultivated; instead this land reverts to the commune, and all six sons receive a share equal to that held by the other members of the community. All together they might hold five to six times the amount of land which their father had held. If the six sons should marry when their father is still alive, then he claims for each one of them an equal allotment of the communal land. Since the sons continue to live in the same household with their father, he does not have to worry about establishing them. On the contrary, a marriage is fortunate for the family. Even if she has no dowry, the arrival of a daughter-in-law means an additional share of the communal property. The marriage and establishment of his daughters is thus the least of a Russian peasant's worries. . . .

From the very beginning the human race has been divided into two categories, the agricultural and the pastoral peoples, as symbolized in the biblical figures of Cain and Abel. Almost all the great races in history fall into these two groups (and, as we know, they are divided into the blond- and brown-haired races). Some are representatives of agriculture and others raise cattle as their means of livelihood. Among the Semites, the Arabs are the shepherds and nomads, the Babylonians and Assyrians the agriculturists. Among the Persians the Iranians are the tillers of the soil with permanent abodes, and the Turanians the nomadic people. The Mongols are nomads, and the Chinese farmers. There are Tatars with a fixed domicile (Chion Buchara) and nomadic Tatars (Nogai). Among the Germanic peoples the Ingaevones had permanent homes and the Suevians were the wanderers. The Slavic race was probably also divided into these two groups. The Wends, the Polish peasants, and the southern Slavs (Bulgarians, Serbs, and Wends) cultivated the soil. The Polish nobility was most likely a nomadic people and the Great Russians originally shepherds.

So deeply ingrained is this division in the human race that the agricultural peoples never become nomads and the pastoral peoples, as long as they continue to dwell in their original homes, will almost never become farmers. Only when the nomads move to other countries where agriculture is already established do they begin to till the soil. However, they never pursue their new occupation with zeal and dedication. They establish permanent homes, but the farmhands, slaves, and women generally work in the fields. This is the custom of the Arabs in Spain and the Turks in Turkey. . . .

In my opinion it is highly probable that the Great Russians were originally a pastoral people who gradually settled down and adopted farming. Only this hypothesis explains many of the peculiarities in the character, the way of life, and the customs of the Russian people.[3]

The entire social and even political life of the nomadic or pastoral peoples rests on the patriarchal principle. The family subordinated to its father and the tribe headed by its chief represent a natural hierarchy. Only in time of need, peril, or war do the tribes unite. In conformance with the patriarchal principle the senior member of the oldest tribe will step to the head of this alliance. As soon as the danger had ceased to exist, the alliance generally dissolves. A new doctrine, a prophet like Mohammed (in recent times the Wahabee)[4] or the call to conquer the world, as in the case of Ghengis Khan, may fire the tribes with enthusiasm. As though driven by instinct, they follow their leader to victory or death. Despotism rests on power; a monarchy, an aristocracy, and a democracy are based on the idea of law. In a patriarchal state the principle of organization and authority is rooted in instinct and custom. The father or patriarch governs with absolute power because nature and custom summon him to rule; the children obey without questioning for the same reason. There are no rights, only duties. It is the father's duty to rule and to provide for his family, that of the children to

3. By the eighth century, however, agriculture had long been established in Great Russia, as archaeological evidence indicates. See George Vernadsky and Michael Karpovich, *Ancient Russia* (New Haven, 1943), p. 327.

4. Wahabee, or Wahhabi, was an austere Islamic sect founded in the eighteenth century. Its adherents, who rejected all veneration of the Prophet, succeeded in capturing Mecca in 1803; see Carl Brockelmann, *History of the Islamic Peoples* (New York, 1960), pp. 352 ff.

obey. Since the nomadic peoples own no real property, the basis for the concept of law with all of its intricacies is lacking. Movable property gives rise to and employs only the simplest legal relationships.

The establishment of permanent homes over the past fifteen centuries, the introduction of agriculture, of Christianity, of the European concept of monarchy, and modern civilization gradually produced a political organism which is nearly identical to that found among the other agricultural peoples of Europe. Nevertheless, the fundamental principles of the original nomadic society are still manifest in the character, the customs, and the entire history of the Great Russians. . . .

The mother's command over the daughters is just as absolute as the father's authority over all his children. The same respect and obedience are shown to the communal authorities, the *starosta* and the white heads and above all to their common father, the tsar. A Russian has one and the same word for addressing his natural father, the *starosta*, his master, the emperor, and finally, God, namely, "father," "little father" (*batushka*). Similarly he calls every fellow Russian "brother" (*brat*), whether he knows him or not!

The common Russian (*muzhik*) knows absolutely no servile fear, but only a childlike fear or awe in the presence of his tsar, whom he loves with a devoted tenderness. He enters the military reluctantly, but once a soldier he harbors no resentment or ill will, serving the tsar with the greatest loyalty and devotion. The famous Russian word *prikazano* (it is ordered) has a magical effect on him. It goes without saying that whatever the tsar commands must be done. The Russian would never resist or defy the tsar's order; indeed, the impossibility of its execution would never occur to him. Even in the case of mere police proscriptions, the Russian does not say "it is forbidden" (*zapreshcheno*) but rather "it is not ordered" (*ni prikazano* or *nevoleno*). The profound reverence shown the tsar is evidenced above all in the Russian's attitude toward everything regarded as belonging to the monarch. He has the greatest respect for the *kazennye*, the state lands or the tsar's property. A Russian proverb says: "The *kazennye* do not die, are not consumed by fire and do not drown in water."

There is almost no case of persons responsible for collecting taxes ever having been attacked or robbed, even though they travel long distances alone and often carry considerable sums of money. In northern Russia, in the province of Vologda, where the customs are untainted and the inhabitants very honest, the tax collector, upon arriving in a village, knocks on every window and cries "kassa." Everyone brings him his tax for the year and drops it into a sack. Knowing he will never be cheated, the collector does not bother to check the amount. When night falls, he enters the first good house and places the sack of money under the icon of the saint. He then looks for lodging and sleeps without a care, confident that the next morning he will find everything just as he had left it!

The national bond which united the Russian people before Riurik is very obscure. Immediately before Riurik we find cities and their territories which, however, were only loosely tied to one another. They had neither a common center nor a common government. We do not know whether these elements were present earlier and then fell into decline but we can assume that this was the case, since the tribes longed for common leadership. In sending for Riurik they said: "Our land is large, but we lack order; come and rule over us." This famous passage from the ancient chronicle of Nestor denotes the political character of the Russians as it is manifested throughout history. The patriarchal ruler, the tsar, appears to be absolutely essential to the existence and perpetuation of the nation. Consequently, we never find popular insurrections which challenge the authority of the government or the tsar as such. Rather, uprisings are directed against individuals and usually for so-called legitimate reasons: for and against the false Dmitrii, for Pugachev, who posed as the banished Peter III, and lastly in 1825 for a similar reason.[5] The people always obeyed the government which ruled over them, even the Mongols. To be sure, they frequently complain about alleged injustices, but, after verbally expressing their grievances, they cease complaining and everyone is content.

Who would be so bold as to venture a plausible conjecture about the origin of the Russians or indeed of the entire Slavic race? Probably after having wandered about the Asiatic and European steppes for many centuries, several nomadic tribes began to settle in the fertile river valleys. We can assume that a large part of the peoples known to Herodotus in ancient Scythia were Slavic tribes.[6] Of course, the true Scythians, that is, the royal Scythians or Scolates, were

5. Haxthausen refers to the uprising of 25 December 1825, but, as he admits elsewhere, this was not directed so much against individuals as against prevailing governmental practices per se.

6. Herodotus distinguished between the "Scyths" and the "Scythian plowmen," the latter of whom, according to Dvornik, were "partly Slavs." Francis Dvornik, *The Slavs: Their Early History and Civilization* (Boston, 1956), chap. 1.

not Slavs. But perhaps the modern Scythians, the Budini and others, are of Slavic descent.[7] It is likely that the Slavs first settled in the areas around Valdai and Lake Ilmen, with Novgorod later their center. At any rate, this is what their oldest chronicler, Nestor, has stated.[8] Branching out in all directions from this common center, the colonies which they founded were located primarily along the rivers. . . . They established a community which cannot properly be called a city in the western European sense of the word. The distinction between a city and a village was unknown to the ancient Russians, who merely differentiated between mother and daughter communities. As long as the supply of food was adequate, they dwelled together in the same place, but, when it became impossible to extract the necessary food supplies from the soil, the commune sent out colonies in all directions. Individual families never established isolated farms; rather, small communities founded villages. These daughter communes maintained very close ties with the mother commune which governed them, and they even called it mother. Hence we find ancient Mother Suzdal, Mother Vladimir, Mother Novgorod, and Mother Pskov. It was in this way that territories arose. This is undoubtedly the meaning of the expression *land*, which is used in all the Slavic countries and whose historical origin is so enigmatic. . . .

The mother commune governed the daughter communes or the land and also offered them protection and refuge when an enemy approached. Although the family and communal organization of the mother and the daughter communes was not essentially different, they were nevertheless gradually distinguished by their different means of livelihood. [In the mother commune,] commerce and industry began to assume a major role, with agriculture declining in importance. The structures erected for its own defense and that of the land gradually gave a different appearance. Because the contacts with civilized nations resulted in an imitation of the external forms of foreign culture, the mother communes took on the features of western European cities. It was primarily the citadel located in the center of the community which gave it an urban appearance. The genuinely Slavic city is always comprised of three parts. In the

7. According to Dvornik, the Budini were "probably Slavs," as opposed to the non-Slavic Scyths. Ibid., p. 13.

8. Samuel Hazard Cross and Olgerd P. Sherbowitz-Wetzor, *The Russian Primary Chronicle, Laurentian Text* (Cambridge, Mass., 1953), p. 53. Dvornik cites archaeological evidence to prove that Slavs settled early in the south of Russia as well, *The Slavs*, p. 19.

center is the citadel (*gorod*) with its walls, towers, and battlements. Surrounding the fortress is the industrial city with a circumvallation. The industrial city is encircled by the agricultural city, which, like our European suburbs, is generally divided into several districts. This layout is so basic that even today Moscow's police precincts are not located next to one another but rather around each other.

Although in principle and in appearance there was originally no distinction between the urban and rural communities in Russia, in the course of time a significant difference emerged. The larger municipalities of Novgorod, Kiev, Moscow, and Iaroslavl have become cities as we know them in western Europe. A middle class has come into being which, to be sure, is basically different from its western European counterpart. While the culture, customs, and views of the Russian middle class do not contrast sharply with those of the rural population, they nevertheless have a particularistic local coloration. The history of Novgorod with its rebellions, divisions, and internal wars offers sufficient evidence of this. It should not be forgotten that Novgorod's contacts with the German Hanseatic cities, which extended over a long period of time, probably brought it the ideas of the medieval German bourgeoisie. Moreover, the history and orientation of Novgorod is unique, and its particularism is alien to the Russian character. Hence these peculiarities are not to be found at all, or only to a very minor degree, in the history of the other cities.[9]

This particularism issues from a local patriotic sentiment which is, as we have already mentioned, alien to the Russian character. But in this particularism one can discern the vestiges of the primitive nomadic nature of the people. The nomad knows no attachment to his place of birth or the land which he has inherited from his ancestors. Born in the tent of the horde, he is forever moving about, using the pastures here and there, but he does not claim ownership to a specific piece of property; all the land belongs to him. His family, his horde, and his tribe are the surroundings to which he is devoted and in them he senses his native land, should he be with them in one place today and somewhere else tomorrow. The only places on earth to which he feels bound are the shrines of his tribe and the graves of his ancestors.

Even today one finds in the Russian little attachment to the soil

9. Haxthausen's remarks on the uniqueness of Novgorod could be extended to Novgorod's immediate dependency (*prigorod*), Pskov. See N. Porfiridov, *Drevnyi Novgorod: Ocherki iz istorii russkoi kultury XI–XV vv.* (Moscow-Leningrad, 1947).

which he temporarily cultivates. His real existence is wandering about on all the highways and byways. Like a nomadic horde he moves about in large caravans with his companions. At home in his village it is only his family, his neighbors, the entire community, above all the individuals to whom he is deeply attached, and not the soil. . . . Without a moment's hesitation he will move to remote areas to establish colonies, if all or even half of the commune takes part and provided only his family and neighbors are among the settlers. The only regret he may have is that he will never again see his village church or the graves of his ancestors. The Russians are imbued with the feeling that the entire country, all Russia, as far as it is inhabited by the Russian race, belongs to all the people and therefore to each member of the tribe. As master of the community, the tsar distributes the land among the various classes of the population with each person being entitled to the use of a share.

To repeat, the Russian feels no profound allegiance to the place of his birth but is imbued with an ardent patriotism. The country of one's ancestors, Holy Russia, the fraternity of all Russians united under the tsar, a common religion, the ancient shrines and the burial places of one's ancestors — all these elements form a vital and harmonious whole which embraces and pervades the Russian's soul. Within this whole everything is personified. Just as every Russian is a brother to every other Russian, in contrast to the foreigner (the *nemets*) and just as he has special names and affection for his most distant relatives, he also regards the inanimate objects of nature as being kindred and gives them the sacred names of kin. He designates God, the tsar, the priest, and every old man as father and calls the church his mother. He always speaks of Russia as the Holy Mother Russia. The capital of the empire is the Holy Mother Moscow and the mightiest river the Mother Volga. The Don River springing from Lake Ivan is addressed as "You, Don, son of Ivan." He even calls the road from Moscow to Vladimir, "Our dear mother, the Vladimir highway" (*nasha matushka Vladimirsha*). Even domestic animals and horses in particular are given the names of kin, such as "little mother," "little brother," etc. The center of all remembrance and Russian history is Moscow, the holy mother of the nation, which all Russians love and revere. Throughout his life every Russian cherishes the desire to visit the mother city, to see the spires of the holy churches and to pray at the tombs of Russia's patron saints, for Mother Moscow has always suffered and shed her blood for Russia, just as the Russian people have always sacrificed their lives for her.

## Chapter Thirteen

Let us return to the Russian rural commune and summarize what has already been said in various places about the settlement and the nature of the communes.

The Russian Slavs never established scattered, isolated farmsteads but always settled in communes. Even in the northern provinces, where the Finns had already settled, the Russians peacefully founded their communes among them. For a long time the Finns remained unassimilated (as today, for example, the Sirianians, Cherlmes, Chuvash, and the Mordvines) until the majority of them, after having adopted Russian Christianity, were completely absorbed by the Russian population. The individual farmsteads dispersed among the Russian communes are probably of Finnish origin, since most of the Finnish tribes settled in this manner. In Estonia and Ingria we can still see them today. The *pustoshe* (or deserted villages) which one finds everywhere and whose names are said to be mainly Finnic may be abandoned Finnish settlements. Also those individual farmsteads known as *odnodvortsy* which are now occupied by Russians undoubtedly were originally Finnish.[10] The fact that these farms represented real property would seem to indicate that they are of foreign origin, since in Russian society the individual is merely granted the right to use the land temporarily. . . .

As their members grew too large in number, the first Slavo-Russian communes established new settlements. At this time the Russians were completely free, the institution of serfdom still unknown. Notwithstanding the fact that patriarchal rule and obedience prevailed, the communes were free. In addition, the daughter communes were probably subordinate to the authority of the mother commune only in certain respects. Even after tsarism had reached its full development, not only the individual communes but also the districts or lands (*zemlia*) which comprised the mother and daughter communes continued to elect their own patriarchal leaders, their *starosty* and white heads. To be sure, the tsars regarded these lands as being under their own administration, and frequently put *voevody*[11] at their head. More often, however, they turned over all the administrative functions to the city or mother commune as had been the custom

10. Most *odnodvortsy*, or one-homesteaders, were descended from minor servitors of the sixteenth and seventeenth centuries whose holdings had been reduced to one farm. See Blum, *Lord and Peasant in Russia*, pp. 478–80.

11. For a detailed study of the institution of *voevoda* and its role in the building of the Russian state see B. N. Chicherin, *Oblastnye uchrezhdeviia Rossii v XVII veke* (Moscow, 1856).

everywhere in ancient times. We find documents dating from the sixteenth century in which Ivan Vasilevich wrote to certain cities and their territories: "Since you are not content with your *voevoda*, I want to remove him and permit you to govern yourselves. Should you do this to my satisfaction and to the satisfaction of the territory, then I shall improve your circumstances with privileges."

At the beginning we thus have the free Slavic commune. However, not all of the land had yet been brought under cultivation. Vast stretches of land, traversed by nomads, lay untilled and were for all practical purposes discovered anew. These lands belonged to the entire nation and to its leader, the tsar, who was entrusted with their distribution. Without encountering any obstacles or resistance, several wealthy, enterprising individuals settled in these newly discovered territories. In addition, the tsars presented their boyars and courtiers with large tracts of land for cultivation and their own personal use. Both groups of entrepreneurs founded villages and recruited settlers, who engaged in farming and cattle raising and who paid the owners a certain amount of rent, which was probably a share of the agricultural produce and a number of young cattle, etc. The status of the *polovniki* in northern Russia is undoubtedly a remnant of this system. This was a true tenant relationship, whereby personal liberty was adequately guaranteed by the freedom to settle elsewhere. However, at an early date one already finds contracts for life as well as hereditary compacts. This contract relationship was called *khapal* or *kabala* (see the journal edited by Professor Pogodin).[12] Only after Tsar Godunov had abolished their freedom of movement on Iuriev's Day, a day of mourning for the people, were the tenants actually regarded as being bound to the soil.[13] Earlier in this work we described in detail how Peter I transformed this relationship into the present system of serfdom by means of the revision tables. Historical documents testify that in very ancient times the boyars and courtiers whom the tsar had endowed with land forced prisoners

12. *Kabala*, a Mongol term, referred originally only to written agreements covering loans to peasants of from one to three years. By the fifteenth century it came to refer to a state of virtual slavery. See Blum, *Lord and Peasant in Russia*, pp. 243–46.

13. The right of tenants to relinquish their tenancy was curtailed by a series of steps, of which the limitation of movement to the week preceding and following Iuriev's Day (Saint George's Day), 26 November, was the first. The final establishment of serfdom, however, was marked by the 1649 Code's lifting of restrictions on the period during which a gentry could reclaim a refugee serf.

of war and other slaves to cultivate the land for their own profit. What remained of this practice may have furnished the model for the ever expanding institution of serfdom in the eighteenth century. We thus have in the earliest periods of Russian history free communes, communities of tenant farmers or semi-serfs, and slave communes. It is improbable that many more free or daughter communes came into being in historical times. In founding colonies the cities began at a very early date to distribute land to the new villages in return for rent to be paid in the form of crops, etc.

The remaining two categories, the tenant and slave communes, multiplied so rapidly that they soon exceeded by far the number of free communes. This is readily comprehensible if one considers that Russia was colonized to a much greater degree than other countries. It should be borne in mind that 150 years ago the area south of Tula and the Desna and Oka rivers was one vast steppe where Tatar nomads roamed, and that as late as 1760 Moscow lived in perpetual fear of their incursions.[14] Today, however, many thousands of square miles of this region are under cultivation and dotted with villages. For many centuries this tremendous colonization effort, which employed the indigenous population, was undertaken almost exclusively by those entrepreneurs to whom the tsar had given land. But in these regions only communes of prisoners of war and slaves (*kholopy*) were established.

Let us now turn our attention to the general character of the Russian people. The sense of unity in the nation, in the commune, and in the family is the foundation of Russian society. Every form of individualism and nearly every form of property, especially land, coalesces in each of these three unities. Except for the nation itself and its representative, the tsar, no one owns real property. All of the property held by the communes and the families is merely granted to them temporarily and thus is not based on the principle of permanent ownership. In every aspect of life the idea of communal property is evident. It constitutes the basic principle of Russian society, whereas among other peoples, the Germanic for example, the principle of communal property applies only in families related by blood or marriage. Among the Russians the family itself is not limited by blood. The servant who raises the son of an aristocrat loves him more than his father and is always considered a member of the

14. This is an exaggeration, for the energetic measures taken in the decades before 1650 caused the Tatar invasions to subside. See A. A. Novoselskii, *Borba Moskovskogo gosudarstva s tatarami v pervoi polovine XVII veka* (Moscow-Leningrad, 1948), chap. 8.

family. He is given the specific national name of "uncle." Anyone who has not understood this most fundamental principle of Russian social life cannot appreciate the profound intimacy of these relationships. Blood is a part of parenthood, to be sure, but not everything. As the peasant commonly says: "Why should I worry about the steer? The calf is mine." He loves and takes as good care of the cuckoo as his own child.

Several sects, specifically the Skoptsy (eunuchs) offer the most unusual example of this. They have wives and children whom they love and care for as if they were their own. Paternal authority, the most absolute of all authority, is not limited exclusively to blood relationship. The adoptive father, the eldest brother, the eldest member of the commune, the *starosta*, and the leader chosen by the *artel*, are obeyed with the same respect. Kinship through baptism and the church is considered to be the equivalent of consanguinity. The elective fraternity of the Serbians, the *krsno-bratstvo*, and the fraternity of the cross as practiced by the Russians are almost more intimate than the relationship among blood brothers.[15] The tsar is the father of the Russian people, but the land of his birth is of no importance. Riurik and the Varangians, who were summoned to Russia, were obeyed as if they had been the chieftains of indigenous tribes. . . . Empress Catherine II, even though a woman and a foreign princess, found the same respect and affection as the native Russian princes. Upon becoming tsarina she belonged to the nation. This profound respect for authority is accorded every person who, by the grace of God, assumes this office.

While the Russian humbly obeys and holds all his superiors in the real or fictive family hierarchy in great esteem, he still feels that everyone is equal. He honors and obeys every father, but he considers himself to be the peer of all his brothers. This sense of equality is most clearly evidenced when the muzhik, the peasant, stands in the presence of the tsar. Knowing that everyone is equal before the tsar, he speaks to him naturally, easily, and without reserve, which a member of the upper classes can seldom do. We can best observe the manifestation of this feeling of equality during all religious celebrations and in church. The peasant has the greatest respect for the *chinovnik* or official; he trembles in the presence of a general, but in church he considers himself to be his equal and even crowds ahead of him. In a Russian church one always

15. Based upon the literal exchange of crosses worn at the neck, as in Dostoevsky's novel *The Idiot*. This act binds both members in a close and holy relationship.

sees the peasants huddled together in the front and the persons of rank in the rear. During a special celebration in one of the churches in Moscow an aristocratic gentleman wanted to go to the front of the church. His servant, a Russian-speaking German, said to one of the peasants standing before him: "Don't you see that the general would like to move forward?" The peasant, however, calmly replied: "Brother, we are standing before God, and in His presence we are all equal."

There is a peculiar instability and mobility in the Russian national character. Nowhere do we encounter rigid forms. The Russian does not like rules or a specific regimentation, nor does he want a fixed position in his life or in his profession. He demands the greatest independence; he wants to be able to move about freely, to remain at home or to take to the road as he pleases. He does not want to be subjected to strict discipline or thrift. The Russian is hospitable and prodigal regarding food and drink, never conserving his provisions. He loves risk, gambling, and speculation. Because a great deal of money passes through his hands, he disregards the kopek. In his family life he will not tolerate sharply defined relationships between parent and child, father and son, husband and wife. He does not permit outsiders to mingle in his domestic affairs. He has no property which is permanently his. Rich today, poor tomorrow! A family's wealth hardly lasts two generations. . . . In his relationship to his superiors, however, he does not want to be free, perferring to be ruled. He loves the authoritarianism of a father, of a *starosta*, of the tsar, and of his master every now and then. Indeed, he would seek this subordinate status if he did not already have it. He does not even mind being squeezed now and again, for oppression awakens and steels his faculties so that he can shrewdly escape unjust treatment. He demands that his superiors be firm and severe, but he does not want to be governed by rigid laws or lifeless constitutions. He loves human arbitrariness. He wants a personal tsar whose authority is limited neither by written laws nor by estates. Just as primitive Christianity had no written word or constitution but was merely based on the practice of a Christian life, the Russian, too, desires that secular life be based on this very principle. Each individual should carry his constitution within, for he then will know his place and his vocation. . . . .

By means of a highly formalistic system in all the official organs and activities of the state, the government since the reign of Peter I has sought to counteract this flighty and unstable quality in the national character, which endangers the stability of society throughout. So numerous are the governmental controls, laws and ordinances that this system is unparalleled in all of Europe. Outwardly there appears to exist an order, uniformity, and security which the most perceptive critic could not hope to improve upon. But we do not intend to extol this system. The best actions undertaken by the various administrative bodies do not follow these regulations. Charlemagne traveled widely to observe conditions first hand and executed his own projects. Where he was unable to go personally, he sent reliable and experienced emissaries, his *missi*, who submitted an exact account to him. After seeing what had to be done, they took the proper measures in his name. Emperor Nicholas also follows this procedure.

Russian national life resembles the land. It is a vast open plain where everything moves about freely and joyfully. But the government constructed a wall around it and left several gates open.

Every impartial Russian who is familiar with his country and his people will acknowledge the accuracy of our comments on the Russian national character and its embodiment in the organization of the family, the commune, and society. It is clear that many traits may have been exaggerated and others not sufficiently emphasized. Furthermore many features are lacking for a truly comprehensive portrayal. The reasons for this deficiency can be attributed to the fact that this book is to the best of our knowledge the first attempt to describe the Russian character based on these principles and also to the fact that this task has been undertaken by a foreigner.

The foundation as well as the entire edifice of the Russian social order constitutes too sharp a contrast to the principles and ideas of modern Western civilization, which are dominant in the educated classes, not to have been sharply criticized. Hitherto these Russian institutions have not been actively defended. But their passive resistance is so strong and they are rooted so deeply *in succum et sanguinem* of national life that superficial attacks are incapable of putting this solid edifice out of joint. Furthermore, no Russian can totally free himself from the inbred inclinations of Russian national character. Western European culture, which will always be merely an adopted culture, cannot eradicate these tendencies. The profound attachment which the Russian still has toward indigenous institutions thwarts every attempt to modify them in their essence. We hope that this foreign, unnational culture will never succeed in seriously threatening or destroying this sanctuary of the Russian people. . . .

In Russia there is no national or family bond without a coordinating focus, a leader, a father, or a master. A leader is absolutely in-dispensable in the Russian's life. The Russian selects a father if God has taken his natural father from him. Even the free commune chooses an elder (*starosta*) and obeys him unconditionally. He is not the delegate of the community, but rather its father with full paternal authority. One must keep this point clearly in mind if one is to understand the position of the tsar. Russian society is very much like a colony of bees, in which royalty is a natural necessity. Just as the colony would cease to exist without its queen, so, too, would Russian society cease to exist without the tsar. In Russia the tsar is neither the delegate of a sovereign people nor the first servant of the state nor the legitimate lord of the land. He is not even a sovereign ruling by the grace of God. He is simultaneously the unity, the leader, and the father of the people. He holds no office; rather, he occupies the position of a parent. He is simply the father in whom the nation recognizes the unity of its blood. This feeling is as much a part of the common man as the awareness of his own being! Hence, the tsar can never err, in the people's opinion. Whatever he does is always deemed right. Every reduction or limitation of his power, even in the well-intentioned sense of the Germanic organization of the estates, appears to be utter nonsense in the Russian's eyes. Ivan IV could thus commit atrocities and the people remained loyal to him and loved him as before. He is still the favorite of the common people and the hero of folk legends and popular ballads!

At the present time in particular, the organization of the Russian commune is of immense political value to Russia. All the western European nations are suffering from an evil which threatens to destroy them and for which no cure has been found: pauperism and "proletarianism." Protected by its communal organization, Russia escapes this evil. Every Russian has a home and his share of the communal land. Should he personally relinquish his allotment or lose it in some way, his children still have the right as members of the commune to claim their own share. There is no *mob* in Russia, only a *people*. This will continue to be the case as long as new, unnational institutions do not create an unpropertied mob, which we hope is no longer to be feared.

Precisely because it is rooted in the basic character of the entire Slavic race and because it developed spontaneously out of the Russian people, the principle of communal organization is the same throughout Russia. To destroy this principle or even to modify it essentially would be, in my opinion, extremely dangerous. The drawbacks of this organization in regard to agricultural progress are too evident to require an explanation. But the political value of this institution outweighs the disadvantages so greatly that they never could be placed on the same scale. Furthermore, I do believe that the detrimental effects can be offset or modified in various ways without eliminating the principle — for example, by restoring the original system of cultivating the land, particularly in the smaller communes or in the subdivisions of the larger communes. This could be accomplished by abolishing the distribution of land and by reintroducing communal agriculture. In my opinion these proposals can be realized among a people so accustomed to obeying authority. I am certain that agriculture could be carried on much more efficiently in this manner and that no one would be at a disadvantage if, instead of dividing the land, the harvest were equally distributed.

I have already mentioned that there still exist in the interior of the forests agricultural communes which cultivate the land in common rather than in individual holdings. But there are also vast areas where the largest part of the land is not distributed among the individual communes but where the land has remained in the possession of one entire territorial commune. At this point we would like to examine one of these large territorial communes more closely. For this purpose we have chosen to describe the commune of the Ural Cossacks, a tribe in which the ancient Russian character and customs have been very well preserved.

### The Commune of the Ural Cossacks

The Ural Cossacks, who probably descend from the Great Russian race, live along the Ural River adjacent to the Kirghiz steppe.[16] They settled on the right bank of the Ural for protection from the Kirghiz hordes. Only in two places do they have settlements on the left bank, which serve also as military outposts. The line which they inhabit begins at Mukhranov, which is approximately 35 miles from Orenburg, and continues for more than 450 miles to Chunev, where the Ural empties into the Caspian Sea. They dwell in *stanitsy*, villages with one to two hundred houses, located about 10–13 miles apart. The river flows through a vast plain which, for the most part, is a wholly sterile salt-steppe and only the lowlands, the banks of the rivers, and particularly the banks of the mighty Ural have

16. As Haxthausen explains, the Ural Cossacks were formed in part by deserters from the Don Cossacks, who were in turn composed of both Great Russians and Ukrainians. See A. Savelev, *Trekhsotletie Voiska Donskogo* (St. Petersburg, 1870).

fertile soil, most of which is meadow land. The Cossack settlers carry on very little agriculture; those living north of Uralsk do not farm the land at all and those who dwell to the south just a little here and there. Tiny gardens can be found near their homes. They live principally from fishing and cattle raising. Initially the Cossacks probably settled voluntarily on the banks of the Ural River. The first settlers were the so-called deserters from the Don, who were later joined by many Streltsy fugitives. At first they organized themselves in their own fashion, and only later did the government lend their communities a greater coherence and unity by several regulations. They are of robust stock, handsome, lively, industrious, submissive to authority, brave, good-natured, hospitable (they consider it a disgrace to accept payment for food and drink), indefatigable, and intelligent. In their legal institutions, customs, and manner of life we can still discover the genuine old Russia.

All the Cossacks are required to serve within the territory from their eighteenth to their twentieth birthdays and outside the territory from the age of twenty to fifty-five, as often as needed. As a rule, the Don Cossacks serve for nine years, three of which are spent outside the territory, the Bashkir and Ural Cossacks for three years from a total of twelve. According to a general regulation they are supposed to fulfill their military obligations in a definite sequence, but in reality this is not the case. Circumstances do not always conform to such lifeless written orders. Let us assume that the man whose turn it is to serve cannot leave home without totally disrupting his affairs. But he is wealthy and his neighbor poor and, furthermore, it is not necessary for his neighbor to be at home. His neighbor will thus volunteer to take his place and, in return, he will provide for his neighbor's family or give him a certain amount of money. The government is prudent enough not to interfere with these arrangements, which develop naturally and without constraint. Every order is thus directed to the entire community rather than to specific individuals. This explains, moreover, why no region can muster its troops as rapidly and efficiently as these Cossacks!

There are approximately 24,000–25,000 men here of whom 10,000–12,000 between the ages of eighteen and forty-five are in the service. In 1837 only 3,300 of these men were inactive and at home. The war necessitated an immediate mobilization of the troops.[17] Four regiments of 550 men each or two-thirds of all the able-bodied men in the territory were supposed to be called. Within

17. Haxthausen evidently refers to the intensification of military action against Shamil in the western Caucasus after 1849.

three weeks they appeared at the designated place fully mounted, armed, and equipped! The order to gather at the marketplace in Uralsk had been passed from commune to commune. The *voiskavoi*, deputy and adjutant of the *hetman*,[18] rode into the crowd that had assembled and, holding the emperor's order above his head, cried out: "*Atamany!* You are ordered to mount your horses and to furnish four regiments!" He then removed his cap, read the order aloud and designated the places where they should gather. And with that the matter was concluded on the part of the authorities. On such occasions the majority of the troops who are ready to march organize themselves in the marketplace. Generally they group together in families. If one out of every five or seven men is summoned to duty, the closest relatives decide upon their delegates. Whoever can afford to leave his home with the least inconvenience and wants to serve goes. The others offer him a certain amount in payment, equip him, and provide for his family. If he is a drunkard, he does not get the money, but instead it will be given directly to his family. The price fluctuates depending upon the circumstances. If only a few men are enrolled, they will each receive a considerable sum, since a large number [of men] are contributing. If, for example, eight or ten men are required to send one man, each of them could easily pay 100–200 rubles. Those who are called to serve in the Imperial Guard in Petersburg, which is, of course, comprised of tall, handsome men (everyone else is rejected) and in which the duty is very difficult, sometimes received 5,000–6,000 rubles. There are approximately 3,000 men serving in the Caucasus. They, too, agree among themselves as to who will maintain sentry duty in the interior. Those who live nearest the posts to be occupied assume the duty, and the others pay them 200–300 rubles. At the time I referred to above, two out of every three men were to be levied, which meant that the third man had to pay the other two. Only the wealthiest and those who were absolutely needed at home were freed from their military obligations. To be sure, they had to sacrifice a substantial part of their fortune for the others. In such a case a settlement is arrived at as follows. One man advances 200 rubles not to go; the second offers 300 rubles and the third 350. They bid until one claims that he cannot afford a larger contribution and offers to go. He then receives the sum that the others have offered to remain free.

To repeat, at that time two out of every three men were to be

18. The German text uses the term *Hetman* but the leader of the Ural Cossacks was titled *Ataman*.

enrolled. The price varied between 900 and 2,000 rubles, which the two recruits divided. Within a couple of days 1,100 wealthy Cossacks had raised no less than 1,500,000 rubles. What great wealth among a people with such simple customs! On the fourth day following the proclamation of the order, the entire population assembled at the marketplace in Uralsk with each of the four regiments together with its officers taking up the position to which it had been assigned. The contracting parties then stepped forward. The man who was to remain behind presented the other two and announced the price which they had agreed upon. They shook hands, the officer placing his hand above theirs, and the contract was concluded. Everyone then returned home and, within fourteen days, the regiments were ready to march. These agreements are always kept, for if they were broken the government would intervene after two weeks and simply seize anyone who could be found.

And what excellent troops they are! All of them depart cheerfully and willingly because it is their own decision and they are paid. Their families are provided for, they are well equipped, and it does not cost the government a penny. Clearly the government could not commit a more serious political error than to attempt to modify this system even slightly. But, nevertheless, several pedants with a love for formalities have come up with the ingenious idea that it is impossible to decorate the Cossacks with chevrons indicating the number of years they have served.

The entire organization of the villages (*stanitsy*) is totally military. Whereas an officer is at the head of every larger village, each smaller community stands under the authority of a petty officer. Both are appointed by the crown and charged with the duties of law enforcement and the administration of communal affairs, etc. In each village there is a complete military guard comprised of fifteen to twenty men. Three men keep sentry at intervals of three to four versts between the villages, one sentinel always standing watch on a high scaffold while the other two, who are below, eat, sleep, and so forth. Always armed to the teeth, the Cossack is never without his musket.

The entire territory forms a social, economic, military, and political unity, whose center is the market town of Uralsk. Formerly the *ataman* and his *voiskavye* governed the entire Cossack state from this point. Today he is assisted by a committee of four counsellors. With the exception of the last two, all the *atamany* have been native Cossacks. The present *ataman*, Kazhesnikov, is said to be an excellent man. The individual villages do not have separate finances; rather, the entire Cossack community has a single budget. The revenues derived from the sale of fishing licenses, which often amount to 100,000 rubles, represent the main source of income. These permits are purchased by the men who are not on active duty and who do not have the right to fish. The salt tax constitutes the remainder of the community's income. Although the Cossacks receive salt for household use gratis, the salt used to pickle fish for sale is taxable. Most of the salt is taken from Lake Inder.[19] The expenditures are for the *ataman* and the authorities and also, I believe, for the pay of those officers who are at war outside of the territory. An ensign receives 240 rubles banco. The ordinary soldier serving within the territory or less than one hundred versts from the Urals, gets no pay; beyond that limit he receives his pay and his rations from the crown.

The economic conditions of these Cossacks are extremely curious. The basis of the right of ownership is the Russian family, its extension, the commune, and its communal property, as we have already described it. According to this principle there is no private ownership of land; rather, this territory measuring seven to eight hundred versts is the common property of 50,000 people! Of particular interest in this respect is the harvesting of the hay. Not only do the individuals not own private property and not only do the villages not have their own meadows, but the meadow lands have always been the property of the entire large Cossack community. The hay is harvested under the supervision of the *ataman* and his aides, the *voiskavye*, and the village officers.

The *ataman* determines the date for the harvesting to begin, which is usually the first of June. An officer is stationed as an inspector at all of the points where there are extensive meadows. Every Cossack who is serving in the army (only they have this right) chooses the piece of land that he would like to mow. The night before the harvesting is to begin, they all appear at their places. At the break of day, the officer gives the signal and everyone begins to mow his piece. On the first day, however, the Cossack simply mows a circle around his plot. Whatever lies within this circle becomes his property, and he can mow it leisurely in the following days with the help of his family. A good deal of calculation and ingenuity is needed to find the right circumference. If on the first day he attempts to mow too large a circle, his neighbors will enter his

---

19. Lake Inder is a saline lake 25 kilometers east of the Ural River and 160 kilometers north of its mouth.

plot where the circle is still open. The object is to mow the largest possible circle and to close it as quickly as possible. The Cossack works with the most incredible output of energy, hardly taking time out for a drink of water, since all work must cease at sunset and everyone must have taken possession of his property within this time limit. Only the Cossack soldier on active duty may mow, with no member of his family being permitted to help him. Before the first of June no one is allowed to mow even the smallest plot of grass and to take the hay home. Should someone discover in the Cossack's home the blade of his scythe attached to the handle, he will be deprived of his share of the hay for the year.

Fishing is also precisely regulated. It is limited to specific times in the winter, spring, and autumn. Whoever dares to catch a fish out of season loses his share for that year. Even if the Cossack happens to find a sturgeon which has been tossed onto the land, he will carefully throw it back into the water rather than take it home. In the winter the *ataman* sets the day for the opening of the season. The operation begins at a point approximately eight versts from Uralsk. All the Cossack soldiers on active duty gather there the night before, each equipped with a fishgig, an icebreaker, and a pick, which is used to help pull the fish out of the water. Behind each fisherman is a horse and a wagon driven by a member of his family. His relatives, however, are absolutely forbidden to help him in the actual catching of the fish. Crowded together in a row along the bank, all the fishermen, having chosen their places, await the starting signal. If someone steps onto the ice before the signal has been given, he will have to forfeit his right to fish for the day. Only he who has been elected *ataman*-for-fishing for that year strolls gravely about on the ice. A cannon stands on the bank, the *ataman* gives the signal, and the cannoneer fires. In the same instant everyone leaps onto the ice, selects his place, chops a hole in the ice and begins spearing fish. In the good spots, which, of course, are sought out, the fish are so abundant that every stab nets a fish. The shallow areas, where fewer fish are to be found, are left for the stragglers. The Cossack's family on the bank hauls the fish away and lends as much aid as possible. Only the Cossack soldier is permitted to step onto the ice and to wield the above instruments. The flurry of activity on the ice is highly interesting. Each person works only for himself, never coming to the aid of his fellows, even though everyone cries out a hundred times: "Brothers, children, help me! I cannot go on!" Of course, no one lends a hand. Whoever calls for help, however, is determined not to assist anyone else, even if he is his cross-brother.[20] The ice breaks, the man balances on the flow, and, to be sure, frequently breaks through and falls into the water. He stands half submerged in the water or swims ashore with his booty. At one point a man left the ice for a moment and gave his fishgig to his neighbor. Plunging both instruments into the water, the latter speared two fish. After having pulled them up, he found it was impossible to fetch both fish out of the water simultaneously. He then grasped one of the spears between his teeth, using both hands to remove the fish. But, alas, the ice was already unsafe. He took off his belt, tied the fish to his leg, and then pulled up the other fish. But the ice gave way and he threw his spear onto the land, clutched the second fish under his arm, and happily swam to shore with the other fish bound to his leg.

The Muscovite merchants are already waiting on the bank, and very brisk trading commences. Generally all the fish are sold on the spot. The price of a sturgeon is determined by its size, with a large fish costing as much as 400 rubles. In order to subsist, a Cossack has to earn approximately that amount each year. For a period of three weeks following the initial catch, they work their way down the river for 250–350 miles under the same inspector and the same regulations.

In the spring the Cossacks fish from boats which are twelve to sixteen feet in length. Artistically hollowed out of trees, these boats are often decorated with sculpture and bound with iron. Everyone gathers on the bank in an orderly fashion long before the activities are to begin. The Cossack stands directly at the river's edge with his hand on his boat; standing at the other end of the craft is a hired Kirghiz. The signal is given, and in the same moment the boat and its crew, the Cossack and his Kirghiz, are afloat.

For the autumn catch, two Cossacks join efforts with their two boats. . . . Between the boats are two nets, one of which has large holes measuring more than half a foot square. The other net, which is of fine mesh, is placed behind the larger one. Upon entering the first net the sturgeon becomes entangled between the two and is thus captured. The fishing season in the spring and in the fall lasts for six weeks. Formerly, all the fishermen assembled at the marketplace in Uralsk. Everyone sat waiting on his sled and as soon as the signal sounded, rushed pell-mell in the direction of the river. But the tumult was terrific and accidents often occurred.

20. See above n. 15.

Today mishaps are very rare. In the autumn they also fish at the Caspian Sea, as far as the Cossack coast extends. Huge dragnets are used, and everyone is permitted to participate. It is forbidden to navigate the mouth of the Ural River up to a certain distance into the sea. For the most part, only small fish and no cartilaginous fish are to be found here. The abundance of fish in the Caspian Sea is said to have diminished considerably, since the water contains too much sulphate of magnesia, etc.

The fish are salted immediately in order to prepare the caviar. While the Cossacks receive the salt for their personal needs without charge, they must, however, pay a tax on the salt used in preparing the fish for sale. By taking the amount of tax revenue, we have calculated that the return from the annual catch is approximately 2,000,000 rubles. A portion of the fresh caviar is always sent post-haste to the emperor in Petersburg by a Cossack officer and is known as the tsar's morsel (*tsarskii-kusok*).

I would like to repeat that one cannot be careful enough in changing the military organization and the economic institutions of this people. If a regular tour of military duty were enforced and the purchase of replacements and the system of compensation, etc. forbidden, one would impose the greatest hardships on them and would completely destroy their natural societal organization. The introduction of another system of civil administration, the distribution of the meadow lands among the communes or individuals, and the systematic organization of the fishery would completely undermine their outstanding *esprit de corps* as well as an incomparable political institution. Officials would have to be salaried, the doors would be open to abuses, corruption, and the mania of regimentation, whereas now only a minimal amount of direction is necessary, which, moreover, is without cost and complications. No people renders so many services to its government as this tribe of Ural Cossacks. I would like to conclude this chapter by applying a well-known maxim to them: *Sint ut sunt aut non sunt!*[21]

21. "Let them be as they are, or are not."

# 14
## *Mission of Russia*

. . . [The Russians are] the most numerous and geographically largest Slavic tribe. We meet here all the prerequisites which lead us to the conclusion that, of all the Slavic peoples, the Russians alone seem to be destined to play a role of world historical significance at the present time. Favored by time, geography, and circumstances, Russia appears to be equal to her mission.

To formulate more precisely the mission which has devolved upon the Russians, we should like to maintain that Russia has been summoned as the mediator between Europe and Asia to transmit the civilization of the one society to the other.[1] In this regard, Russia is still in the ascendant stage of her history, and she can doubtless look forward to a long and glorious future.

The Russian Empire offers several points of comparison, contrast, and analogy with the ancient Roman Empire to which we shall make later reference. One point of comparison is appropriate at this time. Because it included all the civilized nations in the Mediterranean, the Roman Empire by virtue of its location as well as its ordered internal constitution made possible the rapid dissemination of Christianity and the establishment of a uniform ecclesiastical organism. Owing to its power, its extent, its position between Europe and Asia, and its European culture, the Russian Empire alone presents

1. On this point Haxthausen's Russian friend Petr Chaadaev wrote that Russians, "supporting [themselves] with one elbow on China and another on Germany, ought to have united within [them] the two great principles of intellectual nature — imagination and reason," *The Major Works* . . ., p. 37.

a vehicle for the penetration of this culture and hence Christianity to the interior of Asia.

The expressions "to conquer," "thirst for conquest," and "war" have an unpleasant ring. Basic ethics must designate the actions implicit in these terms as unjust and sinful, but they have a different value in world history. What would the human race be without wars and conquests? War necessitated the creation of national organisms, established communities, and the unity of monarchy. War aroused and stimulated all the intellectual and physical energies of nations; war alone made cultural progress possible. War and conquest had as their immediate result the disappearance of the smaller tribes, some of which bore the seeds of decline within and others of which were incapable of material and spiritual advancement because of their isolation. These smaller tribes were then incorporated into the larger and more powerful communities. It was in this way that states arose, in which the individual peoples came into close contact, taught each other, and exchanged their national cultures. Strengthened by mutual assistance, they made common cultural progress. Lastly, the great wars of conquest also established close ties with those peoples living in the most remote areas; they gave birth to the basic concept of all civilization, the idea of the oneness of humanity, which was ultimately perfected and sanctioned by Christianity in the idea of the brotherhood of all men and their equality before God.

It is far more often human passion than human reason that calls forth and guides the events and deeds of world history. The individual's thirst for conquest or the drive to conquer on the part of nations may be unjustified and may exact retribution for the individual in this life or in the next. But the end result, the conquest, is almost always a divine blessing for all mankind, in that it promotes human progress.

In examining the great peoples of history, as well as the deeds and their results, we have before us the most manifold diversity in the paths along which Providence has guided them. Nevertheless there are also many similarities and points of comparison. Developing slowly from humble beginnings, a few peoples gradually spread out over vast areas, absorbing foreign tribes and thus forming large nations which carried their civilization far beyond their original homes. . . . In this regard, we should like to approach our objective by examining the position which Russia occupies with respect to Europe.

More than one hundred peoples speaking a hundred different

languages live within the boundaries of the Russian Empire. However, almost all these peoples dwell on the periphery of this vast territory. The interior is inhabited by a very homogeneous people, the Russians, who number perhaps fifty million souls, whereas the total population of all the other peoples living in the empire does not exceed twelve to fifteen million.

No other European state possesses such a large population of the same nationality. France has only thirty-two million Frenchmen out of a population of thirty to thirty-six million, and Great Britain approximately nineteen million Englishmen among its thirty million inhabitants. Only the German-speaking peoples in central Europe, if we include the Low German dialects of the Dutch and the Belgians, may approach the number of Russians. The Germans, however, are not united into one body politic. . . .

A common tongue is a powerful bond in the internal solidarity of peoples, but a nationality must be borne by a common history and a shared fate. The French and the Spanish can be cited as examples in this respect, but not the Germans. First of all, a true unity of language is lacking. Of what use is it for scholars to assure us daily that all the German dialects constitute a single language when the Flemings, the Swiss, the Swabians, the Mecklenburgians, and the Austrians cannot understand each other and consequently do not regard each other as compatriots? It is true that High German gives the educated a sense of linguistic unity, but the lower classes, the core of the population, cannot speak High German, although they understand it in part. . . . The various German peoples are divided even more by their history than by their dialects. For centuries, each small province followed its own individual development, a history which was often characterized by strife and war with its neighbors. As a result, sympathies hardly exist, whereas antipathies abound. The Bavarian detests the Austrian, the Hanoverian the Prussian, etc. Only in the smaller territories has the old unity of kaiser and empire sustained a feeling of solidarity, and this was the only positive aspect in the national movement of 1848. The tradition of an Austrian emperor was a reality, even though there was little emotional attachment to him; all the rest was scholarly ideology and professorial illusions. The experiences of the past two years have convinced us that those countries inhabited by Germans which have not shared a common history with Germany, such as the German-speaking parts of Switzerland and Alsace, do not have the slightest notion of German patriotism and unity. Schleswig sympathized with Holstein because for centuries they had had common institutions and history and had shared a common antipathy toward the Danes, but certainly no allegiance toward Germany. Lastly, an important cause of division must not be forgotten: namely, different confessions. Although the old struggles have generally ceased, in many regions the various religious parties continue to regard each other as foreigners and sometimes as enemies.

Russia presents a totally different picture. Here we encounter a highly compact nationality. Among the thirty-six million Great Russians, there exists a unity of idiom which is not to be found among any other people. The language of the upper, educated stratum of society is precisely the same as that of the multitude; the emperor and the muzhik speak the same language and even have the same style of speech.

The dialect of the White Russians and the seven million Little Russians is distinguished from the language spoken by the Great Russians, but the difference is not nearly as great as that between an inhabitant of the Harz Mountains and a native of Brunswick. The Ruthenian dialect is further removed from that of the Great Russians, but the Ruthenians have little difficulty understanding the Little Russians.

In addition to the total unity of language, we also find a remarkable uniformity in the habits, customs, and dress of the Great Russians. Whereas in this regard Germany displays the greatest variety, often differing from one village to the next, a diversity more poetic and picturesque than elsewhere, the most absolute uniformity prevails among the Great Russians. This monotony is not poetic, but it vastly enhances political vitality.

Of much greater consequence in respect to political power is the total unity of religion and the church in Russia. This unity is complete among the Little Russians as well as among the Ruthenians except for a small number of the latter who have loyally maintained their ties to Rome. The Great Russians are divided by a schism. The Old Believers dissociated themselves from the ruling church, not for reasons of dogma, which is absolutely the same, but because of divergent practices and ceremonies.

Although the ancient Russian Empire ruled by Riurik was established by Normans who most likely introduced the bases of Germanic institutions and hence the principles of the feudal system, the Normans appear to have been too few in number for these principles to penetrate deeply into the Slavic population. Only in ancient times does one find slight traces [of feudalism] which soon disappeared. On the other hand, the patriarchal character of all popular institutions, which is rooted more deeply in the Slavic and above all in the Russian peoples than in any other European nation, developed fully. In this respect, the Russians most closely resemble the ancient peoples of the Orient. The entire social order with all its relationships and authorities constitutes an unbroken hierarchical ladder, which from the lowest to the highest rung, reposes on patriarchal authority. The father is the absolute sovereign of the household and the children; the family cannot exist without him. . . .

The next rung above the family is the Russian commune, which is the fictive expanded family under its elected father, the elder, or the *starosta*. The *starosta* is generally elected for three years. He governs and one obeys him unconditionally. However, he does consult with the "white heads" on the more important community matters. In many villages it is still the custom for the *starosta* to terminate the functions of his office before the assembled commune by kneeling, laying down his mace, and imploring the forgiveness of the community if ever he should have wronged it! . . .

All of the communes taken together make up the nation, a nation of brothers, who, from the beginning, have enjoyed complete equality and equal rights and who are likewise subordinate to a father, the tribal chief and leader of the nation: the tsar. The authority of the tsar is absolute and the obedience [of his subjects] unconditional. In the eyes of a true Russian, a restriction on the tsar's authority appears utter nonsense. "Who can limit the power and rights of a father?" the Russian asks. "He does not derive his power from us, his children, or from any man, but from God, to Whom he must someday answer." The touching proverb cited by the Russian if he thinks he is being oppressed by his master or a government official, "God is on high and the tsar far away," best identifies the source of all power and expresses his submission to authority. . . .

The Russians are as patriotic as those most patriotic of peoples, the French, the English, and the Spanish. These strong national sentiments demonstrate above all that the Russians belong to the large European family of nations. They also distinguish the Russians from the Oriental peoples who are merely united by one spiritual force, the unity of religion, and to whom the concepts of country and nationality as well as those of political and national freedom, honor, and humanity sound empty. . . .

The unity of religion, language, customs, and dress greatly enhances the intensity of patriotic sentiment. The way of life adds to this. No people travels as widely within their country as the Russians. In almost all the villages there are several peasants who have been in Archangel, Odessa, Kiev, Kazan, and Moscow! More than a million Russians annually travel outside the borders of their own province. And the area of each of these provinces is comparable to that of a kingdom! There are fairs in Russia where hundreds of thousands gather. At the places of pilgrimage, such as the Trinity—Saint Sergei Monastery, one often finds two to three hundred thousand persons assembled to commemorate the anniversary of a saint. That such gatherings, where people get to know each other and exchange ideas and opinions, should arouse and sustain a feeling of national unity is natural. . . .

We have already described the Western conception of Christianity as being realized by the Romano-Germanic peoples in the social and political institutions of the feudal system. The Slavic peoples understood Christianity differently. The basis of the Germanic conception is the voluntary submission of the individual, in both the social and the political sphere, to an order designed or perhaps merely sanctioned by Providence. The Slavic conception is rooted in the childlike sense of obedience and dependence which God has instilled into human nature. It is the submission of children to the father, of the individual to the head of the tribe or community, of the entire nation to its leader or prince, and of everyone to the Heavenly Father, who ordained this family hierarchy. . . . Among the Germanic peoples, religious cognition is the essence of Christianity, while among the Slavs it is religious feeling. That this striving for knowledge is fraught with danger has been demonstrated by the first fall of man. It appears that this endeavor is now leading the Occident to a second fall, to the deification of man and the abandonment of Christianity! The Slavic masses are less susceptible to these perils, for emotion is much more difficult to extirpate and is less responsive to speculative reasoning. . . .

At this point we should like to examine the position of Russia in the large European republic of nations as well as the policy which this position assigns to her with respect to the other states.

In her origin and growth, Russia offers several points of comparison with Rome. Like Rome, Russia arose from insignificant, almost obscure beginnings, expanding very slowly but steadily. The mythical history of Rome commences with two brothers who, together with their companions, built a small city and founded a petty kingdom, whereas Russian history speaks of a tribe which was no longer able to maintain order. Out of a need to be ruled, this tribe summoned a foreign leader and his retinue and submitted to his authority. Soon thereafter, all the other kindred tribes joined forces, and after 120 years their authority had spread over a vast, though thinly populated, area. Russia embraced Christianity and entered the large European family of Christian nations at the end of the tenth century. But divisions sapped the energy of the country, so that it soon succumbed to the attacks of the Mongols and Tatars. For more than 200 years the Russian people groaned under the yoke of their conquerors. That Russia attained national and political unity in her hour of misery and foreign oppression instead of perishing as a state and a people and instead of dividing into factions is testimony to the indestructible vigor of the Russian people. Religion and church, to which the people clung with devotion, served as the common bond. Although the Tatars knew how to conquer, fortunately they were incapable of permanently organizing their conquests. They simply plundered the Russians but permitted them to keep their customs and practices; they did not intermarry with the Russians, and they aroused all the energies of the vanquished by their humiliating treatment. Instead of maintaining and encouraging division, they fortified the Russians' sense of national unity by promoting the union of the smaller principalities under the scepter of the grand duke. The situation then reversed. The Russians not only cast off the Tatar yoke but gradually subdued almost all the Tatar territories. Immediately following the decline of the Eastern Roman Empire in 1453, Russia reentered the European family of nations as an autonomous Christian state (1472).[2] From that time on, Russia slowly but steadily ascended to her present height. She now appears to have reached the summit of her external might but not nearly the peak of her internal greatness.

When the Roman Empire had reached its zenith, Roman customs and virtues were already in a state of decline; luxury and sensuous pleasure were rampant; religiosity and patriotism were fading. Nevertheless, the Romans continued to rule the world for centuries.

Hence Russia, too, can in all likelihood look with promise to the long continuance of her great power, even more so since the Russian people proper, in contrast to the Romans at the time of Augustus, still possess all the characteristics of an unspoiled nature

2. In 1442 Ivan III was married to Sophie Paleologue, a niece of the last Byzantine emperor, in 1480 the Mongol rule was officially ended, and in 1493 Russia entered the first of many strategic alliances with Western nations.

and vigorous youth; a profound sense of attachment to the family and the commune, hospitality, generosity, compassion, a spirit of self-sacrifice, and patience. To these traits is added a physical constitution hardened by an inclement climate and privations of all kinds and capable of withstanding great fatigue. Lastly the Russians have an indestructible and almost naïve faith in the unity of the church and state, an ardent patriotism, and an unshakable consciousness of their own grandeur and power.

One can divide Russia's conquests into three categories as well as three periods. The first category comprises those conquests which the principal tribe and its prince undertook in order to unify the nation and state. For the most part, these conquests fall into the oldest period, when the grand dukes of Kiev, and later the grand dukes of Moscow, gradually united all the territories inhabited by Russians, reincorporating the individual principalities into the main empire. Russia has also conquered or reconquered important territories in modern times, namely the Ukraine, White Russia, Kiev, Little Russia, and parts of Red Russia.

We would like to designate as the second category of conquests those which the Russian people undertook out of an instinctive but obscure sense of the mission with which world history had entrusted them. To this category belong the wars waged to realize the highest interests of humanity, that is, the wars which Charlemagne waged against the Saxons in order to convert them to Christianity, the Crusades, the wars of the Teutonic knights in Prussia, etc. In Russia's case this category includes those conquests undertaken to acquire seacoasts. They appear to have been absolutely necessary to Russia's existence as a world power.

Prior to these conquests Russia had been a huge, landlocked country, cut off from all the seas and consequently from all of Western civilization. Maritime routes provide the easiest and most comfortable means for the propagation of civilization, overland routes being too difficult and inconvenient. After having conquered the Baltic Sea coast, Peter I, like another Archimedes, sought a point there from which he could hoist ancient Russia out of her isolation, her prejudices, her provincialism, and put her on the same level as the rest of Europe. The conquest of the Black Sea coast and the Crimea was, moreover, an act of vengeance against the last empire of the Tatars, who had enslaved Russia for so long.

One can hardly call the occupation of Siberia a conquest, in that Russia simply took possession of a *res nullius*. The semibarbarous hunting tribes which inhabited this region never formed political entities, nor did they consider themselves to be owners of the land. Even today Russia does not interfere with them, although she is gradually introducing Christianity and civilization into this wilderness.

The third category is comprised of conquests motivated by political interests. Poland was partitioned and for the most part subjugated because an autonomous and powerful Polish state was too dangerous a neighbor. Second, an impotent Poland in the hands of an enemy always served as a base for an invasion of Russia, as was learned from the bitter experience under Napoleon. Finland was conquered in order to safeguard Saint Petersburg and to dominate the Gulf of Finland in the interest of the fleet. The northernmost provinces of Turkey up to the mouths of the Danube were occupied so that no other power would be able to establish a position there and also to be in possession of the keys to the Porte if Osman's old, shaky edifice should someday collapse and the scramble for the skin of the lion begin. The proffered crown of Georgia was accepted and Dagestan and Armenia taken in order to gain control of the mountains which protect the frontiers of Russia proper and thereby to be in a position to menace Persia or Asia Minor at will. Lastly, from Siberia, Russia occupied several regions in America so as to secure a firm footing on the continent of the future.

Although we recognize the first two groups of conquests as being justified given the situation and the mission of Russia, we certainly do not intend to try to defend this third category. At most we can invite that people or state which is free of sin to cast the first stone at Russia!

The first two categories of conquest have proved beneficial in that they vastly enhanced Russia's power and greatly expanded her territory. With the exception of the German Baltic provinces, even the second category has been assimilated into Russia. The colonization movement rapidly settled a predominantly Russian population from the interior into these newly conquered territories. The regions around Petersburg and all of southern Russia, which was formerly inhabited or traversed by Tatars, has been transformed into essentially Russian land.

The third category of conquests presents a different case, and it is here that we see a fundamental contrast between the ancient, universal empire of Rome and the Russian Empire. Rome knew how to assimilate its conquests, often in a very short time. It adopted the foreign divinities and introduced its own gods into the land of the vanquished and, by identifying the two cults, established a religious unity. In a short time the language and the customs of the Romans became native to the provinces in a way which still puzzles historians. . . .

In every respect the opposite is true of Russia. Russia cannot transmit to her conquered territories her religion and her church, since both are too national. This national church can provide a homogeneous people with a strong common bond, but a foreign people would first have to surrender its national character and become completely Russified before they could be integrated into the Russian church. (A good example is offered by those Mordvines who, after having adopted the language and customs of the Russians, also embraced their religion.) Russian language and customs were not disseminated in any of the conquered territories, either in Finland, the Baltic provinces, Poland, or even in Georgia, although the latter has the same religion and church as Russia. . . . The countries subdued by Russia possess for the most part a culture which is superior to that of their conqueror. Consequently they have not become provinces of the Russian Empire in the Roman sense of the word but have remained foreign elements or dependencies. Hence only the land of the Russian people and the Russian church will constitute the true Russian empire. . . .

We must emphatically deny the assertion that Russia has been summoned to rule the world and to establish a universal monarchy. It is true that Russia has immense resources at her disposal and for the moment the most favorable chances to conquer the world, but victory would lead to her immediate downfall. With respect to Asia, for example, Russia would simply have to surmount the difficulties presented by the climate and terrain; nowhere would the peoples themselves offer serious resistance. Several isolated regions on this continent, such as Circassia, are of no importance to the conquest of Asia as a whole. In regard to Europe, Russia occupies a geographical position unusually favorable for waging war. She has the broadest base of operations for launching a surprise attack against Europe from all directions (after the necessary means of transportation has been completed, that is, the railroad from Petersburg to Odessa etc.) In addition, her hinterland is so immense that every invading army must of necessity be engulfed. The conquest of the entire country can thus be regarded as only a pipe dream, but even the subjugation of the smallest part of Russia could never be secured. It is not necessary to refer specifically to Napoleon's invasion, but at the present time anyone who is familiar with the country and the people knows that even without the Russian winter he would have been defeated. For war Russia possesses the most abundant resources and materials: iron and all the other metals, wool, leather, hemp, flax, wood (even for the construction of a fleet), etc. But does she possess the *nervus rerum gerendarum*, money? It is generally believed that no European state could presently wage a serious war without having to borrow the money. Russia, however, carried on a brief but very expensive war in Hungary without a loan.[3] Of course, we do not believe that there are immense metal treasures in the vaults of Saint Petersburg; but the resources of the Russian Empire are inestimable and in case of need or simply upon the request of the emperor the people would eagerly sacrifice their property and blood. Lastly, as far as the army is concerned, no state has as many troops as Russia.

Since the time of Catherine II, we have always observed that the armies which Russia initially sent across her borders were relatively small. But unlike the armies of other states, Russian troops became more numerous the longer the war lasted. In the War of 1812, when her very survival was at stake, Russia opposed the huge armies of Napoleon with scarcely 200,000 men, but, at the close of the war in 1815, 300,000 men were actually under arms on foreign soil.

In recent times a complete change has come about. Today Russia possesses in reality, and not simply on paper, a military force stronger than that of any other state, an army which is always prepared for battle and which can quickly be concentrated at a given location.[4] When, in 1849, Russia responded to the Austrian plea for help and entered the war against Hungary, all of Europe believed, as the newspapers sarcastically remarked, that Russia would send at most 50,000 troops across the Hungarian frontier. Contrary to these estimates, Russia provided 120,000 front-line troops and 60,000 reservists, an army so completely and perfectly equipped as had hardly been seen in modern times! Moreover, the troops were, according to the unanimous testimony of all who had the opportunity to

3. This was to suppress the Hungarian Revolution of 1848 and the related invasion of Wallachia in 1848; it nonetheless cost the Russians dearly both because it required considerable financial outlay and because it encouraged them (and Haxthausen) to overestimate their strength on the eve of the Crimean War four years later. See Curtiss, *The Russian Army*, chap. 6.

4. In 1849 troops had been moved from Warsaw toward Hungary via railroad; the absence of rail facilities in southern Russia proved a major factor in the Crimean defeat.

observe them, stalwart and hardy, perfectly disciplined, and eager for combat. And let it be noted that this was not a national but a purely political war, waged by order of the emperor. Although the Russians were in sympathy with the Magyars and opposed to the Germans, whose cause they were supposed to be supporting, this was the order and the army fought with distinction. . . .

We believe that the conquest of Europe [by Russia] will be easy in the future if the social order of Europe continues to deteriorate and if the governments continue to grow weaker, as unfortunately seems to be the case, and particularly if France, the second most powerful European state, is completely debilitated politically by an increasing republicanization or by socialistic-communistic revolutions. But after Europe has been conquered, what then? We have already noted that Russia, in contrast to ancient Rome, has only been able to assimilate those peoples who are of the same blood, the same language family, and the same religion. All other conquests may have offered Russia material advantages, but with respect to her political might they were more of a burden. Russia, because of her very nature, cannot assimilate the defeated civilized countries of Europe simply because their culture is superior to hers. Can one seriously believe that it would be possible for Petersburg to rule Paris, Rome, Vienna, and Berlin, and for a sparsely settled country, a land of steppes, to govern an industrial and heavily populated continent, intersected by mighty mountain ranges and everywhere close to the seas? Russia would have to disarm these countries and, because she could never rely on the indigenous troops, she would have to station her national army there as an occupation force to quell every uprising. This would have a very adverse effect on the population balance in the Russian interior. Furthermore, there is the danger that the army could ultimately be infected by the poison of western European revolutionary fever!

The conquest of European Turkey would be of a different nature. In this region, the inhabitants are for the most part Slavs who are closely related both racially and linguistically to the Russians and, what is even more important, they belong to the same church. Without a doubt the Bulgarians, the Serbs, and the Bosnians would assimilate completely with the Russians within a short period following the conquest. Even the Christian Albanians and the Greeks in Turkey would probably establish close ties with Russia, since they are part of the same religious community.

But Russia cannot subdue Turkey before having conquered all of Europe. And since the conquest of Europe, as we have already demonstrated, could not be permanent, the conquest of Turkey is also merely a dream. As long as the present political system of Europe continues to exist (since 1849 Austria and Prussia have succeeded in lifting themselves somewhat out of a state of anarchy), the various powers cannot allow Russia to take sole possession of Turkey. To prevent this from happening, all of Europe, with England at the head, would join forces in battle. With the latter it would be a war to the death. Even if Russia were victorious for the moment, such a conquest would be precarious and continually challenged by the enemy as long as Europe exists. Common sense itself prevents Russia from playing for such high stakes. Moreover, the advantages to be gained would be very problematic, since the necessity of governing Constantinople from Petersburg would disturb the equilibrium of the empire. On the other hand, the preservation of Turkey offers Russia the most advantageous position. The identity of origin and the religious unity which join the majority of the subjects of the Porte to Russia enhance the latter's influence to such a degree that on every important question Turkey must follow Russia's counsel. All the existing treaties provide Russia with the greatest security and advantages for the development of her navy and trade. Turkey is also well aware that its preservation is of the greatest interest to Russia and that it thus has Russia as a loyal ally who will protect it not only against any foreign enemy but also against internal dissolution. We witnessed this when Mehemet Ali's army threatened Constantinople.[5] Only if Turkey were actually to disintegrate completely from within, which event we do not consider to be likely in the near future, and if it were a question of dividing the remains, would Russia demand her share of the booty!

Since the time of Napoleonic conquest for the sake of conquest, the naked and insatiable passion to conquer is no longer in vogue. In the Russian people there is not a trace of this passion, and in the last twenty-five years at least the government has shown a moderation which Europe did not expect. Following the decisive victories won against Turkey and Persia,[6] Russia modified her frontiers only

5. Russia's defense of Turkey against Mehemet Ali, as the British tirelessly emphasized, was motivated in large measure by her desire to strengthen the Russian hand in Istanbul and to broaden her transit rights in the Bosphorus. See Philip E. Mosely, *Russian Diplomacy and the Opening of the Eastern Question in 1838–1839* (Cambridge, Mass., 1934), chap. 1.

6. Whereas Haxthausen's contention is true for the most recent campaigns, the earlier extension of imperial authority to the south and into the Caucasus was achieved at the expense of Turkey and Persia. See Gladys Scott Thompson, *Catherine the Great and the Expansion of Russia* (London, 1955).

slightly, returning all the conquered territory. In the matter of Cracow, she kept nothing for herself but on the contrary nearly forced Austria to take possession of the city and the province.[7] When Turkey and Austria appealed to Russia for aid against Egypt and Hungary respectively, it was not only the armchair politicians who prophesied that Russia would occupy at least a part of these countries as footholds. *Quod non!* After having provided the requested aid, she immediately withdrew her army!

What is Russia's natural policy vis-à-vis Europe today? To be sure, it is of great concern to Russia that the revolution not gain too much ground and that it not come too near her borders. Even though there is little danger that revolutionary teachings will be adopted by the Russian populace, nevertheless the contagion has already infected Poland, and its spread to the other dependencies, such as Finland, is to be feared. Were a revolution completely victorious in Europe and all the monarchies and governments overthrown, the cry, "All the peoples have deposed their kings, let us do the same!" could lead to at least a temporary catastrophe, given the perverted education of Russia's upper classes.

Sound policy prevents Russia from embarking on a course of conquest and from intervening unbidden in the internal affairs of the European states. In this respect Russia has already learned a bitter lesson, which she has not yet forgotten. Napoleon was at the zenith of his power. Russia's efforts in 1805 and 1806 to check his triumphal course remained futile. She began to submit to the new order of things and even abandoned her alliance with England, the last anchor of old Europe. Russia had not yet understood that for a revolutionary power such as Napoleon's every standstill is a step backward. Thus, in spite of all her concessions, Russia was attacked by him. Only after Napoleon's defeat did Tsar Alexander resolve to reestablish the old monarchial order. He succeeded beyond expectation. Seduced by his success, he went one step further: instead of restricting himself to the restoration of the boundaries of the various states, he also meddled in their internal affairs and institutions. The emperor forced upon the Bourbons the Charter of 1814 which was a misfortune for Europe and an offense for which even Russia has had to pay dearly.

7. Again, Haxthausen's contention may be challenged, for the autocracy was firm in its desire either to suppress revolutionaries or, if that proved difficult, as in the case of Cracow in 1846, to shift the responsibility to the shoulders of others. See R. F. Leslie, *Reform and Insurrection in Russian Poland* (London, 1963), pp. 1–43.

The time may well arrive when Russia will march her armies into Europe for a second time in order to come to the aid of the monarchies in their struggle against revolution and anarchy. Will she make the same mistake again? Certainly not! Her conduct in the Hungarian matter proves that she has understood the principles of sound policy and also intends to practice them. Hence we should not be led to believe that Russia enjoys appearing on the field of battle out of any love of war or ambition or thirst for conquest. She will only intervene if absolutely necessary and never without being summoned. Her real power, her impressive position, offers the European monarchies moral support in the face of anarchy. But, as we have mentioned, only in case of extreme necessity will she provide a significant amount of material aid, for she can be certain that she is sacrificing her money and blood without hope of indemnity, to be paid only with ingratitude. Russia must also be careful not to station her armies for too long a time in anarchistic countries. In our opinion, it would be sheer folly if, after having suppressed anarchy, she were to meddle in the internal affairs and developments of the individual states.

We have not yet referred to Russia's present or future political position vis-à-vis England. It is different from her relationship to the rest of Europe, and we would like to touch upon it very briefly at this point. England is a state whose governmental institutions appear for the moment to be more secure than those of any other European state. At this time it may very well be that England is the only European state whose political power is equal to Russia's. For this reason each looks at the other with jealous eyes. They have innumerable contacts with each other, and their interests are nearly identical in every part of the world. And yet by virtue of their position they are kept so far apart that it would be difficult to say at which point they might come into serious conflict. Russia cannot conquer England, nor can England subdue Russia. They can harass each other and go to battle against each other, but neither can really do the other too much harm. But it is not at all necessary for them to assume a hostile attitude toward each other. On the contrary, Providence has entrusted both nations with the very same mission, namely, to disseminate Christianity and civilization throughout Asia, each in its own way, Russia by way of land, England by way of the sea. There they will someday meet, but this encounter need not be hostile.

The Slavic conception of Christianity, as it is manifested in the Russian church, will never be able to incorporate either the Latin church or Protestantism, because they represent a spiritually superior force. The Russian church enjoys a different position, however, with respect to the Asian peoples. Not only are the Slavs both spiritually and culturally superior to the peoples of Asia, but Slavic religious sentiments must, in our opinion, have a greater chance of acceptance among the meditative and sensuous Asians than any other Christian rite. It is therefore likely that the Russian church will conquer large areas for the Christian faith in the Asian interior when it has developed missionary talents and zeal, which thus far has not been the case. In this regard the English have proved completely powerless. Their missionary societies have made great but totally fruitless efforts. Protestantism can be embraced by peoples who are already Christian but never by heathens or Mohammedans. Experience has shown this to be the case, particularly in Asia. . . .

Both nations are introducing their industrial products into Asia and are in this way gradually disseminating the external forms of our modern civilization. The resulting transformation of the customs and habits of life is paving the way for the larger political and religious upheavals which the Asian interior will obviously undergo.

Wherever Russian and English commerce meet, English products are always preferred to the Russian goods. But such competition is rare. As far as Asia is concerned, Russia is a civilizing country; vis-à-vis Europe she is not. Consequently her culture and her products are being introduced to the peoples of northern and central Asia, to those wholly uncivilized peoples or to those whose culture has fallen into a state of decline, to the Persian, Tatar, and Mongolian tribes, and to northern China. The English products, which are superior to Russian goods, find a market in India and in southern and central China, countries with ancient cultures. Here the Russians will never gain admission or influence, since their cultural superiority is not sufficiently pronounced. . . .

Culturally Russia leans toward Europe. The Russians are a European people and stand at the head of the powerful Slavic race which inhabits more than one-third of Europe. Russia is anchored in the great Christian family of European nations, which is the leader of the human race. Russia received civilization and political forms from the rest of Europe. But with respect to Europe she has no important economic interests to represent; she exports only her raw materials to the European market; her industry cannot compete with that of western Europe. Russia could only conquer, but her conquests would greatly weaken her. There is, however, one paramount interest which Russia must protect with respect to Europe; she must do everything in her power to support and to uphold the principles of law and order, for these are her very own moral foundations. If these foundations were to collapse in Europe, if anarchy were to erupt with full force, it could exercise an incalculable influence on Russia.

In 1830 the Holy Alliance collapsed; France overthrew the principle of legitimacy, the Netherlands followed her example, and Prussia and Austria made only a halfhearted attempt to defend it. Russia adhered strictly to the principle of legitimacy, which she had once accepted out of conviction and which had been sanctioned by oath and treaty. Russia did not want to recognize Louis Philippe and would even have risked a war to prevent the dismemberment of the Netherlands had Austria and Prussia been interested. She always remained aloof from the French king in spite of Louis Philippe's great efforts to draw near to Russia, in spite of the undeniable sympathies which exist between the Russians and the French, and in spite of the manifold material interests which join the two states. To this very day Russia does not have an ambassador in Spain, because the legitimacy of the throne has not been established. She recalled her ambassadors from Brussels and Turin because Polish officers, guilty of breaking their oath, had been accepted into the armies of both countries. Russia also broke off diplomatic relations with Switzerland when the old constitutions were overthrown and a radical government seized power. . . .

Who in 1848 could have prevented Russia from overrunning Europe, from incorporating the remnants of the Prussian and Austrian armies, from crushing the demagogues in Frankfurt and Turin, from coming to the aid of the French legitimists, and from dictating the peace in Paris as well as the new order of Europe? Militarily, this probably would not have been so difficult.

Or at this time when Europe was completely shattered, who would have hindered Russia from taking all the Polish provinces (indeed, with the enthusiastic approval of the Poles), from crushing Turkey and reorganizing the Ottoman Empire with Slavic interests in mind, in which case the realization of a Pan-Slavic universal empire would not have been at all remote. Russia would merely have had to agitate à la Palmerston and then fish in troubled waters, to engage in doubledealing here and there, to support a government in one place and demagoguery somewhere else. Had this been the case, Schleswig-Holstein would have furnished the best occasion as well as a justifiable pretext!

Instead the emperor had in view only the most general and important interests of order, law and monarchy χατ᾿ ε᾿ξοχπ᾿ν. In his eyes these interests outweigh at the present time the seemingly natural but selfish interests of Russia. Under the former political and legal system only some of the Austrian and Prussian provinces belonged to the German confederation. If Russia had been at odds with Austria, let us say, over the mouths of the Danube, she could have waged war and, if lucky, could have conquered Hungary, Galicia, etc., without embroiling the German confederation in the conflict. This would have also been true if Russia had been involved in a dispute with Prussia over Posen and Polish affairs (as was actually the case in 1848 when Russia declared that she would consider certain eventualities to be a *casus belli*). Nevertheless, in 1850 and 1851 the tsar approved almost without hesitation the plans for the entry of all the Austrian and Prussian provinces into the German confederation. Indeed, it is said that he supported the steps which Austria took in this respect, solely in the interest of the monarchial principle. For the strengthening of this principle he regards a powerful but, of course, not aggressive German confederation as desirable and even necessary in the common interest of all of Europe. The German confederation with its seventy million inhabitants would serve to check eventual territorial ambitions on the part of France as well as Russia. . . .

And what is Russia's policy vis-à-vis the rest of Europe? She is on friendly terms with her Swedish neighbors. She protected Denmark when an intoxicated Germany attacked in 1848 and wanted to wreak her anger on this small weak country. Russia maintains her old proven friendship with Holland. On principle she remains distant from Belgium, Spain, Sardinia, and Switzerland without harassing or insulting them. She holds a protective hand over the rest of Italy and Greece without demanding their subordination or anything in return. As for France, the tsar has openly declared that in his eyes a quasi-legitimate constitutional monarchy is a horror because it is based on an inherent lie. On the other hand, he could be on frank and even amicable terms with a republic. For this reason he lends moral support to every French government which endeavors to maintain order, such as the former government of Cavaignac and the present government under Bonaparte.

For a comparison, let us take a look at England's policy, in particular the newest course which she has been pursuing under Palmerston's leadership. Everywhere we encountered the noble lord fishing in troubled waters. He recognized only the basest interests of the shopkeeper policy to which he subordinated everything: rectitude, political principles, trustworthiness, and honor. It is said that in the deepest recesses of his mind he is devoted to the tenets of absolute radicalism. We do not even want to do him the honor of giving credence to this assertion. He loves radicalism but only abroad, since it leads to anarchy and completely paralyzes the political power of these countries. From the ensuing standstill of all industrial activity England can only profit; the finest pecuniary benefits will then accrue to her. The noble lord never questions the justice of his actions. Because of unimportant and often completely unjustified claims on the part of individual English businessmen and plutocrats he immediately employs brutal force but, *nota bene*, only against weak and defenseless countries. With respect to the United States, which always assumes a bold and defiant attitude toward England, he pulls back his claws at once and does nothing more than put forward moderate objections. But in Italy, that unfortunate country, torn by revolutionary fever and socialism, he exploits radical Sardinia in favor of the English manufacturers. For years he has been plotting and directing the most despicable intrigues and stirring up violent propaganda in Sicily, Naples, the Papal States, and Tuscany. In Hungary he intrigued to weaken Austria. He is offering Switzerland his lofty protection in order to keep the fires of anarchy burning for all of Europe. And finally, let us not forget the brutality with which he treated a weak and impoverished Greece! Should not a cry of indignation against such action have gone up throughout all of England, which has always prided herself on her noble sentiments? Instead, the City rubbed its hands with pleasure and the High Tories scarcely managed a weak attempt at censure, even after France and Russia had openly and vehemently denounced this policy.

Having indicated how Russia's cultural interests incline primarily toward Europe, we should now like to explain in what way her material interests are directed for the most part toward Asia. Russia's position on the border between Europe and Asia ought to be viewed as a true mission of Providence assigning her the task of first transmitting European culture to Asia, and subsequently perhaps Christianity. But this mission will not be accomplished by conquest, but by way of humanity, fellowship, and trade. More and more the empire's center of gravity is inclining toward the east and southeast. The colossal fair at Nizhnii Novgorod may soon become more important than all her commercial dealings with Europe.[8]

8. This had nearly become the case by 1852, when the turnover at the

For one hundred years the stream of a mighty colonization movement has been flowing from the west and northwest to eastern and southeastern Russia. Perhaps the time is not too far away when Petersburg will be only a large Russian port in northern Europe, just as Odessa is a harbor for southern Europe; both of them may simply be powerful commercial cities and European outposts.

Having maintained that Russia's policy with respect to Asia has been peaceful rather than aggressive, we would like to demonstrate this in detail. Let us begin at that point where Russia has continually waged war, namely, in the Caucasian provinces. The Caucasian mountain range in its entire length faces the Russian plains. The warlike and rapacious highlanders had always swooped down on the unprotected plains, pillaging and ravaging the countryside and then withdrawing unpunished to their safe mountain fortresses. It was nearly impossible to launch a frontal attack against them, because they had all of Asia behind them. Then Russia acquired Georgia. It was a great burden and embroiled Russia in sanguinary wars with Persia and Turkey, which led to the conquest of the entire region south of the Caucasus between the Black and Caspian seas. This conquest took place before the accession of the present emperor. He had to accept his inheritance. Should he have given up this entire conquered territory and abandoned to the detestable Mohammedan government of Persia or the despotism of the Turkish pashas a Christian people who had voluntarily submitted to the rule of his predecessor? That would have been a crime against humanity and against the true honor of Russia as a Christian state. But Nicholas I has done nothing there but make incredible efforts to pacify, organize, and civilize this region, as well as to wage defensive wars. . . .

For twenty-three years Russia has been at peace with Persia. Prior to this Abbas Mirza had attacked Russia in peacetime.[9] The Russians were wholly unprepared and were forced to abandon several provinces temporarily. But after they had collected their forces,

Nizhnii fair reached 57 million rubles and for all Moscow was only 60 million; both did approximately equal volume of trade with Europe. See M. E. Rozhkova, "K voprosu znacheniia iarmarok vo vnutrennei torgovli doreformennoi Rossii, pervaia polovina XIX v.," *Istoricheskie zapiski* 54 (1955): 299–301.

9. Abbas Mirza was the leader of Persian forces in their unsuccessful defense against a Russian advance along the Araxes in 1812, later defeated again by Paskevich in 1827. These two campaigns lost to Russia most of the Caucasus, and the northern shore of the Caspian. See Brockelmann, *History of the Islamic Peoples*, pp. 420 ff.

Paskevich was victorious,[10] and Persia had to cede to Russia the Tatar lands as well as Armenia. These territories were not inhabited by Persians, nor did they originally belong to Persia. Having been conquered at one time, they were now lost. The inhabitants, Armenian Christians and Shi'a Moslems, who were most cruelly tyrannized and oppressed by the Persian government, regarded the Russians as their liberators. The boundaries were delimited in such a way that Russia would be protected from future Persian attacks. From that time on, Russia has been a good and true friend of Persia; she has encouraged Persia's trade and sought to strengthen and to preserve its government.

Russia's treatment of the Turks in Asia Minor was even more lenient. Russia would have conquered Bayazid and undoubtedly could have advanced as far as Trabizond. In this region, too, the inhabitants were not Turks, but Armenian Christians and Kurds, who only reluctantly tolerated Turkish rule and who regarded the Russians as their liberators. Russia returned most of the conquered territory and merely sought to establish a strategically safe border along the ridge of the Anatolian mountains. She retained Akhaltsikhe, the ancient slave market, in order to check the traffic in Christian slaves, which could not have been eradicated in any other way. Perhaps Russia acted against the principles of humanity in permitting Christian Armenia to fall back under the Turkish yoke. She did not even keep Batum, the most important harbor on the Black Sea, which was actually indispensable to her.

Lastly, in the Far East, Russia's relations with the ancient Celestial Empire, China, are completely peaceful and upright. The borders have been fixed by treaties in which the Chinese duped the Russians everywhere.[11] Trade is precisely regulated. The Russian government oversees the ethics of her merchants and shows consideration for the national practices of the Chinese. Russia exports woolen goods to China, the so-called Meseritz cloth which is now imitated in Moscow. England, on the other hand, ships opium to China in

10. Field Marshal I. F. Paskevich (1782–1856) was appointed commander-in-chief of Russian forces in the Caucasus in 1827; troops under his command occupied Erivan in October 1827, which led to the Treaty of Turkmanchai in 1828, which ceded Persian Armenia to Russia but left both Armenian and Azerbaidjan peoples divided under Persian, Ottoman, and Russian rule. See Curtiss, *The Russian Army*, chap. 2.

11. That neither the Russians nor the Chinese achieved a clear victory in the important 1689 Treaty of Nerchinsk is maintained by Vincent Chen, *Sino-Soviet Relations in the Seventeenth Century* (The Hague, 1966), pp. 118–19 and chap. 9.

order to bring the population to physical and moral ruin. When the Chinese government wanted to stop the import of opium, England began the most unjustified of wars and forced the noble Celestial Empire to poison itself!

To foster her trade, Russia is seeking to open up routes leading to the heart of Asia, to Tibet, that curious land with an ancient culture. In the vast Mongolian steppes she has established Cossack communities which may someday become Europeanized cities connected by trade routes. Is one justified in calling this a conquest? We think not. The Mongols are a political but not a territorial entity. They do not consider the land to belong to them or to anyone but use the free pasture lands as nomads. Consequently, the Cossacks as well as every other people would have as much right to use the land as the Mongol nomads.

Russia will be wary of conquering territory in Asia. She now has safe frontiers and territories inhabited by her own people. Should she conquer regions by force which would constitute an uncertain possession, subject to attack and retainable only by a military presence and at a considerable expense? Russia is interested in seeing that peace prevails in Asia, that the Asian empires prosper and become somewhat civilized, and that they adopt European customs, since Russia's industry and trade will thrive as a result. In comparing the present condition of the Asian empires — Turkey, Persia, China, Bukhara, and Tibet — with that of a hundred years ago, one cannot fail to recognize that their political and social contacts with Europe are more extensive than they were in the past. France contributed somewhat to this development, England played a greater role, and Russia can claim the most credit. In any case, Russia is doing the most to support and preserve the existing states of Asia.

Russia's thirst for conquest is decried throughout Europe. Yet in the past twenty years she has not conquered a single village. England's conquests seldom meet with protests or criticism in spite of the fact that she has been conquering territories and subjugating nations for a hundred years and has more than quadrupled the area of Old England and her population. And seldom does a year go by that she does not conquer new lands.

# Index of Personal Names

# Subject Index

Agriculture, experimentation in, 64–66, 68–69, 83, 166–67, 171–72, 255; economics of, 37–42, 50–59, 78, 84–89, 94–95, 106, 170
Alcohol, *see* Spirits
America, 309, 319
Anarchy, 315, 317, 319
Archangel, 230
Aristocracy, *see* Nobility
Armenia, 123, 195, 309, 321
Art, 17–18, 112, 271–73
Artel, xxviii, 100, 222, 289
Artisans, 30, 34, 43, 212–15, 236
Asia, 315–16, 319, 322
Austria, 182–83, 200–201, 313–14, 317–18
Autocracy, 9–10, 260, 265, 281–82, 285–87, 289–90, 292

Baltic provinces, xvii, xxxiv, 51, 210, 236–39, 249, 252, 286, 309–10
Bank, Imperial Loan, 251
Bazaar, *see* Markets
Black Earth region, 12, 52, 85, 119, 179, 207, 209, 220
Bohemians, 5, 27, 275–76
Boyars, 107, 243, 244, 287
Bulgaria, 5–6, 195, 275, 278, 312
Bureaucracy, German, xv–xvi, 249; Russian, see *Chinovniki*

Byzantium, 243

Caspian Sea, 293, 300, 320
Catholicism, xii, xxxi, 145, 150, 164, 263, 268–69, 271, 275
Caucasus, xix, 4, 157, 179, 295, 320
Census, 83, 86
Charlemagne, 20, 291
Charter of 1785, 257
Cheremiss, 178
Chernigov, 4, 142, 205, 266
*Chin*, 165, 214, 244–47, 258
China, 119, 218, 316, 320–21
*Chinovniki*, 49, 62, 74, 77, 209, 215, 231, 237–39, 246, 249, 253–54, 257–58, 289
Cities, 10, 215, 282–85, 288; legislation on, 27
Civil service, see *Chin; Chinovniki*
Clergy, 12, 48, 95, 135, 244, 258, 261–62, 265–66, 269–70
Colonization, xxv, 12, 14, 160 163–64, 168, 176–97, 288–89
Communes, xiv–xv, xvii, xxiv–xxvii, xl–xli, 5–6, 9–11, 30, 43, 72, 75–76, 79–84, 86, 89, 100, 106, 115, 177, 250, 276–79, 283, 286–88, 292–93, 297, 305
Communism, 93
Constantinople, 261–62, 265, 313
Convicts, 115–16, 189–93

*325*